PHENOMENOLOGY AND DECONSTRUCTION

Phenomenology and Deconstruction

VOLUME TWO : *Method and Imagination*

Robert Denoon Cumming

CHICAGO & LONDON : *The University of Chicago Press*

ROBERT DENOON CUMMING is professor emeritus of philosophy at Columbia University. He is the author of numerous books including *Starting-Point* and the two-volume *Human Nature and History*, both published by the University of Chicago Press.

The University of Chicago Press, Chicago 60637
The University of Chicago Press, Ltd., London

ISBN (cloth): 0–226–12368–5
ISBN (paper): 0–226–12369–3

Library of Congress Cataloging-in-Publication Data
(Revised for vol. 2)

Cumming, Robert Denoon, 1916–
    Phenomenology and deconstruction.

    Includes bibliographical references and index.
    Contents: v. 1. The dream is over—v. 2. Method and imagination.
    1. Phenomenology—History.   I. Title.
B829.2.C85   1991   142'.7'09   91-12696
ISBN 0-226 12366-9 (v. 1)
ISBN 0-226-12367-7 (v. 1, pbk.)

FOR JEANNE

CONTENTS

Translations from the French and German are usually my own. Citations from Heidegger and Husserl are to the German pagination, when it is available in the margin of the English translation, except in the case of *Ideas I,* where I cite section numbers, since there are two English translations in print.

INTRODUCTION

ONE

The Passage Way

Husserl opens the way—Sartre

Access

To come up against a "dangerous ambiguity" that portends a "besetting confusion"— this is hardly an unusual predicament for a philosopher to find himself in. It is also not unusual for him to try to work his way out by resorting to "an example."[1] What is unusual in the case of the philosopher I am quoting, Edmund Husserl, is that his example is a work of art—a notoriously complicated affair. Usually a philosopher who finds himself threatened by ambiguity and confusion prefers to keep his examples simple, lest matters get even further out of hand.

The confusion that Husserl would clear up is ultimately between his phenomenological reduction and what happens when we contemplate a work of art. Both are instances of what he terms a "neutrality modification." I shall not go into the technicalities of the phenomenological reduction now; because of the difficulties in carrying it out, Husserl himself recommended postponing it, even though he regarded it as a "method providing a way of access" (*Zugangsmethode*) to the subject of philosophy and dedicated thousands of pages to expounding it.[2] I would only point out that philosophy becoming to this extent a "way" or "method of access" to itself is not unprecedented. Perhaps the most famous passage in the history of philosophy is Plato's cave, with its delineation of the "passage way" (*eisodos*) that a prisoner (someone who is not yet a philosopher) must be induced to take if he is to become a philosopher.[3]

Indeed it seems possible that one of the distinguishing characteristics of a philosophy is that no other undertaking is as often concerned with how access is to be gained to itself; certainly no science is. Philosophy to this extent becomes an intro-duction to philosophy in the strong sense of Husserl's idiom of re-duction, whereby we are "led back" out of the cave—out of the confines of what Husserl called the "natural attitude."[4]

As a precedent for his phenomenological reduction, as a "way" or "method of access" to philosophy, what Husserl had specifically in mind was not Plato but, rather, Descartes' method. Indeed, in *Ideas I*, from which I have quoted, Husserl had adopted what he later characterized as "the Cartesian way."[5] In adopting it, Husserl had run into another dangerous ambiguity, which can mislead us into confusing his phenomenological reduction with Descartes' "methodical doubt." In fact this danger seems to have encouraged Husserl to coin his own technical term, "neutrality modification," or at least to apply it with the explanation that the phenomenological reduction is not a matter of supposing with Descartes that the external world does not exist. The phenomenological reduction instead involves merely the "neutralizing" of my ordinary belief in its existence, the "bracketing" of this belief and the "setting it aside."[6] My belief itself, as something I am conscious of, survives, but my confidence in it is neutralized.

I have mentioned the danger of confusing the phenomenological reduction with Descartes' methodical doubt for it is a danger that Husserl tried to eliminate much earlier in *Ideas I* than the section I have quoted.[7] But recalling this danger helps us understand the further danger, which is Husserl's concern in this section, of confusing the neutrality modification involved in the phenomenological reduction with that involved in the contemplation of a work of art.

The Example

Keeping this danger in mind, let us now turn to the example Husserl uses to clarify the neutrality modification involved in such contemplation:

> It may be that we are looking at the Dürer engraving *Knight, Death, and Devil*. In the first place, let us distinguish ordinary perceiving, the correlate of which is the *physical thing, "engraved print,"* this print in the portfolio. In the second place, we distinguish the perceptual consciousness in which there appear to us, in the black lines, the tiny colorless figures "Knight on Horseback," "Death," and

"Devil." In aesthetic contemplation we are not directed toward these as objects; we are directed toward what is represented "in the pictorial image [*im Bilde*]"—more precisely, toward the depicted [*abgebildeten*] realities, the knight of flesh and blood, and so forth.[8]

In this passage Husserl would illustrate the difference in how our attention is directed when we imagine the full-size knight from how it was when we actually saw the tiny engraved figures. This difference in direction is effected by the intervention of the neutrality modification.

It is here that comparison with his earlier distinction between a neutrality modification and methodical doubt is helpful: we are not supposing that the lines or figures do not exist; rather, the existence of those lines or figures we previously saw is neutralized as soon as we contemplate what they represent. This neutralizing is a modification, a redirection of our attention. Let me bring out the import of Husserl's example by expanding on it, perhaps somewhat too broadly: our attention was differently directed when, outside the museum, we were threading our way through traffic to cross the street than it is now, inside the museum, when we are looking at the pictures.

Such redirections of our attention we do not ordinarily attend to; they are too familiar. But prying ourselves loose from the familiar ("the natural attitude") is characteristic of the effort to obtain access to philosophy. Again I cite noteworthy precedents—Plato's cave and Descartes' methodical doubt. For Husserl, too, philosophy requires a special redirection of our attention. Indeed, he regards his phenomenological reduction as the most important procedure for meeting this requirement.

Granted the attentiveness required, it seems somewhat curious that Husserl should be so casual in his handling of this example. The phrase that introduces the passage, *Es sei etwa* (roughly, "It may be," or "It may happen"), is a colloquialism, which seems to imply that he could just as well have taken some other print as his example. This implication is perhaps played up by his having the print in a portfolio, where it presumably was lying loose.

Translation

The access route to philosophy that I am now proposing is not followed by Husserl or Descartes or Plato but is reached by understanding the differences between the routes different philosophers have followed. If I were interested simply in Husserl's access route, I would not have started out with a passage two-thirds of the way through *Ideas I*. I have quoted the passage from Husserl only because Sarte quoted it, lifting it out of Husserl into his own philosophy.[9] My noticing Husserl's casualness may have seemed quibbling, but a reason I did so was because Sartre apparently regarded this causalness as unmotivated. (Later I'll suggest a possible motivation on Husserl's part.) At any rate, two phrases in Husserl suffer slight mistranslations in Sartre. Husserl's informal *Es sei etwa* Sartre translates with the formal behest *Considérons* ("Let us consider"), and *dieses Blatt in der Mappe* ("this print in the portolio") becomes *cette feuille de l'album* ("this page in the artbook").

Mistranslations so slight I neglect for the present as seemingly inconsequential. I am interested in larger issues of philosophical translation. In my preliminary volume, *The Dream is Over*, I outlined some of these issues insofar as they can be exhibited by the history of phenomenology. I brought out how pivotal to this history was the relation between Husserl and Heidegger. I quoted Husserl on this relation: he came to the conclusion (in the margin of his copy of *Being and Time*) that Heidegger's philosophy was a "trans-lation" (*Übertragung*) of his own philosophy. My hyphenation was justified by Husserl's employing *Übertragung* in its etymological sense, for he went on to accuse Heidegger of having "transponiert oder transversiert" in *Being and Time* what had been Husserl's own philosophy.[10] In other words, Heidegger's philosophy was a version of Husserl's philosophy, and a perversion.

One of several difficulties I encountered in assessing the respects in which Heidegger's trans-lation is a mistranslation or perverted translation of Husserl was that Heidegger (despite his admiring acknowledgement that his *Being and Time* "would not have been possible if the foundations had not been laid for it by Edmund Husserl") does not in *Being and Time* quote a single substantive passage from Husserl.[11] In Sartre's case, however, we have the advantage of a passage that he has literally translated from Husserl and literally "transferred and transposed" into his own philosophy; through it we can examine the extended sense in which Sartre has in effect trans-lated Husserl's philosophy into terms of his own philosophy. In order to focus on the relation between their philosophies, I propose to explore the passage which Sartre has translated as providing a passage way through which Sartre gains, in Husserl's philosophy, access to his own philosophy. "Husserl," Sartre declares, "opens the way."[12]

Starting Points

I have already indicated something of the passage's original context in Husserl's work: his concern is that the neutrality modification that is involved in the phenomenological reduction not be confused with that involved in a depictive act of the imagination—the act whereby we imagine lines and forms as a depiction of something else. It is because his long-range concern is with the phenomenological reduction—with maintaining its integrity against any confusion—that he uses the example of the work of art simply to draw a distinction. He is not worried over the complexities of the work of art as such, and his use of it as an example leaves them out of account. Thus there is not much point in our worrying about the obvious inadequacy of the passage in Husserl as a treatment of the aesthetic attitude or the work of art.

If I have not lingered with Husserl's concern, it is not just to avoid the additional complexities posed by the phenomenological reduction but to move from Husserl to Sartre's use of him. Sartre's concern is with what he can get out of the passage for his own treatment of the imagination; and he has already announced that in this treatment he is not going to apply the phenomenological reduction.[13] Sartre has quoted the passage because, he explains, it encourages him to "bring together" (*rapprocher*) two different kinds of images: "physical images—paintings, sketches, photographs"—with "images that are termed 'mental,'" whereas the traditional treatment had "ended up separating one radically from the other." Husserl's bringing them together amounts to a new "starting point."[14] To use the terminology I worked out in volume 1, the *rapprochement* effects a shift in *subject*.

There is irony in the situation the historian confronts here. Husserl himself never noticed this new "starting-point"; Sartre is crediting Husserl with originality for having effected this rapprochement when Husserl himself was entirely unaware of his originality.

A rapprochement between what was previously "separated" may be sufficient to effect a shift in *subject*. But to treat a subject distinctions are needed. For this purpose Sartre discovers in the passage he has borrowed a starting point in another respect: "This text can be a starting point for an *intrinsic* distinction between the image and perception."[15] Once a physical image is brought together with a mental image, a distinction is needed (if the treatment is to be phenomenological) between perceiving this physical image (the lines, the tiny figures, that compose the Dürer engraving) and the mental image we can then have of what the physical image represents.

In order not to confuse the two starting points Sartre discovers in the passage, I shall label the first his "starting point with respect to the subject he is to treat," and the second his "starting point with respect to the method he applies to this subject." This labeling, I grant, may well seem heavy-handed, for we do not yet know anything about his method.

When Sartre states, "this text can be the starting point," his "can be" allows for a certain discrepancy between what Sartre is taking over from Husserl in the passage and the treatment he himself has in prospect.

Sartre even admits that this "distinction between the image and perception" is a distinction that Husserl "has not pushed further in his published works." It is thoroughly traditional for a successor to proceed from a predecessor by pushing further a distinction which a predecessor had neglected to push. But it would usually be more accurate to say that he is pushing the distinction not just further but in a different *direction*.[16] Differences in method between Sartre and Husserl will emerge as we watch Sartre push this distinction further and in a different direction. The passage way will turn out a dramatic illustration of how two philosophers can proceed in different directions, even when there seems to be an overlap between them—in the present instance, a text the successor has lifted from his predecessor.

The distinction that Sartre would take as a starting point Husserl does not push at all; he prefers to push something else. What it is would be more evident if Sartre, to get started himself, had not created a "text" in his own philosophy by suddenly breaking off his translation of the passage with the announcement, "This text can be a starting point for an *intrinsic* distinction between the image and perception." But Husserl is not directly concerned with this distinction in this passage, any more than he is concerned to achieve the rapprochement with respect to the subject that Sartre congratulates him for achieving.

Context

Sometimes it is worth the reader's while to take a look at the con-text from which a "text" has been extracted. There is always a possibility that the predecessor's own line of argument has been short-circuited. By taking a look at the context, you can see where the successor, in pushing further and in a different direction—has left his predecessor behind.

A difference in direction is well illustrated by reinstating Husserl's actual example. On the one hand, Sartre begins in the middle of a sentence in Husserl's work: "Let us try to make that clear to ourselves: it may be . . ." To find out what "that" refers to, we have to go back to the preceding sentence, where Husserl explains that "we can be convinced by an example of how a neutrality modification takes place when a perceived object becomes, by an act of the imagination, the depiction of something else."

On the other hand, the reader is well advised to read on in the Husserl after Sartre has obtained what he wanted and he stopped quoting from it. In the next sentence, Husserl's argument is that "the consciousness of the picture [*Bild*] is now an example of the neutrality modification of perception." This is not the example that Sartre would have wanted. But he must have read on too, for once he has created his "text," he does have a second thought and concedes, "What matters to Husserl here is that the positing of existence has received a neutrality modification." Sartre adds, however, "We do not have to concern ourselves with this here." Accordingly, Sartre does not concern himself with why what matters to Husserl here is the neutrality modification. The historian has to intervene on Husserl's behalf and explain that what matters ultimately to Husserl is that his phenomenological reduction, as a neutrality modification, not be confused with an imaginative neutrality modification.[17] The historian can also explain on Sartre's behalf that the neutrality modification is of no concern to Sartre because he is not applying the phenomenological reduction as a way of access to the subject he would treat.

Leeway

When Sartre brushes Husserl off—"We do not have to concern ourselves with this here"—he is acknowledging a certain leeway between Husserl's concerns and his own. More explicitly, Sartre is concerned with the work of art as a physical image; Husserl is not. Indeed, Husserl is here concerned with the depictive act of imagination only insofar as it involves a neutrality modification. He is certainly not concerned, as is Sartre, with working out a general philosophy of the imagination. If he does select as an example a depictive act of the imagination, it is presumably because other acts of the imagination, though also dependent in his phenomenology on a preceding act (or acts) of perception, are less likely to be performed in conjunction with a recently performed act of perception (seeing "the tiny figures") and thus would yield a less succinct illustration of the neutrality modification.

Simone de Beauvoir recalls "the extreme rapidity" with which Sartre wrote his work on the imagination. Sartre was "breathless from following with his pen the movement of his thought."[18] We can speculate that since he was breathlessly getting on with his own philosophy, he did not pause to examine the different direction in which Husserl had been proceeding. Indeed, Sartre may seem to have left so much leeway between himself and Husserl that there may also seem little point in the historian himself becoming concerned with their differences. The two philosophers simply go past each other, as philosophers so often do.

Ambiguity

Nevertheless, I have three reasons for examining the passage. First, the "text" Sartre extracts from the passage in Husserl is crucial to Sartre because it provides him with starting points in two respects, granted that their significance as starting points will become clear only later, in retrospect. Second, the fact that the same passage belongs to two different philosophies provides me with a relatively simple example as a starting point in still another respect—for dealing as a historian with the relations between philosophies. Thus I am not just dismissing Sartre as a careless reader of Husserl.[19] Nor is my objective simply to illustrate a recurrent episode in the history of philosophy, namely, the success with which a successor arrives at his own philosophy coming at the expense of some more or less unwitting damage he does to a predecessor's philosophy, thereby requiring the historian to keep his wits about him if he would restore the original philosophy.

Rather, I am recognizing that Sartre's relation to Husserl is honeycombed with ambiguities. I am not for the present interested either in the particular "ambiguity" (Äquivocation) which (as I began this volume by observing) confronted Husserl in the passage Sartre cites or in the "confusion" (Verwechslung) which Husserl found attendant upon it.[20] I am concerned instead with the ambiguous or equivocal relation between their two philosophies and with the "confusion" as a Verwechslung— that is, as the "mix-up" that takes place when Sartre obtains his own different philosophy in "exchange" for Husserl's. Thus a third reason I am exploiting the passage Sartre cites (and other borrowings from Husserl) is to counter the rigid doctrine of undecidability as upheld by the more debonair deconstructionists, who refuse to recognize the extent to which many ambiguities in philosophy can be due to such mix-ups. It is then up to the historian to sift the ingredients in the mixture.

The History of Philosophy

Sartre proclaims that the passage from Husserl on the Dürer engraving "deserves to remain classic." We might therefore suppose it deserves to remain untampered with. But in fact Sartre's tampering opens up in the passage a passage way from Husserl's phenomenology—a passage way by which Sartre can be shown to reach his own phenomenology of the imagination. Furthermore, the passage opens up a way of access to reach some of the problems the historian of philosophy encounters in dealing with the ambiguities of the relations between philosophers and thus deserves to remain classic in a higher-order sense.

I offered in Volume 1 a preliminary outline of these problems.[21] This general outline I arrived at through a succession of forays, in each of which I singled out for analysis an episode in the history of phenomenology.[22] Now I shall offer a sustained commentary on Sartre's treatment of the imagination, as illustrating the relation between his phenomenology and Husserl's. Why it is necessary now to proceed step-by-step will become clear only when we recognize in retrospect the significance Sartre attached to the sequence he has followed. I respect his sequence in my commentary because (as we shall see) Husserl does not attach the same significance to sequence as Sartre does.

In keeping track of the details of Sartre's treatment of the imagination, I am engaged in what Husserl called "grubby work" (*schmützige Arbeit*).[23] Though he found it indispensable, he still was wistful: "How I would like to live on the heights. For this is what all my thinking craves for. But shall I ever work my way upward, if only for a little, so that I can gain something of a distant view?"[24]

My overall analysis I exposed in Volume 1 as expeditiously as I could, but in the present volume it will come into view slowly and in the distance. Even the passage way I have taken in this chapter will have to face challenges to its reliability.

Method

The preoccupation, that I carry over from Volume 1, is to design a higher-order method for dealing with the relations between philosophers—a method that enables us to understand what is at issue between them, so that it becomes a "way of access" (*Zugangsmethode*) to philosophy itself. Such a method is particularly appropriate to deal with phenomenology. In no other twentieth century philosophical movement has controversy over the relations between the philosophies prominently involved in it contributed so much to its momentum. I do not retain Husserl's other metaphor—the "entrance gate" (*Eingangstor*) that he considered he had opened with his phenomenological reduction.[25] A gate swinging on its hinges suggests that there is a single decisive juncture at which entry is to be gained, when there are several decisive junctures. In my forays in Volume 1 I sorted out (besides the shift in *subject,* with which I am starting here) shifts in *affiliation, level,* and in *method.* These shifts determine broadly the *direction* in which the philosopher is proceeding, and in this broad sense I regard them all as shifts in *method.*

As I stressed in Volume 1, I am not proclaiming that the method I am designing for dealing with these relations will yield a prolegomenon to all future philosophy. The shifts I sort out are merely heuristic devices to assist the historian in discerning some of the more decisive changes that have taken place in the history of philosophy and in deciding whether or not at the present juncture we have reached, or are reaching, the end of philosophy.

The Disciple

Husserl had captured me. I saw everything via the perspectives of his philosophy.—Sartre

The Captive

My main argument in Volume 1 for focusing on the relations between philosophers was the problem they pose the historian of philosophy.[1] But a supplementary argument of mine was that focusing on one philosopher's relations to other philosophers can help discern what was distinctive of his philosophy. Unfortunately, as soon as my candidate for this philosopher is identified, a misgiving has to be confronted before I can continue moving along my passage way. Disdain for Sartre as a philosopher has become so entrenched today that impatient readers may well have put this book aside as soon as they discovered that I quoted a passage from Husserl at the beginning because Sartre had quoted it and in effect incorporated it into his philosophy. That Sartre has been more widely read than any other philosopher of this century elicits only a shrug of the shoulders. Already before his death he had become, by his own account, a "has been."[2] His earlier vogue is now hardly even a matter of historical interest.

My interest in Sartre hangs less on his merits or demerits as a philosopher than on the fact that another philosopher "opens the way" for him and, thereby, becomes his access to philosophy itself. Or, rather, a succession of other philosophers do: before World War II, Husserl; during the war, Heidegger; after the war, Hegel and Marx. I have just refused to assess as either a merit or demerit Sartre's wide readership. But by the time he was winning it, he had turned "toward Heidegger and against Husserl."[3] In consequence, his earlier relation to Husserl never received the attention that it deserves as an example of the problems the historian faces in dealing with the relations between philosophers.

Sartre's prewar relation to Husserl is historically remarkable. "Husserl," he admits "had captured me. I saw everything in terms of the perspectives of his philosophy." In his treatment of the imagination, Sartre reports that he writes against Husserl, "only insofar as a disciple can write against his master." Sartre's work on the imagination was "inspired" by Husserl.[4]

That Sartre's relation as a disciple to a master was not just a casual affair that he stumbled into is of course suggested by his later turning toward other philosophers. But in those instances, he never designates himself as "a disciple." He is never "captured" by Heidegger or Hegel or Marx in the same fashion as he had been by Husserl.

Discipleship, I suggested in Volume 1, is the least complicated, the most accessible, of relations between philosophers, to the extent that a disciple is a philosopher who has not proceeded (or has not yet proceeded) from his master's philosophy to reach an original philosophy of his own. Such discipleship on the part of a philosopher who later became as prominent as Sartre is a rather unusual episode in the history of philosophy. More often a philosopher gets underway because he is sensitive to what he regards as unresolved issues between his predecessors, as is the case later with the wartime Sartre, who would resolve in *Being and Nothingness* the issues opposing Husserl and Heidegger—the issues that he only encountered when he turned "toward Heidegger against Husserl."

The Inventor

I am not claiming that the relation between a disciple and his master is without complications. They become more acute when the historian would bring out what is distinctive of the disciple's philosophy or when the disciple himself puts a premium on his own originality, as Sartre did at the very moment he felt he was being converted to Husserl. He felt in "complete disarray" then, for he was confronted by the possibility that Husserl had "already discovered all my ideas."[5]

This feeling is evident in Simone de Beauvoir's report of Sartre's conversion. She was also on hand while Sartre was writing on the imagination: she characterizes his treatment as "an investigation in which Sartre invented both the method and content, obtaining all its materials from his own experience."[6] Is Sartre here a captive or an inventor?

This is a question that can be raised in the context of his relation to Husserl, for if Sartre is a captive of Husserl, this would make him a distinctively different kind of philosopher from Husserl. Husserl, as a phenomenologist, never recognized that he saw anything via the perspectives of any other philosophy. Instead, he interposed the "philosophical *epochē*," with which he set aside everything any other philosopher had asserted, even about philosophy itself.[7] This *epochē* was his initial access to philosophy, granted that it needed to be followed up by the phenomenological reduction. Thus Husserl never viewed himself as allowing any other philosopher to open the way for him in the fashion that he "opens the way" for Sartre.

Une Défaite

As soon as a historian of philosophy has exhibited his own purposes (as I have), he should attempt to decide how relevant they are to whatever philosopher he would exploit. Sartre's relation as "a disciple" to Husserl as "his master" is not simply something that can be settled by balancing his texts against Husserl's—what I began doing in Chapter 1. Quite independently of Sartre's treatment of the imagination or any other problem, the relation between a disciple and a master was itself once of concern to Sartre. This fact encourages my focusing on this relation as a higher-order problem.

The evidence has become available with the publication of *Sartre: écrits de jeunesse*. These juvenilia are to be used with a certain caution. An investigator of at least one of them once came to the conclusion, "Nothing would enable one to predict that Sartre would become 'Sartre.'"[8] The prediction was too extreme: we shall detect traits of "Sartre" in the juvenilia that will survive his captivation by Husserl and his later turning toward other philosophers.

"Sartre" found it difficult to recognize himself in these writings, and (according to their editors, Michel Contat and Michel Rybalka) regarded them with "a certain diffidence." He viewed "these texts of his youth as those of a stranger he had known long ago."[9] Of course, "Sartre" also confessed, "I no longer recognize myself very well [in the period] before the war"—which would include the Sartre who wrote on the imagination.[10] If we discover someone who is not a complete stranger, we shall eventually have to face the question, Why does "Sartre" have such difficulty in recognizing himself?

Now we can observe that self-recognition is not an irrelevant criterion here, since Sartre's youthful fictional writings, as their editors point out, "are autobiographical in character." The editors are footnoting

Sartre's commitment in one early work (dated 1924) "to write only stories about the events of my own life." [11] The manuscript of the most important of these stories, *"Une défaite,"* they guess dates from 1927, and they identify it as "Sartre's last literary effort that we know about before *Nausea.*" They add that "Sartre certainly experienced the reception of this 'first' novel as an *'échec'"*—in particular, its rejection by a publisher. [12] Thus *"Une défaite,"* became a defeat for Sartre himself. [13]

"Une défaite," seems based mainly on Charles Andler's biography of Nietzsche. [14] Sartre relies on Andler's account of the relation of the youthful "Frédéric" Nietzsche to the aging Richard Wagner (renamed Richard Organte by Sartre) and to Wagner's wife, Cosima. Neglecting other features of *"Une défaite,"* that would be interesting in other contexts, I focus here on the relation between Frédéric and Organte. [15]

What was biographical in Andler is recast in *"Une défaite"* as autobiography. Frédéric becomes a student at the *École normale,* a year older than Sartre was at the time, so that one suspects that Frédéric would be Sartre's age by the time Sartre expected to finish the manuscript. This he never did. The explanation of Sartre's recasting is not that he had adopted Nietzsche's philosophy. As the editors point out, "the twenty-two-year-old Frédéric does not feel any profound affinity with Nietzsche." [16] Rather, Sartre is taking advantage of the fact that Nietzsche was enjoying his first vogue in France, and the biographical information that had become available in French enabled Sartre to deck out his own aspirations. In fact, as the editors point out, Frédéric does "summarize in an awkward but straightforward fashion Sartre's own project as a writer." Frédéric explains, "You understand . . . I want to . . . write. Only, I want to be able to bring together . . . everything I will say as a . . . point of view . . . a single point of view. This point of view I want philo[sophy] to provide me with." [17] These phrases Frédéric stammers out to Organte, whom he would have as his master.

A Master

Sartre's editors line up several respects in which Frédéric is obviously the youthful Sartre, so the finality with which they exclude one comparison with Frédéric is rather surprising:

> No one played in the life of Sartre as an adolescent, then as a young man, the role of an admired master . . . , and he himself has assured us that he had never had the least temptation to select a master for himself: "It is something altogether alien to me," he told us in 1975. [18]

Frédéric was more ambivalent in 1927. I quote a passage from *"Une défaite"* in which he is proposing to select a master:

> He visualized himself as an attentive disciple in the gardens of the Academy. But this humility was not sincere. He conceived the kind of master who would be obscure, upright, and a man of genius, but lacking the necessary power to impose himself on the world, and he visualized himself as taking over his master's doctrine, finishing it, constructing the edifice, and constraining by force his fellows to revere it. But this was one of the dreams of his own feebleness. His forceful days, he accepted the prospect of finding his truth by himself. . . . He had felt how painful was the attitude of a disciple. . . . He felt diminished being passive, simply listening and understanding without reacting. . . . And he understood now he could not, like Phaedrus, Philebus—those handsome young Athenians—resign himself to punctuate with a "Quite so" and a "Without a doubt" the long discourses of Socrates.[19]

At the time Frédéric indulged in these reflections, Sartre had not yet encountered Husserl. Yet their ambivalence provides a closer approximation to what transpired when he did (when he was both "captured" and dismayed at a possible threat to his originality) than his blunt disavowal in 1975 that a master "is something which is altogether alien to me."

At this early stage in *"Une défaite"* itself, Frédéric has not encountered Organte. When he does,

> he suffers unceasingly the same very strong temptation to ask Organte, "Would you be my master?" . . . He was shaken by a painful irony: he now recognized the old lament of his distress, of his lassitude, of his isolation. It was still *the call of the master,* this call which used to resound earlier in him in the epoch of his illusions: "A master, a master! . . . Organte is my master. . . . Alas, I will not follow his advice. I cannot be the disciple of any man.[20]

Frédéric is betraying the same ambivalence as he did before he met Organte.

The Lamentable Frédéric

Three features of Sartre's handling of the disciple-master relation should be acknowledged. First, he was apparently not particularly distressed when Mme Louis Morel, the woman who was partly the model for Cosima, took to referring to Sartre himself as "the lamentable Frédéric."[21]

Sartre accepted his identification with Frédéric, but with considerable self-irony.[22] Second, it may be of some pertinence to Sartre's discipleship that the derivativeness with which Sartre as a child launched his writing career—he plagiarized other writers—carries over in his extensive reliance on Andler's biography. Finally, this reliance in turn finds an autobiographical explanation in a letter written in 1926: "I can hardly interest myself in anything besides the life stories of great men. I try to find there a prophecy of my own life."[23] Once the prophecy is fulfilled and Sartre does in fact become a great man, he can make his claim that finding a master for himself "is something which is altogether alien to me," just as he can also dedicate himself in his later autobiographical work, *Words*, to *not* becoming a great man.

For the present, we can conclude that Sartre as a young man was preoccupied in *"Une défaite"* with the disciple-master relation.[24] He could then hardly dismiss as irrelevant my undertaking to explore his relation to the "master" he later found—the only person he ever so designated.

THREE

The Image

What is going on when I perceive a natural object as aesthetic?—Sartre

The Lineup

The most obvious way we can gauge the extent of Sartre's philosophical discipleship is by comparing his later treatment of the mental image, as "inspired" by Husserl, with the earlier treatment in *L'image,* Sartre's *diplôme.* He had finished *L'image* in 1926, before he read Husserl—at about the same time, he was writing on discipleship in *"Une défaite,"* before he ever became an actual disciple. For the purpose of this comparison, let me line up the relevant texts. After Sartre returned from reading Husserl in Berlin, the professor who had supervised the *diplôme* suggested Sartre rewrite it for publication. But only the first part of Sartre's new *L'image* was accepted by the publisher. Except for a brief phenomenological introduction, this part was entirely a historical survey of the treatment of the image from Descartes to Husserl. I began this volume by quoting a passage from Husserl that Sartre himself quotes in the final chapter of the first part of *L'image,* which was published in 1936 under the title *L'imagination.* This final chapter is devoted to Husserl but looks forward to the prospect of Sartre's own theory, which was not published until 1940, under the title *L'imaginaire.*[1] Since the two parts were originally different portions of the same manuscript, which apparently retained the *diplôme*'s title *"L'image,"* they can be presumed to belong to pretty much the same theory of the imagination. There may then seem no definite need to distinguish them. But in what was published separately as *L'imaginaire*, Sartre did add at least one chapter to the original manuscript, and the possibility cannot be excluded that he also made other minor revisions. Accordingly, I shall refer to *L'imagination* and *L'imaginaire* as two separate works.

Since my interest is in Sartre's relation to Husserl, I restricted myself in Chapter 1 to the final chapter of *L'imagination*, and I shall continue to rely on it for the present. The preceding historical survey in *L'imagination* is evidence primarily of Sartre's incompetence as a historian of philosophy (no rebuke could bother him less); I shall therefore neglect that survey, except where he shows his own hand.

That Sartre wrote the *diplôme* demonstrates one fact: his commitment to the image as a subject demanding treatment was not uniquely due to Husserl's inspiration. Once Sartre did read Husserl, however, he was convinced that Husserl could not have avoided treating this subject: "He has undoubtedly elaborated a theory of the image in his courses and in unpublished works."[2] Since it is unlikely that Sartre had any inside information to back up this "undoubtedly," the strength of his conviction is something that will have eventually to be explained. (I shall try in Chapter 6.) As a matter of fact, Husserl did treat the imagination in a lecture course—but this course was published the year Sartre died (1980), more than forty years after Husserl's own death.[3] Since Sartre never had any access to this course, I shall myself make only supplementary use of it. I have already presented in Volume 1 the argument for relying initially on the prima facie evidence a philosopher himself provides for the relation between his philosophy and another philosophy he finds relevant to it.[4] But I also made clear that this prima facie evidence need not be taken at its face value.

The Subject

To recognize Sartre's previous commitment to the image as a subject is not to deny his debt to Husserl for the shift in *subject*. There is a distinction to be drawn between a "subject" in the loose and weak sense in which we ordinarily use the term and the strong sense in which a philosopher finds a "subject" congenial and amenable to treatment. This strong sense cannot be fully specified until the method of treatment is taken into account, but I can nonetheless illustrate the strong sense now by recalling that Sartre regarded the image as having become a new subject, constituted by Husserl when, in the Dürer passage, he brought the mental image into conjunction with the physical image, from which it had traditionally been separated.

The distinction between the two senses of "subject" is particularly necessary when the loose sense is as indeterminate as it is in what we refer to as an "image." The question has even been raised expressly in "Do We Need the Terms 'Image' and 'Imagery'?"[5] The questioner, P. N. Furbank, does go so far as to assume that "the natural sense of the word 'image'" is "a likeness, a picture": this is the sense in which Husserl takes the term and the sense in which there is some plausibility to Sartre's endorsement of Husserl's bringing the mental image into conjunction with the physical image. In fact, Furbank asserts, "No one would deny that painters and sculptors are concerned with producing 'images' (or have been till very recently)," and so he proposes that "we might begin by thinking about painting." He is adopting more or less the same subject for a starting point as Sartre did. He then finds that he has to argue that an "image" in a familiar literary sense "cannot be a picture." For example, "when one reads . . . 'Macbeth has murdered Sleep,'" one is "baffled" if one tries to come up with a mental picture.[6] Thus he is critical of this usage.

As we would expect, Furbank endorses Sartre's general conception of an "image," but Sartre has been criticized for his "dubious assimilation [of a mental image] to portraiture."[7] Such issues over the "image" as a subject are inevitable, given the looseness of our usage. I leave them to one side, for the very simple reason that they are not issues between Husserl and Sartre. Both of them assume an image is in some sense a likeness, and issues will eventually emerge that can now only be summarized baldly as issues regarding respects in which the image is unlike what it is like.

The Shift in Subject

In the *diplôme*, Sartre conceives the mental image as a likeness, but the *diplôme* also yields evidence that Sartre did not then conceive it as something to be brought into conjunction with a physical image. The *diplôme* is a jumble. But to illustrate the sense in which Sartre was treating a different "subject" then, I might pick out a problem that Sartre takes up that we have already encountered in the Dürer passage borrowed from Husserl—the problem of "aesthetic contemplation." In the *diplôme*, Sartre proposes to determine "what is going on when I perceive a natural object as aesthetic." He latches onto the relation between ordinary perception and "aesthetic perception," as posing the problem of what "is added" to ordinary perception. By virtue of the "surplus" (*surcroît*) involved, Sartre employs for "aesthetic perception" the term *surperception*.[8]

In explaining the process by which this "surplus" is added, Sartre assigns a role to the imagination. All I would take into account is the process as featured by the examples on which he relies. They begin with what is perceived and arrive at its transformation as the result of the intervention of "the aesthetic attitude." An example he reports from his own experience is how a landscape in the Vosges mountains acquires the "aesthetic quality" it has for him, although the landscape would be "without artistic value . . . if it were transferred [as it presents itself to his ordinary perception] onto the canvas of a painter." Sartre also relies on two similar examples from Proust. In the first, "I returned to confront the hawthorns as if I were in front of artistic masterpieces which one believes would be seen better if one stopped looking at them for a moment." In the second example, "Suddenly, a roof, sunlight reflected on a stone, the odor of a path, halted me with a particular pleasure which they gave me and also because they had the air of hiding, beyond what I was seeing, something which they invited me to come and take hold of." Sartre comments: "Thus an object that attracts our aesthetic perception appears ambiguous to us. We try . . . to snatch its secret from it. And that is to do the work of the artist." But he implies that we do not succeed, as Proust goes on to admit.

Our first reaction is that this Sartre of the *diplôme* is very different from the "Sartre" who is known to history. The mature Sartre will be urban and "allergic to chlorophyll,"[9] and there are no examples in *L'imagination* or *L'imaginaire* of landscapes or flowers. This Sartre will also for a while be allergic to Proust. And he does give specific credit for this to Husserl, as we shall see in Chapter 6.

All that we can infer at present is some confirmation of Sartre's acknowledged debt to Husserl for the shift in *subject*—the rapprochement between the work of art as a physical image and the mental image. In the *diplôme,* the work of art is brought in merely hypothetically: with "if it [the landscape] were transferred onto the canvas of a painter," and with Proust's "as if I were in front of artistic masterpieces." The natural object is in the foreground, being perceived. But in *L'imagination* the work of art comes to the fore as initially a physical image that is being perceived, and the mental image with which Sartre is so far concerned is an image of what the physical image represents.

Representation

Representation itself is analyzed differently in the *diplôme* and the later writings, and this too is a difference that can be credited to Husserl. Evidence is found in the other long passage from *Ideas I* that Sartre quotes in *L'imagination.* In this passage, Husserl denies the appropriateness of assuming in phenomenology that representations are to be analyzed as "psychological products." But this very assumption is precisely the one behind Sartre's analysis that I have cited from the *diplôme*. How, he in effect asks, does a landscape in the Vosges come to acquire its "aesthetic quality" in his representation of it, "its artistic value"?

In the passage Sartre translates, Husserl would confute the objection that a representation is merely a psychological "product" or "construct." He envisages the objection as seemingly supported by an example when what is represented is a fiction:

> Could it not be objected that [this phrase is Sartre's interpolation] a centaur playing the flute, a fiction that we freely imagine [*einbilden/ formons*] is thereby a free associating of our representations? But . . . it is a representation in the sense [of] what one calls what is represented and not in the sense that a representation would be a name for a mental experience. The centaur itself is, of course, nothing. This *experience of imagining is not to be confused with what is imagined*.[10]

Sartre halts the translation here. He has reached the conclusion he would extract (with his italics) for his own theory, and he restates this conclusion in the following sentences: "This text is crucial: that the centaur or the chimera does not exist does not give us the right to reduce them to merely mental formations. . . . Husserl restores to the centaur its transcendence."

Sartre is extracting from this example a conclusion that we shall later (in Chapter 6) watch him pursue in his essay "A Fundamental Idea of Husserl's Phenomenology—Intentionality," which Sartre wrote in Berlin when he first read Husserl: an intentional object (in the citation, "what is imagined") I am conscious of as transcending whatever psychological activities (in the citation, the "experience of imagining") are involved in producing my consciousness of it. This distinction I am anticipating now merely in order to suggest that Sartre, once he had become familiar with Husserl and intentionality, would view the analysis in the *diplôme* as having reduced "what is imagined" to the "mental formations" that compose the "experience of imagining."

The example is "crucial" to Sartre because the intentional object is an imaginary fiction. Usually Husserl takes as an example of an intentional object something perceived. (This preference of his I shall discuss in the Conclusion to the present volume.) In the earlier Berlin essay on intentionality, in which Sartre himself stays closer to Husserl, nearly all the examples are taken from perception. The example is not similarly "crucial" to Husserl, any more than is the example of the Dürer engraving, which was a relatively unobtrusive and unimportant example in *Ideas I* and did not enjoy the "classic" status Sartre conferred on it. Yet it can be explained why Husserl picked the example of the centaur. It seemed suited (as Sartre apparently surmised with his translation *formons* and with the reference in his conclusion to "mental formations") to the objection Husserl is envisaging, because the example lent itself to the interpretation of a representation as a "product" or "construct," inasmuch as the centaur is put together out of a man and a horse to which is further added the flute it is playing.

Dismemberment

Having discovered what Sartre gets out of this second example from Husserl, we should turn around and discover what Husserl himself got out of this example. For we have learned from the example of the Dürer engraving that Sartre is capable of creating a "text" which he transfers to the con-text of his own theory of the imagination. In the process, Husserl's analysis has suffered dismemberment. In Volume 1, I dealt in general terms with the way in which a successor can dismember the corpus as a whole of a previous philosophy, in a fashion that can sometimes betray a shift in *subject*.[11] Now we are watching specific arguments being dismembered. If we read on beyond the conclusion Sartre has italicized in Husserl, we arrive at Husserl's own conclusion in the very next sentence: "In the same way [as in the case of imagining], in the case of spontaneous abstracting it is not the *essence* that is produced but, instead, the consciousness of the essence." There is no mention, in Sartre's discussion of this passage, of the term "essence," which Husserl italicizes. There is no mention of the fact that the section from which Sartre is citing this passage is entitled "Ideation, Essence, and Fiction" or that it is a section in part 1 of *Ideas I* which is devoted to "essence" and to the procedure of "ideation" (also labeled the "eidetic reduction"), by which an essence is abstracted.

This procedure itself I shall expound later. For the present, I need only explain why Husserl would select at this point this specific example of an image that is a fiction (just as I explained before why he selected the specific example of a depictive act of the imagination whereby something perceived becomes a physical image). Husserl has selected a fiction because in the case of a fiction, as an image of something that does not actually exist, there is an even stronger temptation to disregard the distinction between an act of consciousness and what it is consciousness of (its transcendent object)—and so to regard the fiction as merely a "product" of the act of the imagination—than there is in the case of something perceived, or even something imagined, that in fact does exist elsewhere.

What Sartre overlooks here is (in the terminology I elaborated in Volume 1) a shift in *level,* which we shall see is accomplished by the eidetic reduction—that is, a shift from the level of particular objects (here, the centaur) to the higher level of essence. (Later we shall see that there is nonetheless a sense in which Sartre's analysis is "eidetic.") But Husserl is concerned here with the objectivity not of what is imagined itself (as is Sartre) but with the objectivity of an essence; consequently, he comes up against the risk that the similarity between something imagined and an essence will be extended and that the skeptical conclusion will be reached that an essence is merely something imagined and does not exist in the same sense in which a centaur does not exist. As he himself puts it, he comes up against the suspicion "with respect to the existence of an essence—is it not a fiction as the skeptics would like us to think?" How Husserl disposes of this suspicion is not my concern here. My point is merely that Husserl is carefully precluding the example from acquiring more general implications. He is keeping the implications of the argument circumscribed. Thus we see (and this is a general point I would stress as an historian) that dismemberment need not entail a loss of generality; it can entail, as is illustrated by Sartre's use of this passage on the centaur and the passage on the Dürer engraving, a loss of specificity and a gain in generality. Where Husserl's arguments usually tend to be circumscribed, Sartre's versions of them become sweeping. But this appraisal is itself too sweeping. We should be more specific.

ONE · INTENTIONAL
ANALYSIS

FOUR

In Passing

Husserl treats the problem of the image only in passing.—Sartre

The Passage Way

The differences between what Sartre gets out
of the two passages that we have watched
him borrow from Husserl and what Husserl
himself provided in them is so considerable
that it is becoming evident that my comparison so far has not done sufficient justice to
the discrepancy between what Sartre is up to
and what Husserl is up to. We were overly
impressed by the fact of the borrowing itself
when we assumed that the passages could become passage ways that we could readily tra-
verse from one philosophy into the other.

There is one discrepancy that Sartre himself admits. Although Sartre is convinced
that Husserl "has undoubtedly elaborated a
theory of the image in his courses and in unpublished works," he has to admit that in his
published works "Husserl treats the problem
of the image only in passing."[1] But Sartre
does not explain why, any more than he explains why Husserl preferred to publish
works on other subjects.

These questions can be answered more
specifically by reviewing the two passages
Sartre borrowed as treating the problem of
the image. Although Sartre in his translations of both these passages is treating the
image directly, Husserl himself is in fact
treating the image only in passing. In both
passages, he is concerned with a possible
confusion: in the case of the Dürer engraving, there is risk of confusing the neutrality

modification that is a feature of the phenomenological reduction with the neutrality modification that is an act of the imagination; in the case of the centaur, there is a risk of confusing the essence we become conscious of by carrying out an eidetic reduction with our consciousness of it. I shall deal with Husserl's preoccupation with disentangling confusions later, but it is already evident that in both our present cases Husserl's concern is with confusions that endanger our understanding of his method as implemented by these two reductions.

The Priority of Method

This is a concern to which Sartre so far seems indifferent.[2] Just as when he exploits the example of the Dürer engraving Sartre never mentions the phenomenological reduction, so he never mentions the eidetic reduction (or ideation) when he exploits the example of the centaur. Sartre never explicitly protests against "the priority of method" in Husserl; on the other hand, as we saw in Volume 1, Heidegger does.[3] But this "priority" cannot be dismissed merely as an interpretation foisted on Husserl by Heidegger, since it is now emerging from our comparison of Husserl with Sartre. Indeed, when Husserl himself wrote a "postscript" to *Ideas I*, he emphasized his two objectives in that work: "The essential *Problemschichten* ["levels at which problems are located"] and the essential *Zugangsmethoden* ["methods of access" to them] are clarified."[4] With the eidetic reduction, Husserl gains access to the level of essences, and this is his undertaking in part 1 of *Ideas I;* with the phenomenological reduction, he gains access to the transcendental level, and this is his undertaking in part 2 of *Ideas I.* There is no evidence in Sartre's use of either of the two examples from Husserl of any concern with these distinctions of level any more than with the methodological procedures for gaining access to the higher levels. These are differences of *direction* here between Sartre and Husserl that can receive further attention only when I have expounded the procedures themselves. But we can tentatively conclude that "Husserl treats the problem of the image only in passing," because he gives priority (at least in *Ideas I,* the work Sartre devoured in Berlin) to problems of method.[5]

The Dürer passage, we thought, yielded Sartre what he called a "starting point" with respect both to the subject of the image and to the distinction in terms of which he proposed to treat it. But we should also take into account Sartre's actual starting point in *L'imagination.* As I mentioned before, at the beginning of *L'imagination* Sartre offers a brief phenomenological introduction before undertaking the historical survey that culminates with the final chapter on Husserl. In the introduction, he starts out brusquely with an example: "I am looking at this white sheet of paper." He then proceeds to a phenomenological analysis of this experience. The example itself is borrowed from Husserl without any acknowledgement. But Husserl came up with this example only in section 35 of *Ideas I*, after having treated the eidetic reduction and when he is in the process of carrying out the phenomenological reduction. Thus the "priority" he assigns these two methodological procedures there is evident.

Even in section 35 he is not starting out brusquely with the example Sartre borrows; rather, he introduces it with "Let us link on [*anknüpfen*] an example." He has explained in the preceding section that "on the basis of examples we can grasp and fix in an adequate ideation the pure essence that interests us." We shall have reason later to doubt the purity of the essence Sartre goes on to grasp by using this example. My only comment now is that Sartre starts out with the example itself, without any methodological ado as to what he is doing. His beginning directly with a particular example, his apparent general indifference so far of considerations of method (at least as compared with Husserl), illustrate his commitment to the principle "toward the concrete," which I explained in the concluding chapter of Volume 1.[6]

I also explained in Volume 1 why I myself would accord a certain priority to method in this history and would single out for consideration how the method elaborated by Husserl as the founder of phenomenology would be transformed by his successors. Encouragement for my attention to this transformation I sought with an analogy between a method and a style. Questions of method have sometimes been thought "a waste of time" among anglophone philosophers,[7] but at least the style of a prominent writer or artist, as compared with other writers or artists, is a matter that is usually supposed by anglophone critics to deserve detailed analysis. If we turn to France, we discover that Sartre's literary style has been carefully dissected by critics, but this transformation of Husserl's phenomenological method, in the work Sartre acknowledges to have been "inspired" by Husserl, has been almost entirely neglected.

Priority of Procedure

Although Sartre himself has so far seemed rather indifferent to Husserl's method, and has not even taken into account the relevance of the phenomenological and eidetic reductions to the two long passages he translates from *Ideas I*, I have already anticipated the importance he attaches to one component procedure of Husserl's method—namely, intentional analysis. When Sartre translates the centaur passage, he halts at "what is imagined" as an intentional object, even though Husserl himself treats it only in passing and goes on to the "essence," which emerges in his analysis from an eidetic reduction.

Already in Volume 1, I observed how Sartre not only dismembers Husserl's corpus, by concentrating on *Ideas I* at the expense of his other works, but also dismembers Husserl's method, by the priority he accords to intentional analysis. I drew a contrast with the most prominent of Husserl's other disciples in France, Merleau-Ponty, who takes up intentionality only after the phenomenological and eidetic reductions. I detected a criticism of Sartre in Merleau-Ponty's pronouncement that "intentionality" is "too often cited as the principle discovery of phenomenology, whereas it is understandable only *via* the reductions." [8]

My interest now is in Sartre's relation, not to Merleau-Ponty, but to Husserl. In order to focus on this relation, I postpone considering what happens in Sartre to the reductions that Merleau-Ponty singles out for attention: I will try to determine first what happens to intentional analysis as the procedure to which Sartre accords priority. Here we can perhaps find enough continuity in method to locate a passage way from Husserl to Sartre.

Even before Sartre undertook a phenomenological treatment of the image "inspired" by Husserl, he vented his enthusiasm for Husserl's procedure of intentional analysis. When he recalls arriving in Berlin in 1933 to study Husserl, he admits he did "not know anything" about him— "not even intentionality." [9] Since he also did not know anything about the reductions, the fact that he singles out intentionality indicates the importance the procedure of intentional analysis acquired for him. A glance, in my previous chapter, at the *diplôme* has suggested that Sartre's singling out this procedure was in some measure due to its having discredited his own previous thinking. The promptness with which this procedure acquired its importance for Sartre is indicated by the fact that his first effort in phenomenology was entitled "A Fundamental Idea of Husserl's Phenomenology—Intentionality."

: *Starting Point*

:   *The concept of intentionality is . . . the concept*
:   *to take one's start from in phenomenology.*
:   *—Husserl.*

Procedures

Before considering the procedure of intentional analysis as it is appropriated by Sartre
in the Berlin essay and applied in his phenomenological treatment of the image, we need to
pay sufficient attention to Husserl's own concept of intentionality. One reason for my
qualification "sufficient" is that I am skirting
an issue that would need to be taken up if I
were dealing with the complexities of Husserl's own development. With respect to the
procedures composing his method, the priority differs from one of his works to another. In
the *Logical Investigations* (1900–1901), he
concentrated on the intentional character of
his analysis. But soon after their publication,
he was dismayed by his failure to clarify the
distinctively eidetic character of his analysis,
and in *Ideas I* (1913) he took up the eidetic
reduction first. He accords the phenomenological reduction priority in the *Cartesian
Meditations* (1931).

These differences do not just raise issues
about how phenomenological method developed in Husserl; that no simple decision on
the priority of one procedure over against another could be reached by Husserl (as it can be
with Sartre and Merleau-Ponty) is itself a significant difference between Husserl and his
successors. But determining its significance
would raise issues regarding the development
of his phenomenology, and these would dis-
tract us from the comparison with Sartre.

Perhaps I should emphasize here that I am not attempting a general exposition of Husserl, only an exposition that seems to me adequate for dealing with Sartre's relation to him.[1] For this purpose, I do have to compile the evidence as to what Sartre neglected or transformed in Husserl, so that we can watch what Sartre is doing from Husserl's perspective; such a compilation, however, will not add up to a general exposition, though it does offer one kind of introduction to phenomenology itself. By virtue of Sartre's commitment to the principle "toward the concrete," he provides a more accessible version of phenomenology than Husserl. Moreover, the procedure of intentional analysis is itself more accessible than Husserl's other procedures. This was true for Husserl himself, and when I take it up before the eidetic reduction (and the eidetic reduction before the phenomenological reduction) I am at least respecting the chronology of Husserl's own development.

In *Ideas I* (on which I rely primarily, as the work Sartre devoured in Berlin)—even though the eidetic and phenomenological reductions come to the fore in parts 1 and 2 as "methods of access" to the subject of phenomenology—Husserl still insists that "the concept of intentionality" is completely indispensable at the start [*zu Anfang*] of phenomenology, that it is a concept from which to take one's start [*Ausgangsbegriff*].[2]

Zigzag

Husserl is not suggesting that after starting out with the concept of intentionality, one can go on to other matters. Recall from my preliminary volume how Husserl zigzags: some initial insight into the procedure is gained; then the procedure is applied to substantive problems; thereby additional insight into the procedure is gained—and so on.[3] Husserl uses a paradox which in effect justifies his zigzagging in handling intentionality: intentionality is "readily understandable of itself and most difficult to understand." It is because it is readily understandable of itself that we can start out from it, as indeed Husserl had in the first of his *Logical Investigations*. One reason why intentionality is most difficult to understand is that it is "the designation of the problems that encompass in its scope phenomenology as a whole."[4] In this sense, consciousness-as-intentional is the subject of phenomenology, so that intentionality is not a specific problem that can be isolated, treated, and left behind when Husserl goes on to treat other problems. My isolating of intentionality just now as a specific problem in Husserl finds its justification only in Sartre's isolation of it in the Berlin essay.

Intentional Reference

Husserl took over the concept of intentionality from Franz Brentano, his teacher. I defer any close examination of their relation: Sartre never showed any interest in Brentano or in Husserl's relation to him. But Husserl did initially elaborate his own concept of intentionality in considerable measure by revising Brentano's terminology. Brentano demarcated mental phenomena as intentional in that they involve "reference to a content," "directedness toward an object" or "immanent objectivity." As Husserl himself illustrates, "In perception something is perceived; in imagination, something imagined; in a statement, something stated; in love, something loved; in hate, hated; in desire, desired; and so forth." [5] We have already encountered this "directedness" in the centaur passage, where something imagined is discriminated.

I shall offer more concrete examples by way of acknowledging, in the first instance, Sartre's principle "toward the concrete," and, in the second instance, one of Sartre's applications of this principle: "Problems can be attacked abstractly by phenomenological reflection. But . . . we want to . . . support our thinking by those fictional and concrete experiences which are novels." [6] This is the shift in *affiliation* that I discussed in Volume 1. Brentano visualized his psychology as an empirical science comparable to physics; Husserl visualized his phenomenology as an eidetic science comparable to geometry and as a more rigorous science than any empirical science; but Sartre eventually dismisses Husserl's contention that phenomenology is a rigorous science as "the crazy idea of a genius." [7] With Sartre (as I argued in Volume 1) phenomenology will become affiliated not with any science but with literature.

In alluding to this shift in *affiliation* now, I am anticipating that we shall find in Sartre more than the analogy I put forward in Volume 1 between a philosophical method and a style. In his case intentional reference actually contributed to the shaping of his literary style, as I shall later demonstrate. In fact, it became in France more generally a kind of recipe for certain literary techniques even with novelists who had no explicit philosophical commitment to phenomenology. What I would take advantage of is the common assumption (despite the diligent efforts of literary theorists) that specimens of literature are more readily understandable than specimens of philosophy. So the initial illustrations of intentional reference I offer as literary:

> The desire a child has for a bicycle is the image of its nickle-plated wheels; the fear of a driver at a crossroad takes the form of a black hood emerging suddenly with the screeching of brakes and the landscape trembling in his windshield. [8]

These examples help elucidate Brentano's terminology. The child's desire "refers to," is "directed toward," the nickle-plated wheels, and it cannot be described without following out this reference. Similarly with the driver's fear. The desire or fear, as Brentano would put it, "contains within itself" something as an object. This object is designated by Husserl in the *Logical Investigations* as the "intentional object." [9]

The Intentional Object

Husserl uses the expressions "intentional experiences" and "intentional acts of consciousness" to identify the "phenomena" that are the subject of phenomenology. What this means methodologically is that phenomenology is an intentional analysis in that the references of these experiences or acts are followed out to their intentional objects. Since intentional analysis is the correlation of these intentional experiences or acts with their intentional objects, it can also be called a "correlative analysis." [10]

The need to follow out the reference to the object is played up by the doctrinal formula that phenomenologists repeat: an intentional act of consciousness is consciousness *of* something. It is also played up by the targeting idiom Husserl adopted: the "something"—the intentional object—is "aimed at" by the intentional act. [11]

To bring out the force of this reference to the intentional object, Husserl finds a terminological innovation appropriate. One respect in which he comes to regard Descartes as his precursor is that Descartes succeeded in discriminating with his *cogito* ("I am thinking") the phenomena that Husserl takes as his subject. But phenomenology includes in this subject what Descartes failed to include—the *cogitata* (the "objects thought about"). As Husserl himself phrases it, "Each cogito, each conscious process . . . bears within itself its *cogitatum*—a reference to what it is consciousness of." [12]

I began this exposition by relying on Brentano's terminology. But there is one important respect in which Husserl finds it misleading—when Brentano speaks of "immanent objectivity" as a "content." In Husserl the object is not strictly speaking "immanent"; it is not "contained" within consciousness; it is not reducible to subjective sense-data. We are "conscious of something as an object": "I do not hear tone sensations, I hear the song of the singer." [13]

As we have already learned from Sartre's use of the centaur passage, the intentional object is "transcendent"—that is, we are conscious of it not as a portion of the stream of our consciousness but as "beyond" it. The terminology is ambiguous, as it would also be to say that this object is "outside" our consciousness or "external" to consciousness. For when the phenomenological reduction is carried out, it is discovered that spatial distinctions do not apply to consciousness. Furthermore, when we speak of what is "outside" our consciousness, and so forth, we risk getting hung up on epistemological problems, which are alien to phenomenology, as to the relation between consciousness and what is presumed "outside" consciousness. Husserl will discredit such problems by adopting formulations that are spatially paradoxical, such as "immanent transcendence" and "transcendence in immanence." [14]

Immediate Givenness

When we follow out the intentional reference of consciousness to its intentional object, we are not trying to get "outside" of consciousness to the real object in the external world. The intentional object is immediately given to consciousness by the intentional reference to it. The object is the "something" that consciousness is "consciousness of." What we hear (to repeat Husserl's example) is the song of the singer. To hear mere sounds instead is to intrude on artificial focus, which would be more effectively implemented in an audio laboratory.[15] Thus our usual term for such aural sensations (or for visual sensations) "sense-data" is misleading; they are not immediately given.

Intentional analysis is accordingly to be distinguished from a causal explanation, in which sense-data as psychophysiological occurrences are understood by referring to whatever other occurrences can be tracked down as their causes. When an effect is referred to its cause, the reference has no explanatory force unless what is referred to is specifiable separately from this effect. But the image the child has cannot be described without following out its reference to the nickle-plated wheels. Of course, once this image has been described, it can also be treated as a psychological occurrence (or complex of occurrences) that is the effect of various causes: light waves refracted from the nickle and striking the child's retina; the psychological conditioning whereby shininess has become associated with the new as desirable in a consumer society, and so forth. But the child's image as such is not consciousness of whatever chain of causes and effects may be involved in its production.

There is another similar confusion from which intentional analysis must be protected: the intentional "act" of consciousness should not be construed as an "action" in the usual causal sense. Consciousness of something is an "objectifying" or "objectivating" act, but it is not consciousness of any occurrence whereby my consciousness confers objectivity on sense-data.[16] The objectivity of the object is itself immediately given.

Causal transactions, involving stimuli and responses, are to be delegated by the phenomenologist to the empirical psychologist for explanation: phenomenology as a descriptive analysis is distinct from the causal explanations of the empirical scientist. To fail to maintain this distinction is one fashion in which one can lapse (from Husserl's perspective) into the "psychologism" I discussed in Volume 1.[17]

Identification

Another immediately given characteristic of an intentional act of consciousness is that it is an act of *identification*. I am conscious of something as an automobile, as a tree, as a triangle, as anger. In other words, the intentional act endows what it is "consciousness of" with a meaning, by the very act of being conscious of it. Thus intentional analysis is an analysis of "meaning-endowing" acts of consciousness. Put more simply, "meanings" are the subject of phenomenology.

To exhibit the characteristics of an intentional analysis, Husserl usually prefers examples of perception. Normally, when consciousness is perceptual, more than a single act of consciousness takes place. But throughout the succession of these acts, what one is conscious of remains identical—that is, the object meant remains an identical pole of reference, despite my perceiving different "aspects" of the object from different angles and despite these successive perceptions being psychologically different occurrences. Thus I am perceptually conscious of something *via* its *Abschattungen* (variously translated as "aspects," "perspective," "profiles," and sometimes as "adumbrations," to retain the etymology of the German).[18] One is conscious of the automobile as having a black hood, of its brakes as screeching. Thus the identification is a "synthesis of identification," which goes through successive phases in which each phase is itself a consciousness of something, so that as new phases enter the synthesis, the consciousness at any moment is characteristically a synthetic unity, as consciousness of the identical object.

The emphasis "at any moment" must not be overlooked. The synthesis in question is not the cumulative outcome of an inductive generalization. We may indeed come to identify inductively what something is. But Husserl is not analyzing this process either as a psychological or as a logical operation; he is, instead, analyzing the experience of perceptual identification. Although this experience is a matter not just of becoming conscious of "aspects" of something but of anticipating other possible aspects that might also be perceived (the back of the automobile, for example), if perception continues, the act of identification is not itself deferred. One can be conscious of something as an automobile even if the only aspect one is conscious of pro tem is its black hood. Phenomenology is accordingly to be distinguished as a science from any empirical science that obtains knowledge by inductive generalization.

If I were merely expounding Husserl, I would now reconsider both phenomenology as an eidetic analysis and the procedure that takes the place of inductive generalization—that is, the eidetic reduction. But this exposition will have to wait until Part 3, since Sartre takes phenomenology as fundamentally intentional analysis.

: # A Fundamental Idea

*The image is only a name for a certain fashion
that consciousness has of aiming at its object.*
—Sartre

Trans-lation

Now that we are sufficiently familiar with
Husserl's procedure of intentional analysis,
we can return to the two texts that Sartre
trans-lated from *Ideas I* into the context
of the treatment of the image he proposes
in *L'imagination*. This reexamination will
bring out how intentional analysis becomes
for Sartre the fundamental procedure for
treating the image.

In Chapter 1 I quoted only the concluding clause of the first sentence of the paragraph into which Sartre trans-lates the Dürer
engraving. In this clause Sartre endorses in
the Dürer passage the *rapprochement* that he
finds between mental and physical images
and that provides him with the subject he
would treat. A shift in *subject* is at stake,
since he considers that mental images have
traditionally been treated separately from
physical images.

Recall how in my Chapter 1 we saw that
Husserl's methodological concern in the
Dürer passage was with the neutrality modification with which a depictive act of the
imagination constitutes a physical image, because this act was likely to be confused with
the neutrality modification that is carried
out by the phenomenological reduction. We
watched Sartre disregard Husserl with a "We
do not have to concern ourselves with this
[the neutrality modification] here," for
Sartre's methodological concern is with the
act of the imagination as an intentional act.

Now we should recognize how fundamental an idea intentionality is for Sartre. A subject does not just lie around waiting to be treated—and, according to Sartre, it was intentionality that enabled Husserl to effect the shift in *subject* Sartre wants. I go back to the clause that precedes the one I quoted in Chapter 1: "In effect, if the image is only a name for a certain way that consciousness has of aiming at its object [that is, if consciousness is intentional], nothing precludes bringing together physical images—paintings, sketches, photographs—with images which are termed 'mental.' "[1] Sartre's *en effet* is not the ineffectual conjunction it often is in French; the Sartre who, according to Simone de Beauvoir, is "breathless" as he writes is not just catching his breath. Rather, the "if" clause has genuine efficacy as a premise.

Even before taking up the Dürer example, Sartre has already claimed that "the very concept of intentionality is an invitation to renew the concept of the image."[2] With this example as Sartre reconstructs it, the concept of intentionality becomes an invitation to recognize that a physical image is not simply a physical thing—an object we can perceive—but has to be constituted a physical image by our becoming conscious of it as a physical image—by the way in which our consciousness "aims" at it, in order to become by means of it consciousness of something else—this consciousness being a mental image.

In Chapter 1 we saw that Husserl failed (in Sartre's view) to respond to this invitation to a renewal, since he did not treat the image "in his published writings," except "in passing." He did not appreciate the novelty of the shift in *subject* by which he had brought together a mental with a physical image. Though he was committed to the novelty of his philosophy, its decisive juncture to him was the phenomenological reduction. Thus his most strenuous complaint against Heidegger was that he did not "understand the novelty of the phenomenological reduction."[3]

If the priority Sartre accords Husserl's procedure of intentional analysis in treating the image has been illustrated by Sartre's adoption of examples (the Dürer engraving, the centaur) that in Husserl himself were relevant strictly to the reductions, the priority that Sartre accords generally to intentional analysis is illustrated by the title of the Berlin essay— "A Fundamental Idea of Husserl's—Intentionality."[4] Sartre never suggested that any other idea was fundamental in Husserl.

A feature of Sartre's trans-lation of the Dürer passage is his use of an idiom: "[T]he image is only a name for a certain way that consciousness has of aiming at its object." We have seen that the idiom itself had been adopted by Husserl. Though the expression "intention" itself had been taken over by Brentano from medieval Latin, Husserl was probably aware that in classical Latin *intendere* could mean "to bend a bow" and "to aim at." At any rate, he explains, "The expression 'intention' presents the specific character of acts in terms of the image of aiming [*abzielen*] at something." [5] In Sartre the idiom becomes pervasive. One reason for this is the extent to which for Sartre phenomenological method fundamentally becomes intentional analysis, which in Husserl was only one procedure among others. Thus Sartre's trans-lation of the example of the centaur into terms of an analysis that is fundamentally intentional is illustrated by the way the idiom intrudes when Sartre translates *Kentaur-vermeintes* not as "the centaur meant" but as "the centaur aimed at [*visé*]."

Transcendence

Husserl's example of the centaur exemplifies to Sartre, we recall, how Husserl would "restore to the centaur its transcendence." How crucial this term "transcendence" is in Sartre's exploitation of Husserl is manifest in Sartre's Berlin essay when he characterizes Husserl's phenomenology at large as a "philosophy of transcendence." Husserl himself never used this label and never would have accepted it.

Instead, Husserl (we also recall) concocted a paradoxical terminology—"transcendence in immanence" and "immanent transcendence." The paradoxes can be explained. On the one hand, we have seen Husserl apply the term "immanent" to the "contents" (sense-data) of consciousness, as distinguished from the intentional object, which "transcends" it. In this specific sense, as Sartre correctly reports, the imagined centaur is "transcendent," just as a perceived physical thing is "transcendent," even though the centaur does not exist whereas the physical thing does. But, on the other hand, Husserl's term "immanent" has another sense when it is applied not to the "contents" of consciousness but to what is immediately given within the scope of consciousness as such. Thus "immanent transcendence" characterizes the transcendence of the intentional object.

Such paradoxical defiance of ordinary linguistic usage illustrates to Husserl the inevitable inadequacy of language, the result of its meanings having been derived (so long as we are confined within "the natural attitude") from our referring to physical things and to their relations in space. When, however, the phenomenological reduction is carried out and we gain access to consciousness at the transcendental level, the spatial contrast no longer holds between what is "immanent" in the sense of "in" consciousness or "within" consciousness, and what is "outside" consciousness; indeed, we can no longer refer to the subject of phenomenology as if it were a realm restricted "within" the limits of "immanence," outside of which is another realm, where natural science, as the science of physical things, holds equal sway. (This is roughly what Husserl took to be Brentano's position.) The supremacy of consciousness as meaning-endowing is vindicated by the phenomenological reduction.

Immanence

I am not trying to state, much less resolve, all the issues that swarm here. I am only drawing attention to some of the implications of a difference between Husserl's terminology and Sartre's use of it. Because Sartre does not apply the phenomenological reduction in the Berlin essay on intentionality (he does not even mention it), he adheres to the sense of "immanent" that in Husserl applies to "contents" of consciousness, and he identifies as "transcendent" the object as given "outside" of consciousness. To this extent, Sartre can be said to remain at the level of ordinary experience (what Husserl terms "the natural attitude") where a simple opposition between "inside" and "outside" still holds.

Accordingly, in his interpretation of Husserl, Sartre carries out a different kind of reduction, one geared to this opposition and propelled by his having taken the idea of intentionality as fundamental:

> Husserl never wearies of asserting that things cannot be dissolved in consciousness [as its contents]. You see this tree here. . . . But you see it at the very place where it is at: at the end of the road. . . . It could never enter into your consciousness.

> [I]n vain would we try . . . , like a child who embraces his own shoulder, to caress, fondle our own intimacy, since ultimately everything is outside, everything, even ourselves: outside, in the world.

Since everything is "outside," Husserl's philosophy becomes a "philosophy of transcendence."

The point of Sartre's endorsing Husserl's philosophy as a "philosophy of transcendence" is to oppose it to traditional French philosophy as the childish "philosophy of immanence" Sartre would mock. It is for the purpose of setting up this opposition that Sartre ultimately finds "intentionality" fundamental: " 'Everything consciousness is consciousness of something.' Nothing more is needed to put an end to the snug [*douillette*] philosophy of immanence." Thus if Sartre oversimplifies Husserl's terminology, it is to achieve the simplicity of this "nothing more is needed." The opposition to which the essay is geared is less between "transcendence" and "immanence" than between Husserl's philosophy of transcendence and French philosophy of immanence. This is a trans-lation of Husserl to which I shall return.

Commotion

A sufficient reason for the precedence Sartre accords to French philosophy is his going on to speak of it as having "formed us." This raises the question, Does Sartre include himself? I suspect that the Sartre who was reading Husserl in Berlin was more preoccupied with denouncing French philosophy at large than with recalling his own personal philosophical formation. I have already said that his *diplôme* was an illustration of the "psychologism" that Husserl criticized from the point of view of intentionality. We have heard Sartre put it, "Husserl never wearies of asserting that things cannot be dissolved in consciousness."

This "never wearies" strikes me as rather an exaggeration. Many other assertions are to be found in Husserl, and it is at their expense that we have been watching Sartre concentrate on intentionality. Even late in life, when Sartre recalls his having arrived in Berlin not knowing anything about Husserl, he singles out "not even intentionality," as I have already mentioned. Yet Sartre will also claim, according to his editors, that his commitment, " 'to the things themselves,' [that is, to Husserl's principle] antedated his coming into contact with Husserl's phenomenology." [6] And this principle becomes so closely associated in Sartre with following out intentional reference as to become hardly distinguishable from it.

Some sorting out is in order. Sartre's claim itself is substantiated by *"Une défaite"*:

> Frédéric was seized with a commotion, each time he noticed the existence of things. He was thinking vaguely: "It is then true that they exist, so true, so full, so categorical, so violent, so independent of all our science and of all the constructions of our philosophy— how deny them? And why is it that their obstinate existence, which does violence to our mind, brings us joy, if we know how to notice it? It is that, if one believes the pedants [*cuistres*], things would be half [constructed] out of ourselves. . . . They would be aware of our ill-smelling breath, they would be soft and warm in our hands. . . . But they are so strange, so hostile, so fresh. . . . Often I neglect them to talk in myself, but I love them for being so wicked [*méchantes*]. I love them because they are not related to me, and they can be loved without commiting incest." [7]

The "joy" of which Frédéric speaks here will become the exultation expressed in the Berlin essay. Was Sartre, as "the lamentable Frédéric," so committed to becoming a disciple that when he finally found his master, he gave him more than his due?

Affiliation

When Sartre exults in a later conversion, he will admit that sometimes a conversion can be well prepared.[8] Frédéric's argument is cluttered as compared with the Berlin essay, but it does suggest how well primed

Sartre was for his conversion to Husserl. How then could Frédéric's "commotion" not disturb the "psychologism" of the *diplôme?* There is considerable evidence that Sartre's philosophical commitments developed more slowly in his *philosophical* writings than when he was "thinking vaguely" in his *literary* writings about philosophical topics. In Volume 1, I observed how Sartre took on social history in his novel *Le sursis,* before he ever tried to take it on in the *Critique of Dialectical Reasoning.* Similarly, when challenged as to why he treated nausea in a novel rather than in a philosophical work, he explained that he didn't have "a solid enough idea [of nausea] to make a philosophical work out of it." [9] So he wrote the novel instead.

This explanation seems philosophically disparaging of the novel. But we should not forget that the prerogative of the novel as a genre is upheld by Sartre's philosophical principle "to the concrete," so that while Sartre concedes, "Problems can be attacked abstractly by philosophical reflection," he would have us "support our thinking by those fictional and concrete experiences which are novels." [10] In fact we shall later see that Sartre views himself as "primarily a writer [that is, of literary works] and secondarily a philosopher." [11] A long-run argument of mine, which will be completed only in the Conclusion to this volume, is that this view of Sartre's is not merely a personal whim, but is buttressed by his philosophy itself. At the same time, I am arguing that his philosophy cannot adequately be understood (and has not been adequately understood by most of his expositors) because they treat it as if it were simply a philosophy, and without regard to its affiliation with literature—as if his literary works were merely popular expositions of his philosophy. The argument is, of course, designed to vindicate my own procedure, expounded in Volume 1, whereby attention needs sometimes be paid to the affiliation of a philosophy. A similar argument could be designed on behalf of the affiliation of Merleau-Ponty's philosophy with landscape painting (specifically Cezanne's), and of Heidegger's with poetry (specifically Hölderlin's), [12] but the argument is more readily designed in Sartre's case, since he is himself the author of the affiliated works.

The Theory of Knowledge

Given Frédéric's "commotion," as going on in some measure in Sartre's own breast, contact with Husserl's phenomenology could have triggered a conversion by supplying in several respects what the youthful Sartre was seeking. First, "to the things themselves," could become an explicit principle, presiding over the direction he had already tended to take in philosophy. Second, once Sartre was supplied with intentional reference, the things could be specified as individual objects. The flavor of what Frédéric was "thinking vaguely" may be Sartrean; what is missing was specificity. At the moment of his conversion, it was an apricot cocktail (or a glass of beer),[13] and after his conversion his examples continue to feature individual objects. Third, the distinction between intentional reference to a transcendent object and immanent mental contents sharpened Frédéric's misgiving over regarding things as our own mental constructs. Finally, there took place a broader shift in *subject* than we have yet taken into account—the theory of knowledge is displaced by phenomenology.

The first paragraph of the Berlin essay is an exposition not "A Fundamental Idea of Husserl's" but of a theory of knowledge that has prevailed in France with the philosophy of immanence. Sartre lines up individual objects: "What is a table, a rock, a house? A certain collection of [immanent] 'contents of consciousness,' an order of these contents that are known." The second paragraph, from which my earlier quotations came, begins with a *contre,* and develops the opposing concept of knowledge as carrying an intentional reference to what transcends our consciousness. The third and concluding paragraph begins:

> I have spoken first of knowledge in order to be better understood: French philosophy, which has formed us, hardly knows anything besides the theory of knowledge. But for Husserl and the phenomenologists, the consciousness that we have of things is not at all restricted to knowledge of them.

Shifts in *level* and *subject* are taking place here from knowledge to other forms of consciousness and, specifically, to imaginative and emotional consciousness, which Sartre will actually treat in his ensuing prewar phenomenological writings.

Unbeknownst to Sartre, Husserl had undertaken a shift in *level* himself. Having analyzed "the higher intellectual acts in the *Logical Investigations,* he had gone on in his 1904–5 lectures to acts, such as the imaginative, as 'underlying' these higher acts."[14] This distinction between higher and lower is traditional philosophical parlance. Husserl had entitled these lectures "The Principal Pieces of Phenomenology and Theory of Knowledge." Granted that this theory is phenomenological, it is still a theory of knowledge. Sartre was unaware of these lectures and of their title, but I shall try to bring out in the long run how the shift in *level* that Sartre ascribes to Husserl in the Berlin essay differs from any Husserl had ever envisaged.

SEVEN

The Illusion of Immanence

We are delivered . . . from the inner life.—Sartre

Method

Our attention to Sartre's treatment of the image has been restricted so far to his transformation of Husserl in *L'imagination*. Now we can go on to Sartre's own theory, elaborated in *L'imaginaire*.[1] Sartre never commented on the difference between his two titles, but a clue is provided by the opposition in the Berlin essay on intentionality between a philosophy of immanence and a philosophy of transcendence. On the one hand, we find surveyed in *L'imagination* traditional theories in which the faculty of the imagination is a fixture in accounting for the internal operations of the mind; on the other hand, the new theory in *L'imaginaire* is reached by Sartre's following out the intentional reference to a transcendent object that is imaginary.[2]

The first section of this first part is a perfunctory two-page discussion of method. He makes no reference to Husserl in this first section, and it is obvious that Sartre does not share Husserl's preoccupation with method. He winds up the section with the conclusion that "the method is simple." So much for the first two lengthy and laborious parts (138 pages) of *Ideas I*, devoted to the reductions. The third part of *Ideas I* is entitled "Methods and Problems of Pure Phenomenology," and it would not be misleading to regard *Ideas I* as a whole as a treatise on phenomenological method.

All that Sartre's "simple" method requires, he explains, is that we "produce images in ourselves, reflect on these images, describe them—that is, attempt to determine and to classify their distinctive characteristics." Throughout we are merely exercising "intuitive insight." But this is not quite the way that Sartre proceeds in the second section.

Since we are concerned with Sartre's relation to Husserl, what strikes us in the second section is the continued absence of any explicit mention of Husserl. In fact, there is no reference to Husserl in the entire first chapter. Our initial impression may be what Simone de Beauvoir reports— that *L'imaginaire* was an investigation in which Sartre "invented both method and content, obtaining all the materials from his own experience."

The Image Theory

A philosopher's method, however, is not always the method he officially sponsors, and Sartre's method is not as simple as he promised in his first section: he does not begin this second section by producing an image and going on to describe it. Instead, he dissects a "double error." There was an advance warning of what we are now in for, but it was so brief I skipped over it. Sartre began the first section on method, "Despite some prejudices to which we shall soon have to return, it is certain that when I produce in myself the image of Peter, it is Peter who is the object of my present consciousness." Rather than beginning the second section by producing an image of Peter and describing what is certain about it, Sartre returns to the "prejudices," which (he now explains) constitute the "double error."

This "double error" is clearly reminiscent of Husserl's discussion of "two fundamental, well-nigh ineradicable errors"—"the 'image' theory and the doctrine of the 'immanent' objects of acts [of consciousness]." The first of these errors Sartre trans-lates as "thinking that . . . the image was *in* consciousness"; the second, he trans-lates by restricting himself to the case in which we think of the object represented as immanent to the image. Husserl's discussion appears in an appendix to the fifth of his *Logical Investigations*, "On Intentional Experiences and Their 'Contents.' "[3] We have already watched Husserl draw this distinction between intentional experiences as refering to objects that transcend them and sense-data as immanent contents, and we have also watched Sartre in the Berlin essay erect this distinction into a sweeping opposition between "immanence" and "transcendence." Thus despite Sartre's debt to Husserl, their philosophies here are by no means the same: I shall spend the rest of this chapter trying to bring out differences.

The appendix illustrates three respects in which Husserl in his published writings treated the image "only in passing." First of all, there is a
shift in *subject* in Sartre. What Husserl is attacking in the appendix as the
Bildtheorie ("image theory" or "picture theory") is not the traditional
theory of the image that Sartre is attacking but the traditional theory of
perception. According to the "image theory" of perception, as expounded by Husserl, "in addition to the [actual] thing itself [located outside consciousness], there is . . . in consciousness an 'image' whose function is to represent it." In his criticism of this theory of perception,
Husserl does refer to the imagination, but his reference amounts to a second respect in which he treats the image "only in passing," for he refers
not to the imagination in general but to a depictive act of the imagination
that is based on the perception of a painting.

Third, the purpose of his reference is not to treat the depictive act of
the imagination itself. He is making the point that it takes a depictive act
to give the painting, which otherwise would merely be perceived, "the
status and meaning of an image"—that is, of something that represents
something else. He makes this point in order to argue that if in the case
of perception there were an object comparable to this painting, functioning within the mind as a "mental image," it would have to be constituted
as an image by an act comparable to the depictive act, so that the object
within consciousness can perform the function of representing comparable to the way something outside of consciousness can. But "since the
interpretation of something as an image presupposes an object already
intentionally given to consciousness, we would plainly have an infinite
regress."

Finally, this treatment of the "image theory" is relegated, as I have
mentioned, to an appendix. The relegation can probably be explained by
the fact that the "image theory" is just that—a theory. At the end of the
introduction to the *Logical Investigations,* Husserl enforces "the philosophical *epochē*" as a withdrawal from any commitment to any theory.
The distinction here is even more strikingly upheld in *Ideas I.* "No conceivable theory," Husserl claims there, "can make us err with respect to
the principle of all principles" whereby what is immediately given to consciousness is to be accepted as knowledge that is valid prior to any conceivable theory."[4] Phenomenology is the descriptive analysis of what is
immediately given, whereas a theory is explanatory—that is, it goes behind what is immediately given and infers causes. What Husserl as a phenomenologist is bracketing when he applies the philosophical *epochē* at
the end of his introduction includes all theories.

However, he qualifies, "no harm will of course be done by occasional
side-references, which remain without effect on the content and character

of one's analysis." [5] The appendix now under our consideration is an extended side-reference. If the errors criticized had not been relegated to an appendix, Husserl's descriptive analysis would have been sidetracked for too long. Sartre is less sensitive to the distinction between an explanatory theory and a descriptive analysis. His attributing a theory of the imagination to Husserl as well as to himself is not just carelessness with regard to a term. We shall see later that theoretical explanation and description mingle in *L'imaginaire*.

Terminology

Another way Sartre does not respect Husserl's demarcation of the subject of phenomenology becomes apparent as soon as we go on from Sartre's trans-lation of Husserl's criticism of the first error to his trans-lation of the second. Since Sartre is trans-lating what was a theory of perception—which Husserl would discredit—into a theory of the imagination—which Sartre himself would discredit—he carries out the trans-lation with a transition from perception to the imagination. He begins with the case of perception:

> When I perceive a chair, it would be absurd to say that the chair is in my perception. My perception is, in accordance with the terminology that we have adopted, in conformity with the idea of intentionality, a certain consciousness, and the chair is the object of this consciousness. [6]

Sartre then goes on to argue that the chair is no more in consciousness in the case of the imagination—"not even in an image of it"—than it is in the case of perception. Here Sartre is apparently echoing Husserl's criticism of the second error, which is "to draw a real [*reell*] distinction" between the "merely immanent and intentional object on the one hand, and the actual [*wirklich*] and transcendent object" on the other. Any such distinction, Husserl insists, is "absurd" (*widersinnig*); it is a failure to recognize that we are engaged in a phenomenological analysis of meaning-endowing acts of consciousness.

Sartre's criterion of absurdity in the passage I have just quoted is not, however, strictly phenomenological: it is a matter, instead, of proceeding "in accordance with the terminology that we have adopted, in conformity with the idea of intentionality." Here again, I do not think Sartre is just being careless in overlooking a clear distinction in Husserl. Yet nothing could be more incongruously unphenomenological (from Husserl's perspective) than persistent clinging to a terminology. Terminology is for him a secondary consideration: terms are to receive their meanings only

in the presence of what is immediately given to consciousness. Considerations of terminological conformity become prominent in Husserl when
the phenomenologist would connumicate to others what he has already
experienced. Thus Husserl dodges a general discussion of obtaining "un-
ambiguous terms" in *Ideas I* with the admonition that "this is not the
place for going more precisely into . . . matters relating to science as a
product of intersubjective collaboration."[7] Since terminology is a secondary consideration for Husserl, I am postponing it until Volume 3, when I
shall return to the general problem of communication between philosophers that I formulated in Volume 1.

The Academic

What does have to be recognized now is that Sartre finds himself in a
phenomenologically ungainly (if not quite *widersinnig*) situation of requiring himself (as he puts it at the end of *L'imagination*, when he is
looking forward to his own theory) "to start over again from zero, to
neglect all the phenomenological literature" that he has spent most of
L'imagination surveying.[8] This starting over again from zero is presumably Sartre's version of Husserl's philosophical *epochē*. Yet it is not quite
the same procedure. Sartre's historical survey is a demonstration of the
inadequacy of previous treatments of the imagination and, in contrast, of
the inspiration derivable from Husserl. But what then transpires in *L'imaginaire* is not a matter of starting from zero and brusquely pushing
aside, as Husserl did, all previous philosophical theories. Strictly speaking, Husserl's philosophical *epochē* entails neglecting in principle all doc-
umentation and consulting instead, in conformity with "the principle of
all principles," experience as immediately given to consciousness. This is
pretty much what Simone de Beauvoir would seem to believe Sartre was
doing when she characterizes *L'imaginaire* as "an investigation in which
Sartre invented both method and content, obtaining all the materials
from his own experience." But, in fact, *L'imaginaire* is loaded with various materials much of which Sartre had previously taken over from philosophers and psychologists in his *diplôme*, before he had encountered
Husserl and the requirement of the philosophical *epochē*.

This is only one illustration of what I tried to bring out in Volume 1
when I risked characterizing Sartre's philosophy as an "academicization"
of experience. The context there was Sartre's contempt for Camus for not
acknowledging his full immersion in history during World War II.[9]
Sartre's report on the war, as the decisive experience of his own life, is a
report that "I was in the exact situation of the Athenians after the death
of Alexander, who turned away from Aristotelian science to assimilate

the doctrines of the Stoics and the Epicureans, who taught them to *live*. [Sartre is indicating that in the same way he turned away, during the war, from the "academic" philosophy of Husserl to assimilate the philosophy of Heidegger, which in contrast was "barbaric."] And then *History* was everywhere around me. Philosophically, first of all: Aron had just written his *Introduction to the Philosophy of History,* and I was reading it." [10]

Of course, it is a banality that no one's experience is immaculate, that it is banalized by having been thoroughly infiltrated by prevailing inter- pretations of experience. Still "exact situation" seems strained—a false note, an "academic" way of apprehending a war experience. The "exact- itude" strikes me as a function of the books Sartre had read, and achiev- ing it seems hardly compatible with his commitment to his own original- ity, which he considered to have been enchanced by Husserl's commitment to immediately given experience.

"Philosophically" may be a less disconcerting apprehension—but in- asmuch as it was "first of all," we must ask, In what respect did *experi- ence* come first with Sartre? Since the apprehension was a matter of read- ing, I became suspicious that Sartre's rebuking Camus for not being fully immersed in history was perhaps applicable to Sartre himself.

Bookishness

Sartre's report on "History" amounts to a report on how he came to be converted to Heidegger. In my present volume, I am focusing on Sartre's relation to Husserl, and I am now suggesting a sense in which the epithet "academic," which Sartre applies to Husserl, might be transferable to Sartre. In Volume 1, I sought some support for its application to Sartre in his own recollection that at this period "there must have remained in me something of the professor." [11] In his autobiography, he prefers to regard himself theologically as a *clerc* and confesses his addiction to "words," explaining how "I began my life, as I shall doubtless finish it—in the midst of books." [12] This bookish Sartre is not the familiar, the reputed, existential Sartre; it is not the Sartre whom Simone de Beauvoir admired, with so much fidelity, for his inventiveness.

When I dealt with Sartre's bookishness in Volume 1, I did not recog- nize its pertinence to one range of his experience, for *"Une défaite"* had not yet been published. Though Sartre's relations to women are beyond my present scope, his amorous experience provides a useful parallel for his war experience, albeit that his amorous experience was considerably more extensive. [13] If one takes "the lamentable Frédéric" to be the youth- ful Sartre, as did the woman who was a partial model for Cosima, it is noteworthy that Frédéric succumbs to the same bookishness with Cosima as he will when he has his was experience.

In lecturing Cosima, Frédéric asks, "Do you know who could provide an admirable rendering of these half-sensuous, half-intellectual impressions we are having now . . . ? Meredith." Cosima concedes, "I have never read him."

"You must," replies Frédéric. Shortly thereafter, Cosima "groans . . . , 'How boring it is. Do you make like a professor all the time?' " [14]

Since we are told that "Frédéric was trying to confront in his mind the vague impression he had of her with the precise and systematic knowledge he had of the English novelist," we can see the parallel—the impressions Sartre had of the war might have remained vague if they had not been systematized in his own mind by the more precise knowledge he thought he obtained from reading Heidegger. An obvious difference is that Sartre is mockingly aware of the disjunction between Frédéric's "vague impression" and "the precise and systematic knowledge" he had obtained from reading books, but there is no self-mockery in Sartre's wartime confession that "if I were to try to figure what I would have made of my thought without these tools [the tools provided by Heidegger for understanding his war experience], I would be overcome by retrospective fear." [15]

The Prophet

With this background, we can return to the issues raised by Sartre's relation to Husserl, as illustrated by the Berlin essay. When I examined it in Chapter 6, I anticipated the phraseology Sartre used in characterizing Frédéric's relation to Meredith, and I suggested that Husserl's concept of intentionality contributed precision and systematization to what Sartre had been previously "thinking vaguely" about "the existence of things." There was a certain "academic" character to the setup of the Berlin essay, in that it was geared to an opposition less between transcendence and immanence than between Husserl's philosophy of transcendence and the French philosophy of immanence.

However, we should recall how Sartre in that essay left the academic world behind:

Husserl has reinstated horror and charm in things. He has restored to us the world of artists and prophets. . . . He has made room for a new treatise of the passions, which would be inspired by that truth, so simple and so profoundly misunderstood by our sophisticates: if we love a woman, it is because she is lovable.

The prospect of this simplification is indeed alluring. And we have seen how alluring it must have been to Sartre, as "the lamentable Frédéric," whose relations to women were not all that simple—he had not yet discovered intentionality.

Nevertheless, Sartre may be getting more out of intentionality than was actually available in Husserl. For there are differences in the direction in which Sartre is proceeding. When Husserl brings "intentionality" to bear against "two . . . well-nigh ineradicable errors," he is thinking of errors committed by theorists—philosophers and psychologists. Even though the ineradicability of these errors has to be explained ultimately by "the natural attitude," Husserl would attack naturalistic theories that reinforce this attitude. But when Sartre explains that "up until now we have been committing a double error," he is addressing all mankind. Most "academic" philosophers, if they are interested in other philosophers, are particularly interested in their errors. An important unacademic characteristic of Sartre is that he is not that much interested. He soon drops the phraseology he derived from Husserl, "a double error," in favor of "the illusion of immanence," to which all mankind are prone, just as they will be relieved (and not just philosophers and psychologists) to be reassured as to the lovableness of a woman. Here Sartre belongs to "the world of artists and prophets."

I don't want to make too much of a prophet out of Sartre. But I still think there is some pertinence in how Frédéric envisages his prospective master and his relation to him:

> He conceived the kind of master who would be obscure, upright, and a man of genius, but lacking the necessary power to impose himself on the world, and he visualized himself as taking over his master's doctrine, finishing it, constructing the edifice, and constraining by force his fellows to revere it.[16]

Husserl may not have actually been "obscure," but Sartre was not aware of him at the time he wrote *"Une défaite"*; Husserl not only was "upright" but he also believed firmly in uprightness (*Redlichkeit*).[17] We have heard Sartre explicitly dub him a "genius," and to the extent Husserl did impose himself on the world, it was posthumously and with some help from Sartre.

I am not insisting on the inerrancy of Sartre's prophecy. What matters here is how Sartre took over Husserl's doctrine when he assumed the role of a disciple. There are shifts in *level* and in *subject* in the Berlin essay, even though Sartre in its concluding paragraph would credit these shifts to Husserl. Knowledge (and thus the theory of knowledge) can be discounted: "The consciousness that we have of things is not at all restricted to knowledge of them." So Sartre is ready to anticipate his treatment of the imaginative consciousness and the "new treatise on the passions," which will turn out to be his *Theory of the Emotions*. Concomitant with the shift in audience, in *level*, and in *subject*, the treatment will itself become imaginative and emotional, as the Berlin essay illustrates. The shifts are discernible even though their outcome may be characterizable as "vulgarization." [18]

The Inner Life

We are now able to appreciate another feature of Sartre's conversion to Husserl. We have seen that the illusion of immanence is Sartre's version of "the error" detected by Husserl of taking references to a "transcendent" object and reducing them to "immanent" contents—to what is contained within consciousness. In the first sentence of the Berlin essay, Sartre had already mentioned the "illusion" that prevails in a "philosophy of immanence." Likewise, in the essay's final paragraph, which I have been quoting, it is from the illusion of immanence that we are being rescued by Husserl's "philosophy of transcendence," in which the idea of intentionality is taken to be fundamental:

> Here we are liberated [*délivré*] from Proust. Liberated at the same time from "the inner life": in vain would we try, like Amiel, like a child who embraces his own shoulder, to caress, fondle our own intimacy, since ultimately everything is outside, everything, even ourselves: outside, in the world.

Sartre's philosophy is regularly interpreted as a philosophy of freedom, but often with insufficient emphasis on the instances when this freedom is liberation from illusion—here, from "the illusion of immanence," "the inner life." Or perhaps, rather, from books that inculcate the intimacies of "the inner life." We can see a trace of bookishness in the allusion to Proust, which precedes "the inner life," and in the allusion to Amiel, which precedes the description of the child.

The "inner life" from which Sartre has been "liberated" by Husserl was in considerable measure his own. The Proust from which he has been liberated he had originally read with "ecstasy" (*ravissement*).[19] It had been the life lived by "the lamentable Frédéric" that Sartre had been. At least Frédéric had been ambivalent about "the things themselves." Recall his lapse, "Often I neglect them in order to talk in myself." They did not matter to him, he also explains, only "the feeling they inspired." Frédéric "spent time trying to find in the depths of his being the fugitive image that had been awakened." He was prey to "the fluid world of Proust: images, impressions, feelings, above all, memories."[20]

We should allow for the self-mockery here, as a juncture at which Sartre would detach himself from Frédéric. In *Jesus la chouette* (1922), Sartre is already mocking those who live "the inner life" by citing Leconte de Lisle, "The inner dream that they never end."[21] Despite such mockery, the philosophical explanations in the *diplôme* (we have observed) are tainted with "psychologism." In the stretch I quoted, Sartre's problem was "What is going on in me when I perceive a natural object as aesthetic?" And in dealing with this problem he resorted to a "a feeling of my-ness" *(moiitié)*, of "intimacy."

The Berlin essay of 1934–35 still remains evidence that the philosophical struggle for liberation was prompted by Husserl. Sartre never quoted Husserl quoting Goethe, "There is nothing to which one is more severe than the errors that one has just abandoned."[22] But Sartre could well have done so: the error Husserl is attacking is "psychologism" and Sartre in his essay is inspired by Husserl to attack French philosophy for the "illusion of immanence"—which is in effect "psychologism"—though Sartre does not acknowledge that he was attacking an error in which he had himself indulged in his *diplôme*.

The struggle against himself continued. In 1939, a month before the Berlin essay was finally published, Sartre wrote in his journal: "After the war I will not go on keeping this journal, or if I do, I'll no longer mention myself. I don't want to be haunted by myself until the end of my days."[23] His juvenilia illustrate how much he needed to get outside of himself. His struggle to do so was already underway in the self-mockery with which he concocted the character of the "lamentable Frédéric," and with which he also tried to detach himself from him. We can now see how the struggle gained impetus from his adopting as fundamental Husserl's idea of intentionality. Sartre discovered not only that the loveableness of a woman was not a psychological construction, and that they were outside in the world, but also that he himself was outside.

Activism

We saw in Volume 1 that the war was a "turning point" for Sartre.[24] I focused on how Sartre concomitantly "turned toward Heidegger and against Husserl." Thus what Sartre then encountered outside in the world was "History." His liberation from "the inner life" then became his turning toward activism and attempting to "smash" the professor in himself.[25]

This turn is traced in Sartre's sequence of historical novels, *Les chemins de la liberté*. The first is *L'âge de la raison*. Sartre was almost prepared to dismiss this novel as "a Husserlian work, which is rather disgusting when one has become a zealous convert to Heidegger." But a conversion to activism is underway in the third volume, *La mort dans L'âme*—the last Sartre completed. The dramatic date was a year after the publication of the essay on intentionality. At the climax of this third volume, the Germans were pouring into France, the phony war about to become a real war, when Sartre's protagonist, modeled on Sartre himself:

> approached the parapet and began firing, standing up. It was an enormous revenge; with each shot he was reeking vengeance on an old scruple. A shot at Lola, whom I did not dare steal from, a shot at Marcelle, whom I should have junked, a shot at Odette, whom I didn't want to fuck. This shot for the books I did not dare to write, this one for the voyages I didn't make, this one for all the characters whom I wanted to detest and whom I tried to understand. He was firing, laws were flying through the air, you will love your neighbor as yourself. . . . He was firing at man, at Virtue, at the World. . . . He was free.[26]

Sartre's protagonist has not yet attained authentic freedom, and it is entirely implausible, Simone de Beauvoir assures us, to imagine Sartre himself with a rifle.[27] But the fervor of this subversive conversion to activism is Sartre's own.

Direction

However reliable the Berlin essay is as evidence of Sartre's conversion to Husserl, it is not reliable as a rendering of the direction Husserl took in his own philosophy. Before Sartre wrote his Berlin essay, when he was still a student in Paris, Husserl had wound up *Cartesian Meditations*, the lectures he gave in 1929 at the Sorbonne, with an invitation to phenomenology, which deserves to be placed alongside the final sentence of Sartre's essay on Husserl, with its recognition, "everything is outside, everything, even ourselves: outside, in the world." Husserl's invitation to phenomenology in the final sentence of the *Meditations* assumes the guise of Augustine's invitation to convert ourselves to leading the inner life: "Do not be willing to go outside; go back into yourself; it is in the inner man that truth dwells." [28]

Sartre did not attend these lectures, for he was not yet converted to phenomenology, but before he went to Berlin, he could have read the *Cartesian Meditations* in a French translation (1931). More important is the philosophical issue itself. A philosophical conversion, like any other conversion, is delineated by the direction in which a philosopher turns. Now we see that Sartre's ostensible conversion to Husserl was a conversion in virtually the opposite direction from the direction Husserl proposed.

We have reached a juncture where it is necessary to correct an impression I may have conveyed in my presentation at the beginning of this volume. When a philosopher would intro-duce us to philosophy—provide us with "a way of access" to philosophy—he often is promoting a conversion that will liberate us from "the cave" or from "the natural attitude" or from going "outside" or from "the inner life," where we can cherish "the illusion of immanence," or from other "prejudices." But, as this listing suggests, he is not likely to be opening up the same access route as that commended to us by another philosopher.

This is hardly news, but the present illustration is notable, since Sartre thinks he is following "the way" Husserl "opens up" for him, when in fact he is proceeding in so very different a direction.[29] This is the juncture at which there is a place for an intro-duction in which to become philosophical is to come to recognize the differences in direction that are at issue between philosophies. I would pin down these differences as the differences in direction which are implicit in the shifts I sorted out in Volume 1.

TWO · RELATIONAL
ANALYSIS

The Shift in Method

Slide, mortals, do not bear down.—cited by Sartre

Simplification

In examining how Sartre transforms what he takes from Husserl, I have so far gone along with what Sartre himself assumes to be the case—that he continues to apply Husserl's procedure of intentional analysis as Husserl conceived it. I have acknowledged a certain deviation from Husserl: intentional analysis is only one of the procedures composing Husserl's method, but Sartre singles it out in the Berlin essay. However, intentional analysis itself is not in Sartre what it was in Husserl.

In the first section of *L'imaginaire,* Sartre claimed that the phenomenological method is "simple." But in the second section, it turns out to be not all that simple. There we have watched him trans-late Husserl's criticism of "the image theory" of perception into a criticism of the traditional theory of the image. In so doing, he is presupposing Husserl's intentional analysis of perception, in order to proceed to his own intentional analysis of the imagination.[1]

Now consider how the transition is carried out in Sartre's own terms: "The object of my perception and the object of my image are identical: it is this chair of straw on which I am sitting. It is simply [*simplement*] a matter of consciousness *relating* itself to this same chair in two different ways."[2] Granted that Husserl might have referred to the real object ("the chair of straw on which

I am sitting") as an abbreviated way of referring to the intentional object—since the intentional object in his analysis is given to consciousness as what the real chair is—still, the intentional object of an act of imagination is not identical in Husserl with the intentional object of an act of perception. Indeed, if it were, an intentional analysis, as Husserl conceives it, could not be undertaken of either act.

Nevertheless, Sartre's transition with the example of the chair is a warrant not just for Sartre's trans-lating Husserl's criticism of a theory of perception into a theory of the imagination but also for undertaking a different kind of intentional analysis. That consciousness in Sartre can be related to an object in two different ways—one perceptual and the other imaginative—justifies his undertaking an analysis that can be labeled "relational."

In Husserl, intentional analysis is not a relational analysis. Intentional reference is not itself a relation in the usual sense, in which the relata can each of them be specified according to what it is separate from the other: intentional reference is instead locked in on its intentional object, and the character of the reference to it cannot be specified except as a reference to this intentional object.[3] Consideration of other respects in which Husserl's analysis is not a relational analysis I shall postpone until I have brought out, for the purpose of eventual contrast, the relational character of Sartre's intentional analysis.

My first step is noting that Sartre is not applying the "simple" method outlined in his first section: "Produce images in ourselves, reflect on these images . . . determine . . . their distinctive characteristics." This proposed method lasts only until "I close my eyes and produce the image of the chair." But then Sartre goes on to recognize that this is the chair that "I have just perceived." To get at the distinctive characteristics of an image, he will now have to distinguish the way consciousness relates to the real chair when I imagine it from the way consciousness relates to the real chair when I was perceiving it.

Observation

How Sartre conducts his relational analysis becomes still more evident in the third section. He again begins with a characteristic of perception:

> When I am perceiving, I am *observing* objects. . . . Take the example of a cube: I cannot know that it is a cube until I apprehend its six sides, but of these I can see only three at a time, never more. I must therefore apprehend them successively. . . . This has all been stated a hundred times: it is characteristic of perception that the object appears only in profiles.

Sartre goes on to use the German *Abschattungen*.[4] He is presupposing Husserl's account of a perceptual "synthesis of identification." But we should not overlook Sartre's admission that something has happened to what he is presupposing. It is a feature of the kind of vulgarization that I have called "academicization" and associated with Sartre's bookishness—in the present instance, however, it might better be called "doctrinalization." Continual restatement has yielded a doctrine in lieu of an immediately given experience. Even the "cube" itself may remain a discernible debt to Husserl, who had used the example of a "die" in his account of the "synthesis of identification."[5]

What is more important now is that Sartre has not left intact Husserl's original analysis of the experience of identification. Once again we have to revise an assumption on which we have so far proceeded: Sartre is not just presupposing Husserl's analysis of perception and then going on to analyze the imagination; Sartre is transforming Husserl's analysis of perception without apparently being aware of doing so. The transformation is Sartre's sliding over distinctions that Husserl had drawn. Such sliding over frequently occurs when a successor simplifies a predecessor's analysis in an attempt to move "toward the concrete."[6]

The most obvious distinction that Sartre is sliding over is the one between perception and observation. In Husserl, observation would involve (in addition to the "synthesis of identification" that is characteristic of perception itself) paying attention to what one is perceiving and, perhaps, to the process of perception itself. But what is more fundamental here is Sartre's sliding over the distinction between intention and attention. Husserl warns that "no selective attention or noticing [*das auszeichenende Aufmerken, Bemerken*] is included in the 'reference' that is involved in . . . 'intention.' "[7]

Later we shall see that this sliding over is Sartre's vulgarization of Husserl's concept of an "intentional act" of consciousness. In other words, there is a reversion in Sartre to the ordinary, familiar sense in which "intentional" implies some degree of attention to what we are doing. Since I have not yet dealt with the eidetic reduction, with which Husserl abstracts what an "intentional act" of consciousness essentially is, I cannot now pursue this issue between Husserl and Sartre.

I shall instead stay with Sartre's sliding over the distinction between perception and observation. This sliding can be detected in the first sentence of Sartre's brief phenomenological introduction to *L'imagination*. The example Sartre uses is itself borrowed from Husserl, as I mentioned earlier. This is Husserl's example: "In front of me in the semidarkness there is this sheet of paper. I am seeing it, touching it." This is Sartre's transformation of Husserl's example: "I am looking at [*je regarde*] this white sheet of paper. . . . I perceive its form, its color, its position."[8] *Je regarde* may fall short of full-fledged observation (though not by much, once I have perceived successively the form, the color, the position of the paper), but it usually implies some minimum of attention, which "I am seeing" need not. In Husserl, the contrast between the paper and the semidarkness is sufficient for me to ensure my seeing the paper in front of me, and it renders any paying attention unnecessary.

Besides some degree of "attention," "observation" usually involves some degree of *attente* ("expectancy"); if we are observing, we are usually "waiting upon" some further perception to confirm or disconfirm what we have been observing so far. Observation, as involving "attention" and *attente,* is intentional activity in the ordinary vulgar sense. Husserl would consider Sartre to have been misled, because "consciousness is often or always accompanied by conation."[9] This is why a distinctively intentional "act" of consciousness has to be "abstracted" in Husserl (by an eidetic reduction, as I have anticipated) from the conative activity ingredient in "attention" and *attente.*

Because "consciousness is often or always accompanied by conation," we do tend in our ordinary experience to remain unaware of the distinctions Husserl is drawing. Sartre's disregarding these distinctions can accordingly be viewed as a reversion, as vulgarization, granted that it finds philosophical justification in his principle "toward the concrete."

Quasi Observation

Why does Sartre, when he slides—"When I am perceiving, I am *observing*—italicize? I suspect it is to emphasize that not "perceiving" but "observing" is the phenomenon with which he would make the transition to the imagination. He is grafting the process of observation onto the "synthesis of identification," which is characteristic of perception in Husserl, in order to go on to describe the process that he himself will call "quasi observation" and that he will claim is a distinctive characteristic of the imagination.

Here, perhaps, we find a resolution to our puzzlement over his earlier use of italics, when he so eagerly concluded that the text on the Dürer engraving "can be the starting point of an *intrinsic* distinction between the image and perception." Any philosopher dealing with the imagination would come up with some distinction between it and perception. But what is the force of the distinction being "intrinsic"? Certainly a general explanation can hardly be derived from the Dürer example. All that could be claimed is that intrinsic to a depictive act of the imagination is the distinction between it and the prior act whereby something was perceived that becomes with the depictive act an image of something else. But the depictive act of the imagination is a very special kind of imagining, whereas Sartre's conclusion is unqualified. When Sartre proposed it, he must have been already convinced that the distinction could be "pushed further" from this "starting point" so as to reach his later analysis, when his conclusion would become general: *intrinsic* to any act of the imagination is an implicit consciousness, which phenomenological reflection can extract, of this act as distinct from some corresponding act of perception. For example (although the force of this example will not emerge fully until the end of *L'imaginaire*), I am implicitly conscious of the object of this act as not being present there in front of me, as the object would be if it were the object of the corresponding act of perception.

The first specific illustration is the phenomenon of quasi observation, which we cannot analyze as a characteristic of the imagination without becoming conscious of it as distinct from observation as characteristic of perception. I anticipate a later example where the distinction is readily drawn. If I am standing in front of the Pantheon, I can observe it, count its columns, and acquire the knowledge of how many they are. But if I imagine the Pantheon, in order to determine the number of its columns, I cannot do so. If, on the other hand, I already know how many columns it has, as a result of previous observation (and I happen to be good at concocting images), I may be able to incorporate this knowledge in an image of the Pantheon.[10] If, however, I became reflectively conscious of what I am doing, I become conscious of my constituting the image as not bona fide observation, which is a process by which I gain knowledge. With quasi observation, I do not gain any knowledge. The process of gaining knowledge is reversed: knowledge previously gained by observation is put to work in order to constitute the image.

Quasi

At this decisive juncture, Sartre's analysis has become significantly original vis-à-vis Husserl's. Yet there is still a terminological link to Husserl's analysis, and this link (though not acknowledged by Sartre) can be taken advantage of to make a comparison. The term "quasi observation" is not found in Husserl, but he does employ the Latin "quasi," as well as its German translation, in describing the imaginary object. Thus he winds up his example of the Dürer engraving (after Sartre has stopped translating) by referring to our being conscious of the object depicted as "neither existing nor as not existing" but as quasi existing [*gleichsam-seiende*]." The pertinent feature of Husserl's handling of the engraving is the "likeness" (*Ähnlichkeit*) that is conferred on the perceivable figures to what we imagine they depict. Even their "quasi existence" is "like" the existence of real things. This "likeness" Sartre will in effect deny in the next section, in which he asserts that "the Imagination poses its object as a nothingness."[11]

The object of an act of the imagination and the object of an act of perception are no longer alike in other crucial respects. When I carry out a synthesis of identification, I become conscious of the cube as the identical cube, even though I am perceiving successively different sides. But the principle of identity does not likewise hold for an object I imagine: I may indeed dream of Jeannie, but she may well have Joan's blonde hair. The principle of individuation also does not hold for the image: when I see Peter, I see him as he is at the moment; however, when I have some momentary image of Peter, it condenses more of what I know about him than I perceived at any one moment. I may imagine him as wearing the suit he had on last week, but with the expression he had on his face yesterday.[12]

Since the imagined object is unlike the perceived object in these significant respects, the "likeness" between them envisaged by Husserl cannot retain the same significance in Sartre. Yet it does gain a significance it did not have in Husserl—as an illusion. This becomes evident later in *L'imaginaire:* the imaginary object "is out of reach," as opposed to the real object I perceive. "I cannot touch it, change its place," as I can the real object I perceive. "Or, rather, I can [now that the illusory likeness to a perceived object supervenes on the previous opposition], but on condition that I do it unreally [that is, imagine doing it], by not using my own hands but phantom hands, which administer unreal blows on this face."[13]

Illusion

This is the Sartre whom we discovered in the second section of *L'imaginaire* and in the Berlin essay, who would deliver us from "the illusion of immanence." We have the illusion that the "phantom hands" are within the scope of our administration, like real hands. This Sartre is on his way to the concept of *mauvaise foi* ("bad faith" or "self-deception"), which he will arrive at in *Being and Nothingness*. I have accordingly felt at liberty to coin the terminology "bona fide observation" to oppose to "quasi observation." But even in *L'imaginaire,* when Sartre reaches "phantom hands" administering "unreal blows," he will be reaching a reflexive juncture at which "I must double myself, make myself unreal." He is leaving Husserl far behind. Anticipating this juncture yields some sense of the *direction* in which Sartre is headed.

We are now in a position to locate the Sartre of *L'imaginaire* more definitely. Let us reconsider how he started out and ended up in his initial section, "Method":

> Despite some prejudices to which we shall soon have to return, it is certain that when I produce in myself the image of Peter, it is Peter who is the object of my present consciousness.
>
> The method [of "a 'phenomenology' of the image"] is simple: to produce images in ourselves, reflect on these images, describe them.

A philosopher's method, I have pointed out, is not always the method he officially sponsors. Sartre did not in fact begin the second section by producing an image and describing what is certain about it; he returned to the "prejudices" that he had mentioned and that constitute a "double error." That was our first clue to what matters to Sartre in the long run— he cares less for finding out, with Husserl's help, what is certain itself (although he will elevate "The Certain" to the title of part 1 of *L'imaginaire* as a whole) than for relying on what is certain, in order to subvert prejudices.

Husserl's philosophy is subversive of prejudices too (those composing "the natural attitude"), and the process of subversion by the eidetic and phenomenological reductions is a sustained methodological undertaking to which the first two parts of *Ideas I* are devoted. But subversion (in principle, at least) is only a first step (or first series of steps) with Husserl; once he is through the "entrance gate," phenomenological analysis proper begins with immediately given experiences.

False Attitudes

We could overlook Sartre's reference to "prejudices" in the first sentence of the first paragraph because it seems as perfunctorily Cartesian as his reference to certainty was in the first sentence of the second paragraph: "It is necessary to repeat here what has been known since Descartes—a reflective consciousness yields data that are absolutely certain." A crude dialectical opposition is being set up between the prejudices and the certainty that will subvert them. But that the prejudices are what matter to Sartre we become aware only when we anticipate, as we now have, the direction in which he will go in the longer run. Four years after the publication of *L'imaginaire,* Sartre will publish *Being and Nothingness*. It is an "analysis of bad faith," in which he will explain that "the description of authenticity has no place."[14]

Of course Sartre's equating "bad faith" with "inauthenticity" betrays a debt to Heidegger. Nevertheless, this debt is not the whole story. For we can see in the retrospect *Being and Nothingness* provides the direction in which he was already headed in *L'imaginaire*. There we have already picked up some clues as to this direction as different from Husserl's. One of these is involved in Husserl's "two . . . errors" becoming transformed first into "a double error" and, then, into "the illusion of immanence."

This direction in which Sartre is going will doubtless become more "precise and systematic" when he is able to latch onto Heidegger's concept of "inauthenticity" and transform it into "bad faith." But it is arguable that Sartre was already proceeding in this direction before he ever read Husserl or Heidegger, although then he was still "thinking vaguely," like Frédéric.[15]

Frédéric himself was not simply vague and a disciple. He was a deluded disciple, and he recognized in the end (at any rate, as close to it as Sartre came in the manuscript of "*Une défaite*") that in his relation to his master, "I have been your plaything."[16] In "Jesus la chouette" the *professeur* is similarly deluded. In discussing with Sartre still another of the juvenilia, "*L'ange du morbide*," Contat volunteers an explanation that would relate it to *Nausea* and Sartre's later works: "There is in it a sort of distrust of false attitudes—the *professeur* is already a prefiguration of the *salaud*." Sartre only half agrees. Though other specific considerations are involved, he admits more generally, "I am very embarrassed by this story, because I do not recognize very well what it represents."[17] His hesitation can be explained in part by his having elaborated in later works (with the help from Heidegger I have mentioned) a conception of "bad faith" that is a more precisely delineated false attitude than any embodied in the characters of all his youthful writings.

Sliding

I am not suggesting that such precision as Sartre derives from Husserl or Heidegger is comparable with theirs. In *L'imaginaire* it is almost entirely a question of how Sartre uses Husserl. One way Sartre gets where he is going is by sliding over Husserl's distinctions. Initially, he slides over the distinction in Husserl between "two . . . errors" and arrives at "a double error." Then he takes Husserl's distinction between "immanent" and "transcendent," simplifies it by pretty much assimilating it to a distinction between "inside" and "outside," and enlists it in constituting "the illusion of immanence." But before Sartre is through, he will take this distinction, which was restricted in Husserl to the theory of knowledge (a subject to which, we have seen, Sartre is indifferent), and extend its scope by allowing it to acquire moral implications—for example, when I rely

not on my own hands but on unreal hands to administer blows to that
hated face. Husserl's original distinction is thereby blurred even further.

We noticed this sliding earlier, in discussing Husserl's distinction between perception and observation. Such sliding is a departure, unavowed
by Sartre, from Husserl's procedure. In Sartre's autobiographical *Words*,
"Glissez, mortels, n'appuyez pas" becomes a motto for his French grand-
mother, whose delicacy and evasiveness Sartre opposes to the crudity and
bluntness of his male Germanic forebears.[18] I risk a further crudity myself: where Husserl bears down Germanically on a distinction, Sartre becomes French and slides over it.

Such sliding over, I have indicated, can be regarded as a symptom of
vulgarization. I am not thereby suggesting that nothing philosophical is
at issue. But we will not be prepared until Chapter 11 to deal adequately
with Husserl's procedure from which Sartre departs when he blurs the
distinctions Husserl draws.

Common Sense

However, another shift in *method* can be discerned, whether or not it is
regarded as symptomatic of vulgarization. When I previously dealt, in
Chapter 7, with the transformation of Husserl's "two . . . errors" into
Sartre's "Illusion of immanence," it was seen to involve a shift in audience
to the vulgar—or, at any rate, from psychologists and philosophers to
"artists and prophets." The shift then may have seemed merely rhetorical.
But the distinction between "immanence" and "transcendence," which is
also involved in Sartre's detection of this illusion, acquires the meaning
that it has in Husserl in the first place—the meaning that Sartre is blurring—only by virtue of Husserl's carrying out the phenomenological reduction, so that the risk is precluded of confusing it with the spatial distinction between "inside" and "outside."[19]

One way in which Sartre avoids confronting the phenomenological
reduction at this juncture is by another slide—or, at least, a rather facile
transition: "Psychologists and philosophers have, for the most part,
adopted this point of view [that an image is "in" consciousness]. That is
also the point of view of common sense."[20] Husserl would have referred
instead to "the natural attitude." The difference is that "common sense"
is itself a fairly commonsense notion, granted that we are likely to appeal
to it when it seems threatened by the highfalutin. But "the natural attitude" is not a commonsense notion; it is a distinctively philosophical concept. In Husserl, we do not even become conscious of "the natural attitude" *as* an "attitude" until we have begun to transcend it by attempting
to carry out the phenomenological reduction.

Still, Sartre's endeavor to undermine common sense can hardly be dismissed as mere vulgarization. His sliding can also be a manifestation of conflation, of the movement, as we noticed earlier, not only "toward the concrete" but toward a relational analysis as well. For distinctions can get in the way of following out relations. I am not suggesting that these are necessarily two different movements: analyses that would respect the concrete usually follow out the relations that compose it. This becomes evident with the advance Sartre envisages for his analysis at the end of the first chapter of *L'imaginaire*. There he proposes to abandon the procedure that he has so far employed and that he characterizes as "simple reflection," whereby the image is "considered as an isolated phenomenon."[21]

Fluidity

In my exposition, Sartre has already abandoned this procedure to the extent that he has, in the first chapter, treated imagining as differently related to the same object as perceiving. But he himself is more impressed by the further transition he makes to relations between imagining and other phenomena besides perceiving. One reason he is more impressed is that he is now explicitly introducing a new criterion that motivates this transition, though it may well have already encouraged the sliding, the movement toward conflation. His procedure so far, he admits, yields a merely "static analysis" of the image. Now he announces, "consciousness of the image is not given as if it were a piece of wood that is floating [*flotte*] on the sea, but as a wave [*flot*] among waves." It is "homogeneous with other consciousnesses which have preceded it and to which it is synthetically related."[22]

The terminology "synthetically related" may have been inspired by his viewing Husserl's perceptual "synthesis of identification" (on which we have watched him graft the process of observation) as the phenomenon that he finds the most temptingly relational and dynamic in Husserl's analysis. But the juvenilia offers some evidence that Sartre was already tempted by fluidity. There Sartre caught "the lamentable Frédéric" in the act of "seeking in the depths of his being" a "fugitive image" that had been "awakened," and Sartre assigned to him "the fluid world of Proust." The psychology that Frédéric had elaborated, Sartre informs us, was "subtle and fleeting as water."[23]

Later I shall examine Husserl's method, to see why it is as committed to distinguishing phenomena as Sartre is to sliding over Husserl's distinctions. But confronted now with the explicit criterion of fluidity that encourages this sliding,[24] I would take up first the transformation thereby taking place in the subject undergoing analysis.[25] Once we have understood this transformation, we shall be in a better position to appreciate the further transformation of Husserl's method that Sartre undertakes in order to deal with the transformed subject.

NINE

The Shift in Subject

Accompanying every perception is an affective reaction.—Sartre

Starting Point

After completing the analysis in *L'imaginaire*'s first chapter, which I have been sampling, Sartre raises explicitly at the beginning of the second chapter the question of the scope of his subject:

> We have described certain forms of consciousness that are called images. But we do not know where the class of images begins or where it ends. For instance, there are in the external world objects that are also called images (portraits, reflections in a mirror, impersonations, and so on). Is the attitude of our consciousness, confronted by these objects, assimilable [*assimilable*] to that which it takes in the phenomenon of "the mental image"? If this is the ... hypothesis, it is necessary to broaden considerably the concept of image in order to bring within our scope a number of consciousnesses with which we have not so far been concerned.

In explicitly raising the question of scope, Sartre does not mention Husserl. Yet we encountered this broadening initially in *L'imagination,* when Sartre translated the passage from Husserl on the Dürer engraving. Now Sartre is on his own.

Sartre does echo his own handling of the Dürer example. In the present passage, *assimilable* is rather awkward, but he employed this idiom when he discovered in the engraving the "starting point" for the "assimilation [of] two different kinds of imaginative consciousness"—physical and mental images. *Assimilation* there apparently meant "bringing together as similar." In my translation of that passage, I avoided the awkwardness of "assimilation" in English by substituting rapprochement, for *rapprocher* was the verb that Sartre used in *L'imagination* when he endorsed intentional analysis: "[I]f the image is only a name for a certain way that consciousness has of aiming at its object," we are able to "*rapprocher* physical images . . . with images that are termed 'mental.' "

The new example Sartre now goes on to provide in *L'imaginaire* is an instance in which physical images are brought together with a mental image. But since the example this time is Sartre's own, it will illustrate how Sartre pushes on in his own analysis beyond what he got out of Husserl's example of the engraving:

> I want to recall the face of my friend Peter. I make an effort, and I produce a certain imaginative consciousness of Peter. The object is very imperfectly reached: certain details are lacking; others are doubtful; the whole is rather vague. There is a certain feeling of sympathy and pleasantness that I wanted to revive when confronted by his face but that has not been recovered. I do not give up my undertaking. I get up and take a photograph from a drawer. . . . It is a fine photograph of Peter. I find again all the details of his face, even some that had eluded me. But the photograph lacks life; it is a perfect rendering of the external traits of his face, but it does not give his expression. Fortunately, I own a carefully drawn caricature. Here the relations between the different features of his face are deliberately distorted. The nose is much too long, the cheekbones are too prominent, and so on. Nevertheless, something that was missing in the photograph—vitality, expression—is clearly evident in this drawing. I find Peter again.
>
> Mental representation, photograph, caricature: these three realities, which are so different, appear, in our example, as three stages in a single process, three moments of a unique act. From the beginning to the end, the goal aimed at remains identical: it is a matter of rendering present to myself the face of Peter, who is not there. Yet the designation "image" is reserved in psychology for the subjective representation alone. Is that entirely appropriate?[1]

Attitude

The conclusion that this example enables Sartre to reach is sweeping:

> The mental image should not be investigated separately. There is not a world of images and a world of objects. But any object,

whether it be presented to external perception or appears to the inner sense, can function as a reality or as an image. . . . The two worlds, imaginary and real, are made up of the same objects. What defines the imaginary world, as what defines the real universe, is an attitude of consciousness.[2]

In a sense, Sartre is merely further pushing the distinction between perception and the imagination that he got from Husserl's example of the Dürer engraving; in a sense, Sartre is merely repeating the argument he offered in his first chapter—that in the case of perceiving and imagining, "consciousness is related to the same object in two different ways."

However, this time round, the world—imaginary or real—looms up in the background—and a considerable burden is put on "an attitude of consciousness," since that is "what defines the imaginary world," or alternatively "the real universe." This is more than we would ordinarily expect of an "attitude." In fact, the ordinary concept of an "attitude" has received a certain philosophical *stiffening*. This is a specific manifestation of philosophical vulgarization I did not take up in Volume 1. The vulgarization of a philosophical concept hardly ever leaves us simply with a vulgar concept. Here the ordinary conception of "an attitude" has received philosophical stiffening from Husserl's conception of carrying out, with the phenomenological reduction, a "transformation" of "the general thesis of the natural attitude" (the thesis whereby the existence of the world, whenever I perceive something, is posited as implicitly in the background). With this transformation, the "transcendental" or "phenomenological attitude" is reached, which is our access to the subject of phenomenology.[3]

Since Sartre is not carrying out a phenomenological reduction, his analysis remains within the confines of the natural attitude. Thus his use of the term "attitude" is, as it were, a renaturalization of Husserl's concept of "attitude" (*Einstellung*). I have already indicated that in Husserl we do not know we are within the confines of "the natural attitude," we do not even know we have any "attitude" so comprehensive in scope, until the phenomenological reduction is carried out.[4] Hence now in Sartre, the term "attitude" does not quite resume its original ordinary meaning but, without any clear warrant, retains something of the philosophical scope accorded it in Husserl.

Aiming

I return from this implicit issue of scope to the explicit, if more humble, issue of scope that Sartre is raising with his claim that "the mental image should not be investigated separately." We were already aware in his first chapter that it had to be investigated in terms of the differences between the way it is related to the same object as a perception. The advance that has since then taken place was anticipated at the end of the first chapter, when he announced that the imaginative consciousness had to be investigated as homogeneous with other consciousnesses which have preceded it and to which it is synthetically related, in a fashion that is now illustrated by the new lengthy example.

In the Dürer example, I was a dispassionate spectator, absorbed in "aesthetic contemplation." In the present example, Sartre's analysis expands to take in a preceding consciousness: "I want to recall . . ." My consciousness thus includes the conation that we have already seen involved in the "attention" and the *attente*, which were phenomena Sartre incorporated in "intention." Concomitant with this expansion is the new expansion of the scope of "aiming." In Husserl, "aiming" described only the way in which the intentional act singles out an object as its "target." When Sartre reports, "from the beginning to the end, the goal aimed at remains identical," intentional reference is being vulgarized, or renaturalized, in much the same fashion as is "attitude." Moreover, intentional reference is no longer by its "aiming" locked in on its target, the way the act of intentional reference is locked into its intentional object in Husserl; instead, the "aiming" perpetuates itself throughout the continuing activity of consciousness, or range of activities. It is this range that a relational analysis will be required to explore. This gain in scope Sartre himself does not explicitly acknowledge. Apparently, he is not aware of it.

Nor does Sartre recognize explicitly the crucial advance here over the Dürer example: now two physical images are brought together. What is thereby accomplished? In my aiming, I engage in the activity of quasi observation—in the first instance, with respect to the unassisted mental image of Peter. I do not achieve my goal: "certain details are lacking; others are doubtful; the whole is rather vague." So I renew my aiming with bona fide observation of a photograph of Peter, which does yield actual knowledge: "I find again all the details of his face." But again I am unsuccessful: the photograph "is a perfect rendering of the external traits of his face, but it does not give his expression." I then resort to the other physical image, the caricature, which yields information that, strictly speaking, is false: "the relations between the different features of his face are deliberately distorted [*faussé*]. The nose is much too long, the cheekbones are too prominent." Yet this time I reach my goal: "Something that was missing in the photograph—lifelikeness, expression—is clearly evident in this drawing. I find Peter again."

At stake here is a sense of identification very different from the one characteristic of a perceptual intentional reference in Husserl. My aim has been to find again the Peter I know, not in the merely cognitive sense but the Peter with whom I identify emotionally. What "I want" in imagining Peter is what Sartre later calls "an affective reaction," which covers the "feeling of sympathy and pleasantness" that I have when I actually see him, and that I want to revive when confronted by his face in my mental image of him, but that I could not secure from looking at the photograph.

This example may seem rather too specific to exhibit the scope of the subject to which Sartre is now committing himself. But he will later announce as a "principle" that "accompanying every perception is an affective reaction."[5] Affectivity will then turn out to be the particularly significant other "wave" that influences the "wave" that imaginative consciousness is.

The direction in which Sartre is proceeding can more readily be visualized if we again anticipate where he will come out later in *Being and Nothingness*. With intention, attention, *attente*, and now affectivity flowing into relation with each other, Husserl's conception of intention is on its way to being transformed into "appetite" (*ad-petitio*). "In-tention" can no longer be isolated as the "act" of "aiming" at the target it singles out; it pervades a range of activities, correlated as a "seeking toward a goal."

Strata

In *L'imaginaire*, Sartre thus takes into account as a motive for producing an image my wanting and my "waiting upon" my affective reaction to it: this is a deviation from Husserl on which Sartre himself never comments and presumably he is unaware of it.

All that Sartre himself has explicitly claimed to accomplish with this lengthy example is to bring together "a number of consciousnesses"— thereby broadening the scope of his subject. But I would add that this broadening also entails a shift in *method*, whereby his analysis becomes more fully relational. This shift can be more readily recognized once we take into account how Husserl sorted out for separate treatment the consciousnesses that Sartre would bring together in relation to one other.

An initial step toward solving problems in Husserl is their separation, and I shall consider this commitment of his to separation in Chapter 11. The eidetic reduction, which is in a sense a procedure for achieving separation, I am considering in Part 3. For the present, it is sufficient to recognize that just as Husserl envisages the intentional act as singling out and isolating the "something"—the identical object it is consciousness of—as the "target" at which it "aims," so we see in Husserl's analysis of intentional acts a higher-order commitment to singling out and isolating one phenomenon from another. Thus from the very start, Sartre, by virtue of his commitment to a relational analysis, is at cross-purposes with Husserl, even when making use of him. But we need illustrations.

Because he is committed to separation, one of the "difficulties of pure phenomenological analysis" to which Husserl is sensitive is the way in which "acts" of consciousness are "built intricately one upon another" in ordinary experience.[6] Consequently, in analyzing these acts, we risk "confusion between radically distinct strata of problems."[7] For instance, examples of an intentional "act" are also examples of many specific kinds of consciousness (perceiving, imagining, remembering, expecting, and so forth). In separating strata, Husserl accords priority to the stratum of the intentional act itself: this is what enabled me in Part 1 to outline his analysis of the intentional act separately. This analysis is then presupposed as prior when Husserl goes on to analyze an act as, specifically, an act of perceiving, or imagining, or whatever.

Sartre seemed to respect the priority of this stratum in his Berlin essay on intentionality as "a fundamental idea of Husserl's." But when a philosopher ostensibly presupposes a predecessor's analysis, it often becomes clearer in retrospect how he is transforming that analysis.

With Sartre's analysis of the example of wanting to recall Peter's face, we have reached a decisive juncture in this transformation. In lieu of Husserl's idiom of *strata,* Sartre resorts to the idiom of *stages.* These are not isolable from each other in the way that "strata" are. Thus when Sartre distinguishes successive efforts to imagine Peter's face as "three stages in a single process, three moments of a unique act," he claims that "from the beginning to the end" of this process "the goal aimed at remains identical: it is a matter of rendering present to myself the face of Peter."

In Husserl, a "process" would not constitute "a unique act": it would remain a range of more or less overlapping psychological activities that have to be sorted out and analyzed in terms of what is essential to separable acts, each of which is superimposed on the lower stratum of another act. Husserl would not accept the way Sartre sets up the example: he declares, "We reject the mythology of activities; we define 'acts' as intentional experiences, not as mental activities."[8] But in Sartre an intentional act "aims" less at a single object that is its "target" than at a variously pursued objective that is its "goal," and the "aiming" itself is sustained intentional activity.

When he redeploys in this fashion the intentional analysis that he took over from Husserl, Sartre does not mention him, and Sartre is presumably unaware of how different from Husserl's is the analysis that is emerging from the example of my wanting to recall Peter's face. But we

had been prepared for this more fluid analysis, conducted in terms of
"stages," when Sartre in effect discredited Husserl's geologic idiom of
fixed strata and adopted instead for the mental image the hydrodynamic
idiom of a wave among waves.

Interplay

The fluidity of Sartre's intentional analysis, as contrasted with Husserl's
in *Ideas I,* is illustrated by the following example in the next section of
chapter 2 in *L'imaginaire:*

> We place ourselves in front of the portrait, and we observe it; our
> imaginative consciousness of Peter is continually enriched; new de-
> tails are continually added to the object: this wrinkle that I did not
> know was Peter's, I attribute to him as soon as I see it on his por-
> trait.[9]

Instead of conducting, as Husserl would, an analysis of the object singled
out by the intentional reference, there are two objects—the one perceived
and the other imagined. When Husserl briefly brought together two such
objects, he was singling out the neutrality modification as a phenomenon.
But the transition that this neutrality modification effected—the transition from perceiving the Dürer engraving to imagining what it represents—operates only in one direction. He never undertook to analyze
what Sartre is analyzing—recurring *interplay* back and forth between the
solicitation of a physical image and the constitution of a mental image.[10]

The *interplay* becomes more pronounced in Sartre when an affective
reaction contributes to it:

> I am looking . . . at a portrait of Charles VIII in the Uffizi in Flor-
> ence. . . . These sinuous and sensual lips, this narrow, stubborn
> forehead directly arouse in me a certain affective impression, and
> this impression refers to *these lips there,* as they are in the painting.
> Thus these lips have a double simultaneous function: on the one
> hand, they refer to real lips long since turned to dust and derive
> their meaning only in this way; but on the other hand, they act di-
> rectly on my feeling, . . . because the colored spots of the painting
> are given, are seen as a forehead, as lips. Finally, these two functions
> fuse, and we have an imaginary state of affairs—that is, the Charles
> VIII who has disappeared is there, present before us. It is him we
> see, not the picture.[11]

In this example we again have two objects—perceived and imagined—as
we did with the portrait of Peter: this time the synthesis of identification,
by which "aspects" are identified with the object, is more fully analyzed.

This synthesis is a very different process from that which Sartre, in his example of observing the cube, grafted onto Husserl's analysis of perceiving the die. Instead of a unilateral identification of each succeeding "side" perceived as an "aspect" of the die, each "aspect" performs a "double simultaneous function." Sartre states, in elliptical terminology that Husserl never could endorse, "Intentionality keeps returning to the image-portrait" in order to perceive other aspects that it then identifies with Charles VIII. When the identification does seem final—"It is him we see, not the picture"—the *interplay* is relocated: at once he has "disappeared" (because he is dust) and yet is "present before us." This final flourish suggests how a procedure that initially entails doubling, by virtue of the requirements of the subject to which it is being applied, can continue in full swing after these requirements would seem to have been satisfied.

Reflexivity

Interplay can take on other guises as Sartre's analysis progresses in the direction we have already discerned—arriving at junctures where the doubling become reflexive. In the following (and much later) example, a previous affective reaction revives and takes precedence in the constitution of the image:

> If Peter made an offensive gesture yesterday that upset me, what first reemerges is indignation or shame. These feelings grope blindly for a moment in order to understand themselves, then, illuminated by encountering the relevant knowledge, produce of themselves the offensive gesture [in an image].

The feelings need not be those that were a reaction to the original perception:

> Once the image is constituted, I can deliberately react to it with a new feeling . . . , which is definitely posed as a reaction (that is, . . . as the appearance of a new synthetic form). For example, I can produce an image that does not have of itself a strong affective charge and before this unreal [imagined] object become indignant or rejoice.

Of course it is also possible, if "yesterday, for example, a gracious gesture of Annie's provoked in me a surge of tenderness," that "my tenderness can, in reemerging, make the gesture reappear unreally [in an image], all charged with affectivity." More interesting to Sartre, however, is the fact that:

it is possible too for me to reproduce the gesture, in order to make the tenderness reemerge. In this case, what I am aiming at is not yesterday's tenderness, any more than at Annie's gesture for its own sake; I want to feel a tenderness that is real, present, but analogous to yesterday's. I want to be able, as it is put quite accurately in ordinary language, "to find again" [*retrouver*] my feelings of yesterday.[12]

This example is more interesting to Sartre inasmuch as the feeling is reflexively induced by my imagining without any mediation by anything external that could be perceived, such as the caricature in the earlier example.

If we are to appreciate such reflexive junctures in Sartre's analysis, we must acknowledge an obvious difference between his examples and Husserl's examples, one of which Sartre himself seems so entirely oblivious that I have so far overlooked it: Husserl favors examples of consciousness of something; in this second chapter of *L'imaginaire*, Sartre is coming to rely on examples of my consciousness of someone.[13] To explain this difference it is not enough to anticipate Sartre's later preoccupation with the other in *Being and Nothingness* and in his play *No Exit*. Sartre himself tells us how he discovered the other in a POW camp in Germany, and it is rather more than a curious coincidence that with the war he also discovered the other in philosophy. In short, he discovered that Heidegger was not just a disciple of Husserl's, as Sartre himself had been in *L'imaginaire*, but a "dissident disciple" who challenged Husserl's solipsism— assuring that not only the conflict between self and Other but, in addition, the conflict between Heidegger and Husserl had to be dealt with in *Being and Nothingness*.[14]

These anticipations are helpful, but the expositor shouldn't jump the gun. The Sartre we are dealing with at this point is the author not of the wartime *Being and Nothingness* but of the prewar *L'imaginaire*. Within the limits of this work, certain explanations are available for Sartre's favoring examples of consciousness of someone. At present we can see that in an analysis whose direction is toward reflexive junctures, my relation to someone can prepare for dealing with my relation to myself. Thus my aim in the initial example was to "find" Peter "again," to *rendre présent* ("render present," "re-present") Peter's face. But eventually it is not Annie herself I would "find again," by re-presenting her in an image; it is my feelings for her I would "find again."

It is true that the *direction* can be better understood if we anticipate how "rendering present" is transformed in the successive examples of a rendezvous in *Being and Nothingness*. The initial rendezvous is between two parties—my "rendezvous with Peter at four o'clock." Since "I arrive a quarter of an hour late," I ask myself, "Has he waited for me?" But the climactic rendezvous is not with a "you" but reflexively with myself. My *attente* maintains the continuity between the two stages: "I wait for myself [*je m'attende*] in the future, where I have a rendezvous with myself on the other side of that hour, of that date, or that month." So crucial a phenomenon in *Being and Nothingness* as anxiety is "the fear of not finding myself at the rendezvous [or worse, because I become more reflexively involved] of not even wanting to be there."[15]

Stages

In his analysis, Sartre is not only proceeding in a *direction;* he is also proceeding by stages.[16] Just as in the initial example of this chapter he corralled successive "stages" of "a single process" whose aim was "to *rendre présent*" Peter's face, so the successive examples in the longer-run analysis can be corralled as successive stages in an analysis of the aim of "rendering present," of "re-presenting" in an image. But we should also recognize that the analysis itself—the way it is being conducted—is developing by stages.

I should add that it is because I would respect the way the analysis is developing that I am offering a commentary in which I sample each stage, instead of undertaking a series of separate forays, as I did in Volume 1. There I was elaborating my own analysis of the *shifts,* by reference to the problems with which they were designed to deal. That analysis having been elaborated, now that I am respecting the development of Sartre's analysis, I appeal to each of the shifts, over and over again, each time it becomes pertinent.

I have already indicated how the analysis in *L'imaginaire*'s second chapter differs from the "static" analysis of the first chapter: it has become a dynamic, fluid analysis. Hence, it is transformed in conformity with its subject, when the wavelike character of this subject is finally recognized. There is, of course, a weak sense in which any respectable analysis develops as it advances, but in Sartre the development is the transformation of the character of the analysis. In this stronger sense of development, a "static" analysis is an undeveloping analysis, whereas a fluid analysis, which is undergoing transformation in conformity with a subject, is a dialectical analysis, in which the *interplay* promoting this transformation articulates the flow into stages.

I would beg the terminological question of whether or not the first chapter of *L'imaginaire* is to be regarded a stage, even though no concept of "stage" is put forward.[17] This chapter is entitled simply "Description," and I am inclined to regard it as merely outlining how Husserl's method of phenomenological description can be applied to the image. It has accordingly been valuable for the purpose of discerning a certain initial continuity with Husserl. It is only in the second chapter, I have argued, that Sartre finds his own starting point for treating the image, by determining the scope of his subject. This starting point he had discovered in Husserl's handling of the Dürer engraving as achieving a rapprochement between the mental image and the physical image. But we have seen Sartre go beyond Husserl in the second chapter by bringing the mental image together with two different kinds of physical image, the photograph and the caricature. Accounting for the difference between one's reaction to these two kinds of image enables him to include affectivity within the scope of his subject and to organize his analysis methodologically in terms of successive stages. But since this is only the first stage of Sartre's analysis, we are not yet in a position to generalize about the sequence of these successive stages. Retrospective generalization will become feasible in Chapter 15.

Expression and Meaning

We exclude much that in ordinary speech would
be called an "expression."—Husserl

Starting Point

Before going on to the next stage in Sartre's
analysis, we need to zigzag. Having reexam-
ined Sartre's starting point with respect to his
subject, we should examine Husserl's. This
reexamination will yield a different perspective on the relation between the two analyses.
Though the Dürer engraving may have originally provided Sartre with his starting point,
this example in Husserl is found two-thirds
of the way through *Ideas I.*

One reason I took up Sartre's starting
point first was that Husserl adopted different
starting points in different works. The eidetic
reduction, with which he started in *Ideas I,*
deserves examination, since *Ideas I* is the
particular work that Sartre devoured—and I
intend to examine the eidetic reduction in
Part 3. But we have seen that Sartre seemingly disregards the eidetic reduction, even
when he makes use of a passage from Husserl that exemplifies it. Taking the eidetic reduction into account could not initially assist
us in canvassing the actual textual evidence
of the relation between Husserl and Sartre.
Here we reach an at least temporary impasse.

We do, however, have textual evidence in
Sartre that will enable us to come a little
closer to Husserl's starting point in the first
of the *Logical Investigations*. Several considerations prompt this selection. From Husserl's own point of view, the *Investigations*
were a "breakthrough" and thus still a

"starting point" (*Anfang*), even after he had written *Ideas I*. Thus he could express the hope that the *Investigations* would "help introduce the reader to the nature of genuinely phenomenological . . . work." [1] In turning to the *Investigations*, I am further anticipating the importance for the history of phenomenology not only of Heidegger's allusions to it in *Being and Time*, including an allusion to its starting point, but also of Derrida's interpretation of this starting point as the starting point for Husserl's entire undertaking in phenomenology, as I pointed out in Volume 1. [2]

In the present volume, the decisive consideration so far is that the procedure that receives detailed attention in the *Investigations* is intentional analysis: we have seen that this is the procedure that Sartre also favors at the expense of the reductions. But the immediate textual basis of a comparison now is that Sartre draws a distinction in the second chapter of *L'imaginaire*—the chapter that we have just begun—and that this distinction apparently derives from a distinction Husserl draws in his analysis of intentional reference in the first of the *Investigations*.

The Sign

Phenomenology is for Husserl an analysis of meanings or, more definitely (once the concept of intentionality is brought to the fore, as it is in the first of the *Investigations*), an analysis of intentional "acts" as *sinngebende* ("meaning-giving" or "meaning-endowing"). "Intentionality" is accordingly for him (as I indicated in Chapter 5) "indispensable at the start." But, in fact, meanings are first encountered in the guise of signs (primarily spoken or written words), which express meanings. Thus the first of the *Investigations* is entitled "Expression and Meaning." The first chapter of this investigation is entitled "Essential Distinctions," and elicits the distinctions that are essential for an analysis of meanings.

What we are looking for now is the first of Husserl's "essential distinctions" that is picked up by Sartre. We have already examined the first section of the second chapter of *L'imaginaire* (a section largely devoted to the implications of the example of wanting to recall Peter's face) and have also sampled the examples of portraits in the second section. But this second section is entitled "The Sign and the Portrait," and it begins by drawing a distinction that seems to derive from the first chapter of the first of the *Investigations*, though there is no acknowledgment of Husserl. At this juncture in Sartre we seem to come fairly close to one of Husserl's "essential distinctions," granted that Sartre reaches it only when his own analysis is well under way.

The distinction that we shall examine in Sartre seems to derive from the following passage in Husserl:

What is involved in the descriptive difference between the physical sign phenomenon and the meaning intention that makes it into
an expression becomes very clear when we turn our attention to the
sign . . . as the printed word. . . . If we do this, we have an external
perception . . . like any other. . . . If this object . . . functions as a
word, its presentation [*Vorstellung*] is wholly altered in character.
The word . . . remains intuitively present . . . but we no longer intend it. . . . Our interest, our intention . . . point exclusively to the
thing meant in the meaning-endowing act. This means, speaking
purely phenomenologically, that the intuitive presentation . . .
undergoes an essential phenomenal modification when its object begins to count as an expression. . . . There is constituted . . . an act
of meaning [*Bedeutung*], which finds support in the intuitive content presented by the word but which differs essentially from the
intuitive intention directed upon the word itself.[3]

Husserl's distinction is differently drawn in Sartre's example:

I approach some heavy black marks printed on a placard nailed
above the door of a railway station. As I read the words Office of
the Assistant Manager and come to realize that it is this office that I
must enter to file my claim, the marks composing the letters suddenly lose their own dimensions, color, location. . . . I have understood. . . . These marks no longer matter, I no longer perceive them;
in fact, I have adopted a certain attitude of my consciousness that
via them aims at another object. This object is the office where I
have business.[4]

Insofar as Sartre is making a transition from seeing a sign to grasping its
meaning, he can be said to retain Husserl's distinction, though his description of this transition is more dynamic than Husserl's: "the meaning
goes out to the thing and lets the word drop." But the comment that
Sartre makes on this transition is without precedent in Husserl: "The
meaning does not return to the sign."

Interplay

Sartre is not merely undertaking, as Husserl is, a transition from seeing a
sign to grasping its meaning. As is indicated by the title of this second
section, "The Sign and the Portrait," he is introducing a second point of
reference not found in Husserl: he is setting up an opposition between the
unilateral meaning-endowing act in the case of the sign and the way in
which (we saw earlier) the portrait is endowed with meaning. In its case
he describes the *interplay* between what is perceived and what is imag-

ined in elliptical terminology that, I suggested, Husserl never could endorse: "Intentionality keeps returning to the image-portrait." Thus the
point of Sartre's comment that the "meaning does not return" in the case
of the sign is to play up this opposition between its unilateral reference
(whereby the word that has been perceived is dropped, and the meaning
goes to the thing) and the *interplay*, in the case of the portrait, between
what is perceived and what is imagined.

In order to stress this opposition, Sartre accentuates in the example
the perceptual materials of the sign. Its "heavy black marks" are more
salient than the "printed word" is in Husserl. These marks have initially
"their own dimensions, color, location." Yet the perceptual "matter of
the sign is entirely indifferent to the object signified. There is no relation
between the Office that is black marks on a white placard and the 'office'
that is a complex object, not only physical but also social." If we are
inclined to protest Sartre's "no relation" (How then am I able to find the
office?), we should remember not only that Sartre is setting up an opposition but also that in his relational analysis significant relations are characteristically constituted by *interplay*.

There can be *interplay* between what is perceived and what is imagined in the case of the portrait because the relation to the portrayed is "a
relation of resemblance," and a consequence of this resemblance is my
affective reaction:

> This painting, which is made to resemble a human person, acts on
> me the way a man would. . . . This knitting of the brows on the
> canvas moves me directly. The calm of this face moves me di-
> rectly. . . . These elements can enter either into an imaginative or
> perceptual synthesis. . . . They are expressive.

Expressiveness

At this juncture, Sartre may seem to have come close enough to Husserl's
analysis of "Expression and Meaning" to permit a comparison. But very
different problems come to the fore in the first of Husserl's *Logical Investigations*. When Husserl contends that "the problems of expression and
meaning come first for philosophers," he is assuming that philosophers
are "directed by general logical interests."[5] Sartre has other interests.
Though we are not yet able to specify them fully, we can see that they are
interests that may well have directed him when he favors consciousness
of someone over consciousness of something, when he brings the sign
into conjunction with the portrait, and when he plays up the meaning of
the facial expression conveyed by the portrait, to which I have an affective
reaction. There is a clear contrast here with Husserl who explains, "We

. . . employ the term 'expression' restrictively: we exclude much that ordinary speech would call an 'expression.'" His definition specifically "excludes facial expression."[6]

The example I have just quoted from Sartre of an expressive face in a portrait is hardly exceptional. If we go back to the beginning of this chapter in Sartre to his example of wanting to recall the face of Peter, we can discern its implications for a comparison with Husserl's analysis in "Expression and Meaning." What was missing in the photograph, though "it is a perfect rendering of the external traits of his face," is Peter's "expression." This is then provided by the caricature. Examples of photographs abound in Husserl's canvassing of physical images, but there is never, so far as I am aware, an example of a caricature. The explanation is that Husserl never sought out an example that would exhibit expression in Sartre's sense. There is a corresponding adjustment by Sartre in the "meaning" of what is "expressed." At stake (reflexively and affectively) is what Peter means to me. This adjustment is further illustrated by another example of Sartre's in his second chapter: "When I am looking at photos in a newspaper, they quite likely can 'mean nothing to me.'" There are, he adds, "instances where the photo leaves me in such a state of indifference that I do not even carry out [on perceiving the photo] the constitution of an image."[7]

The photo, I would explain, means nothing to me because I have no affective reaction to it. Sartre is on the way to elaborating a concept of imaginative meaning in which the affective component is dominant. This is the *direction* in which we shall watch Sartre's analysis develop in *L'imaginaire*.

Faces

Faces, their expressions, portraits, turn up not only in *L'imaginaire* but elsewhere in Sartre's prewar writings. In *Nausea* Sartre's protagonist confronts his face in a mirror and discovers it is "perhaps impossible to understand one's own face. Or perhaps it is because I am a loner. People who live in society have learned to see themselves in mirrors as they appear to their friends." At a later, climactic moment, he confronts the social elite of Bouville *via* their portraits in the museum, and the confrontation ends with Sartre's most famous affective reaction: "Adieu, handsome lilies . . . in your little painted sanctuaries, adieu, . . . our pride and reason for existing, adieu, shits [*salauds*]."[8] The year before Sartre published *L'imaginaire,* he published "Official Portraits" and "Faces." The official portrait "defends a man against himself"—against his "too human reflection" in a mirror.[9]

Although these examples introduce a social dimension, they still illustrate the same characteristic movement that I picked up earlier in the *diplôme,* as well in the Dürer example—from something perceived to something imagined. Now the move is from what the "loner" perceives in the mirror to faces that are imagined as they appear to others, and from "the too human reflection in a mirror" to the face as imagined in the official portrait.

It is worth observing too that although Husserl "excludes facial expression," faces already enjoy a certain prominence in the *diplôme.* Clearly this is one of Sartre's original directive interests that survives, in *L'imaginaire* and elsewhere, his conversion to Husserl. I have previously mentioned Sartre's doctrine of *surperception* (the "surplus" the image can add to what is perceived). Such examples as landscape and Proust's hawthorns may not survive in *L'imaginaire,* but Sartre had also argued in the *diplôme* that "there is never [merely] perception but *surperception* of a human face." This would not always be the case with a landscape.

Sartre had also argued in the *diplôme* that "we are more sensitive to impressions aroused by a grimace, a play of feature." He cites from Tolstoy the example of "a woman who, when she laughed, 'resembled a squirrel.'" It is not (in Sartre's explanation) a matter of our imposing on her face the representation of a squirrel: when "we perceive the squirrel on her face, . . . we are adopting, while seeing it, the affective attitude that we would have toward a squirrel." Thus Sartre's explanation had relied on the affective component. In the *diplôme* there had even been a forewarning in a footnote of the example that becomes Sartre's starting point in *L'imaginaire:* "Our reaction to caricatures, etc. should be investigated."

I shall return in Chapter 12 to Sartre's transformation of the relation between expression and meaning, for we shall then reach the example in *L'imaginaire* that marks his definitive break with Husserl.

The Priority of Method

Our analytic investigations cannot be allowed to wait upon the systematic determination of our subject.—Husserl

Ambiguities

We have again reached something of an impasse between our two philosophers, as a result of Sartre's broadening the scope of his analysis of expression and meaning. Sartre moves to include in his analysis just what Husserl would "exclude" when he undertakes to "employ the term 'expression' restrictively," at the expense of "much that ordinary speech would call an 'expression'"—with his definition specifically excluding "facial expression." Although we cannot here get around this difference between the subjects each treats, we can resume our pursuit of the concomitant difference in method. For when Sartre includes what Husserl would exclude, he is reversing, with his movement "toward the concrete"—which is concomitantly his entry into a relational analysis—the movement of restrictive abstraction in Husserl.

I illustrated this movement in Husserl earlier by considering the way Husserl separates subjects for treatment. The instance I examined was his separation of strata and, specifically, the stratum of the intentional act itself. Sartre, in contrast, locates the image that becomes his subject in terms of a rapprochement between the mental image (to which philosophers and psychologists had traditionally restricted their attention) and the physical image (which they had neglected).

This rapprochement is the relational starting point that Sartre found in the passage in Husserl on the Dürer engraving, but it becomes a fully relational starting point only when one physical image (the photo) is brought into relation with another physical image (the caricature). We were deterred then from seeking the implications of Sartre's initial starting point in Husserl himself because the Dürer example doesn't turn up until two-thirds of the way through *Ideas I*, quite remote from Husserl's own starting point. In addition, Sartre himself was indifferent to what Husserl himself would accomplish with this example.

Husserl was, in fact, using the example of the Dürer engraving to deal with a "dangerous ambiguity" and an attendant "persistent confusion." Husserl's commitment to separation is illustrated not only by his separating specific subjects but also by his general methodological preoccupation with ambiguities and confusions. Ambiguities he considers, are to be treated with distinctions that separate in an ambiguity whatever can lead to a confusion—for instance, in the section with the Dürer example, the confusion of the neutrality modification with an act of the imagination (since such an act is only one species of the neutrality modification).

In Chapter 10, I quoted section 5 of the first chapter of the first of the *Logical Investigations* since that passage seemed the first in Husserl of some substantive relevance to Sartre: his treatment of the sign, in fact, seemed to derive from it. Now I would revert to section 1, for the evidence it will yield of Husserl's own starting point in analyzing "Expression and Meaning." This first section is called "An Ambiguity of the Term 'Sign.'" In this section, Husserl is attempting to disentangle "meaning," which we have seen is to be the subject of his phenomenology, from that with which it is "always entangled [*verflochten*]" when a "sign" is used "to indicate" in "communicative speech." [1]

That Husserl fails in this attempted disentanglement is implicit in Heidegger's analysis in *Being and Time* and explicit in Derrida's analysis.[2] I take note of the attempt itself simply for the purpose of a general comparison with Sartre. But since Sartre treats the "sign" only in passing, while dealing directly with the "portrait," I am postponing Husserl's treatment of the sign until I can take into account Heidegger's treatment of the "sign," "indication," and "communication" in Volume 3 of *Phenomenology and Deconstruction*.

Difficulties

Another problem, however, can be raised now with direct bearing on Husserl's methodological commitment to disentangling entanglements that are ambiguous and confusing. We reached our initial impasse when we ascertained that Husserl had treated the imagination "only in passing," so that Sartre could find in him only "brief allusions" to "a theory of the image" that, Sartre was convinced, Husserl had "undoubtedly . . . elaborated in his courses and in unpublished works."[3] Some of these allusions Sartre garnered in the citations that I've quoted from *L'imagination*. I used the citations to explain the strength of Sartre's conviction that any philosopher equipped with a concept of intentionality would have been committed to a rapprochement between mental and physical images, thereby finding himself in a position where he would "undoubtedly" have to treat exactly the subject that Sartre is about to treat. Thus I took Sartre's "undoubtedly" as betraying the strength of Sartre's own conviction, for there is no evidence that Sartre was actually privy to any information about what Husserl covered in his unpublished lecture courses.

The problem we then face in Husserl, Sartre did not face. Granted that Husserl did in fact treat the imagination in one of his lecture courses, we have to explain why he gave priority to *publishing* other works over publishing this treatment. In a fragment from the period in which he was working on the imagination, Husserl offers a vivid description of encountering difficulties:

> At some point, after prolonged efforts, the clarity we have yearned for seems in the offing. We think that the most superb results are so close that we need only reach out. All the problems seem to be resolved; our critical sense mows down contradictions one after another. And now only a final step remains. We are about to take it, and begin with a self-conscious "therefore," and then we suddenly discover a point that is obscure [but] that continues to loom larger. It grows to a monstrous size, swallowing up all our arguments and reanimating the contradictions that have just been overcome. The corpses come back to life; they leer; they snicker. The work and the struggle start all over again.[4]

There is a lot of temperament here and expense of spirit. But other considerations also are pertinent.

In 1906, while working over materials he had accumulated, Husserl acknowledged writing "many supplements, often handling difficulties."[5] Encountering difficulties, often requiring supplemental analyses, is a general characteristic of Husserl's philosophy. A contrast is inevitable with the facility with which Sartre churned out philosophy. This facility would be evident even if we did not have de Beauvoir's report of "the extreme rapidity" with which he wrote *L'imaginaire,* "breathless" from trying to keep up with "the movement of his thought."[6]

A difficulty is not necessarily evidence of a philosopher's obtuseness. Nor is a difficulty a solid obstacle that any philosopher is likely to run into, blocking his advance. It does not simply lie in wait to ambush him, so that it can "leer" and "snicker." A difficulty that a philosopher encounters is a philosophical difficulty; that is, it is encountered as a difficulty by virtue of the character of the philosophy that the philosopher is elaborating, in which it becomes a difficulty to be dealt with. I remarked when I began this volume that an ambiguity is hardly an unusual difficulty in philosophy. What I would bring out now is that a difficulty takes its particular shape from the character of a particular philosophy. Thus a difficulty for Husserl is an "ambiguity" that portends a "confusion," which is characteristically an entanglement and, as such, is to be dealt with by drawing distinctions that enable the philosopher to disentangle what he would separate out and isolate for treatment. This is the function of the "essential distinctions" that Husserl draws in the first chapter of the first of the *Logical Investigations* and that we have sampled in sections 1 and 5.

There may well have been specific difficulties of this sort that Husserl ran into in treating the imagination, perhaps in separating it from the other topics he treated in the lecture course. In the 1913 introduction to the second edition of the *Logical Investigations,* Husserl recalls some of the difficulties that he has run into since the first edition. In particular, he had become conscious of how "confusingly" phenomena that were the "modifications" of other phenomena were "built one on the other" [7] and, indeed, not in any single fashion but (as he had already put it when he stressed "the difficulties of pure phenomenological analysis") because they were "built intricately one upon another in multiple ways." [8] The subject of the imagination might well be a specific case in point, in that it is a "modification" of perception.

Systematization

There is yet another kind of difficulty that Husserl encountered. In his manuscript on the imagination, he entered the behest: "See also the Time Manuscript! Where everything is worked out anew. So work through together." [9] But whenever Husserl attempted to rework his previous materials, he discovered distinctions that needed to be drawn, and they would proliferate and impede his attempt. He often discovered that "many new distinctions are required in what previously was regarded as simple." [10]

The proliferation of distinctions, particularly in dealing with "difficulties," was one reason that Husserl's manuscripts rarely seemed to him ready for publication. He himself complained, "Most of my work remains embedded in manuscripts. I could almost curse my inability to reach completion." This inability may help explain why he failed to put together "The Principal Pieces of Phenomenology," which included his lectures on the imagination. He also confesses his inability "to rework the universal systematic thoughts that my detailed investigations require."[11] Recall his lament to Brentano (for the letter was written the same autumn that Husserl delivered his lectures "The Principle Pieces of Phenomenology and Theory of Knowledge") that his undertaking was "a troublesome, wearisome, and besides, a groveling task. How I would like to live on the heights. For this is what all my thinking craves for. But shall I ever work my way upward, if only for a little, so that I can gain something of a free distant view?"[12]

Leverage

Husserl's commitment to analytic discrimination may help explain in general his inability to reach completion. But we are more immediately concerned with his specific failure to publish the lecture course on the imagination he gave in 1904–5. What still has to be taken into account is that Husserl was becoming at that time increasingly preoccupied with method. Initially, he would raise methodological considerations, expecting that they would help him deal with substantive "difficulties," only to find that coping with these considerations itself raised "difficulties" that tended to take precedence over the substantive "difficulties."

"The Principal Pieces of Phenomenology" raised problems about the relations of a "piece," as a "part," to the complete "whole." It is perhaps no accident that in the introduction to the third of the *Logical Investigations* (which is entitled "The Doctrine of Wholes and Parts" and which deals with the kind of "part" a "piece" is) Husserl makes the following recommendation:

> Our analytic investigation cannot be allowed to wait upon the systematic treatment of our subject [*die Systematik der Sachen*]. . . . Difficult concepts, which we employ in research that would clarify knowledge and be made to work rather in the manner of a lever, cannot be left unexamined until they emerge themselves in the systematic interrelations of the realm of logic.[13]

Even though Husserl had undertaken the "Principal Pieces" with a view to dealing with their systematic interrelations and had proposed to rework them afterward with this in view, they did not remain all of them equally principal. The first to lose out was "Expectation" (*Erwartung*). The negligible treatment it received is especially apparent to us, since we have begun to see how crucial *attente* is in Sartre. The "piece" that did become principal for Husserl (it was, at least, the only piece that he had published) was "Time." Husserl arranged to have his first research assistant, Edith Stein, pull his manuscripts together; he then turned them over to Heidegger for further editing.

What became crucial for Husserl's own future labors, however, was the phenomenological reduction, which first emerged in the lectures on time and which he wrote out in a "primitive" version during his summer vacation following his delivery of these lectures.[14] The methodological problems of this reduction continued to be a concern of Husserl's and reached a fuller formulation in *Ideas I* (1913). Precisely how this reduction was to be carried out continued to pose one of the most persistent cluster of "difficulties" that preoccupied Husserl for the rest of his life.

Husserl's next attempt to be systematic was in his *First Philosophy* lectures (1923–24). After a first volume raising critical and historical considerations, the second volume was entirely taken up with *The Theory of the Phenomenological Reduction*. By 1924 his interest in the imagination had dwindled.

In whatever measure it may be pertinent to the specific case of the imagination, method in general (and the phenomenological reduction in particular) had for Husserl increasingly gained priority over the systematic treatment of substantive problems. Husserl himself admitted his predicament in an anecdote that Levinas recalls him telling. As a child, Husserl had been given a pocketknife. He found, though, that the blade was not sharp enough, so he kept sharpening it, failing to notice that the blade was becoming ever smaller, until it vanished. Husserl's mood in telling this story was dejected.[15] What he as an adult was seeking to sharpen (if I may be literal about it) were distinctions that would eliminate ambiguities by disentangling confusions.

This too brief sketch of Husserl's career from 1904 to 1924 may be sufficient to suggest a plausible (if only partial) explanation of why Husserl treated the imagination "only in passing." Having treated this subject in a lecture course, Husserl passed up the prospect of a complete revision for publication, as he became preoccupied with method and, particularly, the phenomenological reduction.

Perception and Imagination

Now we can turn our attention to some of Husserl's "allusions" to the imagination in the works that he did publish. I have already supposed that Sartre may have been responsive to the appendix attached to the fifth of the *Logical Investigations,* for he must have been attracted by its title, "Critique of the Image Theory and of the Doctrine of the 'Immanent'

Objects of Acts." But Sartre was likely also to have been aware of the fifth investigation as a whole, since it is entitled "On Intentional Experiences and their 'Contents,' " and it is Husserl's most extensive presentation of the concept of intentionality, which Sartre takes as "fundamental."

Let us glance at one of the three sections of this investigation in which Husserl acknowledges "Difficulties" in their titles—the section where the difficulties have to do with maintaining the essential distinction between intentional experiences and their contents, due to the danger of confusing intentional experiences with mental contents (sense-data) that only "serve as the building stones" for these experiences.[16] We have already recognized that this distinction is picked up again in the appendix and is pivotal in Sartre's Berlin essay on intentionality.

Before we consider how Husserl handles this distinction in this section, we must note another, more specific distinction, also pertinent to Sartre's undertaking, that Husserl handles in a way illustrating the priority he accords method. Husserl alludes to "the relation between perception and imaginative presentation as a much-treated matter of dispute." Any survey of modern philosophy from Descartes on (including Sartre's sloppy history in *L'imagination*) would suggest that this is indeed a much-treated and much-disputed matter. But Husserl in effect takes himself out of this history by relegating his allusion to this matter to a footnote. In this footnote, he is concerned not to resolve the dispute but to explain that it "can have no satisfactory outcome in the default of a properly prepared phenomenological foundation and the clarity thereby obtained in concepts and problems."[17] Thus the distinction between perception and imagination that we have seen Sartre drag out of Husserl's Dürer example, take as a "a starting point," and push further is a distinction Husserl would postpone working over until he prepared the phenomenological foundations for treating perception and the imagination. Some of his preparations we have taken into account: the separation of strata, the taking of intentional experiences as the fundamental stratum, and the drawing of the distinction between these experiences and sense-data in this logical investigation itself.

I return to this distinction. The example illustrating it that I quoted earlier was "We do not hear sounds [but] the song of the singer."[18] In the section we are now considering, Husserl comments on his selection of examples. He explains that "examples that can be used to elucidate this distinction . . . are provided by comparing perception with memory, or comparing either with presentations [*Vorstellungen*] by means of physical images (paintings, statues, etc.), or by signs. But verbal expressions yield the most suitable examples." One of these that he actually elaborates is "the case of someone attentively hearing a completely strange word as a sound-complex, without even suspecting it is a word, and comparing this with the case when he afterward hears the word, . . . in the meantime having become acquainted with its meaning." He hears the same sounds but now the intentional act is performed, endowing these sounds with meaning.

Just as Husserl mentioned only in passing (that is, in a footnote) the distinction between perception and imagination that Sartre took as a starting point, so now he mentions only in passing the example of comparing something perceived with something presented by a physical image. If he had selected this example, it would have brought him closer to the initial "starting point" Sartre found in the Dürer engraving. But Husserl selected verbal expressions instead, which might remind us that he originally started out with the sign as a verbal expression in the first of the *Logical Investigations,* "Expression and Meaning." And we are also aware that Sartre reached the sign only in connection with the portrait as a physical image—accordingly, he treated the sign very differently.

Direction

It is not just such specific differences that matter; there are overriding issues regarding priorities. There is, in the first instance, the priority of method, just illustrated by Husserl's postponement of the substantive problem of the relation between perception and imagination. There is, in the second instance, the priority he accords the sign as a verbal expression at the very start of the *Logical Investigations* and the confirmation of this priority when in the fifth investigation he prefers "verbal expressions" as yielding "the most suitable examples" for drawing the distinction between intentional experiences and mental contents (sense-data). Other issues of priority emerge when Husserl goes on to accuse his predecessors of having elaborated a theory that "overlooks points decisive for concern [*Interesse*] with logic and the theory of knowledge. It does not do justice to the facts of the subject [*Sachverhalt*] of phenomenology; it does not even attempt its analysis and description."[19]

Husserl is making three assumptions here. We have seen, first of all, that he is assuming that certain specific points are decisive (whereas other points are taken to be decisive by Sartre) because he assumes in general that what philosophy is decisively interested in as a *subject* is "logic and the theory of knowledge."[20] Though he would concede that this interest determines what facts will be selected for analysis and description (verbal expressions, for example, rather than the physical images), he is assuming, second, that the discriminating process of selection itself does not disturb or distort the array of facts—that it is philosophically neutral in its *method,* as is the process of analyzing and describing these facts, for these are immediately given.

I have used Sartre's selection of decisive points and his descriptions in order to quarrel with Husserl's assumptions. Thus I am not dealing with these assumptions directly. The evidence I am offering for regarding them as not philosophically inevitable is the history of the phenomenological movement. In Volume 1, I assembled this evidence, while simultaneously working out a method for assembling it. We reach a decisive juncture, at which Husserl's commitment to analytic discrimination falls short, when he refers sweepingly to a "concern" or "interest" by which philosophers are "directed" (*geleiteten*). Neither Heidegger, Sartre, nor Merleau-Ponty (the most prominent successors of Husserl) have retained Husserl's concern for "logic and the theory of knowledge." In Volume 1, I could sort out only very broadly their divergent concerns, using the shifts in direction in which they proceeded and trying to pin down those shifts as involving shifts in *subject,* in *level,* in *affiliation,* and in *method.* In Volume 2, we have already watched Sartre discount the theory of knowledge in the very essay in which he endorses intentionality as the fundamental idea of Husserl's phenomenology and exploits Husserl's distinction between intentional experiences (as referring to transcendent objects) and mental contents (as immanent). Nevertheless, Sartre's divergent concern will require further delineation.

If a phenomenological analysis could do justice to any considerable range of phenomenological fact while remaining neutral in its concern, I would now be analyzing this phenomenological evidence myself, instead of analyzing the evidence of competing phenomenological analyses. Indeed, there would be no competing phenomenological analyses. Not even "analysis" itself is a philosophically neutral conception. Thus we have seen how Sartre transforms Husserl's intentional analysis into a relational analysis. We shall see in the next chapter that not even a "relation" is a philosophically neutral conception.

TWELVE

Relations

*Every analysis that disentangles, renders
unintelligible.*—Merleau-Ponty

The Whole

Sartre did not start out *L'imaginaire* by drawing "essential distinctions." He did not run
foul of Husserl's difficulties in disentangling
what he would treat from its entangling relations to other phenomena. Instead, one of
Sartre's decisive initial moves was to "bring
together" (*rapprocher*) what previous philosophers and psychologists had "separated." [1]
He pounced on the example of the Dürer engraving as providing a rapprochement as a
"starting point," despite its having been for
Husserl an example that had helped him to
distinguish the neutrality modification involved in the phenomenological reduction
from that involved in a depictive act of the
imagination. We have also seen that Sartre, in
following out other relations besides this rapprochement, slides over distinctions that Husserl had deemed essential—the distinctions
between intention, attention, and *attente*.

This issue of method—between what I
would roughly call "analytic separation" or
"analytic discrimination," on the one hand,
and "following out relations," on the other—
is recurrent in the history of philosophy. But
Husserl regards the commitment to discrimination as peculiarly his undertaking:

> We would proceed step-by-step in our
> undertaking, with the utmost caution
> [*Vorsicht*]. . . . So great are the difficul-
> ties, and . . . many new distinctions are
> required in what previously was re-
> garded as simple.

This is indeed *generally the peculiar character* [*Eigenheit*] of phenomenological analysis. Each step forward yields new points of view, from which what was already discovered appears in a new light and often enough presents as complicated [*mehrfaltig*] what originally was accepted as simple [*einfaltig*].[2]

Even though I am concerned in this volume with Sartre's relation to Husserl, I would myself be failing in discrimination if I simply characterized Sartre's intentional analysis as "relational" in comparison with Husserl's intentional analysis. This characterization is too sweeping; comparisons with other kinds of relational analysis are needed. One pertinent comparison here is with Heidegger, who could have lent encouragement to Sartre in adopting a relational analysis. Comparison is also pertinent with Merleau-Ponty, who viewed Sartre's analysis as not sufficiently relational.

The relational character of Heidegger's analysis is manifest in his hyphenated terminology, which is designed to undercut the discriminations of ordinary language, and of traditional philosophy as well. "Being-in-the-world" is the most notorious example. Of course, discrimination has still to be sought, but only while respecting how "the whole of this structure [of being-in-the-world] always comes first."[3]

Up until now in this volume, I have pursued in my exposition a step-by-step procedure, justified not only because this is Husserl's own discriminating manner of proceeding but also because caution is necessary in pinning down the rather refractory evidence of Sartre's relation to Husserl. At last I have reached a juncture at which the whole of a structure comes first, and I can wind up my exposition of a relational analysis by resuming my deconstructive style in Volume 1 and broadening out my comparisons. When Heidegger starts out his analysis of being-in-the-world as a structure, we can detect unacknowledged debts to Husserl's terminology, which may betray some effort on Heidegger's part to make his way from the kind of analysis Husserl offered and reach his own. These debts can underpin a comparison, though at the moment it has to be limited to bringing out the overall difference in the direction in which the two phenomenologists are proceeding.

Parts

For the purpose of this comparison, my account of Husserl's progression in the first three of the *Logical Investigations* is inevitably crude. The whole does not come first with Husserl. He is instead, as I have just recalled, proceeding step-by-step. He is also zigzagging back and forth between substantive and methodological considerations, giving priority to the latter and not undertaking a "systematic treatment" of his subject, as he admits in his introduction to the third of his *Investigations*. Heidegger, in contrast, presents his phenomenological method in his introduction to *Being and Time* before undertaking the analysis of being-in-the-world as a structure. The hazard of determining Husserl's sequence, as compared with Heidegger, any reader can confirm by comparing the two works' respective tables of contents, and he will not find Husserl's sequence much easier to discern if he takes into account Husserl's review of it in his foreword to the second edition of the *Logical Investigations*. There Husserl explains how the first of his *Investigations* "directs the look of the phenomenologist starting out to the initial, already most difficult problems of the consciousness of meaning." [4] For this purpose Husserl elaborates, as we have seen, an analysis of intentional reference as "directed" toward the intentional object, thereby endowing it with meaning. In the second investigation, Husserl goes on to examine essences (or idealities) and "the modern theories of abstraction," which try to account for these essences. His own procedure for reaching them, I have anticipated, is the eidetic reduction, which we shall be considering in Chapter 13. But a criterion we are already familiar with presides over this procedure, as is clear in the second edition from his criticism that he had failed to meet "the requirement of a deep separation of essence." [5] Granted this commitment of Husserl's to separation, he comes up in the third investigation against difficulties in dealing with wholes and in doing justice to the status of parts in relation to wholes. Here I can only observe, for the purpose of the comparison with Heidegger, that a concept that Husserl employs in coping with these difficulties is "the need for supplementation" (*Ergänzungsbedürftigkeit*).[6] Heidegger does not retain this concept. He does not require it, since he is starting out with "the whole" (*Das Gänze*), which "always comes first."

Husserl distinguishes between a "piece" (an "independent part" of a whole—for example, the leg of a table) and a "moment" (a "nonindependent part"—for example, the color of the table, which I cannot be conscious of apart from the surface of the table).[7] Heidegger starts out his analysis of being-in-the-world by declaring,

> this structure is not pieced together but is originally and continually a whole. It affords us, however, various ways of looking at the moments that are constitutive for it. The whole of this structure always comes first, but if we keep it continually in view, these moments, as phenomena, will be made to stand out in relief. And thus we shall obtain . . . objects for analysis.[8]

If Heidegger does not have Husserl's problem of "supplementation," he does have the converse problem of obtaining "objects for analysis," which Husserl does not have, since he starts out with intentional acts singling out intentional objects. But since Heidegger starts out with "the whole," and proposes to "keep it continually in view," his problem is articulating this whole in order to obtain these "objects for analysis." Without damage to the whole he cannot articulate it into "pieces" that are (in Husserl's terminology) "independent parts." Thus the whole in Heidegger is not "pieced together," so he can discard Husserl's term "pieces." But Heidegger can retain Husserl's term "moments" ("nonindependent parts"). Another term Heidegger can retain from Husserl is *anheben:* while we keep the whole continually in view, the moments as phenomena are to be made to *stand out in relief.*[9] The phenomena are not separate "objects" in Husserl's sense.

Negation

Sartre and Merleau-Ponty will yield further evidence about the problem the status of an object poses for a relational analysis. Sartre seems to have suffered a certain hesitancy in *L'imaginaire,* inasmuch as this title does not make clear what is "imaginary." The examples we have adduced so far, as well as his having taken intentionality as fundamental, suggest a reference to the intentional object as imaginary—yet he also considered using the titles *Le monde imaginaire* and *Les mondes imaginaires.* That he could vacilate between *L'imaginaire* and the other two titles perhaps illustrates how he still visualizes Heidegger as a disciple of Husserl, like himself, and so sees no reason to choose between their approaches.[10]

Whether or not the two titles Sartre did not use were inspired by Heidegger, Sartre confronts directly in *Being and Nothingness* (published three years later) the problem of reconciling Husserl and Heidegger, whom he had come to regard, since writing *L'imaginaire,* as having opposed philosophies. On the one hand, in his introduction to *Being and Nothingness* he follows Husserl to the extent of undertaking an analysis of consciousness as intentional. On the other hand, he starts out part 1 by warning that the unity of a relation must be maintained: "One should not separate the two terms of a relation in order to try to rejoin them later." In this context he appeals to his directive principle, "toward the concrete," which in effect prescribes a transition from Husserl to Heidegger:

> Consciousness is an abstraction. . . . The concrete is man in the world with that specific union of man with the world that Heidegger, for example, calls "being-in-the-world."

Sartre regards himself as repudiating here not Husserl's intentional analysis but the phenomenological reduction, conceived as Husserl's having bracketed "the world" in order to analyze consciousness: "To carry out the phenomenological reduction . . . is to start out deliberately with the abstract." In the next sentence, Sartre is applying his principle "toward the concrete" and reversing (as I phrased it at the beginning of this chapter) the movement of restrictive abstraction in Husserl. Sartre then finds himself committed to a totality, which is "not pieced together" (in Heidegger's terminology)—or, as Sartre puts it himself, "It is impossible to succeed in restoring the concrete by adding up or organizing the elements that have been abstracted from it. . . . It is enough to open one's eyes and question in complete naïveté this totality that is man-in-the-world."[11]

However, opening one's eyes is clearly not enough to settle the issue here between Husserl and Heidegger. When Husserl used the visual idiom to convey "the peculiar character of phenomenological analysis," he pointed out that "each step forward yields new points of view, . . . and often enough [the new point of view] presents as complicated what originally was accepted as simple." Seeing is being visualized as discriminating. But Heidegger would have us "keep [the whole] . . . continually in view," so that "objects" emerge for "analysis" only to the extent that they can "be made to stand out in relief."

Sartre (like Heidegger) faces the problem of articulating relations within this totality. This problem Sartre resolves by construing the articulative operations of consciousness as negations, in conformity with the recognition, often featured by a relational analysis, "Omnis determinatio est negatio." But in Sartre the relational context is predominently affective. Reconsider the example I have already quoted in another connection:

> Not-being always appears within the limits of human expectancy [attente].
> Has Peter waited for me? [M'aura-t-il attendu?] I look around the café, the drinkers and say: "He is not there."
> It is certain that the cafe by itself . . . is a plenitude of being.

But as I look around the café, my attention becomes a process of articulation:

> each element . . . tends . . . to emerge against the background constituted by the totality of other objects. . . . In particular the faces . . . hold my attention for a moment ("Could that be Peter?") and . . . promptly disintegrate, precisely because they "are not" Peter.[12]

The Fabric

The status of relations becomes even more salient an issue with Merleau-Ponty, who finds Sartre's dialectic of being and nothingness "too exclusively antithetical" as a process of articulation. What the exclusively antithetical excludes is what Merleau-Ponty would respect—"a vital living interrelation."[13] Unlike the articulations in Sartre's analysis, those in Husserl's analysis are not antithetical. Yet Merleau-Ponty (without acknowledging that he is in effect criticizing Husserl's analysis as an analysis) explains that phenomenology "is a matter of describing, not of explaining or analyzing."[14] He would have had Husserl and Sartre in terminological agreement with him if he had merely distinguished description from explaining and halted there, instead of going on to deny that phenomenology is an analysis.

If I have not been satisfied to label Husserl's phenomenology simply as description but have employed the label "descriptive analysis," it was to avoid blurring the issue that emerges explicitly only in terms of his relation to Merleau-Ponty. The issue can be followed through from one level to another. Thus I recognized earlier that just as Husserl is committed, in his analysis of intentional acts, to the way in which each of them singles out its intentional object as remaining identical throughout our successive experiences of it, so he is committed to an analysis in which he separates one phenomenon from another. Merleau-Ponty himself eventually recognizes how Husserl's procedure is "to disentangle, unravel, what is entangled." But his own insistence on the intimacy of relations prevails with his protest, "Every analysis that disentangles, renders unintelligible."[15]

I have anticipated Heidegger and Merleau-Ponty as a forewarning that Sartre's is only one way of handling relations. Indeed, his is a rather unsteady manner of proceeding, by virtue of his initial commitment to an intentional analysis and his subsequent shift to an analysis modeled on Heidegger's analysis of the whole. Merleau-Ponty's appraisal of Sartre's analysis as insufficiently respectful of relations should also be taken in conjunction with Merleau-Ponty's denial of the priority the concept of intentionality enjoys in Sartre. It is, we have heard Merleau-Ponty protest, "too often cited as the main discovery of phenomenology." Merleau-Ponty himself, instead of adopting—as Sartre does—Husserl's idiom of "aiming" for the way in which the intentional act singles out and isolates its object, deploys analogies that convey his appreciation of "the wonder of interrelated experiences." He presses a reflexive argument, "We are ourselves this network [*filet*] of relationships." Experience is for him a "fabric" (*tissu*).[16] A fabric is not an entanglement, and its disentanglement is an unraveling that deprives it of its character as a fabric.

Landscape

Another analogy that Merleau-Ponty offers tends to undercut Husserl's and Sartre's conception of an intentional object:

> To the player in action the football field is not an "object." It is pervaded by lines of force (the yard lines, those which demarcate

the "penalty areas") and articulated in sectors (for example, the "opening" between members of the other team). . . . The player becomes one with the field and feels the direction of the "goal."[17]

We have already watched Husserl's intentional object, as the object targeted by an intentional act, become in Sartre the goal of an action, and this transformation may have encouraged Merleau-Ponty to adopt the idiom of goal-directedness. But if this player had been able to enter Husserl's or Sartre's analysis, he would not have become "one with the field," as in Merleau-Ponty. The goal is no longer in Merleau-Ponty, as in Sartre, a fairly isolable determinant of the player's sense of direction; his goal-directed action belongs to the relational context of the field, which is "not an 'object.' "

Concomitant with Merleau-Ponty's rejection of analysis (as well as explanation) is "a disavowal of science" and a shift in *affiliation.* "The field," which he takes over not only from football but also from gestalt psychology, can become a landscape, which has the advantage that it can be both a natural landscape and the genre of painting that Merleau-Ponty favors when he commits himself to painting as an affiliate for his philosophy.

I have mentioned that the adult Sartre is not much taken with natural landscape. (He is not, for that matter, much taken with the artistic genre.) But even the example that Sartre employed in his *diplôme* Merleau-Ponty would hardly find sufficiently responsive to interrelatedness, since the issue for Sartre is what "is *added at times* to ordinary perception to render it beautiful"—that is, to render the perception "aesthetic."

"The wonder of interrelated experiences" is virtually a principle for Merleau-Ponty.[18] (It would be fully a principle if the distrust of the discrete it embodies did not preclude his adopting any sharply defined principle.) Consider another analogy Merleau-Ponty adopts:

> Just as the perceived world holds together only by reflections, shadows, levels, the horizons between things, which are not things, and which are *not nothing,* but which rather are the only way *the fields* of possible variation are demarcated . . . , so in the same way the work and the thought of a philosopher are also made out of certain articulations between things said, . . . [which] are *not objects of thought,* since, like the shadow and the reflection, one would destroy them by submitting them to observation that is *analysis,* or to thought that *isolates.*[19]

Analogy

I have quoted this analogy at some length not only as a further illustration of Merleau-Ponty's distrust of the discrete ("articulations . . . are not objects of thought" and are destroyed by "thought that isolates") but also because the philosopher who is being eulogized in this essay is Husserl, who did envisage the intentional act as singling out its object.[20] If Merleau-Ponty is able to overlook the fact that Husserl's philosophy is not intimately relational in the fashion this analogy would suggest, it is in considerable measure because he is not concerned with Husserl's thought in its isolation, but in its intimate relation to the thought of his successors in the phenomenological movement. Thus we can understand the title of this essay, "Husserl and his Shadow," in terms of the analogy to the perceived world as holding together by shadows, and so forth. Husserl's thought is likewise to be seen as inseparable from the shadow it casts in the guise of Merleau-Ponty's thought and that of other phenomenologists.

One reason the character of a relational analysis has needed clarification is that I am dealing myself with relations—with the relations between Husserl and his successors. These relations are subject to the same vagaries in different philosophies as other relations.[21] Merleau-Ponty's preoccupation with "interrelated experiences" helps explain why Merleau-Ponty (as I observed in my previous volume) is the only one of our four phenomenologists who provides us with anything at all in the way of a history of phenomenology. This is also why he fails to provide us with an adequate history: he is too accommodating of his predecessors, except when they are themselves unaccommodating, as Sartre is by being "antithetical"—for example when he pits Heidegger and Husserl against each other. In contrast Merleau-Ponty blurs the issues separating them, in the interest of demonstrating the intimacy of the relations holding between them.[22]

It is possible, of course, that Merleau-Ponty derived his analogy here from Husserl's term *Abschattungen;* however, he does not mention this possibility, perhaps because in Husserl, it is the individual perceived thing that I am conscious of in terms of its "adumbrations," its "shadowing forth," and Husserl could not be said to apply the term in Merleau-Ponty's fashion to "the fields of possible variation," any more than "horizons" in Husserl are relational phenomena in Merleau-Ponty's sense of articulations "between things." That Merleau-Ponty is happy to rely on and multiply analogies—"reflections, shadows, levels, the horizons between things"—itself betrays his commitment to "interrelated experiences, for an analogy, whatever it conveys more specifically, conveys a relation. Thus Husserl is less prone to analogies than Merleau-Ponty.[23]

The Shifts

I return to the issue of expression and meaning, not only as Husserl's starting point in the *Logical Investigations,* but also as fundamental to any phenomenology as an analysis of meaning, so that the differences we have been examining between phenomenologists turn on what expresses meaning.[24] Thus we should not conclude that Sartre's favored examples of faces and their portrayals prevail by virtue of their vividness. Considerations of method are relevant even in his literary works, where vividness would seem at a premium.

Let us reexamine the vivid affective reaction of the viewer in *Nausea* to the dead bourgeoisie who are the subjects of the portraits in a provincial gallery—*salauds*. But first place alongside this example one from Merleau-Ponty which is almost as concrete and almost as vivid:

> We never remain suspended in nothingness. We are always in . . . being, just as a face, even in repose, even in death, is always condemned to express something (there are those whose faces, in death, express surprise, peacefulness, discretion), and just as silence is still a modality of sound.[25]

The differences between the two examples betray the different methodological commitments of Sartre and Merleau-Ponty that we have been exploring in the present chapter.

First there is the shift specifically in *method* which we have seen is implicit in Merleau-Ponty's protest that "the notion of intentionality" is "too often cited as the principal discovery of phenomenology." Sartre's viewer is reacting affectively by attributing with his epithet conscious intentions to the subjects in question, while they were still alive. For the term *salauds,* Sartre explains elsewhere, he applies to those "who try to demonstrate their existence is necessary," despite its contingency.[26] At the same time the viewer is attributing conscious intentions to the painters, as having collaborated in the demonstration in a fashion commensurate with the intentions that had animated their subjects' lives:

> Under the brush, the mysterious weakness of human faces was removed. . . . I reflected that they did not have this necessity while they were still alive. But at the moment of passing on to posterity, they trusted themselves to a painter of renown, to have him operate discretely on their faces the dredging, the drilling, the irrigation, by which . . . they had transformed the sea and the fields.[27]

In Merleau-Ponty consciousness is "dispossessed" of the "sovereign power" that it exercises in Sartre with intentionality. Insofar as Merleau-Ponty still retains a notion of intentionality, a shift in *subject* takes place: "Certain major concepts of Husserl's phenomenology crystallize in the way in which . . . 'intentionality' is transferred from consciousness to the body."[28] This transfer is illustrated by comparing how faces in the passage I have quoted are able to express attitudes "even in death" (and thus no longer animated with conscious intentions), with the conscious intentions expressed by the faces as portrayed in Sartre's museum.

This shift in *subject* can only be delineated if the further shift in *method* is taken into account which has emerged from my comparison of Sartre with Merleau-Ponty in this chapter. In Merleau-Ponty's relational analysis relations "overlap" and are entangled,[29] so that he can criticize (we have seen) Sartre's dialectic of being and nothingness as "too exclusively antithetical." This criticism is conveyed by Merleau-Ponty's initial comment in the quoted passage, "We never remain suspended in nothingness." As the passage goes on, we become entangled in the ambiguities of overlapping relations, but presumably there is the implication that the relations between the psychic and the corporeal, between life and death, are not exclusively anithetical. At any rate, he relies on an analogy (the "just as" of the quotation) to insinuate relevant relations.

Because of this overlapping of relations, an intention itself cannot be singled out analytically; the phenomenologist must trace out "a network of intentions."[30] The body itself cannot be singled out analytically, since "the body is our general medium for having a world." Finally, we have seen that Merleau-Ponty favors natural landscapes and painted landscapes (where one object overlaps another), rather than facial expressions and portraits. If he provides an example of faces in the quotation, I suspect it is because he has Sartre in mind.[31]

Nevertheless, Merleau-Ponty is also protesting, in effect at least, against Husserl when he "excludes facial expressions." Recall his insistence, "Every analysis that disentangles, renders unintelligible." It is high time we examined Husserl's crucial analytic procedure for disentangling—the eidetic reduction.

THREE · EIDETIC ANALYSIS

THIRTEEN

The Eidetic Reduction

Just as the given for empirical intuition is an individual object, so the given of essential intuition is a pure essence.—Husserl

The Shift in Level

In dealing with the relation between Sartre and Husserl, I have not yet provided the justification for focusing on examples—initially on those Sartre borrowed from Husserl, later on the examples, different in character, that Sartre elaborated on his own. Method may enjoy a priority in Husserl it no longer has in Sartre. But one trait the two phenomenologists do share is that they both rely on examples for carrying out an eidetic analysis.

So far I have expounded Sartre's method as if it were merely Husserl's intentional analysis transformed into a relational analysis. Sartre does take intentionality as fundamental and as inviting the rapprochement between the physical and the mental image that yields him his subject. However, in "Method," his brief section at the start of *L'imaginaire,* he makes the claim that "the act of reflection has . . . an immediately certain content, which I will call the *essence* of the image." The term "essence" was not much in vogue in French philosophy at that time and must have been appropriated from Husserl. Sartre also sometimes characterizes his analysis as "eidetic"—as "eidetic description," "eidetic psychology," "eidetic intuition," or simply as an *eidétique.*

Before trying to discover why Sartre might want to avoid the term "reduction," we should determine why Husserl's eidetic analysis took the guise of a reduction. In

Husserl, the eidetic reduction is a procedure for using examples to "lead" our consciousness, as we re-flect on them, "back" from the empirical level to the eidetic level, where whatever is essential in the example is disentangled from what is merely particular to the example. An example we have already considered illustrates the procedure. When Husserl insists, "I do not hear tone sensations, I hear the song of the singer," [1] he is not interested in the particular song being sung, or in music, or in hearing; he is interested in the essential distinction between an intentional experience and mere sense-data.

In the *Logical Investigations,* Husserl was predominantly concerned with clarifying the character of intentional experiences. But in *Ideas I,* he is predominantly concerned with clarifying his procedures for clarifying the character of intentional experiences, starting with the eidetic reduction. In his foreword to the second edition of the *Logical Investigations*— the edition he published the same year, 1913, as *Ideas I*—he admits "the impossibility of lifting the *Investigations* entirely on to the level of *Ideas.*" [2] Husserl is thinking of the shifts in *level* that he carries through in *Ideas I* with the eidetic and phenomenological reductions.

I shall review the examples of intentional experiences I have presented previously, in order to bring out the eidetic reduction implicit in them. When I used the example of a child's desire for a bicycle, I was not interested in the particular child's particular desire for a particular bicycle, or even in desire itself as a particular phenomenon. Similarly, I was not interested in the particular fear of the particular driver, or even in fear itself as a particular phenomenon. With both examples, I was interested in an essence—the essential structure—of an act of consciousness as an act of intentional reference to an object. [3]

The act by which I grasp this essential structure of an intentional act is intuitive, but it is essentially distinct from an empirical intuition. At the empirical level, I am immediately conscious of something particular—my desire for a bicycle with nickle-painted wheels, my fear of an automobile at the crossroads. Between this empirical intuition and an eidetic intuition, there is a distinction in *level:* "Just as the given for empirical intuition is an individual object, so the given of essential intuition is a pure essence." [4]

Recall the comparison with the affiliated eidetic science of geometry that I used early in Volume 1 to bring out the eidetic character of phenomenology. The lines of the particular triangle I have drawn on the blackboard are wobbly. But I can be conscious not merely of this particular triangle but also of the essential structure of the triangle it exemplifies.

Essences

The higher-level status enjoyed by these essences is not metaphysical, according to Husserl. He does not take essences to be real, as Plato is traditionally supposed to have done. Remember that even an intentional object is not a real object (in the sense that it is something that occupies space), and the relation between the intentional object and a real object in the world is not a real relation—so any question about their relation is inappropriate.

Of course, the automobile that the driver is driving exists as a real object, and his driving is a real action. His fear is real, too, and can be a real cause adduced to explain another real action (his depressing the brakes), just as this real action can be adduced in turn to explain the real swerving of the car as its effect. Nonetheless, the essential structure of an intentional act of consciousness, which his real fear exhibits, is not itself real.

My use of this term "act" of consciousness may have long since seemed troublesome, but it is a concept that itself can be purified by an eidetic reduction and, accordingly, recognized not to be one of the gamut of real activities with which it is entangled in my consciousness. Thus, here again, the question as to what "the real" relation is between this logical "act" and these activities is inappropriate.[5] Yet since we have already seen in Sartre that the intentional act is one of these "waves" influencing one another, we have already gleaned some evidence that the distinction in *level* Husserl would establish by the eidetic reduction is weakened by Sartre—evidence that may explain why even though Sartre retains Husserl's term "eidetic," he does not retain the term "reduction."

Introspection

Unless the eidetic reduction intervenes, rendering a phenomenological analysis distinctively eidetic, its procedure is likely to seem introspective. Indeed, phenomenology has frequently been dismissed by its adversaries as nothing but introspection. The issue of *level* here can, to some extent, be clarified by distinguishing between the essences that phenomenological analysis obtains by an eidetic reduction and the general concepts obtainable by an empirical induction.

Introspection is a familiar way of compiling empirical facts and generalizing from them. I ask myself, "Do I really love her?" Usually I attempt to answer the question by introspection: I did miss her on Monday, but on Tuesday I forgot her, and on Thursday I was responsive to the charms of another woman. As a compilation of such positive or negative facts, introspection is comparable to the sometimes more rigorous inductive procedures of the empirical scientist. Like the scientist, I proceed from the particular facts to whatever generalization they may warrant.

Presumably, there presides over my procedure some general sense of what love is, what its meaning is. This general sense may itself still be largely, or entirely the outcome of previous inductive generalizations. It is quite possible that love is so variable a phenomenon (or galaxy of phenomena) as we move on from one particular individual to another, from one particular culture to another, that an eidetic reduction cannot eliminate its particularities so that it is recognizably an essence. This may also be the case with desire and fear. It seems less clearly the case, however, if we move to a higher level and try to purify the essence of "emotion," as Sartre does in his prewar *A Theory of the Emotions*. In any case, we have already encountered an essential structure that Husserl considers indisputably purifiable—intentional reference.

Free Variation

The procedure of purification that the eidetic reduction enforces is a way of handling empirical facts very different from an inductive generalization, whether experimental or introspective. Husserl characterized it as a "free variation." By freely varying the examples of intentional reference (starting from a sound-complex that is heard without the knowledge that it is a word and switching to the same sound-complex after the word and its meaning have been learned; or, moving from the example of the child's desire for the bicycle to the driver's fear at the crossroads), what is particular to each example is eliminated in favor of what is essential to the act of intentional reference. A less elaborate free variation in Husserl is the following lineup of examples: "In perception, something is perceived; in imagination, something imagined; in affirmation, something is affirmed; in love, something is loved; in hate, hated; in desire, desired; and so on." [6] In each example, I am conscious of what is invariant: consciousness is "consciousness *of* something." But it has been necessary to vary the particular examples in order to disentangle this essential structure. Thus the differences between fear of something, desire for something, judgment of something, and so on, assist us in eliminating the variants as irrelevant: "While what differentiates the variants remains indifferent to us," the *eidos* has been "elevated from its milieu." [7]

Free variation eliminates the contingency of "this here," which infects the empirical generalization. Indeed, the phenomenologist need not even start from empirical fact. The driver may have been mistaken that another automobile was approaching the crossroads, but he still feels fear. The phenomenologist may have read this example in a book, or merely imagined this example, and he may go on to imagine, quite "arbitrarily" (*beliebig*), other possible examples, such as the child's desire for a bicycle. It is the arbitrariness with which the examples are to be imagined that warrants Husserl's characterizing the variation as "free." [8] This arbitrariness further justifies his claim that because phenomenology, like geometry, is an eidetic science and does not deal with particular matters of fact, "clear imaginings not only offer . . . foundations as good as but, to a great extent, better than the data of actual perception." [9] That the imagination thus assumes for Husserl a certain methodological importance is a matter to which we shall have to return.

The Engraving

At the moment, we can perhaps resolve our initial puzzlement over three features of Husserl's passing reference to an act of the imagination. I observed two of them, in my Introduction, as Sartre's seemingly minor mistranslations. Sartre began the passage on the Dürer engraving by translating with a formal, "Let us consider the Dürer engraving" Husserl's casual, "It may be that we are looking at the Dürer engraving." Sartre also translated as "art book" what would more accurately have been translated as "portfolio." Perhaps Sartre should not have disregarded Husserl's casualness; perhaps it should be taken seriously, as appropriate to the arbitrariness of a free variation. The "It may be" would seem to imply that he need not necessarily have taken this particular work of art but could have taken any work of art as an example to make his point about the depictive act of the imagination. [10] This implication is perhaps played up by his having the print lying loose in a "portfolio" rather than bound in an "art book."

At the same time, granted he had to pick a particular example, this one seems unnecessarily complex to make the simple point that although whatever we perceive, we take to be real, this attitude can be suspended or neutralized by a depictive act of the imagination? All he needed was any depiction in which our attention could shift from the figures we perceive to the realities they depict. Why did he not pick an example in which the reality is plain, instead of so varied an assortment: the journeying knight is an allegory for the Christian militant; Death is a personification; the Devil is whatever the devil he is. Perhaps, however, a free variation may be involved here. Husserl may be eliminating as irrelevant to the neutrality modification the differences in the kind of reality that each of the three figures claims, thereby encouraging us to transfer our attention to what is essential—the neutrality modification itself.

Picture-Book Phenomenology

If the particular engraving, or differences between the particular figures, were not a matter of indifference, Husserl would have been engaged in what he disdained as "picture-book phenomenology."[11] This was how Husserl mocked the undertaking of phenomenologists who lapsed from the level of eidetic analysis to the level of empirical psychology—in the present instance, introspective, descriptive psychology. He was also sensitive to his own slackness in having characterized his analysis in the *Logical Investigations* as "descriptive psychology."[12] The strength of his commitment to maintaining the distinction of *level* is evident in his starting out *Ideas I* not with an analysis of intentional reference, as in the *Investigations*, but with the eidetic reduction, as necessary to establish the distinction of level in "Fact and Essence" (the title of the first chapter of *Ideas I*).

Sartre's dropping Husserl's term "eidetic reduction" has aroused our suspicion that he may be less sensitive than Husserl to establishing and maintaining this distinction of level. The suspicion is heightened by his insistence that his method is "the description of the image," by his entitling his first chapter "Description," by the brevity of his first section, "Method" (two small pages as compared with the forty-one large pages that Husserl devotes to "Essence and Eidetic Cognition," as secured by the eidetic reduction), and by the simplicity of the conclusion Sartre reaches in this section: "The method is simple—produce in ourselves images, reflect on these images, describe them." Yet Sartre still retains Husserl's term "essence," his analysis is still "eidetic," and such characteristics of imagining as "quasi observation" are essential characteristics. What then is Sartre's procedure?

FOURTEEN

Dialectical Correlation

*We can describe . . . in terms of the variations
. . . the function "image."—Sartre*

Examples

Husserl's eidetic reduction is a procedure
whereby an experience is treated not merely
as a matter of fact but as an example exemplifying an essence. I have stressed that
Sartre, like Husserl, relies on examples. Initial clues as to the differences between Husserl's eidetic reduction and whatever comparable procedure Sartre is employing are the
differences in the character of the examples
themselves. Although there is a certain complexity to the example of the Dürer engraving, Husserl himself made no explicit use of
this complexity. If in the first chapter of *L'imaginaire* Sartre's examples were relatively
simple, and were in fact often borrowed
from Husserl or at least similar to Husserl's
examples, they have become more complicated in the second chapter.

Yet even the borrowed examples betray
certain differences. Recall the first example
with which Sartre brusquely starts out *L'imagination*. The example is seemingly inconsequential and obvious in both Husserl and
Sartre. Husserl used it when he eventually
reached the act of intentional reference in
Ideas I—"This sheet of paper" that is "lying
in front of me. I am seeing it." [1] Sartre starts
out: "I am looking at this white sheet of paper, placed on my table." Sartre, I remarked
earlier, is not "seeing" but "looking at"
something, and "looking" implies that some
degree of attention is being paid to what one
is "seeing."

We are already familiar with what would be, from Husserl's perspective, Sartre's failure to distinguish "intention" as a cognitive performance from "attention," which also involves some volition. There are also other slight differences, which are not just literary refurbishing on Sartre's part. The paper does become "white" in the next section in Husserl, and his seeing then becomes a turning of his look (*Blickwendung*). Husserl is varying his initial example to involve the discrimination of a quality (whiteness): such discrimination would entail some degree of attention. By thus varying the initial example, Husserl would demonstrate that consciousness still exhibits the same essential characteristic of intentionality.

I have skimmed over this stretch of Husserl's analysis to make the point that Sartre, at the very start of his treatment of the image, brings together what Husserl treats with separate examples. We have already found in the Dürer engraving an illustration of a more significant commitment to rapprochement, where Husserl would separate. In the present instance, Sartre is moving—more instinctively than deliberately, I would suppose—"toward the con-crete," by accepting certain related experiences, rather than abstracting, disentangling in Husserl's fashion, one experience from another to which it is ordinarily related.

The Image Family

By the second chapter of *L'imaginaire*, Sartre's examples, we have already observed, are no longer similar to Husserl's. We have watched Sartre launch his relational analysis with the example of wanting to recall the expression on the face of Peter. The example exemplified "three stages in a single process, three moments of a unique act." If Sartre has retained Husserl's term "act," what it now includes stretches it out of shape. What Sartre has lined up as "stages," as "three moments of a single act," Husserl would disentangle as exemplifying essentially distinct "acts"—or, rather, he would have relied on separate, more succinct examples to exemplify each of these "acts." He would, for instance, have separated the depictive act of imagination I performed when I confronted the caricature from my affective reaction to it—or, rather, he never uses so complicated an example as a caricature.

In Husserl, an eidetic reduction as a free variation eliminates as variable—and as such, as irrelevant—the differences that render each example a merely particular state of affairs; in consequence, the invariant, identical essence is left surviving the variation. As he himself puts it, "what differentiates the variants is a matter of indifference."[2] But in Sartre the differences between my purely mental image of Peter's face, what I then imagine on the basis of the photo, and what I finally imagine on the basis of the caricature are not eliminated as irrelevant; they are variations that are instead to be correlated, I repeat, as different "stages in a single process." They are different but still related. Thus Sartre's title for the second chapter of *L'imaginaire* is "The Image Family."

This idiom that allows for differences in what is related would not be acceptable to Husserl. In effect, it disregards the requirement that an essence must remain identical throughout all its exemplifications. An essence in Husserl cannot be familial; indeed, Husserl describes it as "solipsistic." Conversely, Sartre's general accusation in *Being and Nothingness* against the eidetic character of Husserl's analysis is that Husserl was guilty of an "antidialectical isolation of essences." [3] There is no evidence that Sartre ever read the work in which Husserl described the essence as "solipsistic," and I suspect Sartre was able to formulate his accusation only once he had come to appreciate the relational character of Heidegger's and Hegel's analyses.

Nonetheless, if Sartre still characterizes *Being and Nothingness* as an eidetic analysis, it must be that he does not fully appreciate how his procedure departs from Husserl's. Since Sartre has relinquished the label "eidetic reduction," I will indicate his departure by supplying a label for his procedure: it is a rudimentary "dialectical correlation." The extent of Sartre's departure will become more evident once we recognize the further advance Sartre makes with his next example, which is the longest and most complicated in *L'imaginaire*.

Impersonation

Sartre also gets more philosophical mileage out of this example than from any other. I cannot demonstrate in advance that the example will repay the detailed attention I accord it; it seems all too obviously the sort of thing A. J. Ayer had in mind when he accused Sartre and other existentialists of describing "certain psychological states . . . of a rather special character." [4] That it nonetheless acquires quite general implications in Sartre is all the more striking. Since my primary concern is with its methodological implications, I would recall my having revived in my Introduction the analogy, which I drew in Volume 1, between a method and a style. A close analysis comparing the style of two writers or artists is regarded as acceptable in most quarters, and I am merely offering a fairly close analysis of Sartre's transformation of Husserl's procedure of eidetic reduction.

Sartre introduces the example with a summary:

> On the stage of the music hall, the impersonator [*fantaisiste*] Franconay is "doing impersonations" [*fait des imitations*]. I recognize

the performer [*artiste*] she is impersonating; it is Maurice Chevalier. I appraise the impersonation: "It really is him," or "It doesn't come off." What is going on in my consciousness?[5]

Before allowing Sartre to answer this question, it is worth noticing that he refers in the *diplôme* to impersonation as well as to caricature, whereas Husserl never took an impersonation as an example, any more than a caricature. The example is not just too complicated; like the caricature, it involves an affective reaction. When I assert, "It really is him" my "really" is largely an affective reaction, for I *know* it really isn't him. It really is Franconay, and I am only imagining that I am seeing Chevalier.

Another reason Sartre is tempted by this example is that it lends itself to an analysis of the kind which I am labeling a "rudimentary dialectic." This is beginning to be apparent even from the summary. Just as in the case of my effort to imagine Peter, the final affectively satisfactory image (to which we could transfer the phrase "It really is him") was based on the caricature, as opposed to the preceding affectively unsatisfactory image ("something was missing") that was based on the photo, so here the affectively satisfying outcome to the impersonation, "It really is him," is now pitted against the opposing outcome, "It doesn't come off."

The dialectical character of this correlation will require further exhibition later. For the present, I would stress only that it is a correlation in a different sense from that in question when Husserl labels his analysis a "correlative analysis." In Husserl the intentional object and the intentional act targeting it are not, strictly speaking, brought together in a relation at all, for they can never be separated:

There are not two things present in experience. We do not experience the object and beside it the intentional experience directed upon it. . . . Only one thing is present, the intentional experience. . . . If this experience is present, then, eo ipso and through its own essence, the intentional "relation" to an object is achieved, and an object is "intentionally present."

In contrast, Franconay's activity and "what is going on in my consciousness" are two separable states of affairs, and the correlation between them is a loose correlation of causes and effects. If the impersonation does not come off, the effects she intended have not been achieved— but the activity her intention animated can still be considered separately. Moreover, the relation is not unilateral, as is the so-called relation between an intentional act and its object. It is, rather, a co-relation, inasmuch as my own attentiveness, my own readiness to respond, my past familiarity with Chevalier contribute to the impersonation coming off, if it does.

Rapprochement

Co-relation is another instance of the commitment to rapprochement that promotes a relational analysis and that was first evident in the "starting point" which Sartre found in the example of the Dürer engraving. It is a commitment to bring together what was separated, not only in previous philosophies but also previously in the philosophy being elaborated. Thus we find in the succession of Sartre's examples an advance beyond what was separated in his own earlier examples, as well as beyond what was separated in Husserl's examples. In the case of my effort to imagine Peter, the unsatisfactory and the satisfactory mental images were based on separate physical images—the photo and the caricature. Now with the impersonation, the unsatisfactory outcome (the impersonation not coming off) and the satisfactory outcome are both based on the same physical image—Franconay's performance.

Another advance that is also a rapprochement applies the criterion of reflexivity. The physical image that is the basis of the act of the imagination we are to carry out is the body of Franconay herself. She is producing the portrayal, and her production of it cannot be left out of account as could the artists who produced the portraits of Peter and of Charles VIII, whose names Sartre does not bother to mention.

There is yet another difference between the successive examples that Sartre himself explicitly emphasizes:

> The difference between consciousness of an impersonation and consciousness of a portrait derives from the materials. The materials of the portrait itself solicit the spectator to carry out the synthesis, inasmuch as the painter knows how to endow it with a complete resemblance to its model. The material of the impersonation is a human body. It is rigid, it resists.

Sartre concedes that "an impersonation can be as close a resemblance as a portrait—for example, when the impersonator uses makeup." But a close resemblance would not yield the pivotal advance we shall soon discover that Sartre wants to make in his treatment of the image. Sartre's suggestion that the resemblance can be so close in the case of the portrait as to be complete (*parfaite*) may seem rather implausible, but any implausibility betrays his effort to maintain an opposition between the impersonation and the portrait.

Nevertheless, there is a continuity that survives this opposition, and it has to be kept in mind as indispensable to the development of an intentional analysis into a relational analysis that is a rudimentary dialectic. Our recognizing who is being impersonated is still a "synthesis of identification," and to this extent this example is still comparable to the earlier example of the cube. We are still perceiving *Abschattungen* and identifying them with an object. In the case of the portrait of Charles VIII, there were already two objects—the object whose "aspects" I perceive, and the object I imagine, to which I assign these "aspects." But the rapprochement now is dialectical to the extent that the opposition has to be overcome between the "aspects" I perceive and the "aspects" of what I am to imagine: what I perceive is a small, plump, dark-haired female; the Chevalier I am to imagine is tall, thin, blond, masculine. This is why there is a risk of the impersonation not coming off. I may merely see "a small woman making faces."

Fulfillment

Before I can explain how this risk is overcome, and rapprochement achieved, I must pause and import Husserl's concept of "fulfillment." I did not include it in my original exposition of his intentional analysis. Husserl himself did not work out in detail the distinction in his own initial analysis in the first of the *Logical Investigations,* presumably because his "logical interests" encouraged him to bring to the fore verbal expressions, which can convey meanings without benefit of fulfillment. Since I was concerned with Sartre's relation to Husserl, the distinction could wait until it became crucial to Sartre, as it does now with the impersonation.

In earlier expounding Husserl's conception of intentionality, I was aided by an image that he uses in the fifth investigation: "Another ambiguity . . . confronts us. The expression 'intention' sets forth the distinctive character of acts in terms of the image of aiming at something." I did not, however, go on to cite the distinction itself with which Husserl resolves the ambiguity: "We cannot avoid distinguishing a narrower and a wider concept of intention. In terms of our image, to the act of aiming [*abzielen*] at the target corresponds the act of hitting the target." Husserl distinguishes between intentional acts in the narrower sense and "acts that hit the target" (*Erzielungen*).[6] But in rendering the distinction, he usually employs another idiom: intentional acts can be "empty" of intuitive content ("aim" at the target without actually hitting it) or they can be "fulfillments" (*Erfüllungen*), furnished with intuitive content ("hit" the target).

I abbreviate an example that Sartre adapts from Husserl. My companion looks out of the window and reports, "A blackbird is flying across the garden." He is employing a sign, a verbal expression, and I may merely grasp its meaning. Or I may imagine the blackbird, or I may even step over to the window and actually see it. In both the second and the third cases, I obtain "intuitive illustration" of the meaning. The object "blackbird," which I was aiming at "emptily" when I merely grasped the meaning of the word "blackbird," is now "given itself." My aim is "fulfilled." [7]

If the impersonation in Sartre "comes off," it is because the target is hit—Franconay has furnished me with the requisite intuitive content.

Signs

Now we are equipped to deal with how the impersonator is to overcome the oppositions that risk the impersonation not coming off—to wit, that she is small, plump, dark-haired, female, whereas Chevalier is tall, thin, blond, male. The risk is partly overcome by taking advantage of the "essential role" that signs can play "in clarifying and guiding consciousness." Here another advance illustrates Sartre's commitment to rapprochement and correlation. Sartre had previously in effect left the physical sign (the placard Office) outside the analysis of the act of the imagination (and continued this analysis with the example of the portrait), for once the meaning of this sign was grasped, the sign was forgotten. But now signs will be brought within the scope of analysis with an explanation of how they will contribute to the constitution of the act of my imagination.

Signs play their role largely at the beginning of the impersonator's performance, when my "consciousness is oriented with regard to the general situation," and "disposed to interpret everything as an impersonation." At this stage my consciousness "remains empty"—without intuitive content. In short, I know that the performance I am beginning to watch will be an impersonation, but my knowledge is not yet supplemented with any relevant perceptual content or any imaginative content. My consciousness at this stage "is only a question, 'Whom is she going to impersonate?' "

My orientation is a broadened version of the "directedness toward" that Sartre inherits from Husserl's in-tention as an aiming act of identification. Sartre has blended into the act both attention and *attente*, as we saw earlier. There is also a doubling of the object of the act: my consciousness is "directed *via* the impersonator toward an indeterminate person, conceived as the object X of the impersonation." Sartre may be merely taking advantage of familiar usage, whereby an "unknown" is designated an "X"—but his terminology could be inspired by Husserl, who describes "the object" being identified in a "synthesis of identification," as "the determinable [*bestimmbare*] X." [8] What Husserl is describing is the way this object can function for the successive acts of synthesis as the "central point of unity for predicates," which consciousness identifies with the object, in perceiving its *Abschattungen*.

During the process of determination in Sartre "the assignment [*consign*] that my consciousness gives itself is double: it must determine the object X in accordance with the signs that the impersonator will furnish; it must actualize this object as an image *via* the performer impersonating the object." Let us consider the process of determination as distinct from the process of actualization, so long as this is feasible. ("Determination" here reflects German philosophical usage—ultimately the Latin *determinatio*—and it means "specification.")

During the first stage in the process of determination, signs play a cognitive role:

> The impersonator appears. She is wearing a straw hat; she is sticking out her lower lip, she is keeping her head forward. I stop perceiving. I read these signs. . . . The straw hat is initially a simple sign. . . . I recognize that the hat of the impersonator refers to Chevalier.

The simple sign is read the way I read a verbal sign—that is, in the way that Sartre illustrated by my response to the placard Office: I do not linger over what I perceive but, instead, follow out the reference to Chevalier. Though Sartre did not mention it, such a simple sign must similarly have been available for the portrait of Charles VIII, whether it was the identifying name printed on the frame in the Uffizi or in the Larousse. Otherwise I would not have known who it was.

In the case of the impersonation, however, I am not alerted in advance to the identity of the person being portrayed. Instead, "Franconay, without mentioning Chevalier by name, suddenly puts on a straw hat." This is not the same kind of sign as the verbal signs that came to the fore at the start of Husserl's *Logical Investigations*. Because he assumes that a philosopher is "directed by general logical interests," that philosophy is a "theory of knowledge," he selects verbal signs that have the function of conveying cognitive meaning. Sartre's relative indifference to such signs may explain why he did not bother to explain how the spectator knew that the portrait was of Charles VIII. His analysis of what was going on in my consciousness was directed, not by "logical interests" but by his interest in the role played by affectivity. Thus the significant identification of the monarch takes place in terms of "those sinuous and sensual lips, this narrow, stubborn forehead," which "directly arouse in me a certain affective impression."

The straw hat similarly arouses a certain affective impression. It is similar to the "arsenal of signs that have been progressively constituted by advertisements, newspapers, caricatures." We are reminded by the inclusion of caricatures that the weapons in this arsenal have been designed largely for their emotional impact. The straw hat itself has been cumulatively constituted a sign by Chevalier's many performances in which he has given just the right tilt to it to arouse the affective impression of jauntiness.

Perceptual Materials

This reaction to Franconay's performance has not yet taken place. Up to the present juncture, the function of the straw hat as a sign is still cognitive, in the sense that when I follow out its reference, I am merely making the judgment, "She is impersonating Chevalier." For the transformation that is now to ensue, the precedent in Husserl is the actualization that provides intuitive content for a meaning previously conveyed "emptily" by a verbal sign. That is to say, I perceive or imagine what is meant.

An impersonation is more complicated. Remember that the "performance" of my consciousness correlates with the performance going on behind the footlights, and that while "the material of the portrait itself solicits the spectator to carry out the synthesis," by virtue of its "resemblance to its model," the "material" of this portrayal, a female body, "resists" the synthetic operation of identification. For the intuitive materials that perception makes available are identifiable with a small, plump, dark-haired female, but the image I am to actualize is of a tall, thin, blond male.

These intuitive materials "are also only minimally intuitive; they are relations—the rakish angle of the straw hat and the angle formed by the neck and chin." Such materials might be a disastrous disadvantage in Husserl's analysis. If their inadequacy can be compensated for in Sartre's analysis, it is because he conceives *consciousness itself* to operate by becoming conscious of relations and correlating them. Its operating in this fashion in effect justifies the *higher-order* operations of the phenomenologist when he conducts his analysis by reflecting on relations that hold between the operations of consciousness and by seeking their correlation. In other words, consciousness is not the same *subject* in Sartre as it is in Husserl, and its restructuring is concomitant with the shift in *method*. Thus the example of the impersonation is not found in Husserl, but in Sartre the impersonator is catering to this proclivity of consciousness to correlate, to seek a rapprochement. Consciousness in Husserl does not exhibit this proclivity, which would seriously impede his reductive effort to isolate essences.

Sequential Analysis

Our investigation can proceed securely only if it repeatedly breaks with . . . systematic sequence.
—Husserl

Stages

Sartre's relational analysis may find its warrant in the way in which he conceives consciousness to be operating by correlating. But with his analysis a further step is taken: the correlating proceeds by stages. That the significant relations in this analysis are the relations between stages, and their sequence will yield a further contrast with Husserl's analysis. The initial examples in Sartre, which were taken over from Husserl or were similar to his examples (such as looking at the white paper in *L'imagination* or at the cube in the first chapter of *L'imaginaire*), were left behind by Sartre in the second chapter of *L'imaginaire* because they illustrated only "the statics of the image." Sartre's initial advance beyond Husserl toward a dynamic analysis was to introduce movement on the side of consciousness: the intentional "act" of the imagination in Husserl became in Sartre an activity—"a wave among waves."

This activity is brought under dialectical control (with the first example in the second chapter) by its articulation into the "stages" of a development that culminates in the final satisfying mental image of Peter. Yet the physical images perceived—the photograph and the caricature—were themselves still static. As I have already observed, the *imitation* that I am perceiving in the case of the impersonation is in motion, so that the process of development that is going on in

my consciousness is correlated with what is going on behind the footlights.

There is another difference between Sartre's handling of the caricature and the impersonation. Looking at the caricature was the final stage
in my effort to recall Peter, the preceding stages having been the initial
unassisted effort of my imagination and, next, this effort assisted by the
photo. What the example did not bring out fully was the development
from one stage to another. For Sartre's immediate problem was to demar-
cate the subject he was to treat—"where the class of images begins" and
"where it ends." The impersonation likewise develops by stages, but because the development from one stage to another is more fully exhibited,
this example itself represents a higher-order stage—a stage in the development of Sartre's own analysis.

As spectators of the impersonation, we are encouraged to seek a correlation, because we are more conscious of certain relations that are "deliberately altered" by Franconay: "the angle of the straw hat is exaggerated." [1] Certain relations were also exaggerated in the case of the
caricature: "the nose is much too long, the cheekbones are too prominent, etc." Yet there is a difference between the impersonation and the
caricature. Even with respect to the specific role played by signs, the impersonation is only achieved sequentially: if "the angle of the straw hat is
exaggerated," it is because "this is the principal sign and must strike us
first, and the others must be ordered around it."

Recall how in the dialectics with which we are most familiar (for
instance, Hegel's and Marx's), sequences of stages are featured. To abbreviate a famous illustration: First the bud, then the blossom, then finally
the fruit. But the development in Sartre is not this natural and necessary.
On the one hand, the impersonation itself is a performance by an *artiste*.
On the other hand, Sartre himself has intervened and lined up the stages
to advance his own analysis, as we are recognizing by comparing the
place of the impersonation in his analysis with the place of the caricature.
To this extent, his analysis is still "voluntary" and "arbitrary" as is Husserl's eidetic analysis.

As we have also seen, Sartre in effect disavows Husserl's formula for
free variation: "What differentiates the invariants remains indifferent to
us." The differences between the members of "the image family" matter
in Sartre's analysis; the sequence he institutes is their correlation. Thus
the unsuccessful, purely mental image of Peter's expression is played off
against the considerable perceptual information provided by the photo,
and this in turn is played off against the decrease in information provided
by the caricature—while the lack of any affective reaction to the photo is
played off against the affective reaction triggered by the caricature.

Husserl's analysis, in contrast, is not geared to a sequence in which the differences between his examples are correlated. These differences carry no significance that would justify their correlation, any more than would the differences that differentiate any particular example itself and that are eliminated by the eidetic reduction in favor of the essence exemplified by it.

Zigzag

There are, of course, short-run sequences in Husserl, and he does concede that, in the longer run, "systematic clarification, whether in pure logic or in any other discipline, would in itself seem to require a following out step-by-step of the ordering of subjects [*Sachen*], of systematic interconnection [*Zusammenhang*] in the science to be clarified." But this is a requirement he is not prepared to satisfy. For when he accords priority to method, it is on the ground that "our analytic investigations cannot be allowed to wait upon the systematic determination of our subject." He warns, "our investigation can only proceed securely, if it repeatedly breaks with . . . systematic sequence. . . . We investigate, as it were, in a zigzag fashion." [2]

Breaking with systematic sequence in this fashion is justified not just to accord priority to the elaboration of method. As we have observed before, Sartre proceeds with breathless rapidity, but Husserl is sidetracked by "difficulties" in his way. And not just by specific difficulties, which could sooner or later be straightened out, enabling him to resume a systematic sequence that has merely been interrupted: there is a general difficulty, the *Ruckbeziehung* (the "backward relation" or "reflexive relation"), of phenomenology to itself. This difficulty is not unique to phenomenology: "The thinking of the psychologist is itself something psychological; the thinking of the logician is something logical—that is, something that lies within the realm to which the norms of logic apply." It is as a consequence of this reflexive relation that in our "first introduction" to these sciences we "must operate with methodological resources to which the discipline in question can only subsequently give a scientific definite form." When a methodological resource has acquired a more definite form, we have to go "back again to our original analyses." [3]

One methodological resource that, we have seen, Husserl went to work on initially was intentionality. He has informed us that it was "completely indispensable at the start of phenomenology, as a concept to take one's start from." But he presented us with the paradox that it was "readily understandable of itself and most difficult to understand." [4] It was readily understandable because intentional reference is exhibited by all acts of consciousness, including those reflective acts with which the phenomenologist undertakes his analysis. But after he has gone a certain distance, he has to go back later to deal with the difficulties that understanding it presents, in order to give his analysis of it "a scientific definite form." Thus Husserl, having analyzed it in the first of his *Logical Investigations*, goes back to it again in the fifth, and again in *Ideas I*, where some of the difficulties of understanding it are handled by his carrying through the two reductions first.

I have myself zigzagged in my exposition of Husserl. I first considered his concept of intentionality in Part 1, and I have reconsidered it in Chapter 13 in the course of expounding the eidetic reduction. Thus I first started out where he started out in the first of the *Logical Investigations*, and I have started out again where he started out in *Ideas I*. Although this zigzagging in my exposition is feasible because of Husserl's own readiness to break in *Ideas I* with the sequence he followed in the *Logical Investigations*, my justification was that I was having to zigzag between two philosophies. I began with intentionality as the concept Sartre had started out with in the Berlin essay, where he took it as "fundamental," and in *L'imaginaire*. Now I am showing how Sartre's analysis, as not merely an intentional analysis but also an eidetic analysis, differs from Husserl's reductive analysis.

Sequence

At the juncture we have reached, sequence itself is the procedural or methodological issue that has emerged between our two phenomenologists. I reemphasize that the progress of Sartre's analysis is geared to a long-run sequence in which the differences between his examples are correlated (the photo has to be followed by the caricature, and the portrait by the impersonation; in contrast, the sequence of Husserl's analysis is not geared to the differences between his examples, and whatever particular differences attach to an example are eliminated by an eidetic reduction in favor of the essence exemplified by the example. Thus he can afford to break with a systematic sequence and zigzag, since the conclusive moment in his analysis is when an essence is immediately given to intuition. Reliance on his "principle of principles" renders any sequence up to this point methodologically inconsequential, except to the extent he has to position himself to obtain finally immediacy of intuition, granted that this positioning needs to be directed by the two reductions.

Now that a rough contrast has been established between Sartre's commitment to following a sequence in his phenomenological analysis and Husserl's readiness to break with sequence, a juncture has been reached when it is appropriate for me to go over again a contrast between my present undertaking and what I was up to in Volume 1. There I undertook a series of forays to elaborate certain procedures for dealing with the history of philosophy, but specifically adapted to the history of phenomenology. In the present volume, I am refining those procedures by adjusting them to the relation between Sartre and Husserl. Instead of forays, I have sought a continuity of exposition, based on the texts I am expounding. Having begun with an analysis of Sartre's debts to Husserl in *L'imagination* and in chapter 1 of *L'imaginaire* (once different parts of the same text), it became clear—particularly when the impersonation was reached in chapter 2—that Sartre himself was following a sequence in *L'imaginaire,* the development of which, in retrospect, now justifies my having hitched my exposition to it—at the same time that my zigzagging vis-à-vis Husserl was also justified.

The Break

When the impersonation is reached in this sequence, there is a clear break with the kind of example on which Husserl relied. We have seen that, in the first chapter of *L'imaginaire,* Sartre relied mainly on examples deriving from Husserl or similar to Husserl's. But although a wide selection of examples appears in Husserl's lectures on the imagination (paintings and photographs are frequent), he shows little interest in physical images in motion, as is the body of the impersonator. Occasionally he mentions watching a play. But consider this example: "I follow the performance of a play, or I contemplate a painting." [5] He offers the second example as the equivalent of the first, and in the ensuing analysis he does not indicate on which of the two he is in fact relying. Either would serve. The fact that the performers in the play are moving is irrelevant. [6]

We have already seen certain respects in which the impersonation is significantly a new kind of example in Sartre's analysis. First of all, what is going on behind the footlights (Franconay puts on a straw hat, and so on) is correlated with what is going on in my consciousness (I read the sign as a reference to Chevalier), so that we have two correlated sequences constituting this particular example itself. But now we are also taking into account the sequence of Sartre's own analysis: this particular example is not just another particular example, it is pivotal as a new stage in the sequence of Sartre's analysis, as he more fully acknowledges in a later retrospect: "From the impersonation on, what appeared in the imaginative consciousness was not at all like what is seen in perception." Recall that in the preceding example of the portrait (as in all previous examples) what was perceived was like what was imagined: "The matter of the portrait itself solicits the spectator to carry out the act of the imagination because the painter has known to give it a complete resemblance with the original." [7] This is no longer, I repeat, still the case with the impersonator's portrayal: what we are perceiving is a small, plump, dark-haired female, whereas the Chevalier we are to imagine is tall, thin, blond, masculine.

This new stage is a break not just in Sartre's sequence; it is a break with Husserl's analysis of the image as well. Husserl assumes that the act of depictive imagination I carry out with respect to physical images is an act by which I become conscious of a likeness between what I can perceive and what I imagine to be the originals of those images. Thus in the instance of the Dürer engraving, Husserl points out, "The consciousness of the depiction" is a consciousness of "the small grey figures by which . . . something else is depictively presented by a likeness." [8]

At this juncture we are reminded that when Sartre picked up in Husserl's handling of the Dürer engraving "an *intrinsic* distinction between an image and perception," Sartre had to admit that Husserl failed "to push the distinction further." But Husserl could hardly have pushed the distinction further in Sartre's direction without undermining the sense in which he assumed an image to be a likeness. Now that we have reached the impersonation, we see that Sartre is prepared to push the distinction further until what becomes significant in his analysis are respects in which what is perceived (Franconay) is so *unlike* what is imagined (Chevalier) as to set up a virtual opposition.

Hylē

This particular example of the impersonation acquires general implications from a substantive criticism that Sartre makes of Husserl. A substantive criticism is the most obvious way in which a successor breaks with a predecessor. If I overlooked this criticism when Sartre presented it in *L'imagination,* it was not merely because I wanted to take advantage of the debts Sartre was acknowledging there to Husserl in my effort to see if I could negotiate a passage way from one to the other. The criticism itself is not implemented in *L'imaginaire* until Sartre reaches the impersonation.

Continuity between the two philosophies was established by Sartre's accepting intentionality as fundamental in the fashion illustrated by the example of Dürer engraving:

> If the image becomes [in Husserl] a certain way of animating intentionally a hyletic content, it could easily be assimilated to the grasping of a painting as an image through the intentional apprehension

of a "mental content." What is in question are merely two different kinds of imaginative consciousness.[9]

The terminology here is Husserl's and derives ultimately from Aristotle's terminology in the *De Anima* of the soul conceived as the "form" that "animates" the "matter" (*hylē*) of an organic body. As the term is used by Husserl and Sartre, the *hylē*, or "hyletic content," refers to the "impressional matter" that is "animated," furnished with a "form," by the intention endowing it with meaning.

Discontinuity is introduced, the break is effected, by Sartre's criticism that Husserl's distinction between imagination and perception "cannot come from intentionality alone; it is necessary but not sufficient that the intentions differ; the matters too must be different." This is the juncture at which Sartre would push the distinction further. Sartre admits that this interpretation of the distinction in Husserl (as coming from intentionality alone) is "an interpretation that the texts seem to me to authorize but which is not necessary. The fact remains that they are ambiguous and that the problem demands instead taking a definite and clear position."[10]

I have already demonstrated that Husserl is not comfortable with ambiguities. In fact, it is clear and definite in Husserl that the matter animated by the intentional act of the imagination does differ but is like the matter of a perception, since ultimately it comes from a previous act (or acts) of perception. If Husserl does not focus on the problem as clearly and definitely as Sartre would wish, I think it is because Husserl contends that the problem of the constitution of the matter has largely to be left to a causal explanation in empirical psychology. I'll return shortly to this disciplinary difference between the two sciences.

Sequential Variation

Sartre's claim that "the matters too must be different," which he buttresses in *L'imaginaire* with the sequence of examples, is based (we now recognize) on his assimilation of "animating intentionally a hyletic content" to "the grasping of a painting as an image." At the start of the sequence, we have such examples as an engraving (or a painting), in which an act of the imagination is solicited by the perceptual materials:

> Consciousness of the physical image and of the corresponding perceptual consciousness, while differing radically with respect to the intention, have an identical impressional matter. These black lines serve at one and the same time for the constitution of the image "Knight" or for the perception "black lines on a sheet of paper."[11]

The sequence of examples from this rapprochement on, as a starting point, is a sequence in which the perceptual materials are progressively impoverished.[12]

In Sartre's claim we now see why the pivotal stage in this sequence is the example of the impersonation, when what is available to perception (the small, dark-haired female) resists rather than solicits (as in the earlier examples) the carrying out of the act of the imagination. There is further impoverishment of the materials with the ensuing example of a schematic design, until Sartre finally reaches the mental image, which he announces, "completes the sequence," since no perceptual materials at all (no physical image) are any longer available. Sartre can then formulate the question, "Has the mental image the same *hylē* as the physical image—that is, in the last analysis, as perception."[13]

Sartre presumes that the progressive impoverishment of the materials in the preceding examples has prepared him to answer this question—the *hylē is* different—even though empirical psychology has to be enlisted from now on to specify the differences. Before the transition to empirical psychology, Sartre reviews the sequence as preparatory in a final section entitled "From the Portrait to the Mental Image." Similarly, the first part of the title of the pivotal section on the impersonation is "From the Sign to the Image," and we have traced the sequence there as one in which the straw hat is "the principal sign" that "must strike us first," before any image of Chevalier can be constituted. In Husserl there are no such titles implying sequence. In the final section of part 1 of *L'imaginaire*, Sartre asserts that "the profound intention of the act of the imagination [as an act that renders present something not present] has not varied." What has varied have been the materials. But their variation has not been "arbitrary" in the sense that Husserl's "free variation" is. The sequential variation in Sartre has been progressive. At the start of the sequence, we were offered a short-run sequence in which "the goal aimed at remains the same,"[14] since my intention remained to recall Peter. This sequence illustrates the same procedure as the long-run sequence: the perceptual material that the photo of Peter provided was impoverished in the caricature, and it had to be made up for by another factor—the affective reaction. In the long-run sequence, too, variation is not designed to be eliminative, in the sense that it is with Husserl's free variation; instead, a correlation is sought between the successive diminishing of perceptual materials and the compensation (notably, the affective reaction) that makes up for the diminishing.

Sartre uses the sequence as a springboard from which he jumps finally to the purely mental image: "By progressing . . . from the image that obtains its matter in perception to the image that takes it from the objects of inner sense, we can describe and determine via the variations, . . . the function 'image.' "[15] Sartre is apparently unaware that with this comment he is disavowing Husserl's formula, "what differentiates the variants remains a matter of indifference." In Sartre we have seen how the differences are lined up to compose the sequence.

When Sartre jumps to the mental image that is not based on any physical image, he admits he is "leaving behind the secure terrain of phe-nomenological description,"[16] where Cartesian certainty can be achieved (the title of Part 1, remember, is "The Certain"), and turning in Part 2 to empirical psychology, which merely yields "The Probable." But what he is leaving behind more specifically is the rapprochement between the mental and the physical image, which was his own "starting point," even though he thought he got it out of Husserl's handling of the Dürer en-graving.

Since I am concerned with Sartre's relation to Husserl, I shall not attempt an exposition of Sartre's empirical psychology: it is out-of-date and does not illustrate any methodological aspiration comparable to his sequential analysis, which has provided us with a contrast with Husserl's zigzag, as a denial of the methodological significance of systematic se-quence.[17] Now that we understand the pivotal place of the impersonation in Sartre's sequence, I shall return to this example in the next chapter, to get at other respects in which it is the juncture at which Sartre breaks away from Husserl.

SIXTEEN

The Plug

*We usually start out . . . with a confused feeling
of some striking quality or resemblance.*
—Bergson

Bergson

In the section of *L'imaginaire* preceding the
impersonation there was a footnote reference
to the handling of the Dürer engraving in
Ideas I.[1] The impersonation is a break with
Husserl inasmuch as Sartre, in order to deal
with the opposition between imagination
and perception that we have seen emerges
with this example, not only does not refer to
Husserl but also turns to another philosopher, Henri Bergson, whom he usually disdains. An assessment of Bergson was implicit
in Sartre's announcement at the beginning of
the chapter on Husserl in *L'imagination* to
the effect that the "great event in philosophy
before the war [World War I]" was the publication of *Ideas I.*[2] Such an announcement
was a flouting of the received opinion then in
France that the great philosophical events before the war were Bergson's publications.

I am not suggesting that Sartre's unprecedented resort to Bergson here goes so far as
to amount to what I characterized as a "shift
in allegiance" when I dealt in Volume 1 with
a philosopher turning from one predecessor
to another. A more appropriate description
of Sartre's brief conniving with Bergson is the
idiom that Sartre later in his career applies to
Husserl, in disputing Husserl's conception of
philosophy as rigorous science. Regarding
Husserl's own lack of rigor, Sartre general-
izes, "That is the way philosophers think.
They come up with something in order to
plug a hole [in their philosophies]."[3]

I am about to examine the "plug" that Sartre borrows from Bergson and inserts in the philosophy of the imagination that he otherwise regards as "inspired" by Husserl. Sartre never explicitly admits to resorting to plugs himself, here or elsewhere. So before conducting my examination, I would interrupt my exposition of Sartre's relation to Husserl to comment on how my own borrowing the idiom of "plug" is justified in terms of my own deconstructive procedure. For "plug," with its insinuation of extraneous incongruity, is itself a deconstructive term *avant la lettre*.

Deconstruction

When Sartre adopts the term "plugs" he is not only interpreting Husserl, but he is also generalizing about "the way philosophers think."[4] Presumably he is one of them.

As I outlined my procedure in Volume 1, my first step is to recognize the prima facie advantage of utilizing any statement a philosopher makes about another philosophy. Such a statement, I argued, is not merely about another philosophy; it is, implicitly at least, a statement in the philosopher's own philosophy, which is available to the historian if he would track down the implications of the statement. In the present instance, I'll abbreviate this step, inasmuch as Sartre's statement may be not too much more than a quip.

In Sartre's existential psychoanalysis, the activity of plugging holes gains philosophical scope from the way in which being is full of holes ("little pools of not-being").[5] More particularly, being a hole is a large part of the deprivation of being a woman, and it renders her passive.[6] Such a conclusion may not be just Sartre's personal sexism; the idiom can receive this particular application by virtue of Sartre's vulgarizing move "toward the concrete," which tends to the confusion of levels—to a *metabasis eis allo genos,* as Husserl would criticize it. In this instance the confusion would be "biologism," rather than "psychologism."[7]

Granted that the idiom may derive from the deeper recesses of Sartre's psyche, I yet propose it for a more superficial use. I ask why Sartre, given his philosophy, would detect at this juncture in Husserl's philosophy the "plug" that Sartre identifies as Husserl's conception of "passive genesis"? My answer is that Sartre identifies this as a "plug" because such a conception is alien to his own phenomenology, in which Husserl's abstractly *logical* (that is, eidetically reduced) "act" of consciousness becomes, with Sartre's movement "toward the concrete," a *psychological* activity, which, despite this reversion, still retains its active character. Any (feminine?) passivity is, accordingly, extraneous to consciousness.[8] I am not going to try to decide to what extent Husserl's logical conception of an intentional "act" as "meaning-endowing" has *stiff-*

ened Sartre's conception of consciousness as psychological activity, or to what extent Sartre's conception betrays his (male?) "aggressive voluntarism." [9] The only point I am making is that the deconstruction which is involved in Sartre's application of the idiom "plug" is a two-sided affair: the particular juncture at which it is applied to Husserl (as well as the idiom itself) draw implications from the structure of Sartre's own philosophy, even though some of these implications Sartre derived originally from Husserl. [10]

Consistency

Of course, "plugs"—or, to drop Sartre's special idiom, extraneous incongruities—are often detected by philosophers in other philosophies. My procedure is to assume prima facie that any philosophy worth examining is some kind of effort at consistency, whatever else the philosophy may be. Sartre's philosophy is a pretty good test case for making this assumption: after all, he admitted himself that an understandable reaction to what he was proposing to do in *Being and Nothingness* would be *Quelle salade!*[11] To retain his other idiom, *Being and Nothingness* does seem full of holes that he has plugged with borrowings from other philosophies. In Volume 1, I used Heidegger's seemingly more neutral idiom *Versäumnis*, which I reserved for a different application. Expounding Sartre in this volume has prompted the more vigorous idiom of plugging holes. One of my eventual objectives in the present volume is to demonstrate that Sartre's philosophy, insofar as it is a philosophy of the imagination, does manifest a certain measure of consistency, though it still is porous—or, I would prefer to say, rather full of "plugged" holes. I anticipate this objective now since Sartre's handling of the example of the impersonation will be crucial to the measure of consistency that I shall find.

The assumption that a philosophy might be significantly consistent is a concession to it that many deconstructionists will not tolerate for long, since their very undertaking depends on finding in a philosophy a fissure where they can obtain leverage for prying the philosophy apart. Thus any effort at consistency on the philosopher's part can be denigrated as an effort to patch over, or even repress, an inconsistency. And we are not to think their intervention implements a philosophy of their own; they contend that their leverage is merely a matter of allowing the other philosophy to "deconstruct itself." [12]

The Intrusion

This very rough appraisal of a standard deconstructionist strategy I offer for the nonce merely for the purpose of contrasting it with my own deconstructive strategy, which allows for the possibility that deconstruction may be a two-sided affair, going on between the philosophy (or whatever other rubric might be more acceptable) that is implementing the deconstruction and the philosophy that is being deconstructed.

Now I resume the more modest pretensions of my present volume. I have supposed Sartre's generalization "That is the way philosophers think" justifies applying the idiom of a "plug" to Sartre himself. What has to be recognized next is that the plug Sartre borrows from Bergson does not fit into Husserl's philosophy. Instead, it fits into Sartre's own philosophy, at the particular juncture where he is breaking with Husserl's conception of what is imagined as "like" what has been perceived. Where Husserl relied generally on similarity holding, Sartre is posing the problem of dissimilarities: How am I to imagine Maurice Chevalier when I am perceiving these plump, made-up cheeks, this black hair, this female body, these female clothes? To deal with this problem Sartre inserts the plug:

> We must now recall a famous passage from *Matter and Memory:* "A clear distinction of individual objects is a luxury for perception. . . . Indeed, it seems that we usually start out not with the perception of the individual, not with the conception of the genus, but with knowledge of a sort that is intermediary between the two, with a confused feeling of some *striking quality* or resemblance."[13]

This plug, I have anticipated, does not fit into Husserl. What "we usually start out . . . with," according to this passage, is irrelevant in Husserl. What we start out with in Husserl is an example of a particular perception of a particular object, but we leave it behind by applying the reductive procedure of free variation, by which reference to what is particular to the example is discarded in favor of the essence exemplified. This sharp distinction of *level* between a particular matter of fact and an essence must be maintained in Husserl, but it is removed, or at least blurred, by Sartre's opening up room, with his citation from Bergson, for some sort of knowledge that is neither particular, nor general, but intermediary. It is knowledge obtained by informal and incomplete inductive generalizations.

Later I'll assess the damage done to Husserl by the intrusion of this plug. To appreciate what Sartre gets out of the passage, however, we need to adapt its implications by cooking up some such illustrations as the following. When we pass individuals as we walk down the street, we usually start out not by noticing in detail the particular traits that would differentiate them as particular individuals. Usually we are not trying to determine exactly the age of an individual, his features, or what his deportment suggests he is up to; we get by, instead, by applying less specific knowledge that we have previously acquired as to what an old man looks like, a stockbroker, a drug addict, a fashion model. Unless one is a private eye, or a sociologist, one enjoys the "luxury" of being more discriminating only when, for instance, one is indulging in girl watching or boy watching. (Unlike Sartre, I would be gender-neutral.) Bergson is making his point with regard to all individual objects, but my illustration restricts its implications to individual persons, for we have known since the example of the desire to recall Peter's expression that Sartre favors an example of consciousness of someone over Husserl's consciousness of something.

Opposition

The Bergson citation enables Sartre to deal with a problem that Husserl never encountered, since he relied on such examples as the portrait and never examined an impersonation:

> A portrait is a faithful rendering of its model in all its complexity. . . . An impersonation presents characteristic traits as such from the outset. With an impersonation, a model has already been thought through and reduced to formulae[,] . . . to schemata. Into these conventional formulae, consciousness wants an imaginative intuition to flow.

The problem then is "these arid schemata, so rigid, so abstract that they seem to get in the way of [s'opposer à] the imaginative intuition, Maurice Chevalier." How, it has to be explained, are we to overcome this opposition?

Insert the plug, and we can arrive at the following conclusion:

> This dark hair, we do not see as dark; this body, we do not perceive as a female body; we do not see its pronounced curves. . . . The hair, the body are perceived as indeterminate masses, as spaces that are filled. They display sensory opacity. . . . For the first time in our description of imaginative consciousness, we see appear—and in the setting of perception itself—a functional indeterminacy. . . . These qualities, which are so vague and which are perceived only with respect to what is most general about them, are abbreviated for the purpose of the imaginative synthesis. They represent the indeterminate body, the indeterminate hair of Maurice Chevalier.

Now we can begin to assess the damage done to Husserl by the insertion of this plug. "Indeterminacy" could hardly qualify as "functional" in Husserl. For central to his intentional analysis is a commitment to determination (specification), as is suggested by his target-aiming "image" for an in-tentional act. I grant that one is conscious in Husserl of "aspects" of an object that is being perceived, which are as yet "indeterminate," but one is primarily conscious of a determinate object as having these "aspects," which are essentially susceptible of being further specified, whether or not we do in fact go on to specify them. Moreover, Husserl's usual examples are objects that lend themselves readily to the specification of what their "aspects" are: the die, the table, the sheet of paper that turns out to be white.

The Reversal

The explanation is still incomplete as to how the imaginative synthesis is to be achieved. Franconay's portrayal still lacks the sort of determinate (specific) perceptual evidence that the portrait furnishes. Positive specifications must be actualized, "even though there is no prospect of constituting with the body of the impersonator Franconay a perfect analogue of the body of Chevalier. All I have available are a few ingredients that up until now are functioning as signs."

There is also no prospect of making the most of the perceptual ingredients that are available: "If I perceive these arid schemata for their own sake, if I observe the edges of the lips, the color of the straw of the hat, the consciousness of the image vanishes." And "I see a small woman making faces."

Instead of relying on continued perception to acquire more determinate knowledge, which is the way in which I usually arrive at an identification,

> I must carry out a reversal of the movement of perception, begin with knowledge [the knowledge that I have acquired previously in considerable part from perception—from having observed Chevalier on the stage or screen], and determine the [imaginative] intuition as a function of this knowledge. That lip was just a moment ago a sign. I make an image out of it.

I now "see" it "only as a 'large protruding lip,' " because I am "seeing" what I already know about Chevalier's lips:

> Here we encounter again an essential characteristic of the mental image—the phenomenon of quasi observation. What I perceive is what I know, I cannot learn anything from the object, and my intuition is only knowledge that has been weighed down, degraded.

Whatever positive perceptual determinations do survive are largely overcome by being

> joined together by vaguely intuited zones: the cheeks, the ears, the neck of the impersonator function as an indeterminate connective tissue. Here, too, it is knowledge that is primary; what is perceived corresponds to the vague knowledge that Maurice Chevalier has cheeks, ears, a neck. The details fade away.

Sartre is still following in the wake of Bergson's analysis, whereby what one usually starts out from is knowledge that is indeterminate—that is, intermediary between "perception of the individual" and "the conception of the genus."

Feeling

Having used Bergson to explain how what could have been determinative for perception in the impersonation can remain largely indeterminate, Sartre next seems to be using Bergson for the opposite purpose—to explain how the now largely indeterminate person prancing around the stage can be determined, identified as Chevalier. Sartre is not explicit about this second use of Bergson, but when he cited Bergson, he italicized *"striking quality"*: this was a phrase he hardly needed to emphasize then, however, it would explain the part played by exaggeration in the impersonator's performance—that is, the tilt of the hat, the protruding of the lip.

If Sartre is not explicit, it may be because he is aware that when Bergson mentions "un sentiment confus d'une qualité marquante," he obviously has a sense impression primarily in mind. Something else is needed to make up for the indeterminacy of the applicable knowledge acquired from having previously perceived Chevalier. Thus the *sentiment* that in Bergson was primarily a "confused sense impression" (this was all that was needed for Sartre's first use of Bergson) now becomes in Sartre a "feeling," which (we shall soon see) takes over the function of determining what I am to imagine. The plug Bergson has supplied has undergone considerable whittling in the hands of Sartre.

What we have here is an instance of the proceeding that I described in Volume 1 (if I may change metaphors in midstream) as a philosopher's "hit-and-run" encounter with another philosopher. There is no prolonged contact. Sartre's disdain for Bergson can remain largely intact. This is why I would say that Sartre merely gets from Bergson what he needs at this juncture—what he could not get from Husserl. Sartre's defection from Husserl is merely temporary and does not represent the shift in allegiance that I discussed in Volume 1.[14] However, the other shifts that I distinguished there are relevant to Sartre's break with Husserl, and I shall review them in the next chapter, in order to do justice to the pivotal significance of the example of the impersonation.

SEVENTEEN

: # *Toward the Concrete*

*By essence, I understand not merely the structure
but even . . . individuality.—Sartre*

Principles

What may seem as capriciously ad hoc as
Sartre's use of Bergson as a plug is his inter-
rupting his analysis of the impersonation to
adduce "two principles." This interruption is
still another respect in which a break occurs
in the sequence of Sartre's analysis at the
juncture of this example.

Adducing a principle has traditionally
been a decisive proceeding in philosophy.
Principles have been involved in demarcating
the subject of philosophy itself. One way in
which Aristotle distinguished "first philosophy" was as a "science of principles" [*ar-
chai*]. The status of a principle was consoli-
dated in philosophy when it came to refer not
merely to almost any "starting point," as
archē (or *principium* in Latin) could in ordinary usage, but to a principle that continued
to preside (like an *archōn*, or *princeps*) over
the entire subject being treated.

This is the first time in *L'imaginaire* that
Sartre has appealed to principles, so a good
deal must be at stake even though they may
seem dragged in by the heels. In fact, the
overall structure of Sartre's philosophy now
begins to emerge—as an implicit reconstruc-
tion of Husserl's.

What is, of course, most obviously at
stake is universality of scope, as is clear from
the way the principles are formulated:

1. Every perception is accompanied by an
   affective reaction.

2. Every feeling is a feeling of something—that is, it aims at an object in a certain way and projects on it a certain quality.[1]

We shall watch these two principles assist Sartre in solving two problems that he has encountered in analyzing the impersonation. But by virtue of their scope, these two principles preside over more than ad hoc solutions to these problems, which might otherwise seem peculiar to an idiosyncratic example. Implicit in the break in Sartre's sequence and in his break with Husserl that the example introduces are the shifts I sorted out in Volume 1.

First of all, the principles promote enlarging the scope of Sartre's subject beyond the restricted essence of the imagination that would emerge from Husserl's eidetic reduction. The first principle opens up room for *interplay* between the act of perception and the affective reaction to what is perceived. Sartre cannot, as Husserl could, disentangle an act of the imagination from the affective reaction that carries over from an act of perception.

The second principle further expands the subject from an intentional analysis, in which "every feeling is a feeling of something—that is, . . . aims at an object in a certain way," into an analysis which includes the way the feeling "projects on it a certain quality." In Husserl's synthesis of identification, a quality is identified as an "aspect" of the object (the whiteness with the paper), and the identification is unilateral. But Sartre's second principle legitimates including an ensuing activity of consciousness.

The Shift in Subject

My formula "shift in *subject*" was originally designed in Volume 1 to describe the "lurch" that took place in Heidegger's relation to Husserl at the start of *Being and Time,* where phenomenology becomes ontological.[2] There might have been almost as abrupt a break in Sartre's relation to Husserl if Sartre had started out *L'imaginaire* by explicitly avowing his two principles and worked out their implications for an analysis of perception. Instead he seemed initially to presuppose, by and large, Husserl's analysis of perception (as he also seemed to do at the start of *L'imagination*), in order to go on to deal with the imagination.

Further evidence of this shift underway in Sartre is his dealing with the two problems for which he adduced his two principles—the problem of compensating for the abstractness of the knowledge that is conveyed by the signs, and the problem of overcoming both the indeterminacy of the perceptual evidence Franconay's performance provides as to who is being impersonated and the resistance this perceptual evidence presents (insofar as it remains determinate) to constituting the image. When I see the real Chevalier, Sartre explains (applying, in effect, his first principle), "my perception is accompanied by a certain affective reaction," which projects on his face "a certain indefinable quality that could be called his 'meaning.'" When I then watch Franconay, the affective reaction that I had when I saw the real Chevalier is reawakened, and it is now

> incorporated in the intentional synthesis. In correlation, the affective meaning of the face of Chevalier is going to reappear on the face of Franconay. It actualizes the synthetic unification of the different signs; it animates their rigid aridity, gives them life and a certain density. Since it gives to the isolated elements of the impersonation an indefinable meaning and the unity of an object, it can be regarded as the real intuitive matter of the consciousness of impersonation.

"Could be called," might be merely a precautionary admission that this is not what would ordinarily be called "meaning." But Sartre's quotation marks around "meaning" suggest, rather, an otherwise unacknowledged terminological debt to Husserl, for whom meaning is the subject that undergoes analysis in phenomenology.

Moreover, Sartre goes on to equate this "meaning" with "a certain expressive nature—the essence, as it were, of Chevalier presented to intuition," and "essence" is hardly an ordinary word. Thus "could be called" and "as it were" betray the extent to which Sartre is measuring his analysis not just directly against the immediately given evidence of consciousness (as a phenomenologist *ex officio* should) but also against the terminology Husserl had devised in analyzing this evidence.

This academicization of phenomenology in Sartre, of which I took note earlier, should not conceal from us but help bring out the shift in *subject* that is taking place. A "meaning" that is "indefinable" would be a contradiction in terms in Husserl, for whom something is endowed with a "meaning" by a target-aiming act that identifies, and in this sense defines, what it is: I am conscious of something as a table, a triangle, as anger. In Sartre, "meaning" is no longer necessarily cognitive and definable; it can become affective and indefinable, as we began to see when the caricature caught the expression of Peter's face to which I reacted affectively. But "expression" then took on a sense that Husserl explicitly excluded from his phenomenology as an analysis of meaning which was a theory of knowledge.

Given that both Husserl and Sartre employ an eidetic analysis that relies on examples, the shift in *subject* on which I am now commenting emerges with the different kind of example Sartre favors as exemplifying the part played by an affective reaction in constituting an image. It emerges first with the caricature and now even more obviously with the impersonation. Sartre's other examples of the physical image that are found in Husserl are not found in Sartre's *diplôme,* but we have seen that the caricature and the impersonation, which are not found in Husserl, are not only found in Sartre's *diplôme* but are also linked there and that the impersonation is cited there as demonstrating the relevance of "the state of affectivity."

We can conclude that Sartre's preoccupation with the role of affectivity in the constitution of the image antedates his encounter with Husserl. But Sartre did not treat the caricature and the impersonation as examples of a physical image in the *diplôme.* In this respect, Sartre remains indebted in *L'imaginaire* to Husserl for the rapprochement that brings together physical with mental images.

The Shift in Level

In this part of the present volume, I am predominantly interested in what happens to Husserl's conception of essence and in the eidetic reduction with which Husserl reaches the level of essence. I am taking Sartre's qualification "as it were" as implicitly an admission that in Husserl, Chevalier as a particular individual could not have an essence of his own. In Husserl, the distinction in *level* between the particular and the essence is sharp. Husserl explains that "although the relation to the contingent example really existing" is "a point of departure for the eidetic reduction," this *relation itself* is "eliminated [*ausgeschaltet*] by the variation." He adds, "To a pure essence, the factual reality of the particular cases by means of which we advance in the variation is completely irrelevant.[3] In Sartre, there is no comparably drastic eliminative operation of the factual reality, even though in *L'imagination* he explicitly endorses an eidetic analysis and can be presumed to be applying it in *L'imaginaire.*[4]

The change in the status of an essence is possible to detect as early as the opening pages of *L'imagination,* where Sartre started out, first, by perceiving and, then, imagining "a sheet of white paper." He explains that "the [imagined] paper that appears to me at this moment is identical in essence with the sheet that I was looking at before," and he interjects, "By essence, I understand not merely the structure but even its individuality."[5]

There is no reference to Husserl in these opening pages, but if he had brought together an act of perception and an act of imagination in this fashion, he would have of course agreed that I could be conscious of the sheet imagined as the same individual sheet as the sheet perceived. But in analyzing this consciousness of sameness, Husserl would not endorse Sartre's use of the concept of "essence." He would regard Sartre as engaged in the most flagrant "picture-book phenomenology." [6]

Recall how the two levels of particular individual fact and essence are distinguished by Husserl. To be perceptually conscious of something is in Husserl to carry out a synthesis of identification in which something is identified as the same individual thing. But when we reflect on this example, and our consciousness is "led back" to the higher level of essence, we are no longer identifying a sheet of paper: we are recognizing that essential to all acts of perception is the identical structure of a synthesis of identification.

Since an essence is reached in Husserl only by an eidetic reduction that discards the particularities that differentiate an individual case, he does not invest in the particularities of his examples but keeps them succinct (the sheet of paper, the table, the die, and so forth). We have watched Sartre, in contrast, elaborate examples whose particular complications are tendentious—his examples tend to provide indispensable support for the sequential development of his analysis. When Husserl has extracted an essence from one particular example, he can go on to extract by a separate reduction another essence from another example, by again discarding its particularities. But we have seen that in Sartre the differences between the particular examples are lined up in a sequence that exhibits different correlations between the variables (in the instance of the impersonation, signs, perception, knowledge, affectivity) that can enter into the constitution of an act of the imagination.

The Shift in Method

The weakening in Sartre of Husserl's distinction of level may explain why Sartre does not retain from *Ideas I* Husserl's terminology "eidetic reduction." Consciousness does not have to be "led back" the same distance (so to speak) as in Husserl from the particular individual fact to reach the essence. This may be why, in the initial brief section called "Method" in *L'imaginaire,* Sartre does not even mention Husserl but introduces his analysis as if it were merely the Cartesian style of reflective analysis with which his French audience is already familiar.

Nevertheless, once Sartre's weakening of Husserl's distinction of level has been taken into account, we are able to recognize that there is a sense in which there is a shift in *level* in Sartre that is carried out by a reduction, which can called "eidetic" inasmuch as an "essence" is reached. My consciousness, in the example of the impersonation, is being "led back" from Franconay's particular traits—small, dark-haired, with female curves. These particularities are not completely eliminated in the way that the eidetic reduction in Husserl would eliminate particularities, but they are disregarded to the extent that they are not allowed to get too much "in the way" of our identifying "the essence, as it were, of Maurice Chevalier." The "relation" to him (to retain more of Husserl's terminology) is not entirely "eliminated by the variation," and his "factual reality" does not become "completely irrelevant" to his "essence, as it were," which could not qualify as "a pure essence" in Husserl.

Embodiment

The eidetic reduction that survives Sartre's weakening of the distinction of level can be characterized as a "vulgarization" of Husserl's eidetic reduction. "Vulgarization" is a procedure that in Volume 1 we watched Sartre endorse for political purposes—and he might be said to endorse it for more general purposes—by adopting the principle "toward the concrete." At the same time the impersonation is a performance by an *artiste* and so can become quasi-methodological. Thus the step Sartre is taking here can be visualized as a different kind of step from mere "vulgarization." With respect to what it induces, Franconay's performance would seem to be to some extent a *substantive embodiment* of the eidetic reduction that was a distinctively methodological procedure in Husserl.

The first clue we had that Sartre was not simply describing what goes on in the consciousness of someone watching a successful impersonation was that description inherited a certain philosophical *stiffening,* most obviously with such a term as "essence" surviving from Husserl's procedure of eidetic reduction. How is this stiffening to be construed? First, it has to be remembered that Sartre's analysis is relational. In such an analysis, if it is dialectical, the relation usually presupposed as fundamental is the relation between method and subject. Thus Hegel denies that method and subject are merely external to each other: "The form is the immanent becoming of the concrete content," and "the content is in itself transition [*Übergehen*] into form." [7]

What is different about the situation now confronting us in Sartre is that the "form" came before the "content"—that is, the eidetic reduction was conceived by Husserl as a methodological operation on consciousness before it became in Sartre the way consciousness is operated on by the impersonator. The upshot of a philosopher's movement "toward the concrete" is often that we encounter what is set forth as a substantive feature of the subject itself only to discover that it is the unacknowledged residue of some procedure a previous philosopher has applied.

Method and Imagination

I am not merely drawing attention to another instance of "academicization" in Sartre. There is a point to be made regarding Husserl too, to appreciate the complexity of their relation at the juncture of the impersonation. This present volume is not simply (as its title might have suggested initially to the unwary) a report on how Sartre applies the phenomenological *method* he obtained from Husserl to a *subject,* the imagination, which Husserl himself had treated "only in passing." That the relation between a predecessor and a successor is almost always more complicated than that was implicit in my sorting out the different shifts in Volume 1. Moreover, there is a specific complication I have left out so far, even in the present volume, because Sartre himself left it out. When he commented that Husserl treated the imagination "only in passing," he was failing to acknowledge explicitly that Husserl had treated the imagination in *Ideas I,* rather less as a subject than in relation to its *methodological* role in carrying out the eidetic reduction. This is another illustration of the priority Husserl accords method. In fact, Husserl endorses not only (as Heidegger recognized) "the priority of method" but also "The Priority [*Vorzugsstellung*] of Free Imagination" in carrying out the eidetic reduction. "Free imagination" refers to the extent to which one kind of imagination can free itself from the restrictions of perception:

> The geometer operates in his investigative thinking in relation to figures and models, incomparably more in the imagination than in perception. . . . He has incomparably more freedom in reshaping at will the figures he feigns.[8]

The phenomenologist operates analogously in carrying out the "free variation" of the eidetic reduction.

Sartre skips over the geometric analogy, but he does cite from this section of *Ideas I.* Furthermore, Husserl's argument that the imagination plays a methodological role in carrying out the eidetic reduction by freeing us from the sway of perception may have been not without influence on Sartre's description of how the impersonator induces us to free ourselves from the refractory perceptual evidence (a woman who is small and dark-haired) that might otherwise thwart our constituting the image "Chevalier." If so, Sartre does not come upon the imagination as a pristine subject, awaiting his treatment—at least not at this pivotal juncture of the impersonation. Already built into the imagination when it became a subject for Sartre was Husserl's conception of its methodological role in the eidetic reduction.

I shall return to this interpretation of what happens to Husserl's eidetic reduction in Sartre when I can include in my comparison what happens to Husserl's phenomenological reduction in Sartre. It also receives substantive embodiment. But so far I have taken Sartre at his word that he is not applying the phenomenological reduction in treating the imagination. Before I can return, there is also a very considerable difficulty to be faced in my intervening chapters: the impersonation seems too particular, too idiosyncratic an example to support the weight of much argument. Thus before pressing the present interpretation further I shall have to demonstrate at some length that the example is not idiosyncratic in the context of Sartre's philosophy and that it acquires there general implications.

Development

All that I am suggesting now is the general point that I began to make with my quotation from Hegel: the distinction between a procedure that is methodological and its substantive embodiment cannot usually be maintained in a relational analysis if it is dialectical, for its formulation as a method is dependent on the concomitant development of a content. Anglophone philosophers are not likely to be alert to Sartre's transformation of Husserl's method here into a rudimentary dialectic, since we have been conditioned by formal logic to take for granted a formalistic conception of method as obviously distinguishable from any substantive matters. One reason I proposed in Volume 1 an analogy between a method and a style, is that we do take for granted that there is, typically, intimacy of relationship between a style and the content undergoing treatment. With the impersonation the analogy can take more specific hold inasmuch as the performance of the *artiste* displays a certain "style" (presumably not just Chevalier's but her own as well), which I have already suggested is quasi-methodological.

In making this general point, the advantage to the historian of the contrast between Husserl and Sartre is that the relation between method and content can emerge in Sartre only when both are developing in a fashion that would be precluded by Husserl's "principle of all principles."[9] This principle upholds the immediate givenness of essences against any "theory," which would embrace the relations between effects and their causes. The eidetic reduction in Husserl is not a development: whatever is gone through during the variation is eliminated in favor of the grasp of the essence which is immediately given as invariant. But our finally grasping "the essence," as it were, of Chevalier, depends on the preceding re-ductive development, which obtains scope from Sartre's two principles. "Accompanied by an affective reaction" stretches the scope of what is being analyzed beyond what is immediately given in Husserl. In the case of Sartre's second principle, a further extension of scope is implicit in the process of projection. Thus the methodological import of these principles requires a substantive process of development to become manifest—the development of our successive reactions to the impersonator as her performance itself develops.

In addition to the development which is the re-duction induced by the impersonator's performance, a long-run re-duction is induced by the succession of examples that are lined up in Sartre. Just as the example of the impersonation is itself a sequential experience of re-duction (in the sense that perceptual evidence has to be downgraded, to be compensated for eventually by an affective reaction) so at the higher level of the general sequence of Sartre's examples, "starting with the impersonation," the perceptual evidence is downgraded in favor of compensating factors—most prominently an affective reaction. In this long-run sequence our reflective consciousness is being "led back," as the perceptual evidence diminishes, as a basis for the act of the imagination until, when the end of the sequence is reached, the image is purely mental and other factors have to become more decisive if the image is to emerge. We have already seen that there is no long-run sequence in Husserl of comparable methodological significance. Instead he zigzags.

The Hybrid State

The fact remains that Sartre does not retain Husserl's term "reduction." This may be because—I have so far suggested—the distinction of level no longer retains in Sartre the sharpness it enjoyed in Husserl. But its weakening is not just flabbiness on Sartre's part. We have watched Sartre enlist the help of Bergson in order to blur the sharpness of Husserl's distinction of level. The blur is not merely a blur. In the citation from Bergson, "We usually start out not with the perception of the individual, nor with the conception of the genus, but with knowledge of a sort that is intermediary between the two." The intermediary is a juncture that often tempts the dialectician by virtue of the opportunity it affords for *interplay* between two opposed levels. Even though my consciousness is, on the one hand, "led back" (in a fashion that might warrant retaining the term "reduction") from the perceived Franconay to the imaginary Chevalier, it then is likely to find itself "sliding from the level of the image to that of perception." Rather than a unilateral eidetic reduction in which we finally grasp the essence Chevalier, the consummation of the experience of the impersonation is the *interplay* between levels, as the image is constituted at one level only to have it slide back to the other level. Sartre explains:

The face and body of the impersonator do not lose all of their individuality, but the expressive something, "Maurice Chevalier" nevertheless appears on this face, on this female body. A hybrid state develops, which is neither entirely perceptive nor entirely imaginative and which would be well worth describing for its own sake. This unstable and transitory state is obviously what is most entertaining for the spectator in an impersonation.

This climax of Sartre's climactic example is not sheer entertainment itself but "would be," Sartre mentions, "well worth describing for its own sake."

The Break

If Sartre does not tell us why, my suspicion is that it is because an adequate answer can be formulated only in terms of what he has not yet written, not even yet thought out. I'll attempt that answer later. For the present, I take the liberty of suggesting an answer that he would never propose, since he does not share my preoccupation with method. The analysis of the impersonation illustrates not the phenomenological analysis he is supposedly prosecuting but the mixture of phenomenological analysis with a rudimental dialectic.

Having applied to Sartre's relation to Husserl the analysis of shifts I elaborated in Volume 1, I have reached a break in his relation to Husserl. This break is a juncture almost comparable to the "lurch" in Heidegger's relation to Husserl, with which I began in Volume 1. Now it is incumbent on me to consider where I have arrived in the present volume as compared with my undertaking in that preceding volume.

Locating a shift is a procedure for explaining a break that takes place in a philosopher's relation to a previous philosophy or to his own previous philosophy. In Volume 1, I examined what Sartre took to be the most significant "break" (*rupture*) in his life—his exposure to social history during World War II.[10] The examination disclosed that this break involved his discovery that Heidegger was not simply the disciple of Husserl whom Sartre had assumed him to be before the war—as Sartre himself had been. Concomitant with his discovery, a shift in his allegiance took place from Husserl toward Heidegger. To this extent, this break in Sartre's life was philosophical.

The more significant philosophical break, however, was that between Heidegger and Husserl, though it assumed its full significance only when Heidegger reached the end of philosophy, for Heidegger then viewed Husserl as confined within the history of philosophy. But the break between Heidegger and Husserl proved difficult to deal with. On the one hand, Heidegger's employment of phenomenological method in *Being and Time* seemed an assertion of continuity between his own undertaking and Husserl's. On the other hand, Heidegger never quotes Husserl as Sartre does, and the discontinuity, the break, seems final when Heidegger, on reaching the end of philosophy, does not even accord Husserl any significant relation to philosophy's end.[11]

The Mixture

What I could salvage on Husserl's behalf was a verdict of Heidegger's linking Husserl to Hegel inasmuch as Heidegger regards both as committed to "the priority of method." This commitment took on its significance for Heidegger despite his admission that Husserl's phenomenological method and Hegel's dialectical method were "different as they could be." Heidegger's becoming indifferent to differences of method was associated with his becoming indifferent to phenomenology, as well as with his arrival at the end of philosophy. When, earlier in his career, he had been committed to phenomenology, he had been committed to its method, and he would not have linked Husserl to Hegel, for he insisted on the differences between their methods: "To try to reconcile the authentic fundamental tendency of phenomenology with dialectic is to try to mix fire with water."[12]

Such a mixture is illustrated by Sartre's *Being and Nothingness,* and I examined its dialectical component in my *Starting Point.*[13] In *Being and Nothingness,* Sartre acknowledges the influence of Hegel. But *L'imaginaire* was written at a time when he had not yet read Hegel, and he himself never even uses the term "dialectic" in *L'imaginaire.* Thus the admixture, which we have begun to sample, of dialectic to phenomenology in *L'imaginaire* cannot be attributed to any influence on Sartre as discernible as Husserl's influence on him. At the same time, Husserl's influence on Sartre yields more manageable evidence of methodological continuity than is discernible in Heidegger's relation to Husserl, at least in *Being and Time.*

We have gone far enough in ferreting out of the mixture dialectical procedures (such as developing a fluid analysis, which is articulated into a sequence of stages in which oppositions are set up and reversals take place) and far enough in delineating the resulting break with Husserl's procedures of intentional and eidetic analysis to enable us now to face up to the problems posed by another shift in Sartre's relation to Husserl.

FOUR · THE SHIFT IN
AFFILIATION

EIGHTEEN

Literature

There is always literary prose hidden in philosophy.—Sartre

Priority

Another shift is at stake in Sartre's break with Husserl. Since Sartre does not accord method the priority it enjoys in Husserl, my comparison remains one-sided until we do justice to what Sartre does accord priority. But here the comparison becomes more cumbersome, for what Sartre does accord priority seemingly takes us outside philosophy. Recalling how he first became interested in philosophy, Sartre was prompt to qualify, "I have always been primarily a writer [that is, a writer of literary works] and secondarily a philosopher." [1]

Although in this history I am myself according priority to considerations of method, as I explained in Volume 1[2] and re-emphasized in the preceding chapter, they are not restricted to the procedures which in Husserl composed phenomenological method, are transformed by his successors, and are involved in the shifts that take place in Sartre. I am also interested in shifts in *affiliation*.

I offer no apology for my interest in a philosopher who wrote literary works and whose interest in philosophy itself was secondary. On the one hand, the distinction between the two genres cannot be held fixed. We should have known this before; if we didn't, we have learned it from Derrida. There are also those (including Richard Rorty, to whom I alluded in Volume 1) who associate the end of philosophy with its becoming a literary rather than a scientific undertaking. Though a concern of mine is with this shift in *affiliation*—as it bears on the end of philosophy—I would argue (quite aside from this perspective) that what is philosophically interesting about Sartre is much less his philosophy itself than the relation between it and his literary works. There certainly have been more competent philosophers than Sartre around in the twentieth century (not to mention literary works of more merit than anything Sartre wrote), but there is no philosopher who has achieved comparable prominence at once in philosophy and literature.

Fictitious Experiences

There are difficulties, however, in the way of dealing with this relation. First of all, Sartre himself has had little to say about it. Perhaps because he was so determined to accord priority to his literary works, and to keep them distinct from his philosophy, he may have been reluctant to subordinate them to any philosophical analysis of their relation to his philosophy.

One of his few specific pronouncements is the claim in *What is Literature?*, "Problems can be attacked abstractly by philosophical reflection. But we want . . . to live them—that is, support our thinking by those fictitious [*fictives*] and concrete experiences that are novels." [3] What initially catches one's attention here is the verb. "To live" problems is a curious procedure, especially when it takes the guise of "experiences" that are "fictitious." The verb, I suspect, retains a certain methodological significance from the concept of "lived experience" (*Erlebnis*), which Sartre usually translates *expérience vécue*, and which is his version of Husserl's (intuitive) experience. [4] Thus Sartre's idiom "to live problems" might be said to privilege the experiences of novels as immediately given, as over against the abstractness of philosophy, but he is then privileging these experiences in the way Husserl had privileged the experiences of philosophy as immediately given, as over against the inductive generalizations reached in the empirical sciences.

What is still perplexing is Sartre's privileging of "experiences" that are "fictitious." [5] How can these qualify as "lived experiences"?

Here too it may be pertinent to remember Husserl's procedure of eidetic reduction or, rather, Sartre's account of it. In explaining how the "kind of reflection the phenomenologist employs . . . operates on examples," Sartre points out,

> It doesn't matter much whether the individual fact that serves as support for the essence is real or imaginary. What is given as an example, even if it were a pure fiction, because it could be imagined

is necessarily the realization of the essence sought, for the essence is the very condition of its possibility: "It is then allowable (if one likes paradoxes, and provided one understands as it should be the ambiguous meaning of this pronouncement) to state that fiction is the living element of phenomenology, as of all eidetic sciences." [6]

Sartre is quoting the conclusion of Husserl's explanation of the role the imagination plays in carrying out the eidetic reduction.

How striking it is that in quoting Husserl, Sartre has skipped over the illustration that Husserl provided about the imagination's operations in the eidetic science of geometry; Sartre has arrived instead at the sentence in which Husserl reached a sweeping conclusion on which Sartre pounces—as the only definite statement by Husserl suggesting that fiction was relevant to philosophy.

Ambiguity

That Husserl had in fact no philosophical concern with literature presents another difficulty in managing the comparison between the priorities of Sartre and of Husserl. This is one of those decisive junctures at which two philosophers go past each other, so that it may seem overweening for the historian to try to bridge the gulf between them.

My first step is to recognize how method can be said to lose in Sartre the priority it enjoys with Husserl, to whom it assures philosophy's scientific status. We have heard Sartre protest that "Husserl's idea of 'philosophy as rigorous science' seems to me the crazy idea of a genius." [7] Admittedly, this protest becomes explicit only late in Sartre's career (1965). At the time he was "inspired by Husserl" in *L'imaginaire*, Sartre presumably thought of Husserl simply as a genius. [8] But Husserl sought this rigor primarily with his reductions, and we have already seen that Sartre ostensibly does not apply in *L'imaginaire* the phenomenological reduction and that he relaxed the rigor of the eidetic reduction in his own eidetic analysis by weakening the distinction of level in Husserl.

Sartre continues his protest against "philosophy as rigorous science" by claiming, "There is nothing more ambiguous than everything Husserl writes." We have seen that Sartre has in mind the holes that philosophers try to plug in their philosophies. But Sartre would also draw a general contrast between philosophy, as ambiguous, and science, which undertakes to be rigorous; he claims, "There is always literary prose hidden in philosophy—an ambiguity in its terms." [9] The "always" stakes out philosophical generality for this claim. I shall be more modest, and try only to demonstrate in Part 5 that certain specimens of Sartre's own literary prose he could have found hidden in (his version of) Husserl's philosophy. But some more general problems need to be faced first.

NINETEEN

The Work of Art

*Your real objective, it is the book, the painting,
the statue that will emerge under your fingers.
—Apollo.*

The Overlap

During the prewar epoch, Sartre's most important literary work was *Nausea,* just as his most important strictly philosophical work was his treatment of the imagination. It should not be forgotten that Sartre was writing *L'image* (the title his manuscript initially retained from the *diplôme*) at the same time as *Nausea.* In fact, Sartre temporarily "abandoned" the novel to finish *L'image.* When the publisher accepted only the first portion (the historical survey published as *L'imagination*), Sartre resigned himself to the fact that the second portion "would not be published for a long time" and resumed work on the novel, which was published in 1938.[1] It seems to have been a result of the critical acclaim that the novel received that Sartre did not have to wait that long time: he was able to get the second part of *L'image* published as *L'imaginaire* in 1940.

There is a philosophically more significant overlap between *L'imaginaire* and *Nausea.* The final chapter of *L'imaginaire* is entitled "The Work of Art." Late in life, Sartre recalls, "This chapter did not exist in *L'imaginaire.*" Sartre added this chapter, he explains, "because I was asked to treat it." What happened was that Bernard Groethuysen, "who was a German philosopher living in France, said to me, 'But the book has no chapter on art.'" This may be merely what one would expect a German philosopher to say when confronted with a work on the imagination. But it perhaps should be mentioned that Groethuysen had become close to writers in France as famous as André Gide and was influential in publishing circles. Since Sartre had had previous difficulty in getting *L'imaginaire* published, he may have been more than ready to oblige with the requested chapter on art, simply because "I was asked to treat it." [2]

If so, the question still remains, "Why did Sartre not treat it on his own, without being asked? It may not have been just that he lacked German thoroughness. The answer I would propose is that he felt he had already treated the work of art in *Nausea*. This would be consistent with his later identification of his philosophy in its unity with all "the different books that I have produced during a given epoch." [3] But I do not need this postwar hindsight offered when he had become committed to historicism. When Sartre encounters the phenomenon of nausea in *Being and Nothingness*, he is not as long-winded as he is on most topics there. For, he alleges, "I have described it elsewhere." [4] If his having described nausea in the novel rendered further description of it largely superfluous in *Being and Nothingness*, why should not his treatment of the work of art in *Nausea* have seemed to him to render its treatment in *L'imaginaire* largely superfluous?

Contingency

In fact nausea and the work of art are closely linked in the novel by virtue of the *interplay* between them: nausea is the exposure to the experience of contingency—of the randomness, the sloppiness, of living—and salvation from this experience is available in the guise of the antithetical experience of the necessary structure of a work of art. Before we can deal with this opposition, certain contingencies intrude on Sartre's own handling of contingency and should be taken into account, especially since they have some bearing on the relation between his philosophical and his literary writing.

In Volume 1, I showed how indebted Sartre was in his handling of nausea to Heidegger's handling of anxiety. My having argued that Sartre is so indebted may have seemed disconcerting, for nausea is the experience with which Sartre is probably most intimately associated in the usual interpretation—to such an extent, as his *Pléiade* editors point out, "It is enough today to spell the word with a capital letter for it to evoke no longer the physical malady of vomiting but existential anxiety." [5]

However, when Sartre was confronted with the assumption of one of these editors—"Nausea describes an existential experience that you had"—Sartre responded (much, one would guess), to this knowledgeable editor's surprise), "But I never had, strictly speaking, this nausea. I lay claim to it, even so, but philosophically."[6] The editor must have reflected that it was very unexistential of Sartre to have distinguished an experience to which he lays claim philosophically from an experience which he has experienced personally. But the fact of Heidegger's influence here is another instance of what I have labeled the "academicization" of Sartre's experience.

The experience of contingency itself Sartre did lay claim to, at once personally and philosophically—or at least Simone de Beauvoir did on his behalf, when she reported his discovery, to his considerable relief, that Husserl could not claim it. But in fact the experience, at least as described in Sartre's published works, derived from Heidegger.[7]

I am not trying to deprive Sartre of his philosophical claim to what was perhaps his favorite experience. His sense of relief, when he read Levinas on Husserl, that Husserl had not got there first in a publication was undoubtedly genuine. But Sartre was not unaware that the concept of contingency had been around for a long time in philosophy. After all, it had turned up as the topic he wrote on for his *agrégation*.[8]

Sartre's own accomplishment was making a novel out of the experience of contingency, though he himself has a negative explanation to the effect that he "gave the idea [of contingency] the form of a novel because the idea was not solid enough to make out of it a philosophical work: it was rather something quite vague, but which had a strong grip on me."[9]

We have encountered "the lamentable Frédéric" when he was "thinking vaguely" and entertaining a "vague impression [of Cosima]" as compared with "the precise and systematic knowledge" he had of a novelist.[10] I have suggested Sartre was self-consciously bothered by his own vagueness. It may well be that his "idea" of contingency, however "strong" its grip on him, was "something quite vague" until he obtained knowledge from Heidegger, which he regarded as "precise and systematic." For I was able to show in Volume 1 that Sartre's definition of nausea, which is the experience of contingency, is precise because it is a literal translation from Heidegger.[11]

Here is a serious difficulty that I must face now in my exposition. Even Sartre expects an idea to display a certain solidity before philosophy can be made out of it. If in a literary work he can get away with ideas that are vague, how is the expositor to trace their contours in a way that retains philosophical relevance? I will do my best.

Salvation

Sartre distinguishes "two moments" in the writing of *Nausea*. Sartre's protagonist, Roquentin, "thinks he is going to be saved at the end by the work of art." Sartre himself, when he was ending the novel, no longer believed in this salvation. "But," he adds, "I wrote it having him believe it, because that had been the starting point."[12] Sartre had believed in it once.

I am taking up, first, the question, How did Sartre lose his faith? For that is where the emphasis falls in Sartre's own account. He says he lost it in two ways. First, because of his "passion for O, I began to have my doubts about salvation by art, which seemed quite futile, confronted with this cruel purity naked." For "my passion for her, like the flame of a Bunsen burner, burnt away my routine impurities"—including his faith in salvation by art. The other way this impurity was eliminated was by "a conversation with the Beaver [Simone de Beauvoir]," who "demonstrated to me how rubbishy my attitude was." This conversation "finished the job of turning me from this moral theory [of salvation by art]."[13]

The passion for O lasted from "March 1935 until March 1937"—a longish time for a Bunsen burner to burn. I don't want to deny either woman her due. But there is also some textual evidence to consider, since during this period, after completing L'image, Sartre wrote the final version of Nausea, when he had lost his faith. A striking difference philosophically between the two works is that L'image is almost entirely "inspired by Husserl,"[14] whereas Nausea is also inspired by Heidegger's experience of contingency. So I would suggest, as a third factor in Sartre's loss of faith, his turning from Husserl's orientation toward essences to the exposure to the contingent found in Heidegger.

Sartre's faith in salvation by art certainly antedates his encounters with Husserl and Heidegger. I need only cite the end of "Er the Arménian." Apollo is the *maître* who is speaking:

> A moral theory, what stupidity! But to maintain the desire to create a work of art, to search every minute, in every circumstance, materials [for it], to drag his body to the four corners of the world, in suffering, in lechery, in beds of roses, in the shit, in order to collect materials. . . . Life alone will not teach you anything. . . . Your real objective, it is the book, the painting, the statue that will emerge under your fingers. You will live with more ardor than all the rest of them, your body abandoned to the winds like the cast-off corpse of the hanged, twisting at the end of his rope, filthy, bloody, soiled with spit, and with the soul unmoved, unshaken in the bosom of Beauty, which is only what you will make.

Er was briefly intoxicated with this vision, but then became "disheartened" and replied, "No, no. To give oneself to that entirely, one must believe in it."

"Without a doubt."

"And to believe in it, is to believe in oneself."[15]

Making allowance for irony, this still can be taken as a declaration of Sartre's faith.

The doctrine of salvation by art has itself been propounded by so many writers that looking for antecedents is not very illuminating. There is certainly no such doctrine to be found in Husserl. But I am taking a look at Sartre's later *formulation* of this doctrine. Sartre is definite about the conception of art in *Nausea* that underpinned his faith: *Nausea* was "written, starting out with a theory of the work of art . . . as a new essence one was giving to the world." Or again: "Up until two years before *Nausea* [Sartre is presumably referring to 1936, since *Nausea* was published in 1938], I thought that art was entirely the grasping of essence. A work of art was accordingly the creation of an essence."[16] Essences are not featured in Sartre's youthful writings.

Proust is probably the principal source for Sartre's doctrine of salvation by art, and *Nausea* has long since been recognized to be a parody of Proust. "The grasping of an essence" is what a phenomenologist does when he carries out an eidetic analysis, whether he be Husserl or Sartre, whereas "the creation of an essence" is something a phenomenologist would never presume to undertake. What can perhaps be credited to Husserl is the sharpness of the distinction between an essence and the contingent. The curious fact is that although Sartre in *L'imaginaire* weakens and blurs the sharp distinction of level in Husserl between essential, necessary structures and contingent particulars, the distinction remains sharp in *Nausea*.

There is one similarity, however, between the way the distinction is drawn in the two works. The most prominent work of art to which Roquentin pins his faith is the lyric "Some of These Days." One version of the distinction between contingency and the level of essence attained by art is provided when Roquentin listens to the record:

> The voice sings:
>
> > "Some of these days
> > You'll miss me honey."

The record must have been scratched there, because it makes a weird noise. And there is something that clutches the heart—the melody is absolutely not touched by this slight coughing of the needle on the record. The melody is so far away—so far away behind. That, too, I understand, the disk is scratched and worn; the singer is perhaps dead; I, I am about to depart, I am going to take my train. But behind the existent [*existant*] who falls from one present to another, without past, without future, behind the sounds that . . . slide toward death, the melody remains the same.[17]

I don't want to press too far a comparison between what is literary and what is philosophical, but *l'existant* is philosophical jargon, presumably deriving from Heidegger, whereas "remaining the same" is the criterion in Husserl for identifying the essence as it emerges from the free variation of the eidetic reduction. Observe the transition from the merely contingent fact that the record is scratched and worn to the other merely contingent fact that "the singer is perhaps dead," for later we are assured that she is "saved" by her singing, along with the composer of the lyric. Before Roquentin departs, he thinks that becoming the author of the novel will similarly be his salvation.

What I would draw specific attention to is the difference between the way the distinction of level is drawn in Sartre and in Husserl. The affective reaction (what "clutches the heart") in Sartre involves *interplay* between (the level of) contingent fact and (the level of) essence. This *interplay* we watched take place between levels in *L'imaginaire*, although what matters in Husserl is transcending the contingent fact and reaching the essence.

Heidegger could have encouraged Sartre to allow for this *interplay*. Heidegger, as well as the two women, could even have eventually contributed to the undermining of Sartre's faith in salvation by art, by undermining Husserl's privileging of essence as over against contingency. Heidegger's preferred term for "contingency" was *Faktizität*, (Sartre's translation is *facticité*), and Heidegger's analysis of "facticity" as if it had an essence implies some criticism of Husserl's sharp distinction between "Fact and Essence."[18] But I do not want to press this point. We should not forget that Sartre is giving "the idea [of contingency] the form of a novel because the idea was not solid enough to make out of it a philosophical work." The idea did eventually solidify for Sartre primarily as the result of his coming to a better understanding of Heidegger. But if the idea was still, as Sartre admits, "something quite vague," it may have been partly because Sartre did not yet have the definite conception of the relation between Husserl and Heidegger that he has by the time he comes to oppose them in *Being and Nothingness*. Until he has clarified this relation, he will not manage to clarify for his own purposes the relation between Husserl's idea of essence as transcending contingency and Heidegger's idea of contingency as undermining Husserl's idea of essence.

Melancholia

In the present volume, I am focusing on Sartre's relation to Husserl, and I would skirt, except where it bears directly on this relation, Heidegger's influence on Sartre. My skirting Heidegger is signalized by my now dropping the title *Nausea,* which was imposed by the publisher despite Sartre's initial misgivings[19] and which, to a considerable extent, transcribes the experience of anxiety in Heidegger. I am reinstating Sartre's original title, *Melancholia,* which also enables me to concentrate on the ambiguity that is central to the novel—the status of the work of art. To appreciate this ambiguity, more has to be taken into account than art's having originally been for Sartre "the grasping of an essence" or "the creation of an essence" and salvation from contingency.

If, according to Sartre, there is literary prose hidden in philosophy, it might also be said that there is a particular work of art hidden in the prose of this literary work. Dürer's *Melancholia I* is well hidden, and no one guessed the inspiration Dürer had provided until Simone de Beauvoir announced it.[20] There is no mention of the engraving in the novel, Roquentin is not explicitly described as a melancholic, and the mood of melancholy is not itself paraded.

However, there is a crucial juncture in the novel where *Melancholia I* may not be entirely hidden, even though it seems not to have been noticed by critics. This is at the end of the novel, when its starting point is anticipated:

Perhaps one day, thinking precisely of this present hour, of this sad [*morne*] hour, hunched over [*le dos rond*], waiting for it to be time to take the train, perhaps I would feel my heart beat faster and I would say to myself, "That is the day, that is the hour when it all started."

Why is Sartre's protagonist "hunched over" now? Throughout the novel he has regularly been keeping his journal and so could well have visualized himself as hunched over. But at this juncture he is not even writing. He is merely saying to himself what he will someday say to himself.

A possible explanation of this posture is that he is being identified with the figure of *Melancholia I,* who is portrayed in this depressed posture in the engraving. He is being so identified at this final juncture when the novel is being brought within its own scope—hunched over on itself, one might almost say.[21]

Why was the Dürer engraving so important to the writer of the novel as to provide its original title? There are two ingredient questions here. The more general question is, Why was a visual work of art so important to a literary artist? The answer to this general question I postpone until the next chapter. In the present chapter, I restrict myself to the question, Why was it this particular engraving that was so important?

The Hidden Philosophy

That this particular engraving had long since acquired extensive literary significance may partly explain Sartre's devotion to it. But quite aside from later commentaries, literary sources are hidden in the engraving itself. One is the *De Occulta Philosophia*. The ultimate literary source for this "hidden philosophy" protrudes in the engraving, for etched in its upper-left corner (and thus given special status as a title) is *Melancholia I:* this numeration was supposed to have been supplied by no less a philosopher than Aristotle. *Melancholia I* is the kind of depression that afflicts the artist who finds himself unable to create.[22]

Yet there is an ambiguity here, since Dürer has been able to create the engraving at which we are looking. And this engraving may even be Dürer's self-portrait of himself as the artist. Sartre's novel *Melancholia* is itself riddled by the same ambiguity. The "perhaps" at the beginning of the passage I have quoted from the end of the novel is stressed by its repetition. Sartre's protagonist is doubtful about his ability to write: "I don't dare to make the decision. If I were sure I had talent."[23] We are left with the ambiguity unresolved: Is what we have read the novel that the protagonist later did in fact write, or is it only the journal that is ending with his anticipation he will write a novel, which in fact it turned out he was unable to write? The ambiguity was heightened when in 1960 the word "novel" was deleted from the front of the work and from its end, the word "end."[24]

Just as the engraving may have been of personal relevance to Dürer, so it may have been of personal relevance to Sartre, who had a bout of depression in 1935, apparently induced by taking mescaline. But, according to its editors, the novel can also "be read . . . as the expression of an identity crisis" that Sartre was experiencing when he started writing it:

> The year 1931 marked at once an end and a beginning. . . . It is the year of the final failure of a first work on contingency, *The Legend of the Truth*, [which was] finally rejected by the publishers. . . . More generally, it was the year of the failure of all of Sartre's attempts at writing.[25]

I would also point out that when Sartre then began a new work on contingency, he might have experienced the doubt of his protagonist—"If I were sure I had talent" (After all, what reader of the present volume would be sure, judging by the citations I have offered from his youthful writings.) Sartre's uncertainty could have led him to identify himself more definitely with the figure in Dürer's *Melancholia I,* who was unable to create.

If the word "melancholy" is never applied to a mood of Sartre's protagonist in the novel, it is often applied by Sartre to his own mood during the period he was working on the final version of the novel. Indeed, this is likely to have been the period when he adopted the title *Melancholia*. Nevertheless, more is at stake than either Sartre's personal talent as an individual or his protagonist's talent. I would reexamine Sartre's distinction between the "two moments": the moment when Sartre, like his protagonist, believed that "he is going to be saved [from contingency] at the end by the work of art," and the moment when Sartre found that he himself no "longer believed this," though in finishing the novel he continued to have his protagonist believe, because "that had been the starting point."

The Ending

Sartre is suggesting that his loss of faith did not effect the end of the novel—but the end is more ambiguous than he later allows for. Sartre apparently no longer remembers later in his life how his protagonist discredits the doctrine of salvation by art near the end:

> There was a poor jerk who had found he had mistaken the world he was in. He existed, like other people in the world of public gardens, cafés, commercial towns, and he wanted to convince himself that he lived elsewhere—behind the canvas of paintings, with the doges of Tintoretto, with the fine Florentines of Gozzoli, behind the pages of books, with Fabrice del Dongo and Julian Sorel, behind the phonograph records, with the long arid laments of jazz. And then, after having made a complete fool of himself, he had understood, he opened his eyes, he saw he had made a mistake.[26]

If Roquentin now goes on to write the novel, he will be deluding himself that he can live "behind the pages of a book" and making again the mistake he has seen through.

Even when Roquentin does proclaim the doctrine at the very end of the novel, the prospect of salvation incurs a further ambiguity:

> "That is the day, that is the hour when it all started," and I would arrive in the past, but only in the past, at accepting myself.[27]

The French, "J'arriverais . . . à m'accepter" anticipates the resolution of the protagonist's identity crisis. But ambiguity would still subvert this resolution. This would be less evident if I had settled for the smoother translation, "I would succeed in accepting myself." I retained the awkward "would arrive" to render the temporal ambiguity whereby Roquentin looks forward to a future in which he would have been saved in the past.

The sentence that follows—the final sentence of the novel—leaves us with a final ambiguity with its prediction, "Tomorrow it will rain in Mucktown [*Bouville*]." The prospect of salvation by art, when Mucktown is taken as its locale, is endangered, since the work of art (most recently in the novel, the notes of the jazz lyric) manifests an "arid" purity, which we have learned in the novel is to be opposed to the sloppy impurities of contingent existence.

TWENTY

In Person

The engravings were their bodies; the text was their soul.—Sartre

The Knight

I have suggested that the doctrine of salvation by art in Sartre's *Melancholia* bears the marks of a certain philosophical inheritance, especially insofar as it is couched in terms of the opposition between essence and contingency. Sartre's own adherence to the doctrine was reinforced by inspiration he obtained from Husserl's exalting of essence, while his abandonment of the doctrine was assisted by inspiration he obtained from Heidegger's rehabilitation of contingency.

These specific debts to his predecessors Sartre himself does not acknowledge. By way of explanation, he offers instead his own personal experiences. I would be the last to deny that "passion" for a woman can be as searing as "the flame of a Bunsen burner." But I suspect that more than a woman is necessary to save a man from believing in salvation by art. Not even two women would ordinarily suffice—"passion" for one, and philosophical conversation with the other. Whatever Sartre's personal experiences may have been, the philosophical relevance of personal experiences is itself a general issue, and I raised it in Volume 1.[1] Here I am raising it only as an issue between Sartre and Husserl.

Husserl underwent a period of depression more or less comparable to the period when Sartre was writing *L'image,* identifying with the engraving *Melancholia I,* and completing *Melancholia.* During this period,

Husserl's own writing was not going well, and he was not publishing. Like Sartre, he was identifying with a figure in a Dürer engraving, which he mentions in the "Personal Notes" he then jotted down:

> I must go my own way as confidently, as determinedly resolved, as seriously, as Dürer's Knight, in spite of Death and Devil. Yes, life for me has become very serious. The cheerfulness of life's physical pleasures has become alien to me and must remain alien to me. I must live at work, in battle, in passionately earnest struggle for the crown of truth. Cheerfulness is not to be felt: a cheerful heaven above when I boldly and confidently press forward, as is above Dürer's Knight. And God be with me as with him, in spite of us all always being sinners.[2]

As an interpretation of the engraving, this personal note does not deserve much attention. I doubt if any examination of the engraving would demonstrate that the heaven above the Knight is cheerful. But the doubt leads us to recognize how very personal this note is. In his disconsolateness, Husserl is imagining a cheerful heaven—perhaps even how cheerful heaven was above some of his academic contemporaries, whose careers were advancing while his lagged. Unlike them, he indicates in a 1905 letter to Brentano that he has not been "an ambitious instructor, eagerly looking out for the public and the government." Instead, he claims, "I pursue my own course." Hence "I have made enemies of almost all the influential people . . . by the fact that I have chosen my problems myself and have gone my own way. I have not allowed any other considerations to enter than those of the thing itself."[3]

To check out Husserl's interpretation of the engraving, we can rely on the art historian Erwin Panofsky, who has tracked down the engraving's literary source, Eramus's *Handbook of the Christian Soldier,*

> where "death" and the "devil" are discounted as "spooks and phantoms" . . . which . . . must be deemed for naught."
> This is precisely what Dürer expressed in his engraving: the enemies of man do not appear to be real. They are indeed "spooks and phantoms" to be ignored. The Knight passes them as though they were not there.
> The Knight . . . quietly pursues his course, "Fixing his eyes steadily and intensely on the thing itself," to quote Erasmus again.

I grant that Husserl may have been entirely unaware of Erasmus's *Handbook* or, at any rate, of its pertinence to the engraving.[4] But he did think of himself as going his own way "as determinedly resolved, as seriously, as Dürer's Knight." And what he might have identified with in the Knight was (in Erasmus's words) the way he was "fixing his eyes steadily and intensely on the thing itself." At any rate, this is the kind of vigilant steadiness and intensity with which the phenomenologist must struggle to direct his consciousness toward "the thing itself."

The Scholar

We do not know if the engraving *Melancholia I* also lay in the portfolio from which Husserl imagined taking out "The Knight" in *Ideas I*. But the two engravings are themselves related. According to Panofsky, they are two of the three engravings that "form a spiritual unity in that they symbolize three ways of life"—the active life, the artistic life of production, and the scholar's life of contemplation. The engraving Husserl did take out symbolizes the *vita activa:* the Knight is committed to "the life of decision and action." Yet Husserl seems never to have been personally engaged in the *vita activa;* he was too old to fight in World War I. Husserl's sense of identification with the Knight may seem even more curious since the third engraving, "Saint Jerome," to which he does not allude, "opposes the *vita contemplativa* to the *vita activa.*" The scholar is visualized by Dürer as living "in the warm, bright, and peaceful seclusion of a well-ordered study." [5] Visitors to Husserl's house in Freiburg remember seeing Husserl in his study (I presume through a glass door) totally absorbed in his work, much in the fashion of the scholar in the engraving. But Husserl visualized himself instead as leading a life of combat. Indeed, philosophers are often eager not to identify themselves as leading the *vita contemplativa.*

In his autobiographical *Words,* Sartre recalls, "I started out my life as I shall doubtless finish it—in the midst of books. In my grandfather's study they were everywhere." When he had nearly finished his life, he will report, "The only thing I really like to do is to be at my desk and write—preferably philosophy." [6] But needless to say, Sartre never identified with a scholar and a saint. We have seen that in his youth he identified with the artist of *Melancholia I.*

Personal Notes

Husserl's and Sartre's sense of identification with related, but different, engravings may be of some minor interest. What is of philosophical interest in this comparison, however, is that Husserl's personal sense of identification with the "Knight" is of no philosophical interest to him, even though it could explain his selecting this engraving in *Ideas I* or even his alluding to the detail of the engraving as "this print in the portfolio." He really may have had a portfolio of prints out of which, when despondent, he may have taken out this particular print. All of these contingencies are philosophically irrelevant to him.

Nothing, however, may seem more incompatible with the vigilance Dürer's Knight could have embodied for Husserl in his "Personal Notes" than the casualness of the "Es sei etwa" with which in *Ideas I* he took this particular print out.[7] Why is he so offhand about selecting this particular example of a work of art, as if it could have been any other, when he had imagined the Knight as exemplifying his own phenomenological undertaking? I have already hazarded an explanation, which I would now supplement: it is because of the very vigilance with which this undertaking must be conducted. This vigilance Husserl sought to ensure by carrying out the two reductions, which eliminated the contingent as philosophically irrelevant; carrying them out was itself the brunt of the "passionately earnest struggle" that Husserl identified as his own as well as the Knight's. But it was a personal struggle whereby phenomenology became an essentially impersonal undertaking. Thus Husserl can report, "Phenomenology came into my life as an unexpected and uninvited guest."[8] Phenomenology, Husserl explains, does not "deal with the experiences of empirical persons"; it "knows nothing of persons, of my experiences, or of those of others."[9]

The phenomenological reduction, which is ultimately in question at the juncture where the engraving is used as an example, rendered irrelevant any personal reasons Husserl may have had for selecting this particular example. The reduction discloses that the agency of the phenomenological undertaking is not a merely personal ego but a transcendental ego.

The passage I have quoted in which Husserl identifies himself with the Knight in the engraving is from one of the "Personal Notes," which he jotted down in a period of depression. They are merely notes and merely personal. Phenomenology supervenes when the uninvited guest takes over. The negligibility of Husserl's personal experience as contingent may help explain the flourished casualness with which he offered the example.[10]

Interplay

I have traced out the implications of the impersonality of Husserl's philosophy as background for what happens with Sartre. As a result of his weakening of the sharp distinctions that support in Husserl the level(s) occupied by philosophy itself, room opens up in Sartre for *interplay* between the more strictly philosophical and the literary and personal writings.

This *interplay* is illustrated by *Words*, Sartre's autobiography. The "personal" for Husserl could be only a matter of "notes," for once the phenomenological reduction had been carried out, the agency of reflection at the philosophical level was determined to be a transcendental ego. In Berlin, Sartre not only wrote an essay enthusiastically endorsing "Intentionality" as "a fundamental idea of Husserl's phenomenology"; he attacked at the same time another idea of Husserl's—the transcendental ego. Once phenomenology is no longer anchored to a transcendental ego, what Sartre is left with philosophically is the self of self-consciousness. The personal, the autobiographical, can no longer be discounted as philosophically irrelevant.

Words is an account, on the one hand, of how Sartre became a writer—the writer, in particular, of Melancholia—that is, of how he came to believe in the doctrine of salvation by art; on the other hand, Words is an account of how he became emancipated from this doctrine. In short, it is an account of a conversion and a deconversion. But before going into this account, we need to answer two questions: What kind of salvation did Sartre believe in, and in what kind of art?

Salvation

To the first question, the answer seems obvious in Words, where his belief is cast in theological terms:

> I thought I was giving myself to Literature when, in truth, I was taking orders. In my case the certitude of the humblest believer became arrogant evidence of my predestination. . . . I was growing . . . in the compost of Catholicism, my roots sucked up its juices, and I made out of it my sap.[11]

But is this "in truth" the entire truth? Sartre never acknowledged his Catholic composting in any other context. Any belief he had in God evaporated while he was still a youngster.[12]

What is evident from his discussion of his belief in salvation by art in his wartime journal is that it was "a moral and metaphysical theory of the work of art" and that its most important single source was Spinoza. Sartre explains by referring to "Spinoza's term salvation," and he adds, "In Spinoza I found this idea of total transformation."[13] Of course, there is nothing surprising about this: Spinoza has the most powerful analysis of a philosophical conversion since Plotinus and Plato. My point is that Words can easily be read without the reader becoming aware that Sartre's doctrine of conversion was largely philosophical or even that he ever was a philosopher.

A philosophical conversion would hardly have elicited the admiration of the Nobel Prize Committee. What Sartre has cunningly done in *Words* is to trans-late his philosophical belief in salvation into a theological belief, so that he can draw on the rich resources in the compost of French anticlericalism and suck up its juices, in order to dam himself for his role as a *clerc*.

Engravings

I turn to my second question. If Sartre started out in *Melancholia* believing in "salvation by art," his very title poses the problem of the relation between verbal and visual art. Moreover, the title is not the only juncture in the novel at which there is a rapprochement between a text and an engraving. When Sartre's protagonist in the novel looks up his former girlfriend Anny (identifiable as Sartre's former girlfriend and, like Sartre, devoted to Dürer, whom she "closely resembled in one of his self-portraits"),[14] she recalls the engravings that she had encountered as a child in Michelet's *History of France* (where, incidentally, *Melancholia I* is discussed). She had singled out in this history the scenes that were "represented by engravings," because "they must be a lot more significant to be made the subject of these images, which are so infrequent."[15] This correlation reproduces within the novel the correlation between this novel as a whole and *Melancholia I.*

Is it only her own childhood that is being recalled, or Sartre's as well? We have heard Sartre's statement in *Words,* "I started out my life as I shall doubtless end it—in the midst of books. In my grandfather's study they were everywhere." So standard a work as Michelet's *History* must have been there. In *Words* Sartre mentions a Dürer, which may explain why Husserl's "portfolio" became an "artbook" in Sartre's translation in *L'imagination.* But the work that Sartre recalls in particular is the *Grand Larousse*—an illustrated encyclopedia that "took the place of the whole universe. . . . Men and animals were there *in person:* the engravings were their bodies; the text was their soul."[16] We have already encountered the portrait of Charles VIII, which is one of the engravings in that encyclopedia, and it will be picked up again, as the example of a work of art, at the beginning of the added final chapter of *L'imaginaire.*

The prominence that engravings enjoy personally with Sartre may be due in some measure to their occurrence in conjunction with texts back in the epoch of his childhood. But more important is the way in which Sartre treats engravings in relation to the words of texts. Perhaps this problem of the relation between the visual and the verbal is dramatized in Sartre's having Anny recall in *Melancholia* that in Michelet's *History* "the scene that the engravings represented never related to the text of the adjacent pages; one had to go looking for the episode some fifty pages further on."[17] This could almost be a warning about the title of the novel itself: the reader has to wait until the book's final scene for any specific evidence of the relevance of *Melancholia I.*

Since I am clinging to titles, I am perhaps entitled to focus on words in *Words.* The passage I have quoted from *Words* on the relation between engravings and the text of the encyclopedia requires further elucidation. Sartre's italicizing of "in person" (*en personne*) is probably not just for emphasis. It may also be an acknowledgment that a technical philosophical term is being used, bringing with it some *stiffening* in the meaning. Sartre does not usually tolerate such intrusions in his literary works, even though his philosophical works are replete with technical jargon. His edict is that "philosophy cannot be expressed in a literary work," because philosophy "has a technical terminology that it must employ."[18]

If he has made an exception here in *Words,* it must be partly because *en personne* makes fairly good colloquial sense. But in his philosophical works *en personne* is Sartre's usual translation for Husserl's *in eigener Person* and sometimes for the synonymous term *leibhaft* (literally, "bodily"). My hypothesis that Sartre may have been influenced by Husserl's technical usage is suggested by his going on in *Words* to describe the engravings as "bodies."

If we did not take the terminological debt into account, we would miss some of the force of "in person." This terminology (or "present in person") is often used by Husserl to draw the contrast between perception and imagination, as in the following description in his lectures on the imagination: "Perception we characterize as an act in which an object appears as in *its own person,* as present itself. In the case of the imagination, the object does of course appear itself. . . . But it appears not as presented but only as re-presented; it appears as if it were there; it appears to us *in an image.*"[19] Sartre sometimes retains this recurrent contrast in Husserl. Recall when we were confronted with the portrait:

> Charles VIII, who has disappeared, is there, present before us, whom we see, not the painting, and yet we posit him as not being there: we can reach him only "in an image," by the intermediary of the painting.[20]

Are Sartre's quotes implicitly an admission that "in an image" is a somewhat awkward technical expression taken over from Husserl? I am raising here the same question that I raised with *en personne.*

Ambiguity

My concern is not with Sartre's terminological debt to Husserl itself but with the implications it acquires in Sartre. In the passage I have quoted,

Sartre may be playing up an ambiguity by violating the recurrent contrast in Husserl between a perceived object ("an object" that "appears as in its own person, as present itself") and an imagined object (that "appears to us in an image"). He is certainly violating the limits of a phenomenological analysis as an analysis in Husserl of what "appears" to consciousness, for Sartre is stepping outside this analysis with a vulgarizing resort to the colloquial sense in which someone who is dead has "disappeared" from the real world.

There is a similar ambiguity between a colloquial meaning and a vulgarized technical meaning in the passage in *Words*. Once the terminology "in person" has been understood colloquially, Sartre can again be understood as if he were only being colloquial when he announces, "Men and animals were there *in person*." In Husserl, they would not be there "in person" but only "in an image." With the violation of this distinction, a certain philosophical *stiffening* is lent to Sartre's pointing up the delusion involved when he came to believe as a child in salvation by art.

I shall consider this delusion in my next chapter. But the rest of Sartre's announcement needs to be taken into account too. Sartre treats the "person" in question as if he were composed of a "body" and a "soul." I requote: "Men and animals were there *in person; the engravings were their bodies; the text was their soul.*" The idiom is familiar. In Sartre's analysis of the impersonation, as we watch Franconay, "The affective meaning . . . actualizes the synthetic unification of the different signs, animates their rigid aridity, gives them life." I pointed out earlier that the technical terminology here originally derived from Aristotle's *De anima,* in which the soul "actualizes," "animates," gives "life" to the body. This idiom Husserl had extended to the way in which an intention "animates" (*beseelt*) with meaning the physical sign (the word heard or seen). Sartre may be taking advantage of this extension to go on to characterize the text as endowing with meaning the engraving as a physical image. But there is a difference between Sartre's and Husserl's use of this idiom. In Husserl words as signs expressing meanings enjoy a certain priority, since his is an analysis "directed by general logical interests."[21] But in *Words,* words become precarious (as "souls" also do) and need embodiment to be there "in person." The ambiguity between Sartre's and Husserl's analysis, to which Sartre is indebted, as well as the ambiguity between colloquial and technical usage, may contribute to the general malaise in *Words,* where words are not to be counted on as the instruments of salvation.

Dealing with a literary work, it is hard to pin down such philosophical ambiguities. We need to return to *L'imaginaire* and seek some light there on a problem Sartre faced in writing literary works.

TWENTY-ONE

A Moral Theory

I strove to descend: I had to put on shoes of lead.—Sartre

Zigzag

Summoning up Husserl's usage did not yield the full force in *Words* of "in person." To the extent that Sartre adopted Husserl's usage, he was being ironically ambiguous. The child who imagined that "men and animals were there, *in person*" was deluded; they were not there. Sartre may have italicized "in person" in order to stress the delusion. In any case, Sartre is transforming Husserl in somewhat the same way that he did when what had been in Husserl a philosophical "error"— "the image theory"—became in Sartre "the illusion of immanence" to which all mankind are prone.[1] In fact, the child's delusion is a specimen of what I have already called Sartre's moralizing version of this illusion.

Sartre's use or misuse of Husserl's terminology may seem a trivial matter, but larger issues are at stake than were apparent when we first encountered this illusion. To appreciate their scope, we have to postpone until Chapter 22 further dealing with the *interplay* between the verbal and the visual and return to *L'imaginaire*. A continuity I have relied on between *L'imaginaire* and *Words* is that Sartre would discredit the imaginary in much the same way as he would discredit words. But I broke off dealing with *L'imaginaire* because I had reached a juncture where it was not possible to appreciate adequately Sartre's next step there—a criticism of Husserl—unless I first considered *Melancholia* and

Words. If it is necessary to zigzag between Husserl and Sartre, as I have been doing, to get at the larger implications of Sartre's treatment of the image, it is also necessary, even though this treatment is philosophical, to zigzag between *L'imaginaire* and his literary works. I mentioned before that too often the interpreter of Sartre's philosophy resorts to his literary works as if they provided only a simpler, more popular version of his philosophy. In fact, the affiliation of his philosophy with literary works has to be taken into account to understand fully his philosophy itself.

The Shift in Subject

With respect to Sartre's philosophical treatment of the imagination, I accepted as a "starting point" the "distinction" he found in Husserl's handling of the Dürer engraving "between the image and perception." It was, Sartre complained, a "distinction Husserl had not pushed further in his published works." We watched Sartre push it further into an opposition, and this effort reached a climax at the stage of the impersonation. Before examining the next step, I would anticipate the final push in *L'imaginaire.*[2] Husserl's phenomenological distinction between the image and perception finally becomes in Sartre an opposition that is pivotal to "a moral theory." I am borrowing the rubric that Sartre uses in his wartime journal to cover the doctrine of salvation by art, and I am extending its coverage to his critique of this moral theory. To oppose a moral theory is to institute a moral theory.

Sartre's opposing moral theory emerges in *L'imaginaire* with a shift in *subject* that takes place in the final chapter, which precedes the conclusion and which is entitled "The Imaginary Life." The way in which his phenomenology annexes moral implications is illustrated in the following passage:

> To prefer the imaginary to the real is not only to prefer to a mediocre present a richness, a beauty, a splendor that are imaginary, in spite of the fact they are unreal. It is also to adopt feelings and behavior that are imaginary *because* they are imaginary. It is not this or that image alone that is chosen but the imaginary state with all its implications. It is not just an escape from features of reality (poverty, frustrated love, failure of our undertakings, etc.) that is sought but the form itself of reality, its character of *presence,* the responsiveness it demands of us, the subordination of our actions to their object, the inexhaustibility of our perceptions.[3]

The shift in *subject* is initially reflexive (from the imaginary object to our "feelings and behavior"), but it is also a shift in *level* ("not this or that image alone"), which is reminiscent of Husserl's eidetic reduction.

The difference is that Husserl's eidetic reduction distinguishes the essential traits of perception or of imagination, but Sartre's moral theory expands the distinction into a sustained opposition between them. He employs as an example my consciousness of someone: "I wanted Annie to come, but the Annie I desired was only the correlative of my desires. Here she is, but she overflows my desire on all sides; I must begin my apprenticeship all over again." [4] Moral implications have been acquired by Husserl's phenomenological distinction between an object "in an image" and an object perceived "in person." So long as I was imagining Annie, the phenomenon of quasi observation prevailed and could be subordinated to my desires; now that I see her again, my perceptions are inexhaustible, since a perceived object in Husserl has further "aspects" that are still to be perceived.

Here Sartre is again stepping outside the limits of Husserl's phenomenological analysis: what is in question is not simply an object I am conscious of perceiving as present but the "presence" of reality itself.

The Lurch

Now that we have seen how far Sartre himself will push the distinction between imagination and perception, we are able to reassess the lurch that takes place in Sartre's relation to Husserl when Sartre reaches the impersonation. This example enables Sartre to derive a criticism of Husserl from the opposition that emerges between the traits of the Franconay I perceive and the Chevalier I imagine. Sartre's criticism is of Husserl's conception of the imagination as involving "fulfillment." It is the only vehement criticism of Husserl in *L'imaginaire*. Sartre finds Husserl's conception "shocking." [5] Sartre is not usually shocked by the errors of philosophers, unless those errors have moral or (later in his career) political implications.

I have already paraphrased, as Sartre himself does, Husserl's analysis of fulfillment in the *Logical Investigations,* where Husserl distinguished between an "in-tention" in the sense that it is merely an "aiming" at its object as a target (I hear or read the words, "There's a blackbird," and I grasp their meaning) and an "in-tention" in the sense that it is an actual "hitting" of the target (I see or imagine the blackbird) and the "empty" meaning-reference is "fulfilled"—"filled" with "intuitive content."

Husserl takes up the distinction again in *Ideas I:* "Givenness [to consciousness] must not be understood . . . [solely] as perceptual. We do not identify what is *given as itself* with what is . . . *given in person.*" He goes on to point out that "anything objectively presented . . . is given in the presentation [*Vorstellung*]." [6] Thus anything presented "in an image" is "given as itself."

When Sartre finds Husserl's conception of imaginative fulfillment "shocking," he has in mind the distinction between imagination and perception becoming merely a difference in degree, as in the following passage in Husserl: "However far an imaginative presentation may lag behind its object [as perception could present it to us] . . . , it makes the object really presented [*wirklich vorstellig*] to us."[7] Here Sartre would consider that Husserl fails to sustain the opposition, which Sartre himself would sustain, between imagination and perception. In Sartre, instead of making "the object really presented to us," the imagination furnishes us with the illusion of the object's presence. What is there "in an image" is precisely not "given as itself" any more than it is there "in person," though this is what the deluded child of *Words* believes, contemplating image and text in the encyclopedia and coming to believe in salvation by art and literature. In *Melancholia,* Sartre had similarly ironized at the expense of the Autodidact, for whom the encyclopedia that he was spending his life reading in the library "took [as it did for the child] the place of the whole universe."[8] In *Words,* Sartre is ironizing at his own expense. His belief there in salvation is comparable with the moralistic version of "the illusion of immanence"—the illusion that images are within our reach. Recall the example of that hated face, which I imagine beating to a bloody pulp.

How saddled Sartre still is by Husserl's terminology (by virtue of what I have described as Sartre's tendency to "academicization"), even when he is rejecting Husserl, is illustrated by Sartre's retaining Husserl's characterization of the reference of the sign as "empty" (that is, as intuitively unfulfilled) and extending this characterization to the reference of the image. Sartre seems to admit he is using a technical term when he italicizes his description of the imaginary object as "empty" (*du vide*),[9] but in Husserl himself it was only the sign, not the imagination, whose reference is "empty." Sartre's extension of the emptiness of the sign to the imagination itself strengthens the continuity I have already found between his moralizing critique of words in *Words* and his moralizing critique of the imaginary in *L'imaginaire*.

Vulgarization

Here, too, I am not concerned with Sartre's terminological debt to Husserl except insofar as it yields clues that enable me to relate what is happening philosophically in Sartre to Husserl's phenomenology. In Husserl's use of the term "empty" for the reference of a sign, there was no disparagement. In fact, we have seen that the sign comes to the fore in Husserl's *Logical Investigations* because of its importance for a philosophy "directed by general logical interests."[10] This logical direction receives a further illustration from the way in which words as signs are assigned logical meanings. The now pertinent instance is the way in which an eidetic reduction renders the words "empty" and "fulfilled" technical terms by eliminating the experiences to which they colloquially apply. Thus he explains that *Erfüllung* ("fulfillment") must be taken to cover the opposite case of *Entäuschung* ("frustration" or "disappointment")—the phenomenologically idiosyncratic (*eigentümliche*) situation in which "the intended unity [of reference] is frustrated in intuitive disunity." (An example would be my seeing something in the half-light as a tree turning out instead to be a man.) Husserl's treatment of this situation as "idiosyncratic" suggests how idiosyncratic he would find Sartre's example of the experience of the impersonation. But the point Husserl himself is making is that both the terms "fulfillment" and "frustration," as used colloquially, imply some affective state, usually with some moral implications. But these implications are essentially irrelevant to perception or imagination as Husserl treats them.[11]

Sartre's relapse, in using Husserl's technical terminology, into the colloquial is a succinct illustration of the revulgarization attendant upon Sartre's return from the abstract outcome of Husserl's eidetic reduction "toward the concrete." This has been more strikingly illustrated by Sartre's moralization of the opposition between perceiving the real and imagining the unreal, wherein perception and imagination become general attitudes between which we have to choose. A phenomenological theory thereby becomes a moral theory. However, I am at present not concerned with this premonition of Sartre's later existentialist philosophy.

Husserl regards language itself as fashioned by our ordinary experiences, interpreted within the perspective of "the natural attitude." Accordingly, it has to be rectified to apply to the essential and transcendental experiences that emerge when the reductions lead us back from these ordinary experiences. Even if terminology cannot be purified completely, this is not completely disastrous phenomenologically. For phenomenology relies ultimately on essential and transcendental experiences, not on their linguistic expression.[12] There is always a risk though—especially when the phenomenologist would communicate purified experiences, since he then has to resort to linguistic expressions. Husserl would view Sartre as having been mislead by the colloquial use of the expressions "fulfillment" and "frustration." As an illustration, Husserl could point to a passage in *L'imaginaire* in which Sartre lines up a sequence in which the illusion of "fulfillment" (grafted, in effect, onto the "illusion of immanence") is followed by "frustration": "the object we imagine cannot fulfill our desires." Instead, it "is a way of deceiving our desires for a moment, only to aggravate them later, rather like the effect of seawater on thirst."[13] Similarly, when Sartre describes the imaginary object as "empty," he is not simply describing the cognitive experience (for which Husserl reserved the term "empty" when the experience was without "intuitive content") but is also resuming colloquial usage that may include a reference to the experience of unsatisfied desire. The "emptiness" of words as signs is (as I suggested in the last chapter) a moral predicament for Sartre, which it is not for Husserl, whose analysis is "directed by general logical interests."

Idealism

While pursuing the consequences of what Sartre is doing to Husserl's phenomenology by weakening the distinctions of level Husserl would maintain by his reductions, we have lost sight of what Sartre himself considers he is accomplishing. This becomes clearer in certain respects when we go on from the prewar works, which were written while Husserl was still Sartre's "master," to *Words*.

Originally I went on to *Words* because Sartre is committed in *Melancholia* to the prospect of salvation by art, and his conversion is actually traced in *Words*. Although there is no reference to Husserl or philosophy in *Words*, there is one passage that might be read as an allusion. I am picking up on Sartre's perennial theme of liberation, which we initially encountered when he relied on intentional reference to a transcendent object to liberate himself from the French academic "philosophy of immanence." In *L'imaginaire*, Sartre is committed to Husserl and has not yet discovered that Husserl's own commitment to essences is idealism. Nor did Sartre regard himself as an idealist then, though he indeed came to regard himself as one in his later retrospect in *Words*, where he traces in effect a double liberation—from the theological doctrine of salvation by literature and from the philosophical doctrine of idealism.

Perhaps we should rather speak of a single liberation, for Sartre explains his liberation from both in the same breath. I quote more fully than before pieces of this explanation:

> The Larousse Encyclopedia took the place for me of the universe . . . Men and animals were there *in person:* the engravings were their bodies; the text was their soul. . . . Platonist by my station in life, . . . I found more reality in the idea than in the thing. . . . It is in books that I encountered the universe. Hence, that idealism that I have put in thirty years liberating myself from.[14]

Of course, "idealism" here is used in so loose a sense that it would apply to almost any belief in the efficacy of words, to any bookishness.

Sartre's idealism is described in terms of a distinction of level, and his liberation from it in terms of a shift in *level:*

> Everyone has his natural place. . . . Mine is a sixth floor in Paris. The flat ground used to overwhelm me. . . . I reascend to my symbolic sixth floor, I breathed again the rarified air of literature. The universe spreads itself at my feet, and everything humbly solicited a name. Giving it was at once to create it and take possession of it. Without this supreme illusion, I would never have written. . . . I wanted to live in the ether among the airy simulacra of Things. Later . . . I strove to descend: I had to put on shoes of lead.[15]

I doubt if the reference to "Things" (even capitalized) is anything as specific as an echo of Husserl's principle "to the things themselves." It might similarly be stretching a point to pit Sartre's effort to descend to a lower level—"toward the concrete"—in opposition to the effort to ascend to a higher level that is Husserl's eidetic reduction.

What inhibits such a comparison is the difference between literary expressions (the "sixth floor," "simulacra," the "shoes of lead"), on the one hand, and "the technical language that must be employed [in philosophy]" and that explains why "philosophy cannot be expressed in literature."[16]

Although at the end of *Words* Sartre renounces "the impossible Salvation,"[17] the words continue to flow, his commitment to literature continues—or, at least, his *acharnement à écrire.* Thus the problem of literary expression survives his loss of faith in *Words,* as it did in *Melancholia.* Indeed, he characterizes *Words* as a "contestation of literature by literature itself." For "that book I wanted it to be a farewell to literature that would be finely written [*en bel écrit*]."[18]

To write this way poses distinctively literary problems. The farewell to literature takes place within a moral theory an older Sartre opposes to the implicit moral theory of his youth, when he flourished the aesthetic attitude: "A moral theory, what stupidity! . . . Your real objective, it is the book, the painting, the statue that will emerge under your fingers."[19] But now Sartre is setting up another opposition: he would say farewell to literature in the most literary of his literary works, *Words.* The literary problems Sartre accordingly faces he could hardly resolve without benefit of what amounts to an aesthetic theory.

FIVE · AN AESTHETIC
THEORY

TWENTY-TWO

Presenting an Object

*I would like to have an aesthetics where the
literary art would have its place, but in its
relation to the other arts.—Sartre*

Reading

Sartre's theorizing about literary expression
is not very probing, but statements in his
philosophical works can be eked out by in-
terviews. In *L'imaginaire,* Sartre deals phenomenologically with the experience of reading—with what is immediately given to the
consciousness of the reader as he reads. The
experience is again dealt with in *Words:* the
first part is taken up with his "Reading" as a
child, which is adduced to explain the emergence of his commitment, in the second part,
to "Writing."

The phenomenological question I would
raise is, How do words function for the
reader of a literary work as opposed to a
philosophical (or, at any rate, nonliterary)
work? For we felt inhibited in making this
comparison when we found Sartre conveying
his philosophical "idealism" in *Words* as the
point of view he attained from the sixth floor
of an apartment house. As it happens, an
apartment house also turns up in *L'imaginaire* in an example Sartre offers to substan-
tiate the following claim: "The sentences of a
novel are saturated with imaginative knowledge; they are not simply *significations* [that
is, meanings conveyed by words functioning
merely as signs]." There is a difference, he argues, between reading in a bureaucratic report the reference to "The Syndicate of
Apartment House Landlords" and reading
the reference in a novel, "He hurriedly went

down the three flights of stairs of the apartment house." In the second case, "I am thinking of the meaning [of the reference] in the fashion of things [à la façon des choses]."[1] Let me expound this second case on Sartre's behalf: understanding what this sentence means, as one reads it, involves in some measure summoning up imaginative knowledge gleaned from previous experiences one has oneself had of hurrying down flights of stairs in apartment houses. Quasi observation is brought into play, much as it is when I watch Franconay and "see" what I already know about Chevalier.

If I was inhibited from comparing the passage I cited from Words on Sartre's "idealism" with the idealistic philosophy Husserl had reached at the eidetic (and transcendental) level, it was because Sartre in this passage visualized his "idealism" à la façon des choses: the higher level becomes the point of view from the sixth floor, essences become "simulacra," and Sartre has to put on "shoes of lead," such as a diver wears, in order to strive downward, in opposition to his upward buoyancy as an idealist.

Imaginative Knowledge

A similar distinction has to be drawn between nonliterary and literary language when the nonliterary language is practical in its bearing. Reconsider the example we had of a sign as opposed to an "image-portrait." On the one hand, the placard Office was simply a sign: "I read the word on the placard, and I . . . know that I must enter the office to make my claim." Once I have gained this knowledge, "the meaning [signification] conveyed by the sign never returns to it." My reading retains no "intuitive content." On the other hand, "intentionality returns continually to the image-portrait," as I perceive successive "aspects" that I can identify with the person portrayed. I am thereby gaining imaginative knowledge of Charles VIII: "these sinuous and sensual lips, this narrow, stubborn forehead," and so forth.[2]

The title Melancholia likewise differs from Office. It not only establishes a correlation between what the novel is about and what the engraving is about, but as a title it also refers to the novel as a whole,[3] so (if we are aware of the correlation) we keep returning to the possibly relevant "aspects" of the engraving, as we read the novel, until at the end the protagonist is more or less reliably identified with the hunched figure furnished by the engraving.

There is a certain similarity too between the situation of the reader of Melancholia and the situation of the spectator of the impersonation. We would be pressing that similarity too far if we concluded, at least by the end of the novel, that Sartre's protagonist is impersonating the figure in the engraving. But it can be urged that the title initially functions for the reader simply as a sign, comparable to the hat that the impersonator puts on: "The straw hat is at first a simple sign. . . . I do not perceive the hat of Chevaliar *via* the straw hat, but it refers to Chevalier. . . . To decipher the sign is to produce the concept 'Chevalier.'" At the same time, a transition from this conceptual knowledge is induced by "the affective meaning" that Chevalier has previously acquired from our previous response to him "in person," so that the image "Chevalier" is eventually constituted. The affective meaning that *Melancholia I* had previously acquired for the reader (to the extent that he, like Sartre, has been responsive to the engraving, the title itself functioning as Sartre's invitation to be responsive) could similarly contribute to our identification of the protagonist of the novel. But the identification is much less likely to come off in that the title *Melancholia* may well remain almost entirely a sign. Indeed, if an affective identification were more feasible, one would have expected Sartre to have demanded that the novel's original title be reinstated, once he became famous enough to override the publisher who had rejected it.

Intuitive Content

We miss the point of the title, however, unless we take into account Sartre's analysis in *L'imaginaire,* where there is an important difference between the visual experience of looking at an engraving (or watching an impersonation) and the verbal experience of reading. This is one of those instances when considering the relation between a philosopher and a predecessor can yield a clue about what the successor is up to. We have seen that Sartre takes over Husserl's conviction that signs, as compared with perceptions, are "empty" of intuitive content. Since Husserl's *Logical Investigations* were "directed by general logical interests,"[4] signs came to the fore in the first investigation by virtue of their "emptiness." In Sartre, signs were initially peripheral and came up for consideration only when he opposed the sign to the portrait. But they later could become significant in the impersonation, for certain signs can trigger an affective reaction, which "animates their rigid aridity." Thus the reader might react to the title *Melancholia* in a fashion more or less similar to his reaction to the straw hat Franconay puts on and tilts.

But, as we have already noted, Sartre, in opposition to Husserl, also attributes "emptiness" of intuitive content to mental images. Like signs, they are not "fulfilling," and their "emptiness" can be frustrating. Sartre faces the problem of writing in such a way as to encourage in his reader the illusion (which he denounces as a moralist) that mental images are fulfilling; by achieving at times the rapprochement of mental with physical images, Sartre encourages the reader to deploy (with quasi observation) the imaginative knowledge he has gained from having previously observed these (or similar) physical images, thereby inducing an affective reaction. This must have been the solicitation intended by the title *Melancholia* and by the references in the novel to engravings, statues, and paintings.

The general philosophical relevance of these references is suggested by a late pronouncement of Sartre's: "I would like to have an aesthetics where the literary art would have its place, but in its relation to the other arts, for essentially literature says what it has to say by signs and comes into aesthetics only in this one way; in contrast, the other arts create a certain way of presenting an object." [5]

Observe that Sartre says, "I would like to have an aesthetics." He does not pretend actually to have an aesthetics. Even though he offered this pronouncement late in a career in which his philosophical output had been voluminous, he had hardly advanced very far toward an aesthetics, considering that he had as a young man written Simone Jollivet, "I have started a complicated theory . . . on the role of the image with the artist, and it will be very fine. Then perhaps, when it will be finished, I shall have a complete aesthetics." [6] At the beginning of the chapter he added to *L'imaginaire* (and he had added it only because it had been requested), he frankly admitted, "I will not treat here the problem of the work of art as a whole." [7] There would seem to have been ample opportunity in the intervening years for him to have equipped himself with an aesthetics.

Sartre's not having done so is a reminder that he is only secondarily a philosopher—particularly, perhaps, when his literary undertakings are in question. [8] In consequence, I have to take some philosophical initiative myself. But his late statement does highlight one specific feature of this aesthetics that he did not have in mind when he wrote to Simone Jollivet and that provides another illustration of how Sartre could become more precise once he had read Husserl: in Sartre, the literary art comes into aesthetics in a way that is deficient—we have gleaned this from Sartre's having taken over Husserl's conception of the verbal sign as empty.

However, this emptiness is not in Husserl the deficiency it becomes in Sartre, especially when he extends it to the mental image as well. The remedy for this emptiness is also Sartre's own: his literary art, taking its place in aesthetics in relation to other arts, exhibits what I have called the "relational" character of his philosophy. The remedial relation here is the rapprochement on which he pounced as a "starting point" in Husserl's handling of the Dürer engraving—the rapprochement between a mental image and a physical image. His singling out of the visual arts suggests how the deficiency of the literary art is to be compensated for, by emulating their way of "presenting an object."

L'Amorce

If we regard Sartre, as he regards himself, as primarily a writer, then we may now have new light on this "starting point." Since I earlier indulged in some minor quibbles over Sartre's translation of this passage from Husserl, I should perhaps also quibble over my own translation from Sartre. "Starting point" is an adequate translation for the *à l'origine de* in the appraisal with which Sartre follows his translation—"This text can be a starting point for an *intrinsic* distinction between the image and perception." [9] But I should now perhaps admit in retrospect my qualms about using the same humdrum translation for *l'amorce* in the appraisal with which Sartre introduces the passage: "*L'amorce* of this rapprochement is found in a passage of *Ideas* that deserves to remain classic." With this accolade, Sartre exalts the passage to a significance that it did not enjoy in Husserl himself. It enjoys such significance in Sartre not only by virtue of the rapprochement he would achieve philosophically between mental and physical images but by virtue of the rapprochement (we are now recognizing) he would also achieve as a writer in order to present objects. I grant that *L'imaginaire* is a philosophical, not a literary, work; I grant that Sartre's statement that "there is always literary prose hidden in philosophy" [10] he made much later in his career. Yet I think there may be some justification for acknowledging the physical imagery embedded in *amorce,* since what is in question is the *amorce* of a rapprochement between mental and physical images.

Amorcer has the relatively abstract meaning "to start by putting in motion." But we can move toward the concrete with its other meanings, which present an array of objects. These include "to prime" (a pump), "to bait" (a hook), and so "to entice." These might serve to suggest how Sartre's thinking was initially put in motion, primed, enticed by the rapprochement between mental and physical images. But more pertinent to my own initial claim that in this passage Sartre opens up a passage way to reach his own phenomenology of the imagination is the use of *amorce* with regard to railway construction, where it applies to the "initial spur" [*tronçon*] of a way indicating future work to be undertaken.

I am not pretending that Sartre was explicitly aware of the physical images latent in *amorce,* only that it would have been appropriate for him at this juncture to use a word in which physical imagery was latent. Or, at least, it is appropriate for me to bring out objects that the word can present and thereby illustrate what is at stake in "thinking of the meaning [of a reference] *à la façon des choses.*"

It is particularly unlikely that Sartre was aware of *amorce* as applied in railway construction, for he thinks he is only following in "the way" that "Husserl opens up." [11] I should not, however, be accused of unconscionable Derridadaism. When we later examine some of "the future work" Sartre did undertake after *L'imaginaire,* we shall see how the way he began constructing there will branch out in a very different philosophical direction from Husserl. But since philosophy is a secondary undertaking with him, we need to linger first with his literary constructions, in order to see if they have any philosophical implications.

TWENTY-THREE

Le Travail du Style

Anxiety is never experienced as this or that confronting us.—Heidegger

The Phenomenological Novel

One reason Sartre is unlikely to have been explicitly aware of the physical images latent in *amorce* is that he is as deliberately indifferent to style when he writes philosophy as he is preoccupied with it when he writes a literary work. His assertion of this opposition illustrates one of the difficulties we have in dealing with the relation between his philosophy and his literary works: he is himself so determined to maintain the opposition between them that he has little to say about their relation.

Nevertheless, some use can be made of the way in which he maintains this opposition. On one occasion when he would maintain it, he explains that "when I write *Being and Nothingness* [that is, a philosophical work], it is merely to communicate thoughts by signs." We have already heard Sartre explain that "essentially literature says what it has to say by signs." [1] The "essentially" allows scope for something additional—for what he dubs *le travail du style*.

We have seen that signs are "empty" of intuitive content but that "the sentences of a novel are saturated with imaginative knowledge." [2] *Le travail du style* contributes to this saturation. We have seen that a further distinction has to be drawn. Since mental images are also "empty" of intuitive content, the illusion of "fulfillment" has to be induced by resort to physical images, which the reader can imagine he is observing, so that through quasi observation the imaginative knowledge can be activated with which the writer would muster an affective reaction.

My reader is stifling a protest: the rapprochement being credited here to *le travail du style* is a banality—most writers deploy references to physical images in order to solicit mental images. But my immediate concern is not with the originality or the adequacy of Sartre's account in general of *le travail du style,* any more than it has been with the originality or adequacy in general of Sartre's philosophy; it is with the relation of affiliation between his philosophy and his literary works. I have shown that in *L'imaginaire* his "starting point" was a rapprochement he thought he found in Husserl between a physical and a mental image. I am suggesting that, insofar as Sartre was "primarily a writer" and only "secondarily a philosopher," he sought that rapprochement philosophically because it was congenial to and helped shape his *travail du style* as a writer. This congeniality would have contributed little to this *travail* if the philosophical implications had not been more specific. But they *were* more specific, as we shall see when we examine the actual physical images he selected in the course of this *travail.* Indeed, as a result of the philosophical implications, his style did show a certain improvement, as compared with his juvenile style. This is a matter of some slight interest, since exposure to philosophy is often notoriously damaging to a literary style.

I can hardly be blamed for pursuing this argument since literary critics (including Sartre's *Pléiade* editors) have never flinched from characterizing *Melancholia* as a "phenomenological novel." But they have not always made very clear what this means. In particular, they have failed to recognize that there were two very different phenomenologies influencing Sartre—Husserl's and Heidegger's.

It is true that the term "phenomenological" gets bandied around by critics, as do most labels borrowed from philosophy. Sartre himself has not been responsive. Despite the fact that he was writing the novel during his afternoons in Berlin after having spent his mornings reading *Ideas I,* he himself has denied that his reading had any decisive influence on the novel. This denial is consistent with the opposition he would maintain between his philosophy and his literary works. But his *Pléiade* editors insist that "there must have been a certain osmosis between his work as a philosopher and the novel." [3] This biological metaphor seems to me rather an affront to the novel, in which such biological processes as digestion, procreation, and proliferation arouse the protagonist's nauseous disgust. Indeed, if *Melancholia* is a "phenomenological novel," osmosis should be recognized to be hardly congenial with phenomenology, given its insistence on what is available to consciousness.

My first step, then, is to restrict my own attention largely to that which Sartre is highly conscious of; his style is something he "works" over. But I also have a longer-run concern with an analogy between style and method. In working out this analogy in Volume 1, I was working against Sartre, and I now come up against the opposition he would himself maintain between his literary and his philosophical works. I am able to circumvent his opposition by demonstrating the extent to which his *travail du style* does bear the imprint of phenomenological method. At least it does in the one significant specimen of his style I shall select from *Nausea*.

However, I cannot embark on my demonstration without endorsing a warning from Sartre himself. In 1926, Simone Jollivet had complained that he was neither spontaneous or true. In his reply, Sartre makes a transition from his character to literary style: "My basic character is very mixed [*hétéroclite*]. . . . I don't write in my genre, . . . I continually change my style."[4] Sartre's style in *Nausea* is not homogeneous; but the specimen I single out for stylistic analysis is of particular significance.

Description

I have already quoted Sartre on the doctrine of salvation by art as "the starting point" (*le point de départ*) of the novel. He was referring to its "starting point" in the lofty sense of the presiding principle or premise— the prospect of salvation by art—on which his writing of the novel had been based, precluding his abandonment of it as he was finishing the novel. But perhaps a little of what Sartre attempts to accomplish by art, by *le travail du style* (and what he will continue to attempt even after he has lost his faith that this *travail* will assure his salvation), can be pinned down by taking as a sample the novel's actual starting point.

The novel itself provides some justification for singling out this starting point, which appears as a separate "Feuillet sans date" ("Undated Sheet of Paper"). As such, it does not quite belong to the narrative itself, which is composed of journal entries with some indication of when they were written. But the obvious intent of this separate sheet as *le point de départ* is to justify the keeping of the journal itself. I quote the first two sentences: "The thing to do would be to write what happens from day to day. To keep a journal to see clearly."

D'écrire ("to write") is homophonic with *décrire* ("to describe"),[5] and this suggests that the writer's purpose in keeping the journal is description, which is also the purpose of the phenomenologist. Moreover, the purpose of phenomenological description is "to see clearly." Husserl explicitly expounds his phenomenological method in *Ideas I* as "The

Method for Clarification [*Klärung*]," [6] and he regularly employs visual analogies to clarify what this clarification entails.

If Sartre's writing is phenomenological description, it will of course conform to his own conception of phenomenological description rather than to Husserl's. In fact, the differences to which we have been alerted between Sartre's and Husserl's method do help us appreciate what is going on in the "Feuillet." We have recognized that Sartre in his phenomenology broadens the scope of description beyond what was immediately given in Husserl. The criterion of immediate givenness is further broadened in the "Feuillet"; the criterion is stretched to embrace what is happening "from day to day"—*du jour en jour*—as the requirement that is to be met by keeping a *journal*. This is hardly surprising: immediate givenness doesn't allow much time for anything to happen.

Intentional Reference

As a result of this stretching, the comparison between method and style may seem hardly close enough to be promising. But we should remember that Sartre took intentionality to be methodologically fundamental to phenomenological description. Then what initially seems fundamental in the "Feuillet," and characteristic of Sartre's style, is his effort to follow out the intentional reference of consciousness by describing objects. In the fourth sentence, the writer issues himself the behest: "I must tell how I see this table, the street, people, my tobacco pouch, since it is that which has changed." We are reminded of the moment of Sartre's conversion to Husserl: "For years this had been his fervent wish—to speak of things, as he came into contact with them, and that this would be philosophy." [7] Only here it is literature.

The first item in Sartre's list may be a trivial link with Husserl, for Husserl describes in *Ideas I* how a table is seen. [8] Sartre, we recall, in the intentional analysis of *L'imaginaire* also starts off with examples that are the same as, or similar to, those employed by Husserl, but then he goes on to more complicated examples of his own, and the complications betray how his analysis is developing differently from Husserl's.

We must watch out for the complications here, too. One of these is the intrusion of an uncertainty with, "since it is that [*cela*] which has changed." To which of the miscellaneous objects listed does the singular "that" refer? Such uncertainty of reference is a threat to the method of following out intentional reference to the something it identifies by its very consciousness of it as something that remains identical throughout successive changes.

Uncertainty of reference is a trait of the experience of anxiety in Heidegger. In "What is Metaphysics?" the first work of Heidegger's to become available in French, "anxiety is never experienced as this or that confronting [*vor*] us." What *is* experienced is the "indeterminability" of any this or that—the essential impossibility of its receiving any determination." [9]

The pertinence of anxiety is confirmed when the writer refuses in the "Feuillet" to describe something that happened. He reports only, "The day before yesterday it was much more complicated." The complication can be traced to Heidegger, for the writer insists, "If I only knew what I was afraid of, I would have already made a great step forward." Anxiety in Heidegger is without any determinate object. But it is liable to be mistaken for fear, since I attempt to elude anxiety by supplying it with a determinate object, thereby reducing it to fear of something, so I can know what I am afraid of.[10]

Uncertainty of reference becomes in Heidegger a critique of the Cartesian criterion of certainty itself—a criterion that Husserl upheld and that Sartre himself carries over as the title of part 1 of *L'imaginaire*, the strictly phenomenological part. Perhaps it could be said that uncertainty of reference, which we are now encountering in this initial "Feuillet," where keeping a journal is justified, becomes in the longer run uncertainty as to what *Melancholia* refers to—to this journal itself or to the novel that the writer was unable to write because of his affliction with *Melancholia I.*

Nausea

The writer's initial difficulty becomes less to determine the objects of his reference than to get a grip on them, as he will admit in the first entry of the journal proper, where he has trouble with his pipe, his fork, a door handle—trouble which he later diagnoses as "nausea in the hands."

Since uncertainty of reference is a trait of the writer's experience deriving from anxiety in Heidegger, it suggests a shift in Sartre's allegiance from Husserl toward Heidegger. The diagnosis of this experience as "nausea in the hands" confirms this shift as a shift from the visual consciousness of something, which presided in the initial behest in the "Feuillet" "to see clearly," to the tactile experience, which comes to the fore in Heidegger. The writer in the "Feuillet" picks up a rock, which he would skip on the ocean. The rock is not an ob-ject, something confronting him (in the mode of *Vor-handenheit*), which Heidegger criticizes Husserl for taking as primary, but something that should be manipulable (in the mode of *Zu-handenheit*, which Heidegger distinguishes).[11] The tactile idiom in terms of which this distinction is drawn by Heidegger undercuts the visual idiom from which Husserl gains confidence in the immediacy with which the object of intentional reference is given. One takes hold of something in Heidegger in order to do something else with it, and the reference to the something else has to be followed out if one would determine what (to use Sartre's examples) a pipe, a fork, a door handle, is.[12]

However, I cannot leave the impression that to explicate the implications of "nausea in the hands," it is sufficient to discern a shift in Sartre's allegiance from Husserl to Heidegger. Even though nausea is a version of Heidegger's anxiety, it is Sartre's own version, and it is not only a tactile idiom but gustatory, though both touch and taste are experiences of contact. Some of the implications for Sartre emerge from what happens at the beginning and at the end of the episode with the rock. At the beginning, a transition is made, "Naturally I can no longer write anything clear regarding . . ." It is a different word that I have this time translated "clear." It is not *clair* as in the initial characterization of the writer's undertaking—"to keep a journal to see clearly." The writer, I have already suggested, could have drawn the idiom "to see clearly" from Husserl, who regularly exploits the visual analogy in characterizing the application of his phenomenological method as *Klärung,* and Sartre would have found the analogy congenial, since it brought with it the Cartesian methodological conviction that what the mind discovers to be "clear and distinct" is also "certain." But the word the writer now is using that I have translated "clear" is *net.* Its primary meaning is "clean." This shift in idiom introduces us to the impossibility of writing anything "clean" about something as "filthy" (*sal*) as the "mucky (*boueux*) rock that, at the end of the episode, the writer is unable to hold onto. He is contaminated by its filth; he cannot clearly distinguish the nauseous revulsion he feels from what is sticking to his hands. The larger significance of this shift from Husserl's idiom will become evident only when I return to Husserl's characterization of *Klärung* in my Conclusion.

The filthy rock also sets the stage for the locale of the novel, Bouville, where the local notables are stuck in the muck (the *bou*) of being bourgeois.[13] I have already mentioned that the writer will eventually denounce them as *salauds* when he visits the museum gallery and discovers how their progenitors were saved from the contingent, shapeless, muckiness of living—saved by art's having given shape to their lives once they were dead.[14]

Une Défaite

The style is still the man, even though it is also the methodology Sartre put together from Husserl and Heidegger. Indeed, I am not claiming that

Sartre's undertaking in this "Feuillet" is simply to reconcile Husserl and Heidegger. (I did not even claim in Volume 1 that *Being and Nothingness* is simply their reconciliation.) I have already quoted the passage, singled out in *"Une défaite"* by the editors as a "meditation on objects," that "announces developments that take place later in *Nausea* and in Sartre's philosophical work, and it precedes—we would underscore—his discovery of phenomenology."[15] I would also underscore that what survives this discovery, as indisputably a feature of Sartre's own phenomenology, is a feeling for filthiness (*saleté*). The "lamentable Frédéric"

> approached a garbage pail and contemplated it with passion. A little ugly odor of earth, of peelings, of dampness arose. He breathed it in affectedly [*précieusement*]. He rummaged its contents with his look. He admired the stained, damp eggshells, the rotten carrots and a strange humus that was filthy brown. He was seized with a commotion, as he was each time he observed the existence of things. He thought vaguely: "It is then true that they exist."[16]

If there is marked improvement in Sartre's style in *Nausea*, it is partly due to his thinking of "the things themselves" having become less vague (as I proposed earlier) in a fashion that can in some measure be explained methodologically—by his following out reference to these things with the intentional reference he has taken over from Husserl. Thus Husserl does seem to have helped Sartre to trim the juvenile lushness and the (perhaps self-ironizing) *préciosité* of "the lamentable Frédéric." But Heidegger also seems to have come to Sartre's help. Heidegger's distinction between *Zuhandenheit* and *Vorhandenheit* may have encouraged Sartre to accord distinctive significance to tactile experiences and to avoid indulging in such awkward elisions as "he rummaged [*fouilla*] . . . with his look."

Another illustration of how Sartre seems to have been helped with respect to his style by Heidegger and Husserl is found in the first entry of the journal proper. Roquentin reports how "I felt in my hand a cold object that held my attention with a sort of personality." It was "the door handle." The tactile experience would seem to derive from Heidegger's *Zuhandenheit*, though the reversal from hold to held is a gimmick of Sartre's own style or method. But ascribing to the handle "a sort of personality" entails a colder, more effective self-assertion (by virtue of Sartre's taking literally Husserl's methodological commitment to what is immediately given as "present in person"—only the door handle refuses to give itself) than in the passage I requoted from *"Une défaite"* in which Frédéric would refute the traditional doctrine of secondary qualities— "the pedants" who think that "things" receive their "softness and warmth from our hands."

The Shift in Method

I return to the initial "Feuillet." When the writer is unable to hold onto the rock because of what is later diagnosed as "nausea in the hands," his experience may be a literalized version of Heidegger's anxiety, which is the experience that there "is nothing left to hold onto" when "anxiety oppresses us."[17] But what concerns us are the methodological implications of the writer's experiences in the "Feuillet." With the experience of anxiety, intentional analysis breaks down; it cannot handle anxiety, since there is no determinate object for intentional reference to be followed out to. When the writer recalls, "If I only knew what I was afraid of, it would be a great step forward," it would have been a great step forward because it would have been a reassuring return to normalcy; a specifiable object would have relieved the writer of his mood, and he would no longer suspect he is "crazy." If he could have been certain that all these changes have to do with objects, that his mood was fear of something, it would also have been a step forward in an intentional analysis. He would know what he was afraid of, whereas anxiety in Heidegger is "uncanny."

I am not suggesting that this breakdown of intentional analysis is a shift in method that derives uniquely from Heidegger, as if at this juncture Sartre's "style" becomes equatable with Heidegger's method. I don't believe Sartre ever became sensitive to Heidegger's method. What does happen at this juncture, at which Husserl's procedure of following out an intentional reference is thwarted (as it is in Heidegger's "What is Metaphysics?"),[18] is that the writer's consciousness has become dialectical in the rudimentary fashion with which we are already familiar from the relish with which Sartre lines up the opposing traits of Franconay-as-perceived over against Chevalier-as-imagined. Thus the writer's consciousness of the rock is no longer intentional—it is no longer consciousness of something whose identity is immediately given, however one-sidedly one is conscious of it *via* an *Abschattung*. Instead, the writer is conscious of the rock as ambiguous, two-sided—"flat, dry on all of one side, wet and mucky on the other." This dialectical ambiguity is distinctively Sartrean.

The Analogy

In my exposition so far of *le travail du style* in "presenting an object," it should be kept in mind that a style (as I previously indicated) is, typically, not distinguishable from the exigencies of content. Indeed, I explained that one reason I adopted the analogy was that conceptions of method have become so formalistic today as to be usually divorced from considerations of content (the object presented).

An obvious misgiving about this analogy—a misgiving that I have so far brushed aside—is that it apparently does not hold for Sartre himself. With it I am cutting across his distinction between his literary writings, in which he is much concerned with style, and his philosophical writings, in which he is indifferent to it. What can be recognized, however, is that this distinction itself is a by-product of his conversion to Husserl. I have agreed with Sartre's *Pléiade* editors that the "meditation on objects" in *"Une défaite"* "announces developments that take place later in *Nausea* and in Sartre's philosophical works" and that "it precedes . . . his discovery of phenomenology." Although they are themselves disregarding here his distinction between his literary and his philosophical works (as I also am), they do not take note of the fact that the distinction itself does not precede his discovery of phenomenology. *"Une défaite"* (and *La légende de la vérité,* *"Er l'Arménien"*—indeed, any of Sartre's longer juvenilia) is a jumble of the philosophical and the literary. The more recent philosophies by which Sartre was miscellaneously influenced prior to his discovery of phenomenology (Nietzsche, Alain, Bergson) were rather literary in character. None of them employs a technical language. When Sartre makes his claim that "philosophy cannot be expressed in literature," because of "the technical language that must be employed [in philosophy]," the distinction would seem the response of a literary writer to the technical language he encountered in Husserl and Heidegger. When Sartre's allegiance later shifts to Hegel and Marx, he is still responding to philosophers who were not literary and who employed a technical language. Since Sartre's drawing the distinction is the response of someone who was primarily a writer and only secondarily a philosopher, he was satisfied with what was philosophically a superficial distinction.

There are other reasons I have relied on in the analogy between method and style besides those I sketched in Volume 1 and my effort here in Volume 2 to overcome formalism. Questions of style are acceptably raised by art historians and literary critics, whereas the only generally acceptable question of method (when such questions are not dismissed as a "waste of time") is whether or not there is a distinctively philosophical method. The standard version of this old question presupposes that what philosophical method is to be distinguished from (or is not to be distinguished from) is scientific method. My contention is that we can no more speak of a distinctively philosophical method than we can of a distinctively literary or artistic style; there are different philosophical methods, just as there are different styles. And there cannot be any definitive vindication of any philosophical method any more than there can be of any style. In Sartre's case, his method is a mixture of methods, just as some styles are a mixture of styles—as Sartre's is in *Melancholia*.

Nevertheless, there are certain pervasive or at least recurrent traits of Sartre's style besides his methodological debt for intentional reference to Husserl, for the thwarting of intentional reference to Heidegger,[19] and his own resort then to dialectical opposites. To one of these I now turn.

TWENTY-FOUR

En Surcharge

I must tell how I see.—Sartre

Y

Melancholia remains a literary work, not philosophy. We should not press the analogy between a method and a style so far that we disregard this distinction, on which Sartre himself insists. There is another side of the initial ambiguity, *d'écrire/décrire*, still to be explored. The writer proposes "to keep a journal *pour y voir clair—*"to see clearly in it." The *y* is left untranslated in the English translation of the novel by Lloyd Alexander. But this one-letter word is crucial. It intrudes a distinction between writing and phenomenological description.

The phenomenologist relies on the immediacy with which something is given to consciousness. I can see the blackbird clearly without applying to it the word "blackbird," and I can describe it without even knowing it is a "blackbird." Phenomenological description in Husserl claims to describe prelinguistic experiences. The climax of *Melancholia,* the mystical vision of contingency in the public garden, will be a prelinguistic experience: "Things are freed from their names," and Roquentin is "alone, without words." [1]

This climax, however, is not the end of the novel. The end (if it is an end) of the novel (if it is a novel) will be the prospect of salvation by art from contingency, and this prospect will supervene with the writing of the novel itself. The *y* in *pour y voir clair* is the initial insinuation of this prospect.

The distinctive demands laid on the writer begin to emerge in the second paragraph of the "Feuillet." Its opening phrase "For example" seems stylistically rather abrupt. But it can be taken as indicating that phenomenological method is being applied, since it is a method that relies on examples. I quote the first three sentences of the second paragraph:

> For example, here is a cardboard box for my ink bottle.
> I should tell how I saw it *before* and how I now see it
>   Oh well it is a parallelepiped rectangle, it emerges
> from—it's silly, there is nothing to be said about it.

The selection of an ink bottle as an example could have been prompted by the "inkstand" that turns up in *Ideas I;* in the *Logical Investigations,* "I see a box." [2]

However, there is a difference between the writer and the philosopher. Compare the writer's situation here with the situation at the start of *L'imagination.* In the first sentence there, the philosopher is looking at a sheet of paper: "Je regarde cette feuille blanche, posée sur ma table." We visualize the writer of the journal as writing on a sheet of paper, for this preamble is entitled "Feuillet." And the writer is not just trying "to see clearly"; he explains, "I must tell how I see . . ."

The pairing of the ink bottle with its box makes explicit the ambiguity *d'écrire/décrire* in the first sentence of the first paragraph. As a simple geometric shape, the box can be compared with the example of the die, which Husserl describes in the *Cartesian Meditations* and which becomes a cube in *L'imaginaire.* [3] But a difference is that when Husserl selects this example, we recognize he is selecting a simple geometric shape; we do not think of him personally as a gambler, the way we are being made to think in *Melancholia* of the writer as writing.

The writer's effort to identify the box as a parallelepiped rectangle reminds us that Sartre, as a philosopher, had followed Husserl in preferring geometric examples when it was a question of exhibiting, as an essential trait of perception, that it is consciousness of something one-sidedly. "It is characteristic of perception," Sartre had concluded from the example of perceiving the cube "that the object appears only in a series of profiles or aspects [Husserl's *Abschattungen*]. . . . I always see it only in a certain way, which solicits and excludes at one and the same time an infinite number of other points of view." [4]

The writer's recognizing that he does not actually see the box as a parallelepiped rectangle is a philosophical recognition that his own point of view intrudes. This recognition is, of course, preparation for his moving on qua philosopher from trying to become conscious of something that remains identical through successive changes to becoming self-conscious—no longer certain that "all these changes have to do with objects," and anxious regarding his own identity.[5]

We have not yet reached this point in the second paragraph, however. There the writer's recognizing the intrusion of his point of view becomes his alarm over "the danger in keeping a journal: one exaggerates everything, one is on the lookout, one continually forces the truth." In Husserl, directing attention to the immediately given can ensure "seeing" clearly with an intentional analysis. But in Husserl *"Intention is not expectancy; it is not of its essence to be directed to future appearances,"* [6] whereas in *L'imaginaire* intention came to involve *attente*—"waiting for," "expectation," which can trespass on and distort what one sees and render an intentional analysis less reliably rigorous than Husserl assumed.

Words

These difficulties, which could pass as philosophical, are compounded by the trouble the writer is having with writing—with words. Sartre supplies editors whose footnote draws our attention to the fact that after the "it" in the second sentence "A word is left blank." The writer's difficulty may well derive from Heidegger's philosophical uncertainty in following out the intentional reference of his consciousness to an object. But we shall soon see it must also involve uncertainty about the right word to use. The writer admonishes himself: One must [blank] but note carefully. The term *noter* reproduces the ambiguity between a literary and a phenomenological procedure: it can mean "write down a note about" as well as "take note of," in the sense of "notice." That *Melancholia* is written down is stressed by its having editors who themselves provide notes. In the note they append to this blank that the writer has left, they explain: "A word is scratched out (perhaps 'force' or 'forge'); another, superimposed [*rajouté en surcharge*], is illegible." Again the writer must have had difficulty finding the right word. The hesitation of the editors between "force" and "forge" is not just hesitation in deciphering one letter but is a further drawing of attention to how the writer's point of view can intrude, in a fashion comparable to the way a point of view has just been acknowledged to intrude when one sees one-sidedly. "Force" would imply that the intrusion would do violence to the truth of his description; "forge" would imply a deliberate intent on his part to falsify, to fake it.

The implication of the fictionality of what is written, we are prepared for by the "Avertissement des Éditeurs" at the beginning of *Melancholia*. They explain, "These notebooks have been found among the papers of Antoine Roquentin." The explanation itself is ambiguous in its effect. For, as the editors of the *Pléiade* edition point out, "This procedure, which is intended to locate the story in *the real world,* has obviously here an ironic function, since it seems to the contemporary reader as actually admitting a fiction."[7] The device has become that trite a literary convention.

Ambiguity

In the manuscript, the editors had gone in their "Avertissement" to refer explicitly to "the notes that we have added in order to clarify a text that is often obscure."[8] Sartre scratched this sentence out. Presumably, its explicitness detracted from the ambiguity he wanted the notes to retain. Be this as it may, the note itself on the scratching out has a certain relevance to Sartre's own procedure as a writer. Consider the self-commentary he offers forty years later, when he can no longer see clearly enough to write. *Le travail du style* requires rereading, scratching out, and rewriting, inasmuch as it is

> above all a way of saying two or three things at once. There is the simple sentence, with its immediate meaning, and then, underneath, at the same time, different meanings. If one is incapable of rendering in language this plurality of meanings, writing is not worth the trouble.

Sartre's interviewer accordingly observes a distinction between "your philosophical manuscripts that are written . . . almost without scratchings out" and "your literary manuscripts, which in contrast are extremely worked over."[9]

We are familiar with one side of this contrast from Simone de Beauvoir's report on Sartre's writing *L'imaginaire:* "Not being detained by any concern with form, he wrote with extreme rapidity, breathless from following his thought with his pen." Sartre was not detained by *le travail du style*.

One feature of *le travail du style,* which Sartre endorses at the end of his career, is the literary procedure that was followed by the writer of the journal in *Melancholia.* In the "Feuillet" a word had been "scratched out" that offered us the alternative implications of "force" and "forge."[10] That a word was *rajouté en surcharge* implies that still another meaning was added, though it is "illegible." The writer was trying (to quote the interview forty years later) "to give each sentence multiple, superimposed meanings."

En surcharge itself is ambiguous. In the "Feuillet" *rajouté en surcharge* must mean literally "added above." But *en surcharge* can also imply an "overload." In the interview, Sartre explains (without any allusion to the "Feuillet," but elucidating *le travail du style*) that the writer should ask himself, "What can this collocation of words yield with their weight [*lourdeur*]?" For "there are words" that Sartre calls "loaded" [*chargés*] with meaning."[11] Thus when the writer of the journal collocates "force" and "forge," he is attempting to "add" not just more meanings but weight of meaning as well.

Sartre also has a lighter idiom that can be taken as applying to *le travail du style*. When the writer picks up the rock, it is because he has been watching "kids who were skipping stones [*jouaient aux ricochets*], and I wanted like them to throw a stone into the ocean." It may be merely a reminiscence here of Hegel's interpretation of art—of how "man as a free subject" attempts to "enjoy in the shape of things an external actualization of himself," just as "a boy throws stones into the river and now marvels at the circles in the water as an effect from which he gains an intuition of something as his own work."[12] There is a threat to Roquentin's freedom in his inability to hold onto the rock and throw it, and this threat prepares us at the journal's start for the anxiety of the writer at the book's end about his ability to write the novel, which by then has been analogized to the work of art. Even if there is no reminiscence of Hegel, the point of skipping a stone, the dictionary reminds us, is "so as to make it rebound as many times as possible before sinking." This is the kind of play with the weight of language in which the writer engages when he seeks "multiple . . . meanings." I would add that the ricocheting of meanings includes those which were originally philosophical.

Intentional Reference

Sartre's *Pléiade* editors have not only endorsed the usual characterization of *Melancholia* as "a phenomenological novel," but they have also announced, "It is most certainly in Berlin that Sartre became stylistically himself."[13] They are presumably thinking of the contrast between *Melancholia,* which he wrote afternoons in Berlin, and such earlier, unpublishable writings as "*Une défaite.*" But the editors do not explain why Sartre should have become stylistically himself in Berlin. They do not produce any evidence that it was promoted by any literary works he read there while he was working so intensively on *Nausea.*

I would hazard some connection between his becoming stylistically himself and his becoming philosophically himself as a disciple of Husserl. It was in Berlin that Sartre first discovered intentionality and wrote the essay on it as "A Fundamental Idea of Husserl's." I have tried to show the extent to which the "Feuillet" can be read as a phenomenological description, oriented initially by intentional reference to objects. Thus if Sartre claims some forty years later that "there is always literary prose hidden in a philosophy," it can also be claimed that in the literary prose of the "Feuillet" there is a philosophy hidden, which is recognizably Husserl's intentional reference, despite some forcing and forging on Sartre's part. Moreover, we have discovered an incipient shift in allegiance on Sartre's part from Husserl toward Heidegger. It has been discernible in the thwarting of intentional reference.

Granted these philosophical debts, why did Sartre not write a philosophical work? We have heard his admission that when he wrote the novel, he did not have "a solid enough idea [of nausea] to make a philosophical work out of it,"[14] and so he wrote a novel instead. I have extended the application of his admission: he did not have a solid enough idea of the relation between Husserl and Heidegger, from whose anxiety he derived the idea of nausea, to array them in the philosophical opposition that he will set up in *Being and Nothingness.* Yet we have recognized that he is already committed stylistically in the novel to oppositions (as he is philosophically in *L'imaginaire*) and, to this extent, to a rudimentary dialectic in which multiple meanings are arrayed against each other—the "clean" is opposed to the "filthy," and the "dry" to the "wet."

The Turn to the Object

What about the criterion of "solidity" itself? I have taken note of Sartre's predilection for "weight." When he admits he did not have "a solid enough idea [of nausea] to make a philosophical work out of it," he perhaps betrays an associated yearning for solidity. Indeed, nausea—as the experience of the contingent as sloppy, mucky, shapeless—would promote this yearning. In *Being and Nothingness,* consciousness as "empty," as a "nothingness," will yearn for the solidity of "being-in-itself." In *Melancholia,* the yearning for solidity is in some measure satisfied by following out intentional reference to its object. Husserl, in fact, had been credited with making a "turn to the object" (*Wende zum Gegenstand*) in the *Logical Investigations.*[15] When Sartre was converted to Husserl's principle "to the things themselves," he had conflated it with his own principle "toward the concrete," so that the "things" in question became physical things occupying space, whereas in Husserl they had been primarily "essences."

The yearning promoting the turn in Sartre was further frustrated not just by anxiety/nausea but by the mental image becoming in Sartre, as it had not been in Husserl, "empty" of intuitive content. Thus Sartre seeks a rapprochement between the mental image and the physical image that not only yields fulfillment when it is perceived but also can yield the illusion of fulfillment if imagining it is assisted by *le travail du style.*

Sartre has posed this problem of fulfillment in the literary presentation of objects through a comparison with their presentation in the visual arts. There he seems to have recognized that the physical images whose objectivity is most effectively presented are three-dimensional, solid. In fact, critics regularly comment on the frequency of statues in *Melancholia* and elsewhere in Sartre's literary writings.

It then has to be asked, What about Tintoretto, who is referred to in a passage I have already quoted from *Melancholia* and who seems to be Sartre's preferred artist? Sartre's interpretation of Tintoretto's style is pertinent. Commenting on "the weight of the body of Saint Mark" in the painting *Saint Mark Liberating a Slave*, Sartre explains that "Tintoretto's space is not a painter's, but a sculptor's: Tintoretto is a painter who paints with the spatial relations of the sculptor's."[16] Sartre means, of course, that the painting yields the illusion of three-dimensional relations. One respect in which Sartre is attracted by Tintoretto is that he compensates for the limitations of his two-dimensional genre, much as Sartre would for the limitations of his genre as communicating "essentially . . . by signs."

Sartre relies on the objectivity of statues in his philosophy as well as in his literary writings. When the intentional object in the phenomenology that Sartre derives from Husserl—the "something" that one is conscious "of"—is ontologized, with some assistance from Heidegger and Hegel, as being-in-itself (in the phenomenological ontology of *Being and Nothingness*), its solid objectivity, as what consciousness is conscious of lacking, can be rendered as that of a sculptured object. Consider the following description of suffering:

> What we call . . . "true" suffering . . . is the suffering which we read on the faces of others, or rather, in portraits, in the face of a statue, on a tragic mask. It is a suffering which has Being. It is presented to us as a compact, objective whole. . . . Each groan, each facial expression of the man who suffers aims at sculpturing a statue-in-itself of suffering.[17]

Observe that Husserl's idiom whereby intentional reference is an "aiming" survives, but in the phenomenological ontology the insufficiency of the sign, which "aims emptily" (*à vide*), and of the similarly "empty" mental image, becomes the insufficiency of consciousness as such. Thus there is a certain progression in Sartre that has been brought out by taking his relation to Husserl into account: in Husserl, signifying consciousness aims emptily; in *L'imaginaire*, imaginative consciousness also aims emptily; in *Being and Nothingness*, consciousness as a whole becomes empty. This final step Sartre cannot take entirely in relation to Husserl. He now needs the help of Heidegger's "nothingness." Later we shall watch him enlist Heidegger's help here in the "Conclusion" to *L'imaginaire*.

There is another fashion in which Sartre would compensate for the insufficiency of verbal signs and of any merely mental imagery. Though words function as signs—"that is, for the purpose of aiming at something besides themselves"—and though they aim emptily, they are "at the same time themselves objects, and to this extent they are "visible" or "audible." Thus another feature of *le travail du style* is to handle the word not merely as a sign but as a "physical object," comparable to the "colors a painter mixes on his palette or to something that a sculptor chisels."[18]

When the word is also audible (or imagined as audible when we read it), sound effects can be associated with the ricocheting of its meanings. Such effects Sartre illustrates as poetic ambiguity:

Florence is city and flower and woman, it is city-flower and city-woman and girl-flower all at once. And the strange object that emerges in this way possesses the liquidity of *fleuve*, the gentle tawny *ardeur* of *l'or* and finally abandons itself with *décence*, prolonging indefinitely, with the continuous weaking of the silent *e*, its reserved expansion.[19]

SIX · SHIFTS IN THE
AFFILIATE

TWENTY-FIVE

: *Playacting*

> *A hybrid state develops . . . that would be worth*
> *describing for its own sake.—Sartre*

The Focus

I argued in Volume 1 on behalf of a history
that focuses on the relations between philosophies.[1] Sartre's philosophy lent itself to this
focus and, thus, to working out some of the
problems the historian faces generally in
handling the relations between philosophies.
For the development of Sartre's philosophy
involved a succession of shifts in the relations
between it and other philosophies. Before
World War II he declared his allegiance to
Husserl; during the war his allegiance shifted
from Husserl to Heidegger; after the war it
shifted to Marxism, and he dismissed both
Husserl and Heidegger as "minor philosophers."[2]

Maintaining this focus on the relation
between a philosophy and other philosophies
might seem to spell neglect of the integrity of
that philosophy. It might even be suspected
that Sartre did not have very much in the way
of a philosophy that was his own. In fact, so
far I have hardly done much more than enu-
merate features of Sartre's philosophy that
could not be accounted for by his conversion
to Husserl (or to Heidegger). Premonitions
of these features could usually be found in
the preconversion juvenilia (for instance,
when "the lamentable Frédéric" was "thinking vaguely"), despite the presumption that
"nothing would enable one to predict that
Sartre would become 'Sartre.'" In this presumption "Sartre" himself seems to have
concurred by viewing "these texts of his

youth as those of a stranger he had known long ago" (see section *Une défaite* in Chapter 2). If I have not so far attempted to pull these features together and fit them to a structure that could be expounded as distinctively Sartre's own philosophy, it was because any pulling together of what he had himself been "thinking vaguely" might well seem so largely a result of his conversion to Husserl (or Heidegger).

When I interrupted my exposition of Sartre's philosophy of the image in *L'imaginaire* to take the shift in affiliation into account, I had reached with the impersonation a juncture at which the claim can be made that my focus on the relations between philosophers can help bring out what is distinctive of a philosophy. But my concern then was to delineate the shifts in *subject, level, method* and finally in *affiliation* that take place in Sartre's relation to Husserl and add up to an adequate analysis of how he breaks away from Husserl in *L'imaginaire*. The impersonation was an example that Sartre treated without citing Husserl (whom he had just cited in the preceding section), an example for which there was no precedent in Husserl, an example on which Sartre based his most vehement criticism of Husserl in *L'imaginaire*.

Now I would move my focus from Sartre's relation to Husserl to how the break in his relation to Husserl helps bring out a structure that is distinctive of Sartre's own philosophy. But I encounter a new problem with my handling so far of the shift in *affiliation*. Fortunately, its solution will advance my exposition of Sartre.

The new problem is that I cannot pretend that the novel is uniquely the affiliate of Sartre's philosophy; in doing so, I overlook the drama: Sartre gave up the novel as a genre in the 1950s, but he continued to write plays. Although *Nausea* has been categorized as a "phenomenological novel,"[3] Sartre has never been regarded as writing plays that are phenomenological.

This incongruity I can hardly dodge, considering the lengths to which I have gone to demonstrate that the "Feuillet" is indeed phenomenological. But it is an incongruity that can be dealt with by taking advantage of our recognition of how different Sartre's phenomenology in *L'imaginaire* is from Husserl's. Once again, the relevant difference emerged with the impersonation.

To appreciate this difference, however, we must take one more step. A reason I gave for turning from *L'imaginaire* to the novel *Nausea* was Sartre's failure to treat the work of art in *L'imaginaire* until he was specifically requested to do so. I explained that he could have assumed that he had already treated it in *Nausea,* which he was working on at the same time. But there is one genre Sartre does not treat in the novel but does treat in his later appended chapter, "The Work of Art," in *L'imaginaire*— "the art of the drama."

The Starting Point

In ferreting out the relevance of Sartre's plays to his philosophy, we can begin with how he treats "the art of the drama" in *L'imaginaire*. He starts off with the announcement, "It goes without saying that the actor who plays Hamlet makes use of himself, of his whole body, as an analogue of this imaginary character." [4] This may go without saying. But it is not how philosophers inevitably treat the drama in their aesthetic theories, and it suggests how idiosyncratic is Sartre's own treatment. It is this idiosyncrasy that betrays what Sartre is distinctively up to as a philosopher.

Once again a clue is the "starting point" Sartre found for the analysis of the image in Husserl's treatment of the physical image (the Dürer engraving) as an analogue enabling the spectator to have a mental image. Sartre's finding this starting point betrays his own philosophical commitment to an analysis of the image in which the work of art comes to the fore as a physical image. When in this analysis the climactic stage of the impersonation is reached, the physical image becomes the actor's "whole body" and is in motion.

Now we can see in retrospect that the impersonation is climactic not only by virtue of the opposition exhibited between what is perceived and what is to be imagined but also as a premonition of how Sartre conceives the art of the drama. It then seems no accident that Sartre in the appended chapter "The Work of Art" follows the same sequence as we saw him follow earlier from the portrait to the portrayal by the impersonator. In the appended chapter, he first revives the example of the portrait (the portrait of Charles VIII again, but supplemented by another painting) and then makes a transition to the drama with the example of the actor playing Hamlet.

My interest in the previous transition from the portrait to the portrayal by the impersonator was that Sartre was reaching an example that not only is climactic in his own analysis but also entails a break with Husserl. I pointed out that Husserl, in treating the imagination, relies on such examples as portraits and other paintings, photographs, busts, and wax figures. A whole body in movement does not attract his attention. I am now adding that with the portrayal by the impersonator, Sartre has almost arrived at the juncture at which he can treat the drama. In fact, he does refer to Franconay as an *actrice*.[5]

The Shift in Subject

However, in comparing the two junctures, we should not forget that the appended chapter was written later than the rest of *L'imaginaire*. We shall find that this chapter illustrates the beginning of the larger shift in *subject* that emerges in *Being and Nothingness*. But I am not satisfied with following out Sartre's *chronological* development. I would argue that this larger shift is an advance in a *dialectical* development, which should be anticipated now to appreciate more fully Sartre's treatment of the drama in the appended chapter.

Being and Nothingness is characterized by Sartre as "an eidetic analysis of bad faith"; bad faith is a phenomenon that Husserl never found it appropriate to treat. His generalization in the first of the *Logical Investigations,* "We shall always presume sincerity" suggests that he might find bad faith philosophically irrelevant.[6] Its irrelevance, though, is not just a whim of Husserl's. Rather, he is not equipped philosophically to analyze this phenomenon, at least not if it has the structure that it exhibits in Sartre's philosophy.

Alternatively put, Sartre's philosophy in *Being and Nothingness* is structured as an eidetic analysis of a certain kind of structure that Sartre himself characterizes as "metastable." This is one of the few technical terms in *Being and Nothingness* that is not taken over from another philosopher. It is a term in physics, and it is Sartre's own importation into philosophy. Though he does not himself flourish the term, it does pick out the distinctive kind of structure he is committed to analyzing. He explains its application: "bad faith" belongs to "the kind of mental structures" that are "precarious and liable to disintegrate." There is "an evanescence of bad faith, which . . . vacilates constantly between good faith and cynicism."[7]

Though the term "metastable" is not yet used, this structure has been illustrated by the climactic example in *L'imaginaire:*

> The face and body of the impersonator do not lose all of their individuality, but the expressive something, "Maurice Chevalier," nevertheless appears on this face, on this female body. A hybrid state develops, which is neither entirely perceptive nor entirely imaginative, that would be worth describing for its own sake. These unstable and transitory states are obviously what are most entertaining for the spectator in an impersonation.[8]

This structure is metastable in that it is a "hybrid state" that is "unstable and transitory," so that "sliding from the level of the image [of Chevalier] to that of perceiving [Franconay] usually occurs at one moment or another." The "meta" is applicable to the movement by which the perceptual evidence yielded by Franconay's performance is transcended to reach an image of Chevalier, until the image collapses and we slide back.

Sartre's claim should not be overlooked that the "hybrid state" produced by the impersonation "would be worth describing for its own sake." Presumably Sartre is admitting that his present description is only for the sake of advancing his analysis of the imagination, and I accordingly have brought out how it does contribute to this advance. Now I am proposing that the worth in question is demonstrated by the development of Sartre's own philosophy when he takes on in *Being and Nothingness* as a subject the kind of structure that is metastable.

The Shift in Method

Consistent with this structure is the method of its analysis. I commented earlier on how (if and when the impersonation does finally come off) dialectical *interplay* takes place between what is perceived and what is imagined. Comparable *interplay* takes place with bad faith—between the opposites "good faith" and "cynicism." The method that will exhibit such *interplay* differs from an eidetic analysis as conceived by Husserl. The essence (of intentional reference, of an act of perception, or of imagination, and so forth) emerges in Husserl as an invariant structure from a reduction; it is not a "hybrid state" or "unstable and transitory," and it does not "vacillate continually between opposites." Consciousness as analyzed by Husserl allows no leeway for "opposition, illusory appearance, being other [*Widerstreit, Schein, Anderssein*]." [9] When Husserl disdains such goings on, he may or may not be aware that they are fair game for a dialectical analysis, such as Sartre's of Franconay's performance.

The dialectical character of a method is usually evident in how the relation between opposites is handled. But the handling of this relation is itself a (higher-order) development, although it cannot be exhibited adequately except as actually applied to whatever subject is soliciting this development.

Nevertheless, there is some justification for anticipating the *direction* in which a dialectic is headed, as I have, when I jumped on from the climactic example in *L'imaginaire* to the metastable structure in *Being and Nothingness*—or, more generally, when I expounded in my *Starting Point* the more fully developed dialectical component in the method of *Being and Nothingness* before expounding in the present volume the more rudimentary dialectic in his transformation of phenomenological method in *L'imaginaire*.

In *Starting Point*, I generalized that any full-fledged phenomenon in Sartre belongs to the kind of structures that he defines as "metastable." It is a "contradictory composite," for example, and it can undergo a development in Sartre's analysis of it as "ambiguous, contradictory, and unstable"—that is, it first emerges as a phenomenon that is ambiguous, the ambiguity sharpens into an opposition or contradiction, and the contradiction renders the composite unstable. [10]

Reflexivity

The advance that "bad faith" involves (as a later stage in the development of Sartre's philosophy) over the mental state produced by the impersonation is an advance in reflexivity. I may in some very mild sense be deceived for a moment by Franconay's impersonation. But Sartre's analysis of the impersonation is an analysis of "what is going on in my mind" as a member of her audience, not of what is going on in her own mind. Franconay herself is unlikely to be deceived at all as to who she is or as to what she is about in the impersonation. In contrast, "bad faith" is a reflexive phenomenon, and the translation "self-deception" becomes more suitable for *mauvaise foi*.

In a later example in *L'imaginaire*, which I anticipated before in order to bring out the reflexive direction in which the analysis was going, Sartre could be watched making the transition to a reflexive phenomenon where I could be said to be indulging in self-deception. The imaginary object is "out of reach," as opposed to the real object I perceive. Sartre explains, "I cannot touch it, change its place," as I can a real object I perceive. "Or, rather, I can, but . . . unreally, but not using my own hands but phantom hands that administer unreal blows. . . . To act upon these unreal objects, I must double myself, make myself unreal."[11]

There is a similar transition in Sartre's handling of bad faith. *Mauvaise foi* in French, like "bad faith" in English, ordinarily carries a primary reference to interpersonal relations. When the liar deceives another person, Sartre explains in *Being and Nothingness*, he may vaunt his intention of telling her the truth ("I would never deceive you!"); his intention is "playacted, impersonated [*jouée, mimée*]"; it is "the intention of the character [*personnage*], which he is playing in the eyes of his questioner." Here "the lie does not involve the inner structure of his present consciousness." As opposed to such a lie to the other, to the effort to hide the truth from the other, is a "lie to myself," when it is "from myself that I am hiding the truth."[12]

Husserl, I have indicated, always presumed sincerity in his analysis. He never envisaged an intention being "playacted, impersonated." In his analysis, consciousness is straightforward in its intentional reference, for it is locked into this reference as "consciousness *of* something."

The Shift in Level

Before considering Sartre's introduction of the idioms of playacting and impersonation into his analysis of deceiving the other, we need to acknowledge that although Franconay is identified by Sartre as an "actress," the term *personnage* is not introduced with respect to the person she is impersonating, as it is in the case of deceiving the other. Sartre is, I would guess, still so much under the spell of Husserl's eidetic analysis that he retains Husserl's term "essence," while adding a qualification—"the essence, as it were, of Chevalier."

The qualification may be a tacit admission of the shift in *level* on which I commented earlier. I also noticed then that in *L'imagination* Sartre understood by the "essence" of the "sheet of paper" that is first perceived and then imagined "not only its structure but also its individuality." The implications of this shift in *level* vis-à-vis Husserl can now be spelled out more plausibly, for we are usually more likely to project on someone the affective meaning we find expressed by his individuality. One sheet of paper is unlikely to mean more to us than another—not much individuality is at stake.

In the case of the impersonation, however, the problem was that Franconay bore so little resemblance to Chevalier. In coping with this problem, Sartre was assisted by Bergson's recognition that "the sharp distinction between individual objects is a luxury of perception" that we usually get along without. But there is a more important factor contributing to a distinction—the heightened individuality that Chevalier has achieved such that Sartre is almost prepared to credit him with an "essence." If Chevalier were not a well-known performer, a star of stage and screen of some magnitude, Franconay could not bring off her own performance so that a star is reborn and we applaud her—"It really is him." It is not a person she is impersonating but a persona, a *personnage,* created by Chevalier's own repeated performances and by the recognition it has attained from audiences—recognition that includes as a prominent component their affective reaction.

If Franconay can play Chevalier's role, it is only because he has so often played it himself: it displays a degree of generality that has rendered it available for reenactment. The role player is likely to accord more general, more persistent significance to his role than to his own particular and transient activities. The role Chevalier plays might be characterized as that of a *cavalier.* How this pun may have contributed to his performance, Sartre does not take into account. The role might then be characterized in English as that of "ladies' man," granted that this characterization is now too tainted by the mores and talents of a bygone epoch when there were ladies as well as men. A dialectically entertaining feature of Franconay's performance (though this too is not noticed by Sartre) is the reversal, and attendant *interplay,* involved in a woman's playing a man's role that he had played in relation to women.

The Personnage

We are now able to insert Sartre's "art of the drama" in its place in the sequence I have traced from Franconay's performance to the playacting that goes on in *Being and Nothingness*. The example of this art was "the actor who plays Hamlet" and who therefore "makes use of himself, of his whole body, as an analogue of this imaginary character." The actor's making use of himself, we remember, marked an advance in reflexivity beyond the example of the impersonation, in that Sartre becomes concerned with what is going on, not in the consciousness of the audience, but in the consciousness of the actor himself.

Moreover, the opposition was no longer between the impersonator (plump, dark-haired, female) and the impersonated (tall, blond, male). It was posed instead in a fashion we are now better able to take into account—by "the famous paradox of the actor": on the one hand, "certain experts insist on the fact that the actor does not believe in his role [*personnage*]"; on the other hand, "others demonstrate that the actor is taken in [*pris au jeu*]—the victim in some sense of the hero he represents."

In his resolution of this opposition, Sartre concedes, with reference to the second claim, that "the actor may really cry, carried away by his role [*rôle*]." In taking this step, Sartre has lost interest in the actor's "whole body"; he is now concentrating on the tears, as pertinent to what is going on in the actor's consciousness. To the first claim, Sartre concedes, "these tears . . . the actor is himself conscious of them—and the audience with him—as the tears of Hamlet—that is, as analogues of unreal [imaginary] tears." The resolution here is reflexive: "It is the actor who renders himself unreal [*s'irréalise*] in his role [*personnage*]."[13]

From the tears, Sartre moves on to another example of dialectical doubling: "A novice actress can assert that her nervousness has helped her represent Ophelia's timidity." Sartre's interpretation of the assertion is that "she had suddenly rendered her nervousness unreal—that is, she has stopped apprehending it in its own terms and has become conscious of it as an analogue of Ophelia's timidity."

Emotion

In this example (as in the preceding example of the tears) an audience is present. The actress may be aided in making the transition to the timidity of Ophelia, or in maintaining this impression, if the audience apprehends her nervousness as the timidity of Ophelia. A further advance in reflexivity is achieved when there is no external audience. I take an example from the work Sartre wrote after *L'imaginaire*—*Psyché*—and discarded in favor of writing *Being and Nothingness,* on the grounds that it was "pure Husserl" and "not original."[14] (I myself suspect that a shift in allegiance has intervened: Sartre is no longer purely inspired by Husserl, having read Henry Corbin's translation of Heidegger and recognized that his own philosophical mission is to reconcile Husserl and Heidegger.)[15] But from the discarded work, Sartre did salvage a *Sketch of a Theory of the Emotions.*

The example I take from the *Sketch* will suggest how far in fact Sartre's eidetic analysis of emotion is from being "pure Husserl." In the first place, it is an example that does not exhibit the essence of an emotion in Husserl's sense. Instead, like the distinctive examples in *L'imaginaire* (beginning with my wanting to recall Peter's face), this example exhibits a development.

At the first stage, "I stretch out my hand to pick a bunch of grapes. I cannot reach it; it is beyond my grasp." I accordingly alter my conduct:

> I shrug my shoulders, drop my hand, muttering, "They are too green," and go away. This play [*comédie*] replaces the action that I could not carry out. . . . What is at stake is my acting out under the grape vine a little play in order to confer *via* it the quality "too green" on the grapes.

But this is not a quality that I can

> confer chemically on the grapes. I cannot act on the grapes by the ordinary ways. Thus I become conscious of this bitter taste of grapes that are too green, *via* an acting out of disgust.

With this example, Sartre comes within range of an emotion, which (he explains) "is playacting [*un jeu*]." But "it is playacting in which we believe." We are taken in—*pris au jeu.* In the case of the grapes, "the play-acting is only half-sincere. Were the situation more urgent, . . . we would have an emotion."[16]

In *L'imaginaire,* we have become aware of the scope the affective reaction gains once the principle has been laid down that "any perception is accompanied by an affective reaction." The application of the principle is illustrated by the way in which an affective reaction can compensate for perceptual evidence that is lacking or is to be disregarded, as in the case of the impersonation. Now we also become aware of the scope that playacting gains as an ingredient in an emotion. Some other features of this example of an emotion we are already familiar with from Sartre's analysis of the impersonation. The present example is analyzed in terms of the distinction between real action and playacting—just as the example of impersonation is analyzed in terms of the distinction between perceiving a real Franconay and imagining Chevalier. In both cases, I am disregarding perceptual evidence: the grapes are no more "too green" than Franconay is tall, blond, and male. Indeed, we can easily suppose some mental image of their being "too green" could be involved in their transformation. But what is crucial to this transformation is in large measure conferred by my affective reaction of disgust (such as we are familiar with from the "Feuillet"). And this must have been derived from my having in the past bitten into grapes or other fruit that really were too green, just as my being able to confer the affective meaning "Chevalier" on Franconay derived from my having reacted affectively to Chevalier's performance in the past.

Furthermore, much as the meaning would not be available were Chevalier not a star of stage and screen of some magnitude (and were not stage and screen themselves a star system), so the episode under the grapevine would hardly be plausible if it did not gain a certain generality from the folk wisdom that the metaphor "sour grapes" conveys about the bitterness of certain of our frustrations.

The Waiter

There are two crucial examples of playacting in *Being and Nothingness*. There is the waiter who

> attempts to imitate in his walk the inflexible stiffness of some kind of automaton, while carrying his tray with the recklessness of a tight-rope walker by putting it in a perpetually unstable, perpetually broken equilibrium, which perpetually re-establishes by a little movement of the arm and hand. All this behavior seems to us play. . . . He is playing with himself. . . . He is playing at being a waiter.[17]

This may seem a banal example of an individual fitting himself into a social role, but there are several respects in which Sartre shows his own philosophical hand. First of all, how does the waiter play at being a waiter? His playing with the tray is the embodiment of the structure that Sartre characterizes as "metastable," and that we first discerned in the "unstable and transitory" fashion in which, as we watch Franconay's performance, an image of Chevalier was established, only to have it disintegrate, as our consciousness slides back and becomes a perception of Franconay, until the image briefly reestablishes.

Second, in playing his role, the waiter achieves, like the impersonator, a certain level of eidetic generality: "I can be the waiter only in the neutralized mode, as the actor is Hamlet, by mechanically making the typical gestures of my condition, and aiming at myself as an imaginary café waiter through these gestures taken as an 'analogue.' "[18]

Third, the significant outcome in the development is reflexive, self-referential. Indeed, here the example has even become a first-person one grammatically. The unilateral aim of an intention toward its object in Husserl is bent back by Sartre toward the self the waiter imagines himself as being.

Self-deception may be at least marginally involved, in that no one, however mechanical his gestures, can make himself into an "automaton," fitting himself exactly to the requirements of his social role. Whatever expectation of his clients are being met by the waiter's performance, Sartre still insists that more "is at stake than social conditions": I am "aiming at myself as an imaginary café-waiter."[19]

The Seducee

The fashion in which Sartre's analysis of self-deception is structured emerges even more definitely in the other famous example—the woman who is about to be seduced. Again this might seem merely an example of a banal social ritual. But Sartre again shows his philosophical hand with certain departures. The usual emphasis in contemplating the ritual is on the interpersonal relation between the two performers, whereas Sartre's emphasis is on the relation of the seducee to herself. Accordingly, the seducer's intentions are held fixed and left outside the scope of the development: "She knows very well the intentions which the man speaking to her cherishes." No interest then attaches to how he may be deceiving her; only to how she deceives herself.[20]

The relation Sartre would analyze is established by her doubling herself. She is playing two roles: one is the self she is conscious of as the sex object targeted by her companion; the other is the spiritual self for which his "admiration and esteem" are solicited, as "she draws her companion up to the most elevated regions of sentimental speculation." In the case of Franconay's performance, what attracted us in the audience was the *interplay* between our arriving at the level of the image and our sliding back to the level of what we can actually perceive. Similarly, in the case of the woman about to be seduced, what attracts her is the *interplay* between the two roles she is playing, so that "her aim is to postpone the moment of decision as long as possible." This postponement itself, we shall see, involves some measure of self-deception.

Development

Sartre's blending intention into attention and into the *attente* that elicits attention is not only a matter of promoting an analysis which is relational, as contrasted with Husserl's commitment to discrimination, but also of promoting an analysis which is more tensely developmental. We can go back and begin with my observing the cube and cooly expecting to see the other side without making any affective investment in the prospect. *Attente* introduces a certain amount of tension when I want to recall Peter's expression and do not find the mental image I summon up satisfactory, even when abetted by the photo. The climactic example of the impersonation was an "oriented expectation [*attente dirigée*]" and its scope extended well beyond what was immediately given. Sartre was explicit: "The consciousness of an impersonation is a temporal form—that is, it develops its structures in time." As an *attente dirigée*, it is a transformation into a developmental conception of Husserl's conception of the "directedness" of an intention toward an intentional object that is immediately given with the intention itself.

In the role we play under the grapevine, an initial expectation that the grapes are edible is transformed into the opposing recognition they are "too green." But for the example to be an example of how an emotion develops, it would be necessary for the "situation to be more urgent"— that is, for the *attente* to be more intense. Similarly, the waiter, even as a *garçon* in French, is waiting on his clients, attentive to their expectations: "He bends forward a little too eagerly, his voice, his eyes manifesting an interest a little too solicitous for the order of his client."

The *attente* of the seducer intrudes more tension into the development: he expects her to come across. Meantime, the woman "does not want to construe his behavior as an attempt to carry through what is called 'the initial move'—that is, she does not want to recognize the possibility of temporal development which his conduct offers. . . . She does not want to feel the urgency." Sartre's analysis, as an analysis of self-deception, has acquired an existential moral tinge. But what should be recognized is the extent to which the moral criteria by which her behavior is to be condemned are methodological. Her behavior is at once antiphenomenological and antidialectical. If she does not want to feel the urgency, it is because she is feeling it. But the "urgency" is not only an immediately given feeling that she is refusing to acknowledge; it is also a feeling that a temporal development is about to take its course. Thus she is trying to deceive herself not only phenomenologically, with respect to what is immediately given, but also dialectically, with respect to a development that is underway.

At the same time, Sartre's method of describing and thereby exposing her self-deception is "hybrid" (to borrow a term from the example of the impersonation and give it a higher-order application)—at once a phenomenological and a dialectical procedure.

It is difficult to assess this awkward conflation and decide to what extent it assists an analysis of the genuine *interplay* that composes a *bifocal* experience, with the seducee having it both ways (being spiritual and being physical) and with Sartre having it both ways (being phenomenological and being dialectical). On the one hand, Sartre's embracing with his analysis a temporal development does not mean that the methodological finality of the immediately given in Husserl is entirely superseded by the development, though of course there would be less leeway for *interplay* if what the seducee felt were more definitely a "something" than an "urgency" is. On the other hand, when I characterize the dialectic as "rudimentary," I am not just admitting that Sartre's dialectic will be susceptible of further development when he incorporates, later in his career, more Hegel and Marx. I am also admitting that it is rudimentary, in that it is an inhibited, halting, spasmodic dialectic to the extent that the phenomenological moment of immediate givenness is not entirely superseded when it is encompassed in a development.[21]

This assessment applies within the confines of an individual example. But it is also the case that Sartre's prolonged eidetic analysis of an individual example (such as the impersonation or the woman about to be seduced) can delay and seem almost to sidetrack the overall development of his analysis. Thus an individual example can sometimes seem larger in its implications (as I have shown to be the case with the impersonation) than the development to which it is ostensibly fitted. This makes for a rather bumpy sequence.

TWENTY-SIX

The True Novel

To a German philosopher it is stupifying.
—Heidegger

Genres

In Sartre's overall development there are more obvious discontinuities than the shorter-run methodological discontinuity that I have brought out. In dealing with his aesthetic theory, I concentrated on a novel, before acknowledging that he also wrote plays. But what I have not yet discussed is his abandonment of the novel as a genre. He never finished his ambitious tetrology of novels, *Roads to Freedom*.

At the same time Sartre abandoned the novel, he undertook his psychoanalysis of Jean Genet. Thus we have to take into account another affiliate for Sartre's philosophy besides the novel and the drama, and its competing claims are impressive. But before considering Sartre's resort to psychoanalysis, we should contemplate briefly the variety of his genres. Versatility is a talent not much prized by anglophone philosophers. That Sartre seems all over the place in his writings does not add in their eyes to his credibility as a philosopher, it only strengthens them in the conviction that he is a very untidy one.

Heidegger is also sensitive to Sartre's versatility. Instead of responding to the report of French visitors in 1969 that "it is *via* Sartre's *Being and Nothingness* that many of us discovered you in France after the Liberation," Heidegger evaded the reference with his comment, "I have great respect for Sartre. To a German philosopher it is stupifying, a man who knows how to express himself at once philosophically and in the novel, the drama, the essay." [1]

Pity

A direct and honest response to their reference to *Being and Nothingness* would have had to be disparaging on Heidegger's part. It seems not generally known that Heidegger's inability to give direct and honest responses is not restricted to the subject of his Nazi period, granted that this failure dwarfs in its significance anything having to do with his relation to Sartre. When Heidegger was in disgrace after the war, he wrote a fawning letter to thank Sartre for the copy of *Being and Nothingness* a go-between had delivered: "For the first time I am meeting an independent thinker who has experienced in depth the domain from which my thinking takes its start. Your book shows an immediate understanding of my philosophy such as I have not yet encountered." [2] In fact, Heidegger had found *Being and Nothingness* impossible to read and gave the book away, and as soon as he saw a prospect of circumventing the prohibition against his publishing, he was writing the "Letter on Humanism," in which he criticizes Sartre for his lack of understanding of his philosophy. [3] When they finally did meet in 1952 and Sartre mentioned *engagement* (a concept that was crucial to him in *Being and Nothingness* and with respect to which he presumably felt some debt to Heidegger), he saw Heidegger looking at him "with infinite pity." [4]

Quite possibly Sartre did not enjoy being pitied, for he walked out on their session together earlier than had been planned. He found a bunch of roses from Heidegger waiting for him in his train compartment; as soon as the train left the station, he threw them out the window.

I cite Heidegger's infinite pity, and Sartre's childish peeve, as a reminder that whatever the *grandeur* of philosophy, its *misère* is the breakdown of communication between philosophers. In Volume 1, I surveyed the breakdowns between Husserl and Heidegger, between Heidegger and Sartre, and between Sartre and Merleau-Ponty. Now that we have reached midpassage in Volume 2, it is worth remembering that the relation between Husserl and Sartre has come to the fore in my dealing with breakdowns because it is considerably less difficult to deal with than the relation between Husserl and Heidegger or even than the relations between Heidegger and Sartre and between Sartre and Merleau-Ponty. This is so if only because Sartre's relation to Heidegger involves Sartre's interpretation of the relation between Husserl and Heidegger, and Sartre's relation to Merleau-Ponty involves their different interpretations of Husserl as well as of the relation between Husserl and Heidegger. [5]

Astonishment

Another appropriate reaction to these breakdowns would be astonishment. Both Husserl and Heidegger endorse the conviction of Greek philosophy that astonishment (more often translated "wonder") is the motive for philosophy itself. It might also be a motive for working out my *Zugangsmethode* to philosophy, as a method for getting at what is at issue in these breakdowns.

Just as my long-run objective is to take the variety of philosophies into account, so my present objective is to take Sartre's versatility into account. It is a little hard to believe that his versatility could have commanded the sincere respect of Heidegger, as a philosopher who was himself committed "to following only one star." [6] So it would be interesting to know what the German original of the French *stupifiant* was.[7] It could hardly be *erstaunlich,* since Heidegger (as I have just pointed out) endorsed *Erstaunen* as the motive for philosophy itself.

Heidegger also distrusted self-expression, so how could he have respected Sartre's expressing himself in various ways? One way Heidegger did not mention is psychoanalysis, and this is the genre in which Sartre most displays his versatility. His bibliographers recall the reception of Sartre's psychoanalysis of Jean Genet in 1925: "When it appeared, the book was received with astonishment . . . : it in fact eludes traditional categories, since it can be considered at one and the same time a philosophical work, literary criticism, a moral treatise, and a psychoanalytic biography." [8]

There is one traditional genre that this undertaking does not perhaps entirely elude. Sartre will characterize his psychoanalysis of Gustave Flaubert in *The Family Idiot* as "a novel that is *true [un roman* vrai]." [9] Since Sartre left *Roads to Freedom* unfinished at the same time he wrote his psychoanalysis of Jean Genet, and since he never undertook another novel, it would seem that he was giving up novels that were fictions in favor of novels that were true.

Playacting

What concerns me at this juncture are not the traditional genres but to see if there is any continuity in the subject treated in the new genre, the *roman vrai,* with the subject that has emerged so far as distinctively Sartre's. The question can be put more specifically now that we have watched Sartre become preoccupied with role playing or playacting. This is a preoccupation that we have watched carry over from the climactic example of the impersonation into Sartre's treatment of "the art of the drama" in the appended chapter, into his definition of an emotion in the salvaged portion of *Psyché*, into *Being and Nothingness* as an "eidetic analysis of self-deception."

The full title of Sartre's psychoanalysis of Genet is *Saint Genet, Play-actor [comédien] and Martyr*. I concentrate first on his sainthood. *Le véritable Saint Genet* was the title of an eighteenth-century play about the legendary Saint Genet who was converted to Christianity during a mock performance at Rome in which he had acted out Christian baptism. At the end of this performance, he announced that he really was converted, and was duly martyred—to become the patron saint of actors. As psychoanalyzed by Sartre, Jean Genet is also not real but someone legendary—someone he imagined himself being. He is sanctified and martyred in Sartre by his playing the passive sexual role of a woman, and Sartre's oral pun *saint/seins* equips him with fictitious "breasts" for this performance. Thus an extended sense in which Sartre's psychoanalysis is "a true novel" is that it is concerned with the truth of a fiction—that is, with the *interplay* between the real and the imaginary that we are already familiar with from "the paradox of the actor" as well as from the example of the impersonation in which we perceive Franconay but imagine Chevalier.

The same *interplay* is exhibited in *The Family Idiot*, which is not only Sartre's last and longest work but is also presented as a "sequel" to *L'imaginaire*.[10] So explicit a proclamation of continuity between an early and a very late work is exceptional in Sartre's writings and needs to be taken into consideration, for his development might otherwise seem too discontinuous even to be regarded as a development.

I shall illustrate the continuity that concerns me now, by examining in this "sequel" an example that is comparable to the impersonation. Our affective reaction to Franconay was not simply to her "in person," as someone we perceive. Also involved at another level was our affective reaction to Chevalier—the *personnage* whom we imagined *via* her. This dialectical doubling in the way one "sees" can be characterized as *bifocal*.

Bifocal Experience

The comparable example from *The Family Idiot* may seem as eccentric as the example of the impersonation did before I showed how significantly central it would continue to be, even when Sartre treated the art of the drama in the concluding chapter he added later to *L'imaginaire*. So before I take up the new example, I would bring out more fully how significant *bifocal* experiences are for Sartre.

I have already explained how the final chapter of *L'imaginaire* came to be written and added to Sartre's manuscript. It was only as a result of the intervention of a reader who regarded a treatment of the imagination incomplete unless it took the work of art into account. Sartre obliged, but in his concluding paragraph he did not reach a conclusion about the work of art. It seems as if Sartre, having briefly detoured to placate the reader (and perhaps the publisher as well), allowed a preoccupation of his own to reassert itself. It is a preoccupation, methodologically, with dialectical doubling, which produces a *bifocal* experience:

> It does happen that we adopt an attitude of aesthetic contemplation in the present of . . . objects that are real. When this happens, any-one can observe in himself a sort of drawing back [*recul*] in relation to the object contemplated, which slips itself into nothingness. What is happening is that, beginning with this moment, the object is no longer *perceived;* it functions as an analogue of itself—that is, as an unreal image of that which manifested to us *via* its actual presence. This image can be purely and simply the object "itself" neutralized, negated, as when I contemplate a beautiful woman; . . . it can also be the imperfect, blurred appearing of that *which it could be via* what is. . . . The object, presenting itself as *behind* itself, be-comes *untouchable,* out of reach. . . . It is in this sense that it can be said that the extreme beauty of a woman kills one's desire for her. In effect, we cannot at one and the same time place ourselves on the aesthetic level where this unreal "herself" appears that we admire and on the real level of physical possession. In order to desire her, it is necessary to forget she is beautiful, for desire is a plunge into the heart of existence with respect to what is most contingent and ab-surd.[11]

Observe the extent to which the *bifocal* experience being analyzed here is still the subject which Sartre considered a "starting point" in the transi-tion that Husserl had made, with the example of the Dürer engraving, from the object perceived to its neutralization by a depictive act. Sartre still retains Husserl's terms "neutralized" and "analogue." What is not Husserl is the reflexive twist whereby the object "functions as an ana-logue of itself," and produces the *bifocal* experience. What is also not Husserl is the way in which the depictive act of the imagination (the aes-thetic attitude), which is confined in Husserl to works of art, has gained scope in Sartre, permeating our experience.

The Princess

The continuing significance for Sartre of *bifocal* experiences is evident in the "sequel" he wrote more than thirty years later. We are now less likely, I hope, to discount as eccentric the following example from *The Family Idiot:*

If Flaubert was in love with Mathilde, it was in fact in order not to possess her. The thighs and breasts of a princess are never sufficiently regal except for someone who refrains from touching them and limits himself, as Flaubert did, to desiring a glorious body, the abstract, unrealizable image, the place of coincidence between woman as such (conceived as the ideal of femininity) and the aristocracy as such. Yet it was necessary that the real body of Bonapart's cousin should serve as analogue for the image—that is, for Flaubert to exhaust himself in aiming, *via* the cellularity of "this formerly pretty woman," at the undivided space that held her glorious body. *Via* the rough vivacity of "a woman who could equally well have been a tart, who was unreliable and rather shopworn," he necessarily tried to no avail to reach that "blue blood" that seems to him the imaginary essence of the ordinary red blood that flowed in the veins of the princess. It was to deprive of reality [*déréaliser*] the flesh and conduct of Mathilde by the very desire that pretended to be aroused by her grace and that in fact, feeding on itself, had for its primary goal to transcend the reality that was too commonplace.[12]

If we compare Flaubert's affective reaction to the princess with the audience's reaction to Franconay, we recognize again the *bifocal* character of the experience. The same two levels can be distinguished, and the reaction is to an imagined persona or *personnage*.

One obvious difference between the two performances is that the ambiguities and contradictions, which are involved in the *interplay* between levels, are now more strenuously reflexive. Thus at the outset Sartre has stated, "If Flaubert was in love with Mathilde, it was in fact not to possess her," while at the climax his "desire" is "feeding on itself."

Doubling

I raise what has become my recurrent question about Sartre: Does the methodological preoccupation with dialectical doubling, which was manifest in *L'imaginaire* and is now manifest in the Flaubert example, betray the inspiration of Husserl, or is it original with Sartre, at least in the sense that it preceded his conversion to Husserl?

We had half an answer to this question when we reached the impersonation, which was not an example found in Husserl. But now I would go back before Sartre's conversion. The preoccupation is already manifest in the *personnage* Frédéric finds in his master, and even more manifest in his relation to Cosima. In Frédéric's reaction to her, there is a precedent for Sartre's rendering of Flaubert's reaction to the princess, and Frédéric's reaction takes place in much the same fashion as one's reaction in *L'ima-*

ginaire to a beautiful woman as an "object presenting itself as *behind itself*" In "*Une défaite*" "behind Cosima, Frédéric had created a redoubtable fictional being, which he did not represent to himself but which was made out of his disarray."[13]

Here the affective reaction takes over at the expense of the representation. But in the still earlier "*Andrée*," which Sartre's editors date to 1923–24 and characterize as "autobiographical," the narrator speaks of himself as "the victim of the *personnage* that I had imagined." But he soon boasts, "I had become someone."[14] In the *Carnet Midy*, which the editors date to the same period, we find an entry under "Illusion," where Sartre deals with a very specific illusion, associated with one's body image:

> What dictates most of our attitudes is a certain representation that we have of our external form. It is not always the same: our acts, the attitudes of our body awaken in us memories of images representing creatures carrying out similar actions. I smile, with my finger in the air, and in an obscure way I believe myself to be de Vinci's John the Baptist.[15]

This example and another in the same entry he embroidered on when they become the reflections of Frédéric:

> The movements [of the person making like John the Baptist] will in a short time be controlled by this belief [that he is John the Baptist]. He will be treated as affected, he is only living in his error, indulging in the thick growth of illusion. The same explanation holds of mature women who play they are little girls. They forget their age, their wrinkles, their spread; all that they feel with their bodies are the supple gestures, the pert sway. They believe themselves to be twenty years old.[16]

These reflections are now the preamble for Frédéric's gaining an image of himself as elegant. In real life, we know such elegance was not Sartre's own accomplishment; Sartre as "the lamentable Frédéric" is trying to make like his alter ego, Paul Nizan. Comparable role playing, or at least the doubling, Frédéric goes in for in relation to himself. He speaks of his "love" not only for Organte but also for "that mysterious Empedocles who was only myself."[17] Of course, the striking instance of such doubling is Sartre's casting himself, as "the lamentable Frédéric," in the role of the youthful Nietzsche.

Sartre's preoccupation with role playing receives elaborate illustration in the relations between "the lamentable Frédéric" and women. I have already cited his relation to Cosima. But it is worth noticing how Sartre starts out "*Une défaite*," when he must have had more confidence than later in the story when he loses control. The first heading hints at what I would describe as his predisposition to dialectic: "Two Points of View toward Frédéric." I shall consider only the first. At the start of the story, Frédéric is breaking off with Geneviève—with "une brutalité composée." The theme of "the master" is introduced: "When entering her apartment, he again finds himself the master of the room. As he had before when merely seeing this woman whose submissiveness he knew, he felt in his body the premises of a bitter and morose pleasure [*jouissance*]." But now he mainly "wanted to compose [for himself] a nice role and to observe." Needless to say, what he is able to observe is that she too, "though infinitely sad, was at her ease in [a] . . . role prepared for months."[18] The mature Sartre could carry matters further. He provided his mistresses with roles in the plays he prepared for them. "Other men," one of his secretaries commented, "gave their women jewels; he gave his plays."[19]

The dialectical doubling involved in Frédéric's reference to "that mysterious Empedocles who was only myself" may well be the sort of thing Sartre has in mind when he discounts the first version of *Nausea* (begun in 1931, but the manuscript is lost) as having been "almost a symbolic novel[,] . . . which I had Castor [Simone de Beauvoir] read the start of." He recalls her having said, "It is lamentable because of the symbolism; it is boring; by all means, speak of certain things, contingency, but it should be in terms of the concrete, the real."[20] We can agree that the style of "the lamentable Frédéric" is indeed lamentable. Yet we have found that a certain movement "toward the concrete," the real, is already discernible in "*Une défaite.*" But the implication of Sartre's later quoting of his and de Beauvoir's appraisal of the early version of *Nausea* is that there is little or no continuity between his earlier abstract symbolism and the later version written in Berlin in 1933–34. I have suggested instead that there is some continuity at least in the manipulation of two levels we find both in "*Une défaite*" and at the end of Sartre's career in *The Family Idiot*. If his style has improved, it is not due to any simple, one-way movement toward the concrete, the real, but to less clumsy manipulation of the relation between the level of the real and the level of what Sartre and de Beauvoir refer to as symbols. Accordingly, I return to the example of the Princess to assess the long-term effects of his conversion to Husserl on this manipulation.

Substantive Embodiment

We have already seen how Sartre's analysis of the impersonation becomes more "precise and systematic" as a result of this conversion: the identification of Franconay as Chevalier becomes at once a synthesis of identification and a sort of eidetic reduction. The same two procedures are involved in Flaubert's identification of the Princess. Flaubert's being "led back" to an "imaginary essence" can be taken almost literally as the substantive embodiment of the methodological procedure of eidetic reduction, in that the body of Mathilde is brought into play, as was the body of Franconay. But such substantive embodiment also illustrates Sartre's commitment to a dialectic, in which form is conforming to content. This I pointed out before.[21]

Something else is now worth noticing. In the case of the impersonation Sartre had hesitated with his qualification, "the essence, as it were, of Maurice Chevalier." Now more than thirty years later, he is no longer as respectful of the terminology of his quondam master when what is now identified is an "imaginary essence." What is at issue is not just a technicality. The "as it were" seemed an implicit admission that there was a distinction of level in Husserl and that Sartre himself was not quite maintaining the distinction. In Husserl (if he could have considered this example) the identification of Franconay as Chevalier would be an imaginative synthesis of identification, carried out at the level where there are individual objects. An eidetic reduction is also an imaginative operation so long as it is merely the "free variation" of examples, but it is one from which an essence emerges to be grasped by a distinctively intellectual intuition.

At one point in The Family Idiot, when Sartre is dealing with a personnage in a play, he refers explicitly to Husserl's relying on the imagination in arriving at an eidetic intuition: "The imaginary has a function analogous to that which Husserl assigns to it in eidetic intuition." The analogy, it should be observed, is to how the imaginary functions in playacting: "What is imagined by the actor is the man who is the plaything [le jouet] of a passion: Harpagon does not exist [any more than the "essence" does in Husserl], he is play-acted [on le joue]; and the actor is not miserly, perhaps, or if he is, no one cares [to this extent his performance, like Franconay's, is an eidetic reduction that eliminates as irrelevant his characteristics as an individual]; what is true are the dialectical moments of the process by which the passion emerges [du processus passionel]."[22] Miserliness as the "essence" of Harpagon's character emerges as he becomes the "plaything" of this passion in successive episodes as the play develops. Sartre's interpretation betrays the traces of combining an eidetic reduction, as a negative operation, with a synthesis of identification, as a positive operation—only this time Sartre is explicitly labeling it "dialectical." I would add that Sartre's combining the two operations itself amounts to a rudimentary dialectic.[23]

Sartre's use of the term "essence" and of the "analogy" to "eidetic intuition" (which have justified my looking for methodological antecedents in Husserl) may jar stylistically. But some of Sartre's ability to manipulate the two levels in a less clumsy fashion than he had in his juvenilia seems traceable to the two operations in Husserl, granted that the preoccupation with role playing and with the attendant doubling of levels seems itself to have been original with Sartre—or at least to have preceded his conversion to Husserl.

Imitation

In surveying this preoccupation of Sartre's, we have arrived at a more definite conception of his privileged subject. It is not the imaginary, either in *L'imaginaire* or in its "sequel"—the psychoanalysis of Flaubert. It is the relation between the imaginary and the real. Insofar as Sartre's philosophy is a philosophy of the imaginary, it is more crucially a philosophy of *imitation*. This time I leave in French the term that up until now I have been translating "impersonation," for the French brings out the fuller scope of Sartre's subject. To deal with an imitation is to deal with what is imagined in terms of that which is real that it is an imitation of.

This is a broad as well as antiquated framework for aesthetics. Having recognized Sartre's scope, it is also necessary to recognize how selective he is. Recall his warning in the added chapter that he was not going to provide a complete aesthetics: "I don't want to treat here the problem of the work of art as a whole." What Sartre did want to treat becomes clear in the concluding paragraph from which I have cited; it is in the relation between an aesthetic attitude and a moral attitude. This is not just because he is committed to a relational analysis, as we discovered earlier when it turned out that Sartre's interest within aesthetics was in "the literary art, but taken in relation to the other arts"—that is, the visual arts. It is because he was recovering from his belief in the moral doctrine of salvation by art, as we have learned from his youthful writings and from autobiographical remarks. This belief could have encouraged him in his youth to undertake what he expected would be "a complete aesthetics."[24] Then his rejection of this belief may help explain why he never followed through in this undertaking.

Also recall his report that he had rejected this belief by the time he was finishing *Nausea*. In the next to the last paragraph of *L'imaginaire*, he refers to the "nauseous revulsion" one feels when the symphony, which one has been "absorbed" in listening to, comes to an end and "consciousness regains contact with existence." This is the only reference to nausea in *L'imaginaire*. But the problem faced in *Nausea* had already in effect been posed in the last part of the original manuscript of *L'image*,

"The Imaginary Life." Thus, after the detour of writing, as he had been requested, on the work of art, Sartre picks up the problem of the imaginary life again, in order to undercut finally the confusion that underlies the doctrine of salvation by art: "To say that one 'adopts' toward life an aesthetic attitude is to confuse . . . the real and the imaginary."[25]

Sartre's preferred examples of this confusion are male reactions to women, as we discovered in the concluding paragraph of *L'imaginaire:* "We cannot at one and the same time place ourselves on the aesthetic level where this unreal 'herself' appears that we admire and on the real level of physical possession." So be it. But it is clear that Sartre himself (at least so long as he believed in salvation by art) extrapolated women to the unreal level by transforming them into fictional characters. The most notable example is Simone Jollivet. It is not certain what "the beautiful novel" was that he promised, "I shall write for you."[26] But she was in part the real-life original for Cosima ("behind" whom, we have seen, Frédéric "created a redoubtable fictional being") as well as the original for the Anny of *Nausea.* As for the other Simone, it is remarkable that Sartre apparently never extrapolated her in any of his fictions.

TWENTY-SEVEN

The Writer

The problem for me was . . . to understand what it meant to be in . . . the imaginary—that is, to make a work of art.—Sartre

Personalization

Now I would make a transition from the role the princess plays as a *personnage* for Flaubert to the reflexive process by which Flaubert becomes a *personnage* for himself. To this process Sartre attaches the term "personalization."[1] The distinctions that are pivotal in Sartre's analysis of personalization are less distinctions in *level*, which we encountered in Husserl, than distinctions of *stages*, which we have encountered in a primitive version in *L'imaginaire*. In a dialectic, stages belong to a development whose direction is determined by the outcome to be reached; they are stages by which Flaubert becomes the author of *Madame Bovary*—that is (to bring out the reflexive character of this outcome), someone who can proclaim, "Madame Bovary is myself."[2]

The first stage in the process of personalization is the development by which Flaubert became an "Imaginary Child"; the second stage, the development "From the Imaginary Child to the Actor"; the third stage, the development "From the Actor to the Author." I shall concentrate on the second stage because of its relevance to playacting and, thereby, to the drama as a genre. Sartre's psychoanalysis is not simply a "true novel" about a novelist; a significant component is Flaubert's self-dramatization, and I shall take the preceding and succeeding stages into account only insofar as they bear on this second stage.

Sartre reports that "at seven years, Flaubert wanted to be a great actor." Thus "the writer in him is to preserve the characteristics of the actor and his style something of his playacting." [3] That Sartre does not trace in a linear fashion how Flaubert became a writer but, instead, intrudes a stage when he wanted to become an actor may have as much to do with Sartre's own preoccupation with playacting as it does with Flaubert's development. [4] After all, in Sartre's own account in *Words* of how he himself became a writer, his playacting as a child was decisive. But what is more explicit in *The Family Idiot* than in Sartre's account of how he himself became a writer is how Flaubert's style preserves something of his playacting.

Style

The fourth and final volume of *The Family Idiot,* for which Sartre only compiled notes, was to have been a "study of the style of *Madame Bovary.*" [5] Even without this volume, we are able to see that this analysis of style would have expanded its scope beyond Sartre's conception of style that I considered earlier. Sartre planned to deal with "a style of life infinitely condensed in the swiftness of a sentence, in its resonance, in the stretching out of paragraphs or of their brusque interruption." [6]

In Sartre's analysis of style, which I earlier applied to *Nausea,* style was worked over with reference to "the totality of the episode, the chapter—and beyond—of the entire work." [7] The "beyond" I illustrated by reference of Sartre's title to *Melancholia I.* Now style expands to become the style of life that is "condensed" (and so forth) in the literary features of the work. This conception of a literary style as embodying a style of a life assumes that "objectivation in the work [*Madame Bovary,* for example] is a moment in a process of personalization, in that the contradictions . . . of Flaubert are all of them in his novel but integrated imaginatively in the unreal object that he presented." Here we have another respect in which the novel is true, granted that it is true to the fictionalized life of someone who identified "Madame Bovary" as "myself." Just as acting is not confined in Sartre to the theater, and "the aesthetic attitude" is not confined to the work of art, so style is not confined to the written work.

Sartre introduces playacting into his analysis by making the transition, with which we are familiar from *L'imaginaire,* from the portrait to the portrayal. In both cases, he retains the double reference, which was the "starting point" he discovered in the Dürer engraving, to the physical image that can be perceived and to the object that I imagine. Thus "when I look at a portrait, the canvas, the spots of color that have dried, the frame itself, constitute the analogue of the object—that is, of the man, today dead, who served as model for the painter." [8]

The portrayal then again provides a reflexive advance in that the physical image is the actor himself, who

> aims at revealing an object that is absent or fictional *via* the totality of his individuality: he treats himself as the painter treats his canvas and his palette. Kean walking across the stage at the Drury Lane Theater lends his walk to Hamlet. . . . The perception of the spectator becomes unreal [*s'irréalise*] in the imagination; he does not observe the mannerisms, the gait, the "style" of Kean; he thinks he is observing those of the imaginary Hamlet. [9]

Sartre then goes on to the "paradox of the actor," as in his treatment of "the art of the drama" in *L'imaginaire,* and includes the same example of "nervousness." What is new here in *The Family Idiot* is the " 'style' of Kean."

Self-Identification

Acting and playacting had previously acquired extended implications in Sartre. The comparison with the actor had been a feature of Sartre's analysis of the reflexive moment in the waiter's performance in *Being and Nothingness:* "I can be the waiter . . . as the actor in Hamlet, by mechanically making the typical gestures of my state, and by aiming *at myself* as an imaginary café waiter through those gestures taken as an 'analogue.' "

His plays themselves are a genre whose adoption by Sartre receives some of its justification from his preoccupation with playacting. [10] When he adapted Alexandre Dumas' *Kean,* Sartre intrudes the same distinction as in *Saint Genet* and in *The Family Idiot* between the real and imaginary, but with a somewhat different twist. Kean, Sartre explains, is in reality "an actor who does not stop acting when he leaves the stage" but who "acts out his life, until he no longer recognizes himself," who "in the end is no one." [11]

In *The Family Idiot,* however, a new distinction complicates the process of self-identification. In Sartre's analysis of Flaubert's personalization, "Acting met Flaubert's need to escape from his own persona, which was inconsistent and tiresome, by substituting for it the being of a role [*personnage*]." Thereby, "over against the fragility of the persona he has improvised, he thinks he has found the most assured protection. . . . Consistency, *Selbständigkeit*, stability[,] . . . in short, being, are on the side of the *personnage*." [12]

In drawing a distinction between the persona and the *personnage,* Sartre relies on the analogy with an actor who plays a role; thus, this more complicated analysis can perhaps be examined against the background of the analysis of the impersonation. There the predominant traits of the physical image (Franconay's body in motion) no longer resembled what was to be imagined, as had the initial examples of the physical image (the photo or portrait of Peter) that was "the basis" for the mental image. Yet the procedure on which the impersonation was modeled was still Husserl's synthesis of identification.

So long as only Flaubert's persona is involved, the problem of his self-identity is still comparable to the dialectical problem of identifying as a tall and blond male the person that a small and dark-haired female is impersonating. The image we in the audience were conscious of was "unstable" and, thus, comparable to the unstable, fragile structure of the persona of which Flaubert is conscious. Now, however, Sartre is introducing a distinction that he had not drawn in dealing with the impersonation. Flaubert's *personnage* ("role"), as opposed to his persona, is designed to be consistent and stable.

Here we have a more complex illustration of a hybrid, metastable structure. The first such structure we encountered was the "unstable and transitory state" of arrival at, and then sliding from, "the level of the image [of Chevalier] to that of perception [Franconay]." Later we encountered the structure again when bad faith "oscillates constantly between good faith and cynicism." We are now encountering it in Flaubert's "need to escape from his own persona." As in the case of his affective reaction to the princess, his affective reaction to himself is bifocal. It is constituted by two ingredient movements: one (for which Husserl's synthesis of identification is a discernible model) is the movement by which Flaubert feels himself identified with his persona; the other (for which the eidetic reduction is a discernible model) is the movement by which he escapes from this persona, "substituting for it the being of a *personnage,*" which is meant to be consistent and stable but which in turn collapses, sending him back to his persona again. Although Husserl's two procedures are still discernible, they can be correlated only by Sartre's tracking them with a procedure that is dialectical.

The Work of Art

In his analysis of Flaubert's personalization, Sartre also employs an example of an actress, which is similar to the example of the impersonation:

> With any analogue, one disregards what gets in the way. When an elderly actress plays with skill the role of a young woman, one lets oneself be carried away; one does not take the wrinkles into ac-

count, one "sees" the youthful beauty that she represents. Certainly old age is not suppressed entirely but remains as a sort of sadness, as a "that's all it amounts to" of the secret disillusion that is aroused at this moment not with the actress in the role but with beauty in general. Thus the masculinity of little Gustave colors the aimed-at object . . . with a certain hermaphroditism.[13]

I shall not follow out the implications Sartre pursues with the "Thus" until I have examined the example of the actress.

Observe in this example the *interplay* between what is perceived and what is imagined. Just as I disregarded (in a fashion reminiscent of Husserl's eidetic reduction, if less eliminative) peculiarities of Franconay ("This dark hair, we do not see as dark, this body, we do not perceive as a female body"), so I disregard the particular wrinkles of the elderly actress, and a certain essentiality, coefficient of generality, is attained, whereby "beauty in general" is at stake. But it becomes ambiguous with the concession "that's all it amounts to," and accordingly metastable—like the other precarious structures Sartre favors.

I return to the implications that are carried over in Sartre's conclusion, announced by the "Thus." There might be, I volunteered, a certain sexual ambiguity in Franconay's impersonating the male Chevalier, who was a "ladies' man." Now the ambiguity takes the form of "a certain hermaphroditism." The context is Sartre's analysis of the first stage in the process of personalization, "The Imaginary Child." "A certain hermaphroditism" will remain a feature of Flaubert's sexual playacting. In Flaubert's own words, "I would like to be a woman, in order to be able to admire myself, strip myself naked[,] . . . to gaze at myself in brooks."[14] In the short run, Sartre is claiming that

> Gustave is a beautiful child: so he is told. This reputation incites him to push this beauty to extremes; he makes himself woman (he who would be horrified to be effeminate), because woman is the object of perfect art.[15]

In the longer run, Sartre has in mind how "the author of Madame Bovary acquired his sense of identity as expressed in his 'Madame Bovary is myself.'" But in a still longer run, the allusion that Sartre intrudes on Flaubert's behalf to "the object of perfect art" betrays Sartre's own continued preoccupation with the doctrine of salvation by art, to which he had been committed in *Nausea:*

> Roquentin thinks he is going to be saved at the end by the work of art. . . . That had been my starting point, my initial idea. . . . The problem for me was . . . to understand what it meant to be in the imaginary—that is, to make a work of art.[16]

At the same time, this is the doctrine from which Sartre himself had been exorcised, as reported in *Words,* so that he can explain in *The Family Idiot* that Flaubert has come to "represent for me the exact[!] opposite of my own conception of literature—total disengagement from social and political problems, and the pursuit of a formal ideal."[17]

A Hybrid State

My immediate concern is with the short run, where the reflexive "in order to be able to admire myself" is taken by Sartre as "the clue" to the child's masturbation fantasies:

> It is possible for the child . . . to imagine that he is another who caresses a real woman—himself. . . . His hands are those of another, they descend slowly from his breast to his sides, to his round thighs. . . . From his image he apprehends only the caressed flesh, neglecting the meaningless details, such as his penis or his male chest.[18]

At this point Sartre suspects his reader of protesting, "This is impossible." It is then that he inserts the example to elicit conviction about how details can become neglected as meaningless: "When an elderly actress plays . . . the role of a young woman . . . one does not take the wrinkles into account, one 'sees' the youthful beauty that she represents."

The details still get in the way of the child's attempt to imagine himself a woman, and they promote the *échec* and "collapse" of the attempt, except for "brief moments of tension when the illusion is attained."[19] Thus Gustave's "hermaphroditism" can be analyzed in much the same terms as the female Franconay's attempt to impersonate the male Chevalier. It too is "a hybrid state . . . that is neither entirely perceptive nor entirely imaginative" but "unstable and transitory," since his consciousness cannot be kept, any more than that of Franconay's audience, from "sliding from the level of the image to that of perception."

Enough of Sartre's analysis of the sexual role played by the child Flaubert in becoming "The Imaginary Child" has been expounded to bring out the pursuit of an identification that is at stake, as in the impersonation. Sartre justifies lingering over the complications because he would argue that it is "not necessary to have recourse to homosexuality to characterize the sexual behavior of Gustave." Such an interpretation of his sexual identity, I would add, would be undialectical, as compared to the ambiguous "a certain hermaphroditism" that Sartre would accredit. When Sartre extrapolates to Flaubert's adult sexual behavior, he concludes that Flaubert "fucks to render himself unreal [*baise pour s'ir-*

réaliser]" and that the process of derealization "is heightened because he is trying to identify himself with the woman he is possessing, to steal from her the sensations that she appears to experience: this convulsed, swooning flesh, it is himself."[20] This is the Flaubert who is on his way to the identification "Madame Bovary c'est moi."[21]

Such an identification is not established once and for all. It is ongoing. "To imagine," Sartre explains, "is at one and the same time to produce an imaginary object and to render oneself imaginary [*s'imaginariser*; on this I have not insisted enough in *L'imiginaire*]."[22] Thus Flaubert "becomes double [*se dédouble*] during his narration; as *story-teller* he is *an other*." Sartre's "enough" would seem to signal the extent he regards a reflexive move as an advance in his analysis.

The Conversion to Dialectic

Philosophy is concerned with man, who is at once agent and actor.—Sartre

The Synthesis

That role playing or playacting is a continuing preoccupation of Sartre's became evident as soon as the example of the impersonation was supplemented with examples of self-deception from *Being and Nothingness* and with the shift in the affiliate from the novel to the drama. I then went on to show in Chapter 27 how this preoccupation carries over in Sartre's psychoanalysis of Flaubert. But so far I have neglected a further shift in the *affiliate*, whereby this psychoanalysis, as compared with Genet's, is backed up with a more or less Marxist social analysis. Is what Simone de Beauvoir calls Sartre's "conversion to dialectic" not a break in the continuity I have been tracing?

Sartre's Marxist dialectic, especially in the *Critique of Dialectical Reasoning*, confronts the expositor with many problems I cannot go into here. But *The Family Idiot* is presented by Sartre as a "sequel" not only to *L'imaginaire* but also to *Questions de méthode,* which outlines Sartre's attempt to reconcile psychoanalysis with Marxism.[1] Consider one juncture in *Questions* at which this combination is effected. Sartre complains that "the contemporary utilization" of Marx by "self-styled Marxists" is "superficial and dishonest." The instance to which he appeals is the claim that "the avowed goal of the Brissotins [during the French revolution] is a mask, that these bourgeois revolutionaries

presented themselves as illustrious Romans but that the objective consequences really defined what they were doing." Sartre demures, "We
should be more careful." He interprets Marx as attempting "a difficult
synthesis of intention and consequences," and he proposes as Marxist

> a new idea of human action. Imagine an actor who plays Hamlet
> and is caught up in his playacting: he crosses his mother's room in
> order to kill Polonius hidden behind a tapestry. But that is not what
> he does: he crosses a stage before a public . . . in order to earn his
> living, to win fame, and this real activity defines his position in so-
> ciety. But it cannot be denied that these real consequences are in
> some fashion present in his imaginary action. It cannot be denied
> that the movement of the imaginary prince expresses in a certain
> distorted and refracted manner his real movement or that the way
> in which he believes himself Hamlet is his own way of knowing
> himself to be an actor. To return to our Romans of 1889, their way
> of calling themselves Cato is their manner of making themselves
> bourgeois. Everything is there. It is one and the same thing to pro-
> claim oneself Roman and to want to halt the Revolution, or, rather,
> one would halt it the more effectively the more one can pose as Bru-
> tus or Cato. This thought, though obscure to itself, gives itself mys-
> tical ends that envelop the confused knowledge of its objective
> ends.[2]

I have a strong suspicion that it may be Sartre himself who is exhibiting
with this example "a new idea of human action," in order to carry out a
difficult synthesis of his phenomenology, as an analysis of intentional actions, with an analysis that follows out their objective consequences.

Pris au Jeu

Of course the seeking of a synthesis is not a phenomenological undertaking, as Husserl conceived phenomenology, any more than is the reflexive
moment of self-identification, conceived as the moment when one is
"caught up" and "taken in" (recall Husserl's "we shall always presume
sincerity"), as the Brissotins were when they made themselves bourgeois
by believing themselves to be Roman. This moment when a *bifocal* experience is produced is not phenomenological, but it is pivotal in Sartre's
"eidetic analysis of self-deception." Indeed, when Sartre accuses certain
Marxists of being "self-styled" and "dishonest" he is probably implying
that they too have succumbed to self-deception, though he pulls this particular punch by also dismissing them as merely "superficial." Indeed if
"superficial" can be understood literally, Sartre is stressing that these

"self-styled" Marxists are incapable of envisaging the distinction of level that is required to analyze a *bifocal* experience such as self-deception. At any rate he only accuses them, more simply, of being "dishonest."

We encountered the reflexive moment when one is "taken in" (*pris au jeu*) when Sartre's treatment of "the art of the drama" became a discussion of whether or not the actor is "taken in—a victim in some sense of the hero he is impersonating." Now these bourgeois revolutionaries are similarly the actor-victims of the heroes they imagine themselves as being. We are reminded of how Sartre himself as a child became taken in by his own role playing—the victim of the heroes he had read about and imagined himself to be.

The shift is that the reflexive moment of self-identification (when the revolutionaries are caught up in the Roman roles they are playing) is to be incorporated in a Marxist analysis in which it is recognized that one can "halt the Revolution [short of the consequences it otherwise would have had] more effectively the more one can pose as Brutus or Cato."

There are obvious differences between an actor on the stage being caught up in a role and the self-deception in which political agents are prevalently enmeshed. If Sartre seems to ride roughshod over these differences, it only illustrates how compelling the theatrical analogy remained for him, even when he became a self-styled Marxist:

> Today I think that philosophy is dramatic in nature. . . . Philosophy is concerned with man, who is at once agent and actor, who produces and plays his drama. A play . . . is the most appropriate vehicle for showing man in action—that is, man.[3]

Two Methods

Insofar as man is an "actor," he is, roughly speaking, assignable to psychoanalysis for investigation; insofar as he is an agent, he is, roughly speaking, assignable to Marxist social history. I introduce the qualification "roughly speaking" because there is neither any simple separation of the two methods nor any simple synthesis; rather, there is *interplay*, since man is "*at once* agent and actor." Sartre himself has spoken only roughly, using two not entirely compatible idioms. On the one hand, the "real consequences" are "in some fashion present in [the actor's] imaginary action"; on the other hand, the "mystical ends" of the revolutionary posing as Brutus or Cato "envelop the confused knowledge of [the] objective ends."

For Sartre himself in *Questions de méthode*, to treat man as a subject is to "employ conjointly . . . two methods"—the psychoanalytic and the Marxist.[4] Although he seems to regard this conjunction as unprecedented, is it not comparable to the dialectical maneuver with which he undertook in *Being and Nothingness* "a synthesis" of Husserl's phenomenology with Heidegger's ontology—or, more specifically, of Husserl's eidetic analysis of consciousness with Heidegger's existential analysis of man as "being-in-the-world"? Thus there is a sense in which Sartre's own distinctive method, even before his encounter with Marxism, was already the conjoint application of two methods that had been applied by predecessors to different subjects.

After his encounter with Marxism, Sartre still relies on "the *methodological* principle that holds that certainty starts with reflection," [5] though he relies on it without bothering to explain that this is the same Cartesian principle that he adopted as phenomenological at the start of *L'imaginaire*. Just as earlier in *Being and Nothingness* he seeks a reconciliation, he now claims that this methodological principle "in no way contradicts the principle that defines the concrete person in his materiality. . . . Reflection is a starting point [and, in this sense, a principle] only if it throws us back immediately among things and men, in the world." Again Sartre's maneuver is reminiscent of his reconciliation of Husserl and Heidegger in *Being and Nothingness,* where he had started out with an analysis of consciousness, then recognized that "consciousness is an abstraction," and made his move "toward the concrete," which he identified as Heidegger's "being-in-the-world." To describe the movement itself, Sartre still retains Heidegger's idiom of *Geworfenheit*—we are "thrown back." [6]

The maneuver presents us with a conflation comparable (both in its awkwardness and in the *interplay* it permits) to that considered at the end of the last chapter: to rely on the certainty yielded by reflection as a starting point is to endorse Husserl's "principle of principles" and rely reflexively on what is immediately given to consciousness; but Sartre transfers "immediately" so that it applies to our being "thrown" in Heidegger "into the world," and in Heidegger this being "thrown" deprives what is given to consciousness at once of its immediacy and of its reliability.

Nevertheless, we should also see how Sartre effects the reconciliation in his own terms. Where the starting point for the Marxist social historian would be some technological development, the invention or utilization of some tool, Sartre starts out with the individual person and his immediately given experience, as constituted by the reflexive moment when he makes himself his own tool. To spell this out: where the Marxist social historian would start with the lever, the wheel, the stirrup, the pulley, the steam engine, Sartre would start with the reflexive experience of this person's own instrumentality when he utilizes the tool. The transformation of the structure of his own experience then has to be taken into account in dealing with his becoming a worker, or a kind of worker different from a type characteristic at a previous stage of social history. In other words, technological development is more than man's transformation of his external environment; his reflexive self-transformation is also involved. Thus when the tool that is introduced is a machine, we are dealing with a technological development visualized by Sartre not as lying at the base of the substructure and generating a sequence of effects that extend into the superstructure and eventually imposing themselves there on individual consciousness. Instead, we start with the individual consciousness.

Sartre's analysis of consciousness is still an eidetic analysis of examples, as in Husserl, only the experience in question is *bifocal* and dialectical: "Girls working in a factory are ruminating a vague dream," but they are "at the same time traversed by a rhythm external to them." What is immediately given is not quite immediately given but involves a mediating external factor and the emergence of a dialectical opposition. Thus "it can be said that it is the semiautomatic machine that is dreaming through them." The rhythm of the machine was "so alien to a girl's vital personal rhythm that during the first few days it seemed more than she could endure." But "she wanted to adapt herself to it; she made an effort." So she "gave herself to the machine," which "takes possession of her work," until finally "she discovers herself *the object of the machine*." [7]

A dislocating dialectical reversal has taken place: the machine is no longer her tool; she has become its tool—*pris au jeu*. But the machine cannot qualify as a subject. We are left with the contradiction that she is no longer quite the subject of her own experiences.

Anthropology

Such an analysis is a more full-fledged dialectic than we came across earlier in Sartre. Yet it is not entirely unprecedented. Even though the impersonation is a much simpler example, we can perhaps still recall Franconay playing the role of Chevalier. In fact, Sartre uses the same idiom. The relation of impersonation, Sartre concluded:

> is a relation of *possession*. An absent Maurice Chevalier chooses, in order to manifest himself, the body of a woman. Thus originally an impersonator is someone possessed. Perhaps this is the fashion in which should be explained the role of impersonation in the ritual dances of primitives. [8]

The brusque reversal here was not only remote from Husserl but also so implausibly extravagant (an absent Maurice Chevalier choosing) that I skipped over it. Yet its very implausibility suggests how tempting Sartre found what in a dialectic would be a reversal, even before he became familiar (belatedly, by his own account) with Hegel and Marx.

Sartre was also not then aware that the relevant anthropology was not that of primitive man but a philosophical anthropology to which he apparently became responsive only with his reading (or misreading) of Heidegger. These are debts Sartre does not acknowledge when he himself elaborates his own philosophical anthropology in the *Critique of Dialectical Reasoning* and *The Family Idiot*. Similarly, he no longer acknowledges debts to Husserl's phenomenology and prefers to present his own psychoanalysis as a transformation of Freud's.

The announced "subject" of *The Family Idiot* is "what can be known of a man today," by applying conjointly the methods of Marxist social history and of individual psychoanalysis.[9] Sartre defines man as a "meaning-endowing being (*être signifiant*)."[10] This definition is a loose conflation of Husserl's conception of consciousness as intentional (as performing meaning-endowing acts) and of Heidegger's conception of man as a "being" who is "there" in the concrete sense that he is in "a situation."

In the example with which Sartre expounds his definition, the situation in which the individual finds himself is in a room with others. He performs an intentional action: he gets up from his chair and crosses the room in order to open a window. Since I am in the same situation, I understand his action, for embodied in it is his intentional consciousness endowing the room with the meaning "too warm."

The window he opens is the consequence of an intentional action. It has been endowed with a meaning, for its design indicates how the worker who made it was conscious of it as something to be pushed up or down or to be swung out. But his action remains anonymous: the design does not express (or no longer expresses) his personal intention as a particular individual.

In contrast with the worker's anonymous action, the individual who gets up to open the window identifies not only the room as "too warm" but also himself by how he gets up, crosses the room, and opens the window. For he performs these actions deliberately, or impatiently, or however. His action thereby expresses a more general intention on his part about how he would perform or should perform. He is not merely an impersonal "agent" opening the window; he is an "actor" as well.

The phenomenology that survives here is Sartre's own "vulgarized" or "naturalized" version—a "picture-book phenomenology" of everyday life. The phenomenological analysis can be conducted by anyone else in the overheated room. Distinctions in *level* are almost flattened, and intention has almost reverted to its colloquial sense. As an "act" that is still "meaning-endowing," it has become merely an ingredient in an intentional action, whether it be the crossing of the room or the making of the window.[11]

Understanding the intentional action recounted in this example is not just the conflation of phenomenology with a sort of Marxism but also the deflation of any distinctively phenomenological procedures. Understanding itself is no longer obedient to "the principle of principles" but has become a process of development. We have reached a juncture at which Sartre hardly still belongs to the history of phenomenology, at least insofar as it derives from Husserl. The time has come to review the development of Sartre's philosophy, in order to bring out what is generally distinctive of it with respect not to its subject, or to its affiliation, or to its method, but to the way in which it developed.

SEVEN · THE ITINERARY OF
· A THOUGHT

TWENTY-NINE

Le Travail de la Rupture

> I transform a tranquil evolutionism into a
> revolutionary and discontinuous
> catastrophism.—Sartre

Discontinuity

At the beginning of Part 6, I recalled the shifts in allegiance that punctuated the development of Sartre's philosophy: before World War II, he was converted to Husserl; during the war, his allegiance shifted from Husserl to Heidegger; after the war, it shifted to Marxism, and he dismissed both Husserl and Heidegger as "minor philosophers." Despite these shifts, I was able in Part 5 to discern a continuity—Sartre's preoccupation with role playing or playacting—a subject that he shared with none of the other philosophers to whom he successively declared allegiance and that also survived the shifts in the affiliates he sought for his philosophy.

Although this continuity manifests Sartre's own preoccupation, it is not quite the continuity that Sartre himself sometimes proclaims. Late in his career, he was asked, "Have you ever left phenomenology?" He replied, "Never. I continue to think in those terms. I have never thought as a Marxist, not even in the *Critique of Dialectical Reason*."[1] This claim could have encouraged my undertaking in the present volume, but I have honored it with the qualification that the phenomenology that he has never left is the phenomenology that emerges definitely in *L'imaginaire* only at the stage at which he leaves Husserl's phenomenology behind with the example of the impersonation. Sartre's phenomenology is predominantly a phenomenology of *imitation,* and his preoccupation with role playing antedates his conversion to phenomenology.

There is another conclusion to be avoided with respect to Sartre's development. It should not be concluded that the discontinuities between the successive periods in this development are simply due to the divergencies between the philosophies to which Sartre's allegiance successively shifted. When Sartre opposes Heidegger to Husserl in *Being and Nothingness,* it is to reconcile their philosophies in his own philosophy. Neither the opposition nor the reconciliation should be envisaged as taking place in the context of either of their philosophies. Both betray instead a rudimentary dialectical method in which issues are formulated in terms of oppositions and resolved by overcoming those oppositions. This method is a specific feature not of his predecessor's philosophies but of Sartre's own philosophy, and it is even extended by him (as I have shown in the previous chapter) to embrace his reconciliation of psychoanalysis and Marxism.

There is another respect in which the discontinuity in the development of Sartre's philosophy is not due simply to the divergencies between the philosophies to which his allegiance successively shifts but betrays a distinctive trait of his own philosophy. At first blush this trait may seem largely his own shoulder-shrugging indifference to continuity. This indifference is manifest in an interview that was first published in English under the title "The Itinerary of a Thought." The interviewer began by producing evidence of discontinuity in this itinerary: "the typical concepts" of *Being and Nothingness* disappeared from the *Critique of Dialectical Reason,* though the interviewer granted that some of them "reemerged" in *The Family Idiot.*

Sartre responded brusquely, "The fundamental question here, of course, is my relation to Marxism." [2] He does not refer to any of the concepts his interviewer had carefully listed. Sartre's so obviously not having dealt with the question may explain why the evidence cited by the interviewer was cut out and why the title itself was changed from "The Itinerary of a Thought" to *Sartre par Sartre* when the interview was published in French. The episode suggests how Sartre leaves almost entirely to his expositors the task of determining the itinerary of his thought.

Le Point de Rupture

Let us begin with his "relation to Marxism," since Sartre is insisting that this is "the fundamental question." Important features of this relation (perhaps the more important) are beyond my scope here, since taking them into account would require what the interviewer had in mind—a careful examination of the pertinent concepts. What Sartre does distinguish broadly are two stages in his relation to Marxism. As a student he had read *Capital* and *The German Ideology,* but he explains, "I had understood everything clearly, and I understood nothing at all. To understand is to transform oneself [*se changer*]."[3] The sharpness of the opposition, of the discontinuity, between the two stages is characteristically Sartre, as is the pivotal significance of reflexivity. The conception of understanding involved is not Marxist, and in this respect his "relation to Marxism" is not itself Marxist.

In one of his activist stances, Sartre might well endorse Marx's eleventh thesis on Feuerbach—"Philosophers have only interpreted the world differently; the point is to change it." But Sartre's conception of understanding imports into the process of change a reflexive moment of self-transformation. He labels what happened to him as "in religious language a conversion."[4] One possible explanation of Sartre's indifference to the question of continuity with his past philosophy is the very fervor of his conversions. Let us accordingly examine his final conversion. After this conversion Sartre could still fluctuate about the exact distance between himself and Marxism or the program of the French Communist party. His conversion was the moment he could no longer fluctuate about what he was opposing—anti-Communism: "The last ties were broken; my vision was transformed. An anti-Communist is a dog: on that I do not yield. I shall never yield. . . . I had reached the point of rupture."[5]

The last ties ruptured were to Sartre's own bourgeois class. Of the moment of this conversion, Sartre reports, "I swore to the bourgeoisie a hatred that will end only when I do." Such hatred was once a rather routine performance on the part of French bourgeois intellectuals. What I would draw attention to is not just Sartre's vehemence but its exact delineation. His stress on "the point of rupture" is such that rather than employing himself the term "convert" (indeed, it is not clear what precisely he was converted *to*), he prefers "traitor," which brings out what he has been converted *from* and would subvert.[6]

Moreover, the stress is reflexively on his opposition to himself and on his ensuing self-transformation. But his initial commitment to self-transformation came earlier. It was not only to World War II as a disruption but also to disruption itself. In the journal he then kept, he confesses, "The essential form of my pride is to be without solidarity with myself." Indeed "any time anyone seems struck with the permanence of my self, I become distracted by uneasiness."[7] This initial commitment to self-transformation would help explain why he "could no longer recognize" who he had been "before the war"; he was committed to rendering himself so transformed as to be unrecognizable.[8]

Subversion

I want to take this example out of its sociopolitical context. Swearing hatred to the bourgeoisie, "a hatred that will end only when I do," is obviously commendable, but there are other implications of Sartre's maneuver that we are in danger of overlooking, especially since it seems here (as it will often seem later in this chapter) as if such maneuvers were merely personal on his part, when in fact they do acquire a certain philosophical generality. Consider a more or less comparable maneuver without sociopolitical implications. It is reported by Mathieu (Sartre's version of himself in *Les chemins de la liberté*) but it has been carried out, by Daniel. While Mathieu has been scavenging for money to pay for an abortion for his mistress, Marcelle, Daniel (whom we are already aware is homosexual) has decided to marry the mistress—ostensibly at least so she can have the child, which he insists she wants. Daniel's decision seems very particular, but it becomes the occasion for the ineffectual Mathieu to reflect on the nature of an act:

> He was fascinated by Daniel. He thought: "Is that freedom? He has *acted;* now he can no longer turn back. It must seem strange to him to feel behind him an unknown act, which he already no longer can quite understand and which is going to turn his life upside down. Myself, everything I do, comes to *nothing.* The consequences of my acts are stolen from me. I can always retrace my steps. I don't know what I would give to perform an irremediable act." [9]

There are certain roughly similar ingredients in Sartre's conversion and Daniel's decision, at least as visualized by Mathieu: freedom being exercised as a rupture, a conversion that is subversive and irremediable.

I have no vested interest in reminding readers that existentialism once flexed moral muscle in a fashion that today seems almost as quaint as Sartre's anti-anti-communism. All I am pretending to treat here is a problem for the tamest historian—the problem I posed in Volume 1 of how to adjust continuity and discontinuity in treating a development, including the development of a philosophy. [10] My recommendation is that some attention be paid to the adjustment the philosopher himself made.

When Sartre becomes a "traitor," he will subvert a whole set of attitudes that had been his own. Some of these attitudes had been so much his own, were so recalcitrant, that their subversion was a "cruel and long-range undertaking." [11] This subversive undertaking may have been his most drastic conversion, but some of its lineaments can be traced in his initial conversion to Husserl before the war. Even though it was milder, and to a philosophy he would later discount as contemplative, it intruded discontinuities: "Husserl had captured me." And Sartre reports how, "I saw everything *via* the perspectives of his philosophy." Indeed, a measure of self-subversion was a feature of Sartre's attempt "to break my personal prejudices and grasp the ideas of Husserl, starting from his own principles and not mine." [12] To this extent, this initial conversion was also self-transformatory subversion.

Personal Rupture

I should perhaps not have taken out of its context Sartre's report of his final conversion. It is offered in his memorial essay on Merleau-Ponty, by way of explaining how his conversion, as a break with what he had himself been, was involved in his break with Merleau-Ponty. History provides the agency for the rupture of their personal relation:

> History chooses actors, transforms them to the marrow by the role she imposes on them, and then with the slightest change, she dismisses them to take on others. [13]

A personified "History" is hardly a Marxist conception. But my present concern is the survival in this setting of the conception of the actor playing a role, which is different from and larger than himself, and which we first encountered in the impersonation.

In *Being and Nothingness* the role played by the woman about to be seduced is played without any extenuation of her responsibility. Now, when the theatrical analogy is introduced, it is extenuating in that the only leeway left the individual is for improvisation:

> As in the *Commedia dell'Arte,* all that is up to us is improvising the rupture. We come out of it badly, but well or badly, we play the scene and go on to others. [14]

Sartre's more general theme is how "each of us was thrown to the opposite extreme of the other." [15]

The opposition between them at the personal level cannot readily be distinguished from the opposition between them at the philosophical level:

> Merleau, smiling, took care not to rupture anything and not to let anything break loose; the placid dandyism of his caution . . . should have achieved completion in [a] philosophy of the continuous. [16]

But would not the opposition Sartre discovers between them at both levels achieve completion in Sartre's philosophy as a philosophy of the discontinuous? At any rate, this philosophy provides justification for breaking loose—for what Sartre calls *le travail de la rupture.*

Sartre explains that he and Merleau-Ponty were engaged in this *"travail* in the sense that Freud has clearly shown that mourning is a *travail."*[17] Sartre adds, "There are psychologists and psychiatrists who regard certain developments of our inner life as the result of a *travail* that it undertakes on itself." This reflexive dimension gains further scope from Sartre's conflating it with *"existence* in Kierkegaard—resistances overcome and re-emerging unendingly, efforts unendingly renewed."[18]

Since this is a distortion of Kierkegaard, we can suspect something distinctively Sartrean is at stake, as we have whenever Sartre distorts Husserl. One feature that is distinctively Sartrean is the metastable structure: "resistances overcome and reemerging unendingly." There is also a certain incongruity in Sartre's conjunction *un travail de la rupture,* for "efforts unendingly renewed" may be characteristic of "mourning" in Freud, but a "rupture" is characteristically sudden and complete.

A crude version of this conjunction is already found in *"Une défaite."* It begins, "Frédéric had left Geneviève with a brutality he had carefully composed," and this is identified as a "rupture." But its composition has involved what will become later in Sartre the less deliberate *travail*—"a slow interior justification had taught him to hate her."[19] In Sartre's psychoanalysis of Flaubert, the *travail* becomes "rumination," which Sartre analyzes at elaborate length.

For present purposes, I focus on the more dramatic moment. As a personal performance on Sartre's part, the rupture is not restricted to his relations to others. Once he was given a projective test as to which design "gave him the most feeling of speed." He picked out a "speedboat that seemed to take off from the lake. . . . Speed is measured in my eyes not so much by the distance covered in a certain specific length of time as by the power to break away [*le pouvoir d'arrachement*].[20]

Philosophical Ruptures

Sartre's personal dedication to *le pouvoir d'arrachement* extends to the philosophical level:

> Violent, I like exploding. . . . From explosion to explosion, mistakenly abetted by a theory [Husserl's] of "the intuition of essences," badly interpreted, I was headed for a Megarian ideology of the discontinuous.[21]

In contrast, "contradictory truths with Merleau-Ponty never come into conflict; there is no risk of their blocking the movement, provoking an explosion." Sartre adds, "Also, are they genuinely contradictory?"[22]

Sartre's recurrent resort to the idiom of the "explosion" is an obvious manifestation of his continuing commitment to discontinuity. In Sartre's Berlin essay, he imposes this idiom, without any warrant, on Husserl's idea of intentionality:

> Husserl sees in consciousness an irreducible fact that no physical image can render. Save, perhaps, the rapid and obscure image of explosion. To know [given that knowing is intentional] is to explode toward—to break away from our damp gastric intimacy.[23]

With equal lack of warrant, Sartre imposes the idiom on Descartes: "Descartes is an explosive thinker [*un penseur à explosions*]. . . . In rejecting anything in between thought and extension, he demonstrated a temperament that was catastrophic and revolutionary; he sliced and hacked, leaving to others any concern with stitching up again."[24]

Slicing and hacking is a more convincing appraisal of Sartre's own philosophy than Descartes': Sartre does apply the idiom of explosion to his own temperament: "I made *un moteur à explosions* out of my soul."[25] Does not his temperament (like Merleau-Ponty's in Sartre's appraisal) achieve completion in his philosophy? Is not the continuity that prevails throughout Sartre's development as a philosopher a commitment to discontinuity, to *le travail de la rupture*, to a *pouvoir d'arrachement* manifest in his successive conversions to other philosophies?

The Image

More fundamental than any of these conversions is Sartre's commitment to conversion itself. Consider his rendering of a conversion as set forth in perhaps the most exuberant passage in the frequently ponderous *Being and Nothingness*:

> These extraordinary and marvelous moments when the previous project collapses into the past in the light of a new project which emerges from its ruins . . . in which humiliation, anxiety, joy, hope are delicately blended, in which we let go in order to grasp and grasp in order to let go—these have often appeared to furnish the clearest and most moving image of our freedom.[26]

Sartre's exuberance displays his dialectical predilection for the "metastable"—structures that are "ambiguous" and "contradictory" and, so, "unstable." Sartre's philosophy is conventionally interpreted as a philosophy of freedom. Earlier I did emphasize the extent to which Sartre sought in Husserl's phenomenology liberation from—from the "illusion of immanence" perpetuated by French philosophy, from the "inner life" consecrated by Proust.[27]

I shall return to the interpretation of Sartre's philosophy as a philosophy of freedom when I am reaching the end of my own exposition. What I would anticipate now is that Sartre's philosophy can be distinguished from the miscellany of other philosophies of freedom by the fact that the most moving image of our freedom is a conversion. This image is the most moving inasmuch as our freedom is, in the instance of a conversion, composed dialectically of opposed movements, as we "let go in order to grasp and grasp in order to let go," and inasmuch as these opposed movements involve opposed affective reactions—humiliation, anxiety, joy, hope—to what is transpiring.

What also should be brought out is why an "image" of our freedom is in question. This is a juncture, solemnized by my title, *Method and Imagination*, at which method can be seen to conform to the subject to which it is applied: our freedom (as a "contradictory composite" and hence a metastable structure, when it is exercised in the instance of a conversion) can be displayed only by an image, which is a phenomenon that obeys neither the principle of identity or the principle of individuation, and thus itself has a contradictory and metastable structure.[28]

Sartre complains that conversions "have not been investigated by philosophers." Such a complaint I described in Volume 1 as a *Versäumnis*—a "negligent omission."[29] It can sometimes be made up for by a philosopher's turning to an affiliate for assistance. Thus Sartre appeals to how conversions have been handled in literature. He cites Gide and Dostoevski. He could also have cited the conversions that take place in his own literary works. On these his comment is, "The characters in my plays and novels reach their decisions suddenly and in a moment of crisis. A moment, for example, is long enough for Orestes to carry through a conversion." Regarding this preoccupation of his with sudden, disruptive conversions, Sartre offers a personal explanation: "These characters are fashioned in my image, not as I am, of course, but as I would like to be. I transform a tranquil evolutionism into a revolutionary and discontinuous catastrophism."[30]

The Writer

What I have singled out for attention is the succession of Sartre's revolutionary and discontinuous philosophical conversions—to Husserl, to Heidegger, to Marxism. But we should not lose sight of how Sartre envisaged himself: "I have always been a writer first of all, and only secondarily a philosopher."[31] Reconsider the last of his conversions:

I had reached the breaking-off point [*le point de rupture*]. . . .
In religious terms . . . it was a conversion.
I wrote at top speed, rage in my heart, gaily, without tact: even

with the best-prepared conversions, when they explode, there is joy in the storm, and the night is black, except where the lightening strikes.[32]

Observe the guise taken by this conversion—Sartre's writing "at top speed."

Such philosophical conversions are in a sense secondary; the conversion which remains a primary and continuing preoccupation to him is the process of self-transformation by which a man becomes a (literary) writer:

> The reason I produced *Words* is the reason why I have investigated Genet or Flaubert: how does a man become someone who writes, who wants to speak of the imaginary? This is the question I sought to answer in my own case, as I sought it in the case of others.[33]

When Sartre rectifies other philosophers' neglect of conversions, it is not simply by investigating conversions in literature but by investigating conversions *to* literature.

The three works in which Sartre treats his converts—Genet, Flaubert and himself—belong to the genre I have so far recognized as a "contradictory composite" having the metastable structure at once of "un roman *vrai*" and "un *vrai* roman," rather than leave it unclassifiable—"a philosophical work, literary criticism, a moral treatise, and a psychoanalytic biography."[34] But in these works the philosophy of literature becomes a philosophy of conversion.

When Sartre in *Words* answers in his own case the question, "How does a man become someone who writes?" he refers primarily to himself as the writer of *Nausea*. We have seen that *Nausea* itself is a novel about how its protagonist may have become the writer of the novel *Nausea*, just as "the true novel" (*The Family Idiot*) is a novel about how Flaubert became a novelist and, more specifically, the writer of the novel *Madame Bovary*. Indeed, essentially the same statement that Sartre makes about his psychoanalyses of other writers, he makes about the problem he faced in *Nausea:* "The problem for me was to understand . . . what it means to be in the imaginary—that is, to make a work of art."[35] *Words*, we have seen, is divided into two parts. In the first, "Reading," Sartre canvasses the roles with which he came to identify in what he read as a child; in the second part, "Writing," he traces how he acquired his role as a writer.

What has not yet been recognized is that role playing is not a subject that Sartre deals with generally, as a social psychologist would. Rather, Sartre focuses specifically on conversions as role shifts that are decisive, disruptive, reflexive self-transformations. Thus Sartre's psychoanalysis of Genet is an analysis of Genet's successive conversions as the shifts in roles that are conveyed by Sartre's titles: Genet's "First Conversion" is to crime, his "Second Metamorphosis" is his transformation into an aesthete, and his "Third Metamorphosis" is into a writer.[36] In the stretch on "Personalization," which concerned us in the psychoanalysis of Flaubert, the successive role shifts are indicated by Sartre's titles: "From the Imaginary Child to the Actor," "From the Actor to the Author," "From the Poet to the Artist," "From the Gesture to the Role." The succession culminates in "Loser Wins" as a "Conversion."

In the analysis of "Loser Wins," Sartre explains,

> One becomes an Artist by *conversion*. . . . One has been constrained by a long succession of frustrations [*échecs*], to carry out *a radical reversal,* and having become oneself image, to dissolve the real into the imaginary.[37]

"Loser wins" is one of the metastable ways this movement is structured. It is the dialectic whereby "to die to the world is to be reborn as an artist." "Defeat" becomes "victory."[38]

This had been Sartre's long-standing perspective. At the end of the fragments of "*Une défaite,*" we are offered some "last words" on a "fruitful defeat," for the time is approaching when Frédéric "will only know victories."[39]

However, becoming an artist is not the final radical reversal in Sartre. It can be succeeded—and is so succeeded in Sartre's psychoanalysis of not only himself as a writer but of Genet, of Flaubert—by a disruptive movement of deconversion. The movement of conversion by which Sartre came to believe in the doctrine of salvation by art, and thus came to be "someone who writes, who wants to speak of the imaginary," is reversed by the movement of deconversion whereby at the end of *Words* he "relegates the impossible Salvation to the storeroom of theatrical props."[40]

We have seen that conversion is itself a "contradictory composite" and hence a metastable structure. Now we see how there supervenes the further contradiction and instability of a deconversion. Sartre's coming to understand in *Words* how he had been converted to literature is itself his undergoing in some measure deconversion. Similarly Sartre's coming to understand in *The Idiot* Flaubert's conversion is, as it were, to deconstruct Flaubert's conversion by exposing the structure of its movement. The deconversion can culminate in the discrediting of the dialectic by which "the loser" (who meets with an *échec* in life) "wins" (as a writer).

Sartre did succeed in discrediting himself as a writer, but he cheated. He did not give up writing any more than Flaubert did. I have already indicated that during World War II Sartre became committed, not only to its disrupting his life, but also to disruption itself. He confessed then in his journal:

> Vis-à-vis Gaugin, Van Gogh or Rimbaud, I have an inferiority complex because they knew how to lose themselves. Gaugin by his exile, Van Gogh with his madness, and Rimbaud, more than all of them, because he knew how to renounce even writing. To reach authenticity, something must crack. . . . But I have preserved myself from cracking. I am bound to my desire to write. Even in wartime I fall on my feet, because I soon think of writing what I feel and what I see. . . . I leave something *intact* in me, which is a resort to a dirty trick [*saloperie*]. . . . There is no real loss [*déperdition*] in prospect for the writer who is about to lose himself, since he is writing even so.[41]

Even while failing to recognize that he had originally established this ambiguity at the end of *Nausea*,[42] Sartre continued to display it until the end of his life.

Earlier I mentioned that Mathieu (the protagonist in the novels that include the period when Sartre was keeping this journal) Sartre identifies as himself. But there is one drastically important attribute Mathieu lacks—he is not a writer, merely a philosophy professor. He also is slated to play an active role in the Resistance. Here all that Sartre could offer on his own behalf was play with another ambiguity "I was a writer who resisted, and not a resister who wrote."[43]

THIRTY

Radical Renovation

The succession passes to . . . Sartre.—Delacroix

Novelty

Keeping Sartre's commitment to rupture in mind, I would now reconsider the two junctures at which Sartre explicitly makes a break with Husserl during the prewar period when Sartre is still a "disciple" and Husserl the philosopher who "opens the way" for Sartre's treatment of the image. The first of these two junctures I considered earlier, as the final and decisive move in Sartre's pushing "the distinction [between imagination and perception] that Husserl . . . did not push further." Sartre pushed the distinction until it became an opposition between the imagination and perception; this opposition lent pivotal significance to the particular example of the impersonation, in which we are to imagine Chevalier even though his traits are opposed to the perceivable traits of Franconay.

At this juncture, the explicit break with Husserl was Sartre's criticism that the distinction between imagination and perception "cannot come from intentionality alone; it is necessary but not sufficient that the intentions differ [as they do in Husserl]; the matters too must be different." This criticism brought Sartre to the following appraisal of Husserl: "It would seem then that Husserl, while having laid the foundation for a radical renovation of the question of the image, remains a prisoner of the old conception, at least with respect to the matter of the image, which would remain for him the sensory impression reemerging." [1] Even when Sartre was "captured" by Husserl, he did not remain a prisoner of the old conception.

The criterion that is implicit here is novelty. It holds for Sartre not only at the level of the theory of the image but also at the level of the image itself, which emerges as a new phenomenon, irreducible to any previous sensory impression. The integrity of Sartre's subject is thereby assured.

The issue here antedates Sartre's conversion to Husserl. He had already raised it in his *diplôme* in a fashion that illustrates the relevance for him of literature as an affiliate. The issue is whether or not the "images" of the (literary) "writer" are "new"—and, if so, "How does he create them?" It is evident (quite aside from this specific problem of the image) that Sartre placed a certain premium on novelty, both as a philosopher and as a writer. Indeed as a man, for we have seen how exuberantly Sartre analyzes a conversion in terms of "a new project" that emerges from the "ruins" of the old. I would not separate the exuberance he derived from the novelty of the "project" and the exuberance he derived from contemplating the "ruins" of the old. The two are dialectically linked, and my stress on the subversive character of his conversions in Chapter 29 needs to be supplemented by some recognition of his commitment to the new. "What comes first," Sartre has explained about himself, "is always what I have not yet written, what I plan [*je projette*] to write." [2] This explanation can also be taken as a supplementary explanation of why he has left to his expositors the retrospective task of tracing the itinerary of his thought.

Romantic Theories

Having recognized the scope of Sartre's commitment to novelty, we can settle down to the substantive problem of the novelty of the image—or, more familiarly, the problem of the creative imagination. Because it is a problem that Sartre had faced before he read Husserl, because it is a problem that Husserl did not face directly, I would allude to Sartre's treatment of it before going on with Sartre's criticism of Husserl. Sartre's treatment seems to me of little merit, and the problem itself is a hoary locus classicus with which we are familiar mainly in the version propounded by Coleridge in the *Biographia Literaria*. [3] We are aware of it in this version because it impinges on issues in literature; as Sartre's version also does.

I restrict myself to his simplistic historical survey in *L'imagination* or, rather, to those phases that have some bearing on Sartre's own "radical renovation." A first chapter, "The Great Metaphysical Systems" (Descartes, Hume, Leibniz) is followed by "The Problem of the Image and the Effort of Psychologists to Discover a Positive Method." The history in this second chapter, though, does not in fact begin with this effort but with a counter-to-fact: "The problem of the image could have received from Romanticism a true renovation." [4] What Romanticism had to offer in psychology was the conviction that "an abyss which cannot be crossed separates the conception of an object that is absent or imaginary—that is, the image—and the real sensation produced by a present object, that these two phenomena differ not only in degree but in nature." [5] This Romantic view appealed to Sartre, even though it is phrased here in the words of one of their adversaries, who did not approve of abysses. But perhaps it is worth noting that to discover an "abyss," Sartre did not have to wait until he read Kierkegaard and Heidegger.

Sartre fits this Romantic view (as we would expect) in stark opposition to the preceding metaphysical systems of "Descartes, Hume, and Leibniz," to whom he attributes as "an hypothesis shared in common . . . that image and sensation are identical in nature." The rest of Sartre's second chapter is largely taken up with what went wrong. On the one hand, the Romantic view was itself "more of a general atmosphere, rather than a well-defined doctrine." On the other hand, "the general atmosphere quickly changed," as the effort took over to discover a positive method. Then "deterministic and mechanistic science . . . conquered the generation of 1850." [6]

The Successor

In *L'imagination,* one footnote still alludes to a Romantic theorist who undertook in 1836 "a new theory of the image." [7] But we have to consult the *diplôme,* not only for a more extensive exposition of Romantic theories but also for a more drastic regret over their eclipse: "One cannot say," Sartre protests, "that psychology has progressed or that it has left the speculative Romantics behind. It must be said, to the contrary[,] . . . that psychology has gone backward and sacrificed the complexity of things to achieve clarity." But, unfortunately, "Romantic theories had no future."

Nevertheless the Romantics did find a successor. In the *diplôme* Sartre offered a diagram that sorts out the relevant psychologists by schools and assigns a lineage to each. Apparently inspired by Sartre's repeated phrase in the diagram, "The succession passes to," Sartre's supervisor, Henri Delacroix, entered under the names Sartre listed as "Romantic Theories" Sartre's own name. He thus became the successor to the theorists he himself had listed as eclipsed.

If the "Romantic Theories" that are dealt with at some length in the *diplôme* are not dealt with in *L'imagination,* a plausible explanation is that Sartre no longer needs them as predecessors; Husserl has become in the meantime his unique predecessor, and his psychology is not, like theirs, "speculative" and "a general atmosphere rather than a well-defined theory."

I would now explore what survives in Sartre of the Romantic "abyss." We have seen that he insists on pushing the distinction between the image and sense perception further than Husserl had. He insists here that the "matters" involved, as well as the "intentions" are different. He also protests against the fulfillment that takes place with sense-perception also taking place with the imagination in Husserl:

> The image, Husserl states, is a "fulfillment" of "meaning." Examining impersonation has, instead, led us to believe that the image is a meaning that is degraded, that has descended to the level of intuition. No fulfillment is involved; what is involved is an essential change.[8]

Degradation

This protest I reported previously only insofar as it seemed pertinent to Sartre's conception of *le travail du style.* I have not dealt with the distinctively philosophical issue Sartre stresses: "What preoccupies me above all else is what may be called . . . the degradation of knowledge."[9]

This "degradation" is involved in the trait of the imagination that he initially analyzed as "quasi observation," as opposed to the bona fide observation that is a trait of perception. With the impersonation, "we again encounter an essential trait of the mental image—the phenomenon of quasi observation. What I see [by observing Franconay] is what I already know [that Chevalier wears a straw hat at a tilt, and so forth]. I learn nothing from [observing] the object, and my intuition is merely knowledge, weighed down, degraded."[10] This "degradation" is "a radical modification" of the knowledge previously acquired by observation, or (as Sartre put it before) "an essential change."

Why does this "degradation" of knowledge preoccupy Sartre above all else? Perhaps partly because he puts the same premium on knowledge being new as he does on images being "new." When I "see" what I already "know" about Chevalier, it is merely old knowledge. However, his very selection of the term "degradation" is puzzling. The word is evidently to be taken in its etymological sense, for Sartre follows up "the image is a meaning that is degraded" with the elucidation "that has descended to the level of intuition."

In Volume 1, I entered a debate over the attempt to understand a philosopher "in his own terms." Sartre's case poses a problem, since so many of his terms are literally taken over from other philosophers. Sartre's use of the term "degradation" is a succinct illustration of how what Sartre has to say can often be accounted for only in terms of his relation to another philosopher. Expositors of Sartre frequently go wrong by focusing entirely on Sartre and not giving their due to the philosophers from whom he obtains his "plugs." Here the fact that the term is introduced in criticism of a "theory" of Husserl's that Sartre singles out as "shocking" should have been a sufficient clue. Turn to the pertinent chapter in Husserl, "The Phenomenology of the Levels of Knowledge" and specifically to the section, "Identification and Fulfillment." After all, Sartre is dealing with the problem of how we identify Chevalier and how Husserl regards imaginative identification as fulfilling. Husserl explains that he "has equated fulfillment with knowledge (in the narrower sense) . . . and thereby with only certain forms of identification that bring us nearer the goal of knowledge [*Erkenntnisziel*]." The idiom suggests that he is distinguishing between "aiming at" the goal or target [*Abzeilen*] with an "empty" verbal sign and "hitting" [*Erzielen*] with a perceptual or imaginative fulfillment. He goes on to explain, "In fulfillment our experience is 'This is the thing itself.' " But, he cautions, "This 'itself' must not be understood too strictly, as if some perception must be given that brings the object itself to actual phenomenal presence." Though he adds that "it may be that in the progress of knowledge, in the gradual ascent by levels [*stufenweisen Emporsteigen*] from acts of poorer to acts of richer fulfillment of knowledge, we must at length always reach perceptions that are fulfilling. . . . The relation of fulfillment is of a character that admits of differences of degree.[11]

What Sartre must have found "shocking" in Husserl is that the difference between imaginative fulfillment and perceptual fulfillment is merely a difference in degree, as are the differences between different perceptual fulfillments. In Sartre himself, the difference involves a "de-gradation," in the etymological sense of a descent in level. It is this descent that is a "radical modification." The "modification" is "radical" in that it is a movement in the opposite direction, amounting to a dialectical reversal: previously I was acquiring new knowledge, and Husserl employs the idiom of ascent for this acquisition (the movement of ascent was traditional in accounts of induction); now this movement in Sartre is reversed, for I am observing only what I already know about Chevalier, and Sartre employs the idiom of descent (the "meaning that is degraded . . . has descended from [the level of knowledge] to the level of intuition").

Frustration

"Degradation" also has its usual pejorative moral sense for Sartre. I quoted before a passage that illustrates the shift in *subject* whereby the opposition between perception and the imagination is no longer merely phenomenological for Sartre but also becomes pivotal to a moral theory. Now I would bring out how a prerogative of the real we perceive is its novelty:

> The real is always new, always *unpredictable*. I wanted Annie to come, but the Annie I desired were merely the correlative of my desires. Here she is, but she overflows my desire on all sides; I must begin my apprenticeship [the inductive process of acquiring knowledge] all over again.

As we recognized before, what "we imagine cannot fulfill our desires"; instead, it's a way of deceiving them for a moment, only to aggravate them later, rather like "the effect of seawater on thirst." [12]

We are reminded that what is at issue here in Sartre is not a simple opposition between traits of an imaginary and a perceived object but the opposition as well between the feelings we adopt toward each. In other words, "fulfillment" itself—or its opposite, "frustration"—are not simply the cognitive phenomena they become with Husserl's eidetic reduction but are vulgarized (or naturalized) by Sartre and recover their ordinary reference to the fulfillment or frustration of our desires. A final reason, I suspect, why Sartre is preoccupied with "the degradation of knowledge" is the compensatory part that then has to be played by emotional phenomena in making up for this degradation—in the case of the impersonation, our affective reaction to Chevalier. They do not intervene in this fashion in Husserl. This crucial difference between Sartre and Husserl has broader implications than I have yet considered, and these I shall take up in my Conclusion.

However, there are first some problems to be faced that are posed by Sartre's own conclusion to *L'imaginaire*. Degradation and frustration are the traits of the image that are stressed in the chapter "The Imaginary Life," which precedes his conclusion, but they do not reappear in his conclusion itself. Instead, the imagination is exalted as free, which may be what we should expect if Sartre is heir to the Romantic tradition of the creative imagination. That should be the last chord on which I would like to hold the pedal down at the end of this volume. Unfortunately, questions of method that were so skimpily treated at the beginning of *L'imaginaire* encroach in Sartre's conclusion and entail considerable adjustments in his relation to Husserl.

EIGHT

CONSCIOUSNESS AND
IMAGINATION

THIRTY-ONE

Radical Conversion

Consciousness, carrying out a radical conversion,
... constitutes itself as imagining consciousness.
—*Sartre*

The Concession

Earlier I explained how Sartre, at the request of his publisher's reader, Bernard Groethuysen, added to *L'imaginaire* (as originally written) a concluding chapter, "The Work of Art." But in *L'imaginaire* (as published) the "Conclusion" is composed of this chapter and a preceding chapter, entitled "Consciousness and Imagination."

This chapter turns out to be not the kind of conclusion any expositor likes to face when he would wind up and reach his own conclusion. He finds himself asking, Is this a conclusion to the work that I have been expounding? Sartre presents it as if it were. The first sentence of the chapter, the sentence that ushers us into the "Conclusion" as a whole is, "Now we can raise the metaphysical question that has slowly been revealed by this investigation in phenomenological psychology." [1] Have we been aware that a metaphysical question was being slowly revealed? Even the term "revealed" (*dévoilé*) is unprecedented; there has not been a previous revelation in *L'imaginaire*.

Our surprise is compounded when Sartre explains that he is formulating this metaphysical question of the imagination not "from the phenomenological point of view" but in terms of a "critical analysis"— that is, a "regressive analysis," in which he proceeds from what is given as a phenomenon to the "condition" that renders the phe-

nomenon possible. The question then becomes, "What must consciousness be in general, if it is the case that the constitution of the image is
always possible?" Sartre's justification is that this is "the formulation that
our minds, habituated to pose philosophical problems from Kantian perspectives, will best understand." [2]

A scholar might well find this concession to a French audience evidence that this chapter was a later addition, for it suggests that the manuscript has been in the hands of a reader (perhaps the publisher's, perhaps
Groethuysen) who could have warned Sartre that he couldn't get away
with phenomenology in France, that he had better dilute it. However, I
cite this concession not to support any scholarly hypothesis but, first, for
its interest for the history of phenomenology. When Sartre made this concession, despite his having himself been entirely converted, phenomenology had not yet made any considerable inroad in France. Second, the
concession illustrates how insensitive or indifferent Sartre is to the priority that method had for Husserl and that would preclude the cavalier
substitution of "Kantian perspectives" for "the phenomenological point
of view."

Since this history of mine is a history of phenomenology, I am not
going to take the substitution into account. Instead, I would first link the
"Conclusion" up with the criticism of Husserl I was considering in Chapter 30. Sartre admits that the metaphysical question "may seem entirely
new and even pointless to French psychologists." [3] This Sartre explains as
due in part to the fact that for them "there is no general problem of the
imagination," since images are merely "reemerging sensations." Here we
can at last see in how strong a sense what I termed in my Introduction a
shift in *subject* takes place in Sartre: with his "radical renovation," he
pushes the "distinction between the image and perception," which he
originally picked out of Husserl's handling of the Dürer engraving, further than Husserl did—indeed, to a point at which the image becomes a
distinct subject. We have seen it is distinct from perception not only with
respect to its intentionality (as it already is in Husserl) but also with respect to its "matter," and in that it does not provide the intuitive fulfillment that perception does. In the "Conclusion," Sartre will arrive, with a
final push, at an ultimate distinction.

Negation

The answer Sartre eventually reaches with his Kantian regress is that

> The condition that is essential for a consciousness to be able to
> imagine is that is possible for it to pose a thesis of unreality. But it is
> necessary to be more specific about this condition. It is not at all a

matter of consciousness ceasing to be consciousness *of* something. It enters into the very nature of consciousness to be intentional. . . . But consciousness must be able to . . . pose objects that are affected by a certain character of nothingness in relation to the totality of the real. . . . The act of negation is constitutive of the image.[4]

This answer is hardly Kantian. Also startling is that Sartre has to reassure us here, in concluding *L'imaginaire*, that he still regards consciousness as intentional. What is transpiring is that Sartre, while pretending that he is translating his treatment of the imagination into a Kantian "regressive analysis" and then merely being "more specific," is in fact translating it into terms of negation. This translation does yield another version of the distinction—indeed, the opposition—that we have so long watched him pursue: an act of perception poses a thesis of reality; an act of imagination a thesis of unreality.

I shall not try to decide the scholarly question of whether this chapter was the original conclusion or a revision of it or whether it was a new chapter appended along with the other new chapter, "The Work of Art." In any case, this chapter was presumably written later than the previous chapters.

The scope of its title, "Consciousness and Imagination," suggests that this chapter was not only written as a conclusion but that it also is in effect transitional to *Being and Nothingness,* where Sartre's concern is with consciousness at large and no longer restricted to the imagination. This transitional character of the chapter is evident from his translation of the problem of the imagination into terms of negation. Not only are there no explicit references to Husserl, but there are frequent references to Heidegger and resorts to his terminology. Thus the term "reveal," which we encountered in the first sentence of the chapter (it turns up again twice in the second paragraph), is rather a giveaway, for it translates Heidegger's *erschliessen,* and it occurs again at the beginning of *Being and Nothingness.*[5] The issue here is not terminological pedantry, for *erschliessen* is a very different operation than any envisaged by Husserl.

Sartre is undeniably in the process of being converted to Heidegger, granted that evidence for his conversion is not complete until *Being and Nothingness.* Henry Corbin's anthology translated selections of Heidegger's works and was published in 1938, but Sartre could have read "What is Metaphysics?" on negation earlier.[6] In any case, the disarray in this chapter is such that there would seem little point in examining Sartre's treatment here of the problem of negation if it is merely a rough transition, with Sartre slouching toward *Being and Nothingness,* though its hour has not yet quite come round. But with a little patience on our part, the disarray will prove illuminating. After all our laboring over *L'imaginaire,* we can hardly skimp what has had conferred on it the dignity of a "Conclusion."

The Phenomenological Reduction

Sartre's relation to Heidegger is not my concern in the present volume. I am concerned instead with what has happened to Sartre's relation to Husserl when he concludes a work that he emphasizes had been "inspired by Husserl." Although there is no explicit mention of Husserl in the "Conclusion," although in the first paragraph he has in effect been shunted aside by Sartre's substituting "Kantian perspectives" for "a phenomenological point of view," the second paragraph begins: "After the phenomenological reduction, we find ourselves in the presence of the transcendental consciousness that is revealed to our reflective descriptions." But we were reminded in the first paragraph that our "investigation" was "phenomenological psychology." And we have not forgotten Sartre's initial admission that although "the essential proceeding of phenomenological method is the [phenomenological] 'reduction,' the *epochē*—that is, the bracketing of the natural attitude," he is not qua phenomenological psychologist "carrying out this *epochē,* but remains at the level of the natural attitude."[7] Now in the "Conclusion," the phenomenological reduction is presumed to have taken place, somehow blended with a Kantian regress to the transcendental conditions of experience. But the blend itself is a blur, since Sartre is overriding the distinction between the Kantian regress and Husserl's reduction: the transcendental conditions of experience are inferred in Kant as beyond experience; in Husserl, "transcendental consciousness" becomes, "after the phenomenological reduction" (as Sartre puts it), an immediately given experience.

Fortunately, this disconcertingly different analysis in Sartre's "Conclusion" can still be compared with Sartre's earlier analysis, for Sartre retrieves the same example of the portrait of Charles VIII in both chapters of the "Conclusion." The second chapter, "The Work of Art," begins: "It seems it is time to derive some conclusions from the long investigation in which we have taken as an example, a statue, or the portrait of Charles VIII, or a novel." Sartre then goes on:

> What follows will have to do essentially with the existential status of the work of art. And we can now formulate the principal conclusion: the work of art is an unreal.
>
> That appeared to us previously when we were considering as an example, for an entirely different purpose, the portrait of Charles

VIII. We understood, first of all, that this Charles VIII was an object. But it was obviously not the same object as the paint, the canvas, the real layers of paint. So long as we were considering the canvas and the frame for themselves, the aesthetic object *Charles VIII* did not appear. . . . It could not be given to a realizing consciousness [*conscience réalisante*]. It will appear at the moment when consciousness, carrying out a radical conversion, which presupposes the nihilation [*néantisation*] of the world, constitutes itself as imagining consciousness.[8]

The only hitch is that much of this had not "appeared to us previously when we were considering . . . the portrait of Charles VIII." The distinction between the perceived painted object and the imagined Charles VIII was drawn, with considerable emphasis instead on the part played by our "affective impression"—an emphasis that Sartre seems to have forgotten.

Prière d'Insérer

In dealing with this stretch of the disarray, we have to allow for the "entirely different purpose" that Sartre is now entertaining and that helps explain his misremembering what had "appeared" to him earlier. The explanation can be eked out by consulting Sartre's *prière d'insérer*, since he is likely to have written it even later than the "Conclusion." I quote from it his statement of his own position:

The distinction between images and sensations can absolutely be founded only on a difference in being. Only a phenomenology of consciousness and of Being can renew the problem of the imagination in order to distinguish existentially the object "*en image*" from the perceived object.[9]

I interrupt the quotation to observe that we now have an explanation of Sartre's reintroducing the example of the portrait of Charles VIII with reference to "the existential status of the work of art." Moreover, the "absolutely" and the repeated "only" manifest the conviction of a convert. "Only a phenomenology of consciousness and of Being" (which he has not capitalized previously) represents a synthesis of Husserl and Heidegger in a "Phenomenological Ontology"—to cite the subtitle of *Being and Nothingness*. In our last chapter, we became familiar with Sartre's criterion of novelty; now what he proposes to accomplish with this synthesis is to "renew the problem of the imagination" in a new fashion—"in order to distinguish existentially the object '*en image*' from the perceived object." Sartre never previously characterized the distinction between the object '*en image*' and the perceived object as drawn "existentially."

I resume the outline of *L'imaginaire* in the *prière d'insérer*: "I have tried here to describe with the phenomenological method certain special objects that present themselves . . . to consciousness, and that are distinct from 'real' things by the fact that their being is a nothingness of being, and that I have named *imaginaires,* to avoid using the old word image, still soiled by sensualism [that is, the failure to distinguish the image from sensations] and positivism." But Sartre has in fact retained the old word in the body of *L'imaginaire!* I continue with the outline:

> Their investigation [the investigation of the *imaginaires*] has led me to the phenomenological examination of "The Imaginary Life" [that is, the last part of *L'imaginaire* preceding its conclusion]. . . . Finally, by a natural regress, I have been led to ask, What must consciousness be in its intimate nature for *imaginaires* to be given to it in general? It then seemed to me that the imaginary could occur only against the background of the nihiliation [*néantisation*] of the World.

The foreshortening in this outline is remarkable, quite aside from Sartre's sponsoring of new terminology. Though the phrase *"en image"* (in the second sentence I have quoted) is used again in his handling of the example of Charles VIII (as it was the first time), and derives from Husserl, what comes to the fore in the outline are the last chapters of *L'imaginaire*.

The first point I would make is that the *rupture* that we have watched take place between works in Sartre is taking place within this work, which happened to be delayed in its publication. After Sartre rejected the doctrine of salvation by art, he had Roquentin go on believing it because it had been the initial premise of *Nausea*.[10] But he is less respectful of the integrity of *L'imaginaire* as a philosophical work. Sartre demonstrates his *pouvoir d'arrachement* by admitting, "My best book is that which I am in the process of writing."[11] This admission can be extended (at least in the case of *L'imaginaire*) to read "The best part of any book I write is the part I am in the process of writing." I would construe the "then" in "It appeared to me then [*Il m'est apparu alors*]" as referring not to the time when he wrote *L'imaginaire* (though this may have been Sartre's intent) but to when he was finishing *L'imaginaire*. "Appeared to me" may be the normal idiom for a phenomenologist, but we are aware of the facility with which the appearances can sometimes change in Sartre, since he has already reported in his "Conclusion" that it "appeared to us previously" (that is, "when we were considering as an example . . . the portrait of Charles VIII") what had not actually appeared to us previously. Thus I am suggesting that he did not anticipate the "Conclusion" while he was writing the body of the work and that what is at issue in the "Conclusion" has not in fact (as he indicates at its beginning) "slowly been revealed" during the course of his analysis. It struck him only when he reached the "Conclusion," and it struck him "then" because he was being converted: he was beginning to "let go" of Husserl in order to "grasp" the "revelation" he was obtaining from Heidegger, along with the term "reveal." Here I am concerned only with how what he is obtaining from Heidegger effects what he retains from Husserl.

The Epochē

Having inserted the *prière d'insérer,* I return to the "Conclusion" and to Sartre's reintroduction there of the example of the portrait of Charles VIII. What catches our attention is the claim that "the aesthetic object *'Charles VIII'* . . . will appear at the moment when consciousness, carrying out a radical conversion, . . . constitutes itself as imagining consciousness." This conversion did not take place when the example of Charles VIII was first deployed. Indeed, though there was a kind of self-transformation featured by the impersonation and by the actor playing Hamlet, we did not encounter the term "conversion" before in *L'imaginaire.* Yet conversion will become a prominent preoccupation of Sartre's in later works.

Why, too, should the conversion be "radical"? Does this only betray Sartre's own predisposition to discontinuity? The rupture involved is an ultimate rendering of his "distinction between the image and perception." We have been aware that Sartre has been looking for an "abyss" here ever since he read Romantic theories for his *diplôme.* But Sartre's terminology also seems reminiscent of Husserl's presentation of the *epochē,* which the phenomenological reduction involves as a "Radical Modification [*Änderung*] of the Natural Thesis." This thesis is "a positing of the existence of the world" and it is intrinsic to "the natural attitude" as a tacit concomitant of any act of perceptual consciousness of something. Sartre retains the term "thesis" in explaining that perceptual consciousness involves a "thesis of a realizing consciousness"; he formulates its opposite, imaginative consciousness, as "positing a thesis of unreality."

However, Sartre has also taken a step beyond the object—"the work of art" which is "an unreal" ("a nothingness")—by attributing to consciousness the ability "to pose objects affected with a certain character of nothingness in relation to the totality of the real." This step he had not taken in his original analysis of consciousness in the portrait of Charles VIII.[12] But now, when I become "conscious of the portrait of Charles VIII *en image,* I immediately no longer consider the painting as a "part of the real world." Alternatively put, "consciousness, in order to produce the object '*Charles VIII*' *en image,* must be able to negate the reality of the painting, and it can negate this reality only by drawing back [*prenant du recul*] in relation to reality taken as a totality." *Prenant du recul* translates Husserl's *epochē.*[13]

Although Husserl does employ the idiom "conversion" of the phenomenological reduction, he expressly denies that the reduction involves the "presupposition of not-being," which he associates with Cartesian doubt, and he refuses to allow the "suspension" (*Aufhebung*) of the thesis [of the existence of the world] to undergo "transformation into the antithesis, the positing into negation." How does Sartre pull off this transformation?

THIRTY-TWO

Nothingness

The epochē is no longer a miracle, an intellectual method.—Sartre

The Conflation

The puzzling expression in the "Conclusion" to *L'imaginaire, néantisation du monde,* Sartre could have obtained from Husserl, who argues later in *Ideas I* that "although the being of consciousness . . . would necessarily be modified by the *Vernichtung der Welt,* its own existence would not be effected." But this is a different argument from that pursued by Sartre; it has nothing to do with the image, or the work of art, or even with negation. Nor does Husserl suggest (as Sartre does) that the reduction "presupposes" this *Vernichtung der Welt.*[1]

Furthermore, there is a definite incongruity in what is transpiring in Sartre. On the one hand, he incorporates (we have just seen) Husserl's *epochē* as my "drawing back [*prenant du recul*] in relation to reality taken as a totality." On the other hand, the world as a whole in Sartre also "draws back [*recule*]." The incongruity between these two movements can be explained only by suspecting that the second movement is Heidegger's "Zurückweichen vor [das Nichts]," which Corbin translates "un movement de recul devant [le Néant]."[2] These two movements are opposed in such fashion as hardly to be reconcilable even in Sartre's loose-jointed dialectic.

Indeed, I would speculate that if Sartre did feel any discomfort over the incongruity of this conflation, it could have encouraged him to work his way toward *Being and Nothingness,* where he will set Husserl and Heidegger in opposition to each other. But he has not gotten there yet. Thus I would infer that Sartre's "Kantian" regress is less from the phenomena to a condition it presupposes than a regress from Husserl's phenomenology to Heidegger's ontology. We have another illustration of what I earlier called Sartre's bookishness: despite his contempt for the academic, despite his effort to "smash" the "professor" in himself,[3] Sartre remains a professor of other philosophies, from which he has difficulty in disentangling himself in order to arrive at a distinctive philosophy of his own.

Even after the slovenliness of Sartre's conflation of Husserl with Heidegger is acknowledged, we still have to face up to the discrepancy in Sartre's handling of the phenomenological reduction. Does he or doesn't he? On the one hand, we have his initial admission that although "the essential procedure" of Husserl's method is "the [phenomenological] 'reduction,' the *epochē,*" he himself is "not carrying out his *epochē* and remains at the level of the natural attitude." On the other hand, at the beginning of the "Conclusion" his "after the phenomenological reduction" assumes that it has been carried out; later we encounter it in the guise of the "radical conversion."

Now that we have recognized that the phenomenological reduction in Sartre presupposes negation, it will help if we anticipate his argument in *Being and Nothingness* against Heidegger's handling of negation. References in *Being and Nothingness* back to *L'imaginaire* are rare. But Sartre does recall his having argued in *L'imaginaire* that if "we begin by taking the image as a reemerging perception [the position he has been attacking ever since the *diplôme,* as we saw in the last chapter], it is then radically impossible to distinguish it from present perceptions. The image must include in its very structure a nihilating thesis [*thèse néantisante*]."[4] All that is of interest to us now is the complaint against Heidegger that this argument supports—that his theory "cuts off . . . nothingness from any concrete negation." Sartre's principle "toward the concrete" promotes this complaint: "If I emerge in nothingness *beyond* the world [this is Sartre's interpretation of Heidegger's nothingness as transcendental], how can this extra-worldly nothingness provide a foundation for those little pools of not-being which we encounter at each moment within being?"[5] One of these would be the "nihilating thesis" that "the image must include in its very structure." The fate of Husserl's phenomenological reduction in *Being and Nothingness* is comparable, and we get a foretaste of it in *L'imaginaire,* where it is already conceived as at once a transcendental operation and as an operation within the world that is integral to any act of the imagination. Thus the answer to my earlier question is that Sartre does carry out the phenomenological reduction, but not in Husserl's sense.

Confusion

The incorporation of the phenomenological reduction (its "thesis of un-reality") in any act of the imagination, as opposed to an act of perception (with its implicit thesis of the reality of what it is consciousness of), I have characterized as Sartre's ultimate move in pushing further that distinction, which he found as a "starting point" in Husserl's handling of the Dürer engraving but which Husserl himself had not "pushed further." But Husserl himself used the example of the Dürer engraving in order to clarify the neutrality modification, which is intrinsic to an act of the (depictive) imagination, whereby one becomes conscious of a portrait no longer as a painting but "as an image." This ultimate push is the ultimate irony, inasmuch as Husserl undertook this clarification of the neutrality modification not out of concern with either the work of art or the imagination but, ultimately (as we saw at the very beginning of this volume), because of "a dangerous ambiguity" that portends "a besetting confusion." The danger he envisaged was confusing "the neutrality modification [as such—and, thus, in the crucial instance when it is a phenomenological reduction] with an act of the imagination." Thus the dramatic denouement in Sartre's relation to Husserl is that although Sartre initially recognized that "the essential procedure of phenomenological method is the reduction," [6] he eventually succumbs with respect to this reduction to the very "confusion" that Husserl sought to avoid in the section on the Dürer engraving where Sartre found his "starting point."

If this confusion were simply a confusion on Sartre's part, it would hardly merit attention. But it is also, on the one hand, a vindication for his shift in *subject* and for the scope of his subject. In Husserl, the phenomenological reduction is the "entrance gate" by which we leave the real world behind and enter the transcendental realm of the ideal, which is "unreal." But in Sartre, the imaginary apparently becomes coextensive with "the unreal." Not only does no room remain for Husserl's idealism, but the imaginary takes over the scope reserved in Husserl for the ideal. [7]

Toward the Concrete

What Husserl would regard as a "confusion" is, on the other hand, a shift in *method* on Sartre's part in conformity with his principle "toward the concrete": what is distinctively methodological in one philosopher (in the present case, Husserl's phenomenological reduction) can become a substantive operation (an act of the imagination) in another philosopher. When this transformation took place in the previous case of the eidetic reduction, I pointed out that this outcome of the principle "toward the concrete" can also be regarded as consistent with Sartre's own method becoming a rudimentary dialectic in which "form" cannot be disassociated from "content."[8] Method perversely regains the priority Sartre himself does not accord it: not only was the methodological procedure formulated by Husserl prior to its becoming a substantive operation in Sartre, but this substantive operation in Sartre can itself hardly be understood without recovering its erstwhile methodological character in Husserl.

In my Conclusion to Volume 1 of this history, I explained how the principle "toward the concrete" presided over the elaboration of Sartre's philosophy in relation to both Husserl and Heidegger. This Volume 2 has added detailed illustration of how this principle promotes Sartre's "vulgarization" (or "naturalization") of Husserl. This is not, however, the complete undermining of the distinction in *level* in Husserl between the transcendental and the natural attitude. Consider the comparable transformation that the phenomenological reduction undergoes when Sartre rejects Husserl's transcendental ego. There, in conformity with the principle "toward the concrete," Sartre's triumphant outcome is that the reduction "is no longer [as in Husserl] a miracle, an intellectual method, a learned procedure: . . . it is at once a pure event transcendental in its origin and an always possible accident of every day life."[9] Sartre's "no longer" marks a juncture at which what had been "an intellectual method, a learned procedure" becomes concretely embodied in a substantive performance, somewhat *stiffened* by its methodological heritage.

As an example, Sartre cites the case of "a young bride," who "was afraid, when her husband left her alone, of going to the window and summoning passersby like a prostitute."[10] Sartre's diagnosis is a conflation of Husserl with Heidegger. On the one hand, Sartre finds that "the natural attitude [in Husserl] is entirely coherent and does not provide any of those contradictions that, according to Plato, lead the philosopher to undertake a conversion. Thus the *epochē* emerges in Husserl's phenomenology as inexplicable."[11] On the other hand, Sartre finds a motive for the *epochē* (concretely for the young bride's "bracketing" the behavior required of her as normal) in anxiety as analyzed by Heidegger.[12]

Anxiety itself I have to leave to one side, since I cannot take into account here Sartre's debt to Heidegger's analysis of it. But in Sartre, it is consciousness of one's "vertiginous freedom." This dizziness of the bride I would diagnose as due in some measure to *interplay* between the transcendental and mundane levels.

We have been examining a somewhat similar conflation between the transcendental and the mundane in a grandiose version of the *interplay* we watched take place earlier in *L'imaginaire* between the level of the unreal, which is imagined, and of the real, which is perceived. The concluding chapter, "Consciousness and Imagination," is transitional to *Being and Nothingness,* where *interplay* will take place between "little pools" of nothingness and transcendental nothingness.[13] *Interplay,* whereby "an always possible accident of everyday life," or an ordinary act of imagination or negation, can implicate "a pure event transcendental in its origin," may help explain some of the attraction Sartre's philosophy once gained among the unlearned as "existentialism"—an attraction that Husserl's phenomenological reduction, as "an intellectual method" for reaching a purely transcendental level, could never have exercised.

THIRTY-THREE

: # *Freedom*

The imagination . . . is consciousness as a whole
insofar as it actualizes its freedom.—Sartre

The Progression

I have accounted for the attraction of "vertiginous freedom" in Sartre as having been due
to *interplay* between the transcendental and
the mundane. Another rendering of the scope
of freedom in Sartre is that his entire philosophy has often seemed to require interpretation in terms of the ramifications of the concept of freedom. Two recent studies are
attempts to satisfy this requirement: Christina Howells's *Sartre: The Necessity of Freedom* and Thomas W. Busch's *The Power of
Consciousness and the Force of Circumstances in Sartre's Philosophy.*

Howells launches her interpretation in
the following fashion:

> As philosopher, dramatist, novelist,
> critic, and moralist, Sartre's major
> preoccupation was, throughout his life,
> always the same—freedom, its impli-
> cations and its obstacles. It is a critical
> cliché—and Sartre himself contributed
> to its dissemination—to view the pro-
> gression of his thought as moving away
> from a conception of absolute freedom
> towards a mature position which takes
> into account the constraints and condi-
> tioning of the external world.

Busch similarly argues that Sartre's "unifying
concept" is freedom, but his title plays up the
same change that is reported by Howells as a
"critical cliché." [1]

Can I get away with a lengthier work on Sartre than either of theirs without the concept of freedom being allowed more recognition? Only briefly alluded to in the *Transcendence of the Ego,* it is elaborated for the first time in the "Conclusion" to *L'imaginaire.* This elaboration I can hardly shirk, granted that Sartre's mature position is only a peripheral concern of mine.

What I would examine, from the restricted angle of this "Conclusion," is only the framework itself that is taken over from Sartre by Howells and Busch to interpret "the progression of his thought." How could it occur to Sartre (to anyone) that his freedom was "absolute?" But let me begin with the position he progresses to; for more plausible than "absolute freedom" is his coming to accept "the external world" or "circumstances" as constraining conditions. Sartre gives an account of this progression in the interview "Sartre par Sartre," which I mentioned had previously been entitled, when it appeared in English, "The Itinerary of a Thought." A possible explanation I offered for the change in title, was Sartre's having brushed to one side the philosophical evidence, as to his itinerary, which the interviewer had presented. Sartre brushed it aside with the pronouncement, "The fundamental problem is my relation to Marxism."[2] I argued that, if this is the fundamental problem, what is interesting about it is that his relation to Marxism is not itself Marxist, and is most readily understood by taking into account the earlier philosophical works he is brushing to one side.

The Prisoner

What concerns me now is Sartre's explanation of his progression. I quote the sentence after the pronouncement: "I would try to explain by my autobiography certain aspects of my first works, for it is of assistance in understanding why I so radically changed my point of view after the Second World War." I interrupt with a reminder that I have argued that this radical change is to be in some measure understood by comparing it with previous radical changes in his point of view: his prewar conversion to Husserl and his conversion during the war to Heidegger.

Having based my own explanation on these comparisons, I come up against Sartre's explanation in the rest of the first paragraph:

> I should say, in a simple formula, that life has taught me "the force of circumstances." In fact, I should have begun to discover this force of circumstances as early as *Being and Nothingness* because I had already at that time been made a soldier which I did not want to be. I thus had already had the experience of something which was not my freedom and which controlled me from outside. I was even

made a prisoner, a fate I had sought to escape. . . . Thus, I was beginning to discover the reality of the situation of man amid his circumstances, which I called "being-in-the-world." [3]

The "simple formula" may indeed be too simple, for Sartre is giving a
counter-to-fact explanation, even though it is introduced by the assertion
"in fact." What Sartre is apparently claiming is that, with his concept of
"being-in-the-world," he should have been able to acknowledge the force
of circumstances as he had experienced it during the war.

I am not just putting forward the obvious—that once Sartre's relation to Marxism becomes fundamental, what is meant by "the force of
circumstances" and by "world" undergoes a radical change. I am also
commenting on Sartre's progression, which is blurred in his counter-to-
fact explanation of what he "should have begun to discover." Sartre is
not giving another "progression" quite its due, which was already underway in his thinking and which he himself had previously picked out with
another simple formula—"toward the concrete"—and found implemented in Heidegger's concept of "being-in-the-world." If we step outside
the never-never land of the counter-to-fact, we can restore the facts by
recalling how Sartre turns from Husserl toward Heidegger in *Being and
Nothingness*: "Consciousness is an abstraction. . . . The concrete is man
in the world . . . which Heidegger . . . calls 'being-in-the-world.' "[4]

What Sartre's later account of the force of circumstances leaves out is
the fate he did not escape as a prisoner of war: he read *Being and Time*
and it became a destiny. In Volume 1 I managed a transition from the
constraints and conditioning of the external world to the constraints and
conditioning of other philosophies on the elaboration of Sartre's philosophy. I argued that his wartime circumstances exercised their constraints
in considerable measure by virtue of his reading of Heidegger. Indeed it is
in these very terms that he himself then formulated a problem of freedom:
"To understand the respective roles played [generally] by freedom and
destiny with respect to what is called 'succumbing to an influence,' I can
reflect [specifically] on the influence Heidegger has exercised on me." [5]

Once his relation to Marxism became fundamental to Sartre, he
played down, not just Husserl and Heidegger, but intellectual influences
generally. Perhaps he felt a danger of "idealism" in accepting them. He
had come to view "idealism" generally as a philosophy which is circum-
stanceless, or rather which disavows circumstances, including those conditioning its own emergence. Even in his own case, to reach the circumstances of his life, Sartre had to descend from idealism by putting on
shoes of lead. [6]

Absolute Freedom

Perhaps Sartre's most notorious contribution to the dissemination of the "critical cliché," whereby he moved away from a conception of absolute freedom to a taking into account of constraints and conditioning, is an admission that both Howells and Busch quote. Sartre recalls his initial commitment to absolute freedom and finds it "very symptomatic" of his once prevailing "state of mind" that he called his early plays a "theater of freedom." He is "scandalized" at his having said in "a prefatory note" that "whatever the circumstances, and wherever he may be, a man is always free to choose to be a traitor or resist." Then he confesses, "When I read this, I said to myself it's incredible—I actually believed that!"[7]

Indeed what is almost "incredible" is Sartre's confession. Philosophers sometimes discard previous convictions, but they usually are still able to give reasons why they believed what they once believed. Discarding previous convictions as "incredible" is sufficiently unusual to deserve explanation. When Sartre believed in freedom as absolute, he was a phenomenologist. Thus his belief should have been an immediate deliverance of his consciousness. How then could he ever get around to rejecting it?

In order to come to closer grips with Sartre's concept of freedom as absolute I would have to expound *Being and Nothingness,* which is beyond my present scope. I cannot do much more than examine the context in which he first comes up with this concept—in the "Conclusion" to *L'imaginaire.*

Procedure

Since I am concerned to exhibit my own procedure, as well as this context, permit me to compare my own interpretation with Howells'. She quotes Sartre in the first sentence of her interpretation of *Being and Nothingness.* This is a significant juncture in anyone's interpretation of Sartre, since *Being and Nothingness* is usually regarded as his major philosophical work and it is at any rate his most influential. But she is not quoting *Being and Nothingness* itself, but *L'imaginaire,* so that she is in effect making a transition from an earlier work, which she has been expounding, to a later work. Before considering this transition and her quotation, reconsider my demonstration of how difficult it can be to follow such transitions through in Sartre.

What complicates Sartre's transition from the prewar *L'imaginaire* to the wartime *Being and Nothingness* is his conversion in between to Heidegger. This is not just a matter of his "succumbing to an influence"; what survives as distinctively Sartrean is some of the exhilarating freedom that he associates with a conversion, when "one lets go in order to grasp and grasps in order to let go." The structure of Sartre's earlier philosophy collapses, as a project "inspired by Husserl," and the structure of "a new project" emerges.[8]

This assimilation of the transition to the structure of a conversion I have offered as illuminating, but it should not be overdone, since Sartre warns us against his tendency to "transform a tranquil evolutionism into a revolutionary and discontinuous catastrophism."[9] I have put sufficient emphasis already on his *travail de la rupture* and on his commitment to "radical renovation." Also, since he obtains the concept of "project" from Heidegger and presents it himself, along with the "conversion,"[10] in *Being and Nothingness*, I will only suggest that an adequate treatment of his concept of "freedom" would take these concepts into consideration too. But even if we put exhilaration aside, and become pedantic, the evolution from *L'imaginaire* to *Being and Nothingness* is hardly tranquil.

Discontinuity

In the sentence with which Howells begins her interpretation of *Being and Nothingness* she, half concedes between the two works the discontinuity I call "a shift in *subject*," but then denies it: "In *Being and Nothingness* Sartre does not discuss imagination *per se*, but since it is identified with [now she quotes *L'imaginaire*] 'consciousness as a whole insofar as it actualizes its freedom,' it *necessarily underlies the entire work*."[11]

An unanswered question is raised by this sentence with its quotation from *L'imaginaire*: Why should Sartre not admit himself that he is presupposing his previous analysis of the imagination as underlying his entire later work? To find out what Sartre does in fact presuppose in *Being and Nothingness*, the expositor should consult its introduction. Here he is likely to find presuppositions that will help explain why Sartre is treating there not the imagination but "consciousness as a whole." The first is something that "Heidegger expressed very well when he wrote (though speaking of being-there, not of consciousness): 'The "how" (*essentia*) of this being . . . must be conceived in terms of its existence (*essentia*).'" The second proposition is a definition:

> Certainly we could apply to consciousness the definition which Heidegger reserves for being-there and say that it is a being such that in its being, its being is in question. But it would be necessary to complete the definition and formulate it more like this: *consciousness is a being such that in its being, its being [is] in question insofar as this being implies a being other than itself.*[12]

This is the only italicized statement in Sartre's introduction. I would claim that any attempt to get at what necessarily underlies *Being and Nothingness* as "an entire work" would include Sartre's interpretation of "what Heidegger expressed very well" in the first statement, Heidegger's "definition" in the second statement, and how Sartre finds it "necessary to complete the definition and formulate it."

I reemphasize, *Being and Nothingness* as "an entire work" is beyond my scope here. I can merely make the further claim that these necessarily underlying propositions are not found in *L'imaginaire,* not even in its "Conclusion." They are all Sartre's later (mis)interpretations of Heidegger. Although this "Conclusion" is transitional in Sartre's thinking, he does not arrive at *Being and Nothingness.* There Sartre makes a new start. Thus a certain discontinuity intrudes between the two works, just as it intrudes between *Being and Nothingness* and the *Critique of Dialectical Reason,* in which Sartre turns toward Marxism. Hence I suggest that we would come closer to explaining why Sartre is treating "consciousness as a whole" in *Being and Nothingness* itself if we were to recognize that Sartre is transferring to consciousness certain propositions of Heidegger's regarding being-there and that accompanying this transfer is a criterion of totality, which becomes explicit for Sartre (or at least reinforced) as a result of Heidegger's insistence that being-there, as being-in-the-world, "is not pieced together, but is originally and constantly a whole." [13]

In His Own Terms

I see no need to repeat here my arguments in Volume 1 regarding attempts to understand a philosopher "in his own terms." [14] This seems to be Howells' endeavor, and it is always worthwhile, even when the constraints and conditions a philosopher has been subject to seem more obviously other philosophies than the force of circumstances. But in Sartre's case the endeavor encounters the almost insurmountable difficulty of what I have called his "bookishness" (or the "academicization" of his experience). This difficulty no expositor has acknowledged before; it seems so unphenomenological of Sartre, so out of keeping with his existentialism.

Sartre's "bookishness" does not mean that I have been able to put Sartre's "Writing" back into the books he was "Reading"—to retain the pair of rubrics in terms of which he organizes his autobiography in *Words.* He is not philosophically the plagiarist he reports himself as having been in his juvenile literary efforts. But meanings do cling to the terminology he borrows, and I have tried painstakingly to determine the extent to which he was "captured" by Husserl in *L'imaginaire* and the extent, as de Beauvoir proclaims, he "invented both method and content, obtaining all its materials from his own experience." Sartre has emerged from my exposition, not just as ill-digested Husserl, but as inventive.

Given that Sartre has been the most widely read philosopher of this century, it has seemed worth determining how inventive he was (especially since his philosophy puts a premium on novelty and freedom) and wherein he was inventive. I don't see how this can be done except by following a procedure such as mine. Because it is this procedure itself that I would defend, I am placing it alongside Howells' comprehensive attempt to interpret Sartre in his own terms.

What are Sartre's own terms? *Sartre par Sartre* begins with the interviewer's question (revised): "How do you see the relation between your previous philosophical writings, in particular *Being and Nothingness,* and your present theoretical work—say, since the *Crique of Dialectical Reason?*" This question regarding the relation between his own works, we have seen Sartre answers in terms of his relation to another philosophy: "The fundamental problem is my relation with Marxism."

An expositor of Sartre need not bog down in all the details of Sartre's debts to other philosophers, but there should be some acknowledgement that a distinctive trait of his philosophy is the very extent of his indebtedness to them.[15] The relations between philosophies cannot be held fixed as the historian moves on from expounding one philosopher in his own terms to expounding another philosopher in his own terms. The relations change, since they are differently determined in each successive philosophy, granted that the historian may have reasons for offering a different appraisal of these relations from those built into a philosophy itself.[16]

Transitions

Sartre does make a transition, in the sentence that Howells quotes, from the imagination to consciousness as a whole, but he makes this transition in *L'imaginaire* from his analysis of the imagination in the body of that work to its "Conclusion." Thus what still has to be examined is the immediate context of Howells's quotation. What we observe first is that the quotation is a specific conclusion. Howells cites, "The imagination . . . is consciousness as a whole insofar as it actualizes its freedom." She does not cite the preceding phrase, "We can therefore conclude."

How did Sartre reach his conclusion? I cite the preceding paragraph:

> The very condition of the *cogito,* is it not above all doubt—that is, at once the constitution of the real as world and its nihilation of this point of view itself, and the reflective grasp of doubt as doubt, does it not coincide with the apodictic intuition of freedom?

Howells can hardly be blamed for not citing this jumble of arguments, but it is not entirely obvious how without them Sartre could have reached his conclusion.

"Apodictic intuition" is Husserl's terminology. It is what I referred to as an "immediate deliverance of consciousness" (at the eidetic-transcendental levels). As such, it is phenomenologically irrefutable, so that I could raise the question, How was Sartre eventually able to reject it? The *cogito* and the "doubt" are of course Cartesian. But Descartes is left behind as soon as Sartre paraphrases the "doubt" as "at once the constitution of the real as world and its nihilation."

Despite the distortion imposed here by Sartre's rudimentary dialectic, we recognize Heidegger's "nihilation," which (according to Sartre) the "radical conversion" of Husserl's phenomenological reduction "presupposes." What we did not previously recognize is that this is the juncture at which the concept of freedom enters Sartre's analysis. That it does not come up in *L'imaginaire* before its "Conclusion" is something (one would have thought) that some scholar preoccupied with freedom in Sartre might have noticed, especially if he were concerned about how freedom became absolute.

Transcendental Freedom

If the concept of freedom has not come up before in *L'imaginaire*, it would seem to be because the phenomenological reduction has not previously been implemented. For it did come up at this particular juncture earlier in *The Transcendence of the Ego*. Observe how it in *L'imaginaire* enters with an argument for the necessity of freedom:

> In order for a consciousness to be able to imagine, it is necessary for it to be able to derive from itself a position of withdrawal [*recul*] in relation to the world. In a word, it is necessary that consciousness be free. Thus the thesis of unreality has yielded the possibility of negation as its condition, but this is possible by virtue of the nihilation of the world as totality, and this nihilation is the other side of [*l'envers de*] the freedom itself of consciousness.[17]

This *recul*, I have already mentioned, is the *epochē*, which is the crucial moment in Husserl's phenomenological reduction.

Freedom enters here with the phenomenological reduction not by virtue of any interpretation of Sartre's own that he imposes; freedom was already in Husserl himself a feature of the reduction as a "radical modification of the natural attitude." He explained that this "transformation [*Umwertung*] is a matter of our absolute freedom [*Sache unserer vollkommenen Freiheit*]."[18] Moreover, the context in Husserl is an effort to distinguish his reduction from Descartes' doubt, which likewise (according to Husserl) "belongs to the realm of our absolute freedom." Apparently not even Sartre's interpretation here of Descartes is natively French but derives, rather, from Husserl's interpretation.

The distinction Husserl drew here between himself and Descartes was, as I indicated earlier, that "the *presupposition of non-being* . . . is a feature of the substratum of the attempt to doubt," so that "it can be said that his [Descartes'] attempt to doubt universally is properly an attempt to negate universally.[19] But Husserl does not retain this "presupposition" for his reduction. If Sartre does, it is not a simple reversion to Descartes' doubt as interpreted by Husserl. It is, rather, that Sartre is again conflating Husserl with Heidegger. Designating it a "conflation" brings out one respect in which the transition here in *L'imaginaire* is not the same as the transition from *L'imaginaire* to *Being and Nothingness*. Here Sartre turns "toward Heidegger" without turning "against Husserl." At significant junctures in *Being and Nothingness,* he will turn "against Husserl" when he turns "toward Heidegger." But in the "Conclusion" to *L'imaginaire* there is no recognition that the two philosophers are opposed. In short, Sartre's relation to Husserl and Heidegger is different in *Being and Nothingness* in part because he envisages the relation between them differently. They can no longer simply be conflated, but have to be reconciled.

Sartre's concept of freedom in the "Conclusion" does not come out of thin air but is provided by the conflation:

It is because he is transcendentally free that man imagines.

But in its turn imagination . . . is the necessary condition of the empirical freedom of man in the middle of the world. For, if the negating function of consciousness—what Heidegger calls transcendence—is what renders possible the act of the imagination, it is necessary to add reciprocally that this function can be manifested only in an act of the imagination.[20]

Here we have the same dialectical doubling—freedom as at once transcendental and mundane (now alternatively termed "empirical")—we had with nothingness. We also have again a coalescence of what Sartre takes to be the reaching of the transcendental level by the phenomenological reduction in Husserl with the what he takes to be the movement of transcendence in Heidegger.[21] It is difficult to avoid the suspicion that the necessity of the concept of freedom in Sartre must have been reinforced by its having entered Sartre's philosophy from two different philosophies.

Originality

Sartre is in a peculiar situation with respect to what was to become, according to virtually all his expositors, the crucial concept of his philosophy. Even though "freedom" enters his philosophy as an immediate deliverance of consciousness, he seems not to have been particularly conscious of it until it became an "apodictic intuition" when he read Husserl or when what he read in Husserl seemed corroborated by what he read in Heidegger.

"Freedom" is not one of the philosophical topics listed in *Carnet Midy* (1924). The most philosophical of Sartre's early writings, *La légende de la vérité* (published in part in 1931, a year before Aron drew Sartre's attention to Husserl and phenomenology), is wide-ranging, but "freedom" does not come within its range. In "*Er l'Arménien*," the most philosophical of his preceding writings, "freedom" is alluded to: "Wickedness = freedom = *disinterested* feeling. One does not do evil for its own sake, but as a work of art. . . . Art is a species of wickedness." [22] In the equations, "freedom" is so confined between other concepts as to retain little meaning of its own. And how quickly Sartre moves on! "Freedom" receives no further consideration, since his continuing concern in the passage is with the work of art.[23]

Perhaps the extraneous sources of his original concept of "freedom" (the fact that its source was not simply an "apodictic intuition" for Sartre) may make it easier to explain how later he could pry himself loose from this concept of freedom and find his ever having accepted it "incredible."

Of course, the derivation of Sartre's concept of freedom from other philosophies does not spare the historian from trying to examine it in the context of his own philosophy (as Howells does). But when he discovers the extent to which other philosophies are involved in the formulation of Sartre's philosophy, the suspicion might dawn that its own context may sometimes be almost too porous, or too plugged with other philosophies, for it to hold together on its own as an original philosophy.

The Gas Leak

A subject that has emerged as more distinctively Sartre's own philosophy is the image. Whatever credit Sartre would give to Husserl for his treatment of this subject, we have seen that Sartre was already committed to it in his *diplôme* before he had ever read Husserl. When Sartre did become converted to Husserl, the image still was for Sartre a subject that Husserl had treated only "in passing." The continuing significance of this subject to Sartre has been recognized by expositors ever since Sartre presented his three volumes on Flaubert as a "sequel" to *L'imaginaire.*

What, then, is the relation between this subject and the subject of freedom, which, I have been arguing, came into its own for Sartre only after he had read Husserl and Heidegger? The notorious characteristic of this relation is an ambivalence in Sartre, which is as much of a "critical cliché" with expositors as his "moving away from a conception of absolute freedom towards a mature position which takes into account the constraints and conditioning of the external world." On the one hand, Sartre offers the positive concept of the imagination that we have just been examining, whereby "the imagination . . . is consciousness as a whole insofar as it actualizes its freedom." This positive concept, I have observed, emerges only in the "Conclusion" to *L'imaginaire.* On the other hand, he offers in the body of *L'imaginaire* a negative concept of the imagining as all-encompassing escapism. "It is not," we have heard Sartre explain in *L'imaginaire,* just an "escape from features of reality (poverty, frustrated love, failure of our undertakings, etc.) that is sought [by imagining], but the form itself of reality." [24]

Here almost anyone who expounds Sartre on the imagination—indeed, almost anyone who expounds Sartre—cites his later statement, "Every man is a gas leak, by which he escapes into the imaginary." [25] Presumably they cite it as an instance of the vividness he is sometimes good at. Presumably because it lacks this vividness—indeed, is rather clumsy—they overlook the preceding sentence, "In my book on Flaubert, I investigate imaginary persons—people who, like Flaubert, play roles." This sentence illustrates the linkup between the imaginary and role playing—the linkup that previous expositors have neglected but that I have followed up, once my attention was drawn to it by Sartre's break with Husserl in *L'imaginaire,* as soon as he reached the stage of the impersonation.

Flight

Sartre does not derive from Heidegger his preoccupation with role playing, any more than he gets it from Husserl. With respect to this subject his philosophy, I have argued, is original. But I might illustrate one more time the understanding of Sartre that can be gained by taking his relation to another philosopher into account, by going on from the clumsy sentence to the next one—the vivid, regularly quoted sentence with the "gas leak," which conveys an escapist concept of "freedom."

As is always done, to retain the vividness of "Tout homme est une fuite de gaz par laquelle il s'échappe dans l'imaginaire," I translated *fuite* by "leak." This translation is accurate enough, yet I suspect that *fuite* also translates the German *Flucht*. For in Sartre's discussion of anxiety, where he acknowledges his debt to Heidegger, Sartre refers to "various modes of behavior [one may adopt] with respect to . . . anxiety—in particular, modes of flight." The ensuing discussion of "flight" derives from *Being and Time*." [26]

Sartre sometimes pairs *fuite* with his crucial term *projet*, which he also takes over from Heidegger and uses unremittingly. In *Being and Nothingness*, much of Sartre's basic terminology comes from Husserl and Heidegger. Nevertheless, expositors often fail to seek the specificity with respect to the meaning of Sartre's terms that can be obtained by seeing how his use of the same term departs from Husserl's or Heidegger's usage. Thus Howells quotes Sartre's statement, "You can consider every project is a flight, but you should also consider that every flight is a project," and she explains that here Sartre is criticizing "psychoanalysis for remaining on a non-dialectical level." [27] But the burden of Sartre's criticism, the dialectic he would impose, is more readily appreciated when we recognize that these terms are not only not ordinary usage or psychoanalytical usage but also that the meanings of the two terms, which are already conjoined in Heidegger, have been altered by their relation having become in Sartre a dialectical flip-flop. [28]

Sartre has thereby come up with a structure that is "metastable." This term initially captured our attention as one that Sartre seems not to have taken over from any previous philosopher. Just as there is a certain originality in the scope Sartre accords to the playing of imaginary roles as a subject, so there is a certain methodological originality in the scope he accords to the way role players are doubled up on themselves to constitute metastable structures. The self-deception involved is only the most obvious illustration of this structure. It is here that we find a certain originality in Sartre's treatment of freedom: his conception of freedom itself as "vertiginous" (granted its derivation from Kierkegaard and Heidegger), his conception of the conversion as "the clearest and most moving image of our freedom," as well as his conception of the imagination itself, which is ambivalently at once (in his later terminology from Heidegger) "flight" and "project."

This ambivalence is usually analyzed by Anglo-American expositors as an inconsistency—a vacillation on Sartre's part between a "negative" and a "positive" conception of freedom. What they thereby demonstrate is a failure to recognize not merely that imagining might be an ambivalent performance but also that there are phenomena that seem to lend themselves to a dialectical analysis. Here as elsewhere the questions of method raised by Sartre's analysis of the imagination would be more readily appreciated by comparison with the philosopher who inspired this analysis.

Conclusion:
Questions of Method

I cannot see the way things look.—Stendhal

The Shift in Subject

Now that the questions that were raised by Sartre's conclusion to *L'imaginaire* are out of the way, I would myself raise in conclusion certain questions of method. These questions are implicit in *L'imaginaire* as a whole, but they lack the explicitness such questions attain in Husserl by virtue of the priority he accords method. They will also provide a final illustration of how the structure of Sartre's philosophy is exhibited in relation to Husserl's by the shifts that my own method sorts out.

In dealing with Sartre's relation to Husserl, I began in Chapter 1 with the shift in *subject*. However, not until we reached the "Conclusion" of *L'imaginaire* was it fully evident in what respects the image became Sartre's own distinctive subject. To provide a more adequate account of how this subject is a shift from Husserl, it seemed helpful to determine what the subject for phenomenology was for Husserl. For we soon recognized how in undertaking his own treatment of the imagination, Sartre tended to presuppose Husserl's treatment of perception. In Husserl himself, acts of the imagination were treated as dependent on prior acts of perception, and in his lectures *The Principal Parts of Phenomenology* a treatment of perception preceded the treatment of the imagination. Husserl is not thereby necessarily endorsing Merleau-Ponty's insistence, in *The Priority of*

Perception, that phenomenology accords priority to perception. This is an issue that should be taken up in terms of Merleau-Ponty's relation to Husserl, though it may well be that Merleau-Ponty is the more insistent on the priority of perception because he is defending his own approach against Sartre's in *L'imaginaire.*

At least it can be observed here that Husserl's according of priority to *examples* from perception has some bearing on his treating the imagination as a subject (in Sartre's phrase) "only in passing." Reconsider the example of perceiving a sheet of paper, since Sartre used almost the same example at the start of *L'imagination.* Husserl uses the example to analyze the essential structure not of an act of perception but of an act of intentional reference. When he has analyzed this structure with this example, he claims that the same analysis of intentional reference holds for other acts of consciousness:

> As we are conscious of things in perception, so we are also conscious of them in recollection, in [imaginative] re-presentations, which are similar to recollection. . . . Of these essentially different experiences, obviously everything is true that we have adduced regarding experiences of perception.[1]

This inference (I pointed out earlier) is an abbreviated eidetic reduction: these other experiences are canvassed as different to demonstrate that their essential structure as intentional acts emerges as the same. Thus any priority accorded to the example from perception is not inconsistent with a certain priority that in Chapter 11 we saw Husserl accord method. For intentional reference, as it emerges from this eidetic reduction, justifies Husserl's intentional analysis as a methodological procedure.

Clarity

If their essential structure as intentional acts is the same, why accord any priority to an example of perception in carrying out this eidetic analysis? A criterion for awarding this priority becomes explicit in a section of *Ideas I* entitled "The Role of Perception in the Method of Eidetic Clarification."[2] The purpose of an eidetic reduction is clarification. Indeed, we saw earlier that Husserl defines phenomenology itself as "The Method of Eidetic Clarification [*Klärung*]."

Clarity is a criterion that can be met in Husserl (as in Descartes) only by securing distinctness. Earlier we also saw how integral to Husserl's method is the drawing of distinctions: "What is characteristic of phenomenological method is . . . that each step forward yields new points of view, from which what was already discovered appears in a new light, and often enough presents as complicated what originally was accepted as simple."[3]

Had the supremacy of these criteria of clarity and distinctness not been in question, there would have been no justification in Husserl's own terms for my beginning the present volume with a section two-thirds of the way through *Ideas I* simply because Sartre had found that Husserl's handling of the Dürer engraving there presented him with a shift in *subject* as a "starting point."[4] For at least it could be said that in this section, Husserl was characteristically drawing a distinction in order to clarify a "dangerous ambiguity" that portends a "besetting confusion."

Husserl's criterion of distinctness discredits the kind of relational analysis that Sartre undertakes when he advances beyond the static analysis of his introductory chapter, where he is relatively close to Husserl, to his own treatment, in which the imagination was appraised as "one wave among others." From this appraisal Sartre derives, as an implicit criterion, fluidity of treatment. This is a criterion that Husserl in effect rejects because of its threat to clarity: "That which floats before us in fluid unclarity [*fliessender Unklarheit*] . . . must . . . be made perfectly clear."[5] If the unclarity of an experience is associated with its fluidity, then clarifying the experience requires an analysis in which its essence becomes fixed.

Emotion

What is methodologically at issue here between Sartre and Husserl is not the simple issue of "the priority of perception" (as asserted by Merleau-Ponty) but the issue of priority with respect to the selection of examples for the procedure of eidetic analysis. In Sartre it is the role of affectivity, as the most influential of the "waves" that is brought out by Sartre's crucial examples—the caricature, the painting of Charles VIII (the first time it is used), the impersonation. When Husserl encounters an emotion as a possible alternative example, he defends his own preference: "Outer perception, with the collaboration of reflection turned back on it, provides clear and stable examples." Maintaining this collaboration is one of the problems with respect to an emotion:

> Anger, when reflected on, may dissipate [*verrauchen*], or its content may be rapidly modified. It is also not always available like perception. . . . To investigate it reflectively . . . is to investigate an anger that is dissipating. The process, to be sure, is not without meaning [*bedeutungslos*], but it is perhaps not what should be investigated. In contrast, outer perception, which is much more accessible, is not dissipated by reflection. . . . If it be said that perception also has its differences in clarity—for example, in the dark, in fog, and so

forth—we will not let ourselves be drawn into detailed considerations of whether these differences are completely comparable. It is sufficient that perception is not normally befogged and that clear perception is always at our disposal when we need it.[6]

Husserl's misgiving about the suitability of an emotion, Sartre apparently managed to overlook when he was digesting *Ideas I* in Berlin. For in the Berlin essay on intentionality, Sartre announces that Husserl has "opened the way for a new treatise on the passions."[7] This treatise would turn out to be Sartre's *Theory of the Emotions,* which was the only portion of his general treatise on phenomenological psychology, *Psyché,* that Sartre salvaged for publication.

When Simone de Beauvoir asks, near the end of Sartre's career, "Why did you save *The Theory of the Emotions* . . . when you did not the rest of *Psyché?*" Sartre replies, "Because the rest of *Psyché* repeated Husserl's ideas, which I expressed in a different style but which nonetheless was pure Husserl; it was not original, while *The Emotions* I saved for their originality."[8] I would conjecture that because of Sartre's indifference to considerations of method, it does not cross his mind that a methodological misgiving was a reason for Husserl's having neglected the emotions.

Criteria

The criteria behind this misgiving also emerge in the passage I have quoted. Husserl's rather patronizing admission that the process by which anger dissipates "to be sure, is not without meaning," yet "it is . . . not what should be investigated," and his evasive, "we will not let ourselves be drawn into detailed consideration of whether these differences are completely comparable," since "it is sufficient . . . ," betray his commitment to the criteria of clarity, distinctness, and stability. They stand in contrast with the confusion, the darkness, the fog that can descend on us with anger and the fluidity with which it is likely to dissipate.

The different criteria that are involved in Sartre's break with Husserl can be brought out by reviewing the pivotal example of the impersonation. The comparison here between Sartre and Husserl I could not pursue further when I first encountered this example, for it then seemed too idiosyncratic to bear much weight. I first had to demonstrate the range of implications that this example eventually acquires in Sartre: it was not only climactic in his analysis of the imagination but was also an initial manifestation of a preoccupation with role playing that persists throughout Sartre's career, whatever his genre—literary, psychoanalytic, or social theory.

With the example of the impersonation, still more than with the caricature (the other example of Sartre's not found in Husserl), an affective reaction makes up for the inadequacies of perception. Franconay's performance supplies perceptual evidence that cannot become either clear or distinct (insofar as it does, it gets in the way of the impersonation coming off), and the image of Chevalier that is the outcome of her performance is metastable—an "unstable and transitory state." It is (in the terminology with which Husserl discounts the suitability of anger for analysis) liable to dissipate.[9]

The Shift in Method

The emergence of different criteria in Sartre is congruent with a shift in *method*—from a purely phenomenological analysis to a rudimentary dialectic that follows out (again to retain terminology featured by Husserl's discrediting) "a rapid modification of content," whereby the spectator moves from what he can perceive to what he imagines, only to slide back again. The instability of this movement no longer discredits this example in Sartre or even renders it marginal. Whereas Husserl is dismissive— something so transient "is not what should be investigated"—Sartre finds it "worth investigation for its own sake."[10] I continued the investigation by considering "self-deception" (the subject of *Being and Nothingness*) as an illustration of the "metastable."[11]

Recall how a crucial step in Sartre's adaptation of Husserl's analysis to the example of the impersonation occurred when Sartre introduced "a confused feeling." At this juncture, Sartre had to discard Husserl temporarily in favor of Bergson.[12] Incorporating "a confused feeling" in his analysis was itself an implicit repudiation of Husserl's criteria of clarity and of the distinctness and stability of experience on which attaining clarity depends.

Sartre's distrust of clarity is not a reaction against Husserl; it antedates his conversion to Husserl. When in his *diplôme* Sartre defended "Romantic theories" and disparaged the "scientific" theories that eclipsed them, he admitted that the Romantics had constructed "systems" that were "obscure, metaphysical, and contradictory." But he repudiated their "scientific" successors as succumbing to the "thirst for clarity for the sake of clarity." Sartre accordingly adopted the historical perspective to which I drew attention in the previous chapter: "It cannot be said that psychology progressed . . . , nor that it left the speculative Romantics behind. It should be said, to the contrary, that after 1870 psychology has regressed and sacrificed the complexity of things in favor of clarity."

In the historical survey in *L'imagination,* Sartre's distrust of "clarity" and deference toward "the complexity of things" becomes more explicitly methodological as a commitment to a relational analysis—or (in his own terminology) to a "synthesis" as opposed to an analysis. He characterizes Romanticism as "a return to l'*esprit de synthèse*" and "the determinist and mechanistic" associationist psychology that succeeded it as commitment to l'*esprit d'analyse:*

> Mechanism sought to resolve a system into its elements and implicitly accepts the assumption that these remain rigorously identical, whether isolated or in combination. There follows naturally that other assumption: the relations between the elements of a system are external.[13]

In other words, the assumption Sartre would repudiate is that elements can be separated out and treated without taking into account the relations between them. At the end of *L'imagination,* Sartre is looking forward to his own treatment of the imagination with his concluding statement, "Every mental fact is a synthesis."[14]

Priority of Method

Sartre has to concede that some prephenomenological philosophers and psychologists have employed the concept of "synthesis." But he protests: "The whole trouble is that they have *arrived at the image with the concept of synthesis,* instead of deriving a certain conception of synthesis by reflecting on the image."[15] Here Sartre is in effect denying the priority of method. He urges:

> The solutions provided for the great problems of the imagination seem *demonstrations of method* rather than positive results. Instead of proceeding directly to the thing and formulating the method on the basis of [*sur*] the subject, they first of all define the method . . . , and *apply it then* to the subject, without suspecting that in providing themselves with the method they were at the same time forging the subject.[16]

There is probably an echo of Husserl's principle "to the things themselves" in Sartre's recommendation that we should proceed "directly to the thing." But it is in order to arrive at "the things themselves" that Husserl relies on method. Since Heidegger retains Husserl's principle and even turns his own version of it, "to the subject itself," against Husserl's according priority to method (on the grounds that method thereby becomes the subject for Husserl) the issue of the relation between method and subject will come up again when I deal with Heidegger and Husserl.[17]

One question of method that has been settled by dealing in the present volume with the relation between Sartre and Husserl is that Sartre's opposing the two alternatives (arriving directly at the thing and formulating the method on the basis of the subject, or first of all defining the method and then applying it to the subject) is naively simplistic. Not the whole trouble, but part of it is Sartre's conflating Husserl's principle "to the things themselves" with his own principle "toward the concrete." He even goes so far as to regret the "toward," proposing instead to "start out from" the "concrete as a totality." [18] The philosopher who would start out so indiscriminatingly is unlikely to be entirely clear about what he is doing. In fact, instead of arriving (as he proposes) directly at the image and deriving a certain conception of synthesis by reflecting on the image, Sartre arrived indirectly at the image with a concept of synthesis he derived from Husserl's synthesis of (perceptual) identification. All that he then needed to do (with the impetus supplied by his rudimentary dialectic) was to arrive at an opposing conception of (imaginative) quasi observation. [19]

Reconsider, too, his analysis of how we identify Chevalier as the person whom Franconay is impersonating. This analysis again reproduces at one level Husserl's analysis of the synthesis of identification. But it is not just Chevalier himself who is being identified, but "the essence, as it were, of Chevalier." Thus I was able to argue that the process of identification was the substantive embodiment of Husserl's methodological procedure of eidetic reduction, which (we went on to see) continues to be embodied in role playing generally, as Sartre analyzes it. Sartre's analyses have illustrated that there is no arrival at the subject itself that is so direct as to be the simple elimination of considerations of method. If there were, I would not be justified in distinguishing shifts in *method* (in the present instance from a purely phenomenological method to a phenomenological method with an admixture of rudimentary dialectic) from shifts in *subject* (in the present instance from examples primarily of perception to examples of perceiving a physical image and imagining a mental image).

Proceeding

I am not suggesting that the influence of fully formulated conceptions (such as Husserl's synthesis of identification or the eidetic reduction) is the whole story. There is another respect in which Sartre's behest that we should proceed directly to the subject is too simplistic. Sartre seems to suppose that what gets in our way are just assumptions and doctrines (such as those he associates in *L'imagination* with "mechanistic and deterministic science"). Even he can overlook what is more concrete: whenever we think we are proceeding directly to a subject (as Sartre thinks he is when he treats the image), we are already enmeshed in ways of proceeding, even though they may be wispy, when we are "thinking vaguely," like "the lamentable Frédéric." These ways of proceeding are implicitly methodological procedures, and they become explicitly these procedures as soon as our thinking becomes more "precise and systematic." [20] But we are more likely to overlook their methodological implications if we do not accord method any priority, especially if we are also writing with "extreme rapidity," like Sartre—"breathless from following with his pen the movement of his thought." [21] In slowing this movement down, I have been able to ferret out methodological implications by taking advantage, for the purposes of comparison, of the explicitness of Husserl's methodological commitments.

Levels

I am not suggesting that Husserl's methodological commitments are always explicit. Sometimes the comparison with Sartre helps render them explicit. When, for example, Husserl recognizes how "confusingly" phenomena are "built on each other" in ordinary experience, he is not just describing his subject—"the things themselves." [22] He is betraying his own methodological commitment not only to clarity but also to the feasibility of the discrimination needed to achieve it. For Husserl is adopting the analogy to construction with the assumption that phenomena that are "built on each other" can be taken apart. Another analogy, which reinforces this assumption and provides a more obvious contrast to Sartre's analogy to "waves," is geologic: if "logic" has "achieved so few tenable results," this is due in part "to confusions of radically separate strata of problems." [23]

Achieving a fixed separation of strata precludes the *interplay* that Sartre's relational analysis permits, as was illustrated by "the confused feeling" he imported from Bergson when he temporarily discarded Husserl. But I did not pause to take into account then the stratum that Husserl distinguishes as fundamental: "Every intentional experience is an objectifying [or objectivating] act, or is founded upon such an act." The objectifying stratum is fundamental: "Objectifying acts have the unique function of providing other acts with the represented object to which these other acts may then refer in their new ways." One of these new ways may be an affective reference. A feeling or an emotion is a "secondary act," to be analyzed as a higher-level act superimposed on the fundamental level. [24]

Interplay

If Sartre had considered this stratification in Husserl, he could hardly have avoided rejecting it with his argument against what he calls "the primacy of representation," which he finds instanced by the traditional assumption that "a representation is always necessary to provoke a feeling." Sartre is ferociously blunt, "nothing is more false." [25]

Sartre counters the primacy of representation with examples of how the synthesis of identification is carried out:

> It is the [real] love that I feel for Annie that makes her unreal [imaginary] face appear, and not her unreal face that provokes a surge of love for her. In a parallel fashion, if Peter made yesterday an offensive gesture that upset me, what first reemerges is indignation or shame. These feelings grope blindly for a moment in order to understand themselves; then, illuminated by encountering the relevant knowledge, produce of themselves the offensive gesture. [26]

Another example:

> It has happened to me . . . that I have felt an extremely precise desire. Affectively its object is strictly determined. . . . Only I do not know what it is. Do I want to drink something cool and sweet? Do I want to go to sleep? Is some sexual desire in question?

Sartre brings out the implications of this last example:

> Briefly, the desire is a blind effort to possess on the representative level what has already been given to me on the affective level: *via* the affective synthesis, desire aims at a beyond of which it has a presentiment without being able to come to know it. The desire is directed on "something" affective that is given to it at present and that it apprehends as representing the things desired. [27]

Levels are still distinguished here by Sartre as they are by Husserl, but Sartre does not keep them separate:

> The image is a kind of ideal for the feeling. It is for the affective consciousness a condition in which desire would be, at the same time, knowledge. The image, if it is given as the lower limit toward which knowledge tends when it is degraded, is also given as the upper limit toward which affectivity tends when he attempts to know itself.

With this *interplay* taking place between levels, the image becomes "a synthesis of affectivity and knowledge," [28] but we need only recall the synthesis of affectivity and knowledge that was involved in the image identifying Chevalier to be reminded that Sartre's conception of this synthesis still derives from Husserl's synthesis of identification, granted that it is a drastic revision.

The character of the knowledge that enters this synthesis Sartre explains with the example, "I love the delicate long white hands of a certain woman." What is in question is "not an intellectual knowledge. . . . The love projects on the object a certain tonality, which could be called the affective meaning of this delicacy, of this whiteness." In Husserl, feeling is never "a kind of knowledge."[29] The only kind of knowledge he recognizes would be covered (roughly) by what Sartre calls "intellectual knowledge." Sartre is again sliding across a distinction that Husserl finds indispensable.

Although Sartre is no longer alluding to Husserl at this juncture, most of his technical terminology still derives from him ("is given," "aims," "directed"). But Sartre's analysis displays a fluidity that Husserl would not tolerate. Thus the implications of the terminology Sartre retains from Husserl are slackened. In Husserl, the "aim" of an intentional act is essentially locked into the "target"—the "something" that it is consciousness "of" and that it is objectifying and representing. But in Sartre, we have just seen, I aim at "a beyond." This slackness is illustrated not only by Sartre's sliding across Husserl's distinctions but also by consciousness's not being directed "to" something but being "directed on [sur] something."[30]

The Shift in Affiliation

With the example of the "delicate long white hands," Sartre has reintroduced the concept of "affective meaning," which we first encountered in the impersonation. Another example is a passage Sartre cites from a story by D. H. Lawrence:

> It was always the one man who spoke. He was young, with quick, large, bright eyes that glanced sideways at her. He had a soft black moustache on his dark face, and a sparse tuft of beard, loose hairs on his chin. His long black hair, full of life, hung unrestrained on his shoulders. Dark as he was, he did not look as if he had washed lately.[31]

I am not concerned with the story itself but with Sartre's elucidation of his citation: "Even while Lawrence seems only to be describing the form and the color of objects, he excels in suggesting the mute affective structures that constitute their most profound reality."[32] The qualification that

"Lawrence seems only to be describing" can be taken (in the context of *L'imaginaire*) to imply that he seems to be providing a phenomenological description (granted that it is at the vulgarized level of "picture-book phenomenology"), but it brings in another dimension of style besides that which I used the "Feuillet" to illustrate—the way in which style can be designed to secure an affective reaction.

On the one hand, terminology again survives from Husserl's intentional analysis: "Indians" would not be referred to by Lawrence as "objects." On the other hand, "their most profound reality" is Sartre's own terminology: even if we overlook the fact that the phenomenological reduction in Husserl would set aside any reference to "reality," the terminology is incompatible with Husserl's intentional analysis, in which the most fundamental level is that where objectification is achieved. "Affective meaning" we examined before as a departure form Husserl;[33] its replacement by "affective structures" is a further departure, whereby "affective meaning" becomes susceptible of a relational analysis.

Earlier I pointed out that the concept of "affective meaning" would have been to Husserl an incomprehensible confusion, a contradiction in terms. But with this concept, Sartre has taken a step on his way toward the "novel that is true." If we had not anticipated Sartre's analysis of Flaubert as his most persistent effort and the longest work of his career, we might have missed the shift in *affiliation* that is implicit in Sartre's citing Lawrence as illustrating "affective meaning."

In *L'imaginaire*, Sartre also cites his own favorite novelist:

> I cannot see the way things look. I have only my childhood memory. . . . I see images. I remember their effect on my heart.[34]

This pronouncement of Stendhal's, which is in its philosophical effect a denial of the priority of perception, gained for Sartre before his conversion to Husserl the importance it still retains in *L'imaginaire*. In the *diplôme* it is climactic—at the beginning of the final section.

Citing this pronouncement in the *diplôme*, Sartre even endorses Stendhal as "certainly having gone furthest in the analysis of images." Presumably "furthest" implies a comparison with the philosophers and psychologists whom Sartre had been discussing in the *diplôme*. When Sartre later read Husserl, the pronouncement would not just have discredited Husserl's preference for "clear perception," as "always available"; it would thereby have also discredited the visual analogy with which Husserl would convey the cognitive reliability of eidetic insight. At the same time, the pronouncement assures memory and the affective reaction the place more generally in our experience that our memory of Chevalier and our affective reaction to him secured in the example of the impersonation.[35]

Role Shifts

Sartre's elaborating the concept of "affective meaning" is a break with Husserl that I have taken in conjunction with two other breaks: his criticizing as "shocking" Husserl's concept of the imaginative fulfillment of meaning, and his criticizing the reducibility of the imagination to previous perception(s). These three issues separating Sartre from Husserl are linked, since it is the inability of perception to play its traditional role in relation to the imagination that makes room for the affective reaction to intervene and compensate for the inadequacy of perception.

I have also insisted on the linkage that is implicit in the context in which these three issues emerge together—in the example of the impersonation, where Franconay plays the role of Chevalier. With this example, role playing comes to the fore in Sartre's analysis of the imagination, and the example marks his definite break with the direction taken by Husserl in his analysis, "directed," as it is, "by general logical interests." [36]

I have further argued that Sartre's preoccupation with role playing becomes more specifically a preoccupation with role shifts, and most specifically a preoccupation with those decisive role shifts that are conversions. With this argument I have advanced from the particular example of Franconay to an illustration of the general interests manifested by the development of Sartre's philosophy. Such an illustration could not be achieved without raising the methodological considerations that are raised by my sorting out the shifts in *method, subject, level,* and *affiliation* with which a philosopher arrives at his conception of philosophy itself. Thus it can finally be recognized that what is crucial to the impersonation is not that a dark-haired, curvacious female can play the role of a tall blond male; it is that the "role of affectivity in consciousness of the impersonation"—that is, in constituting our consciousness of the role she is playing. This role of affectivity is a *higher-order role shift,* with "affectivity taking the place of the strictly intuitive elements of perception in order to actualize the object as an image." This higher-order role shift takes on general significance in Stendhal's pronouncement. In watching Franconay we no longer see the way she looks. Perception yields little more than what we already know (that Chevalier juts his jaw and wears a straw hat at a rakish angle). Given the opposition between what is perceivable and what is to be imagined, Franconay's performance can only come off if there is a reawakening of the affective reaction we had when we originally perceived Chevalier, so that the "affective meaning of the face of Chevalier will appear on the face of Franconay." [37]

This higher-order role-shift is implicit in Sartre's discrediting of "the primacy of representation" and eventually in his writing, as a "sequel" to *L'imaginaire*, of a "novel which is true." This higher-order role-shift (and the concomitant accrediting of "affective meaning") also would legitimize the conversions whereby a Genet, a Flaubert, Sartre himself become "imaginary persons"—that is writers, who in turn re-imagine other imaginary persons, as Sartre does with Genet, Flaubert, and himself. It would also legitimize Sartre's becoming "primarily a writer" and only "secondarily a philosopher."

Epilogue: The End
of Philosophy

You are sometimes presented as the last of the philosophers.—Pingaud.

Sartre completed his theory of the imagination in 1935, the year that Husserl announced "the dream is over"—the dream of "philosophy as rigorous science." [1] If Husserl had been confronted with this theory, as the "radical renovation," for which Husserl had, according to Sartre, "laid the foundations," [2] I suspect Husserl might have regarded it as another piece of evidence that the dream was over, much as he regarded (as I suggested in Volume 1) Heidegger's *Being and Time* as evidence, despite Heidegger's similarly crediting Husserl with having "laid the foundations" for that work.

However, certain hesitations restrain me from concluding that "the dream is over" with Sartre's philosophy. First of all, even though Sartre's undertook a "radical renovation" in *L'imaginaire*, radical renovation has been a frequent aspiration during the history of philosophy, and it does not entail in any sense giving up on philosophy.

Second, Sartre himself makes no claim on his own behalf that he is a harbinger of the end of philosophy. Once he was informed by an interviewer, "you are sometimes presented as the last of the philosophers. This is a way of saying that philosophy is dead." [3] In response Sartre does not refer to Heidegger or Derrida, whose renderings of the end of philosophy had not yet perhaps been fully exhibited. Instead, he finds the end of philosophy illustrated by its fate in the United States:

In a technocratic civilization there is no longer any place for philosophy, unless it translates itself into a technique. That is what is happening in the United States: philosophy has been replaced by the
social sciences. What continues under its name is a sort of vague
reverie, very general reflection.

Of course if philosophy has been replaced by the social sciences and otherwise survives only as a vague reverie or general reflection, it has come
to an end.

Yet this reflection on Sartre's part is itself too vague and general. The
history of philosophy should be accorded an ending commensurate in
some measure with what philosophy has been; its history should not be
allowed to end in technique, reverie, or whimper. Thus an important reason for not associating Sartre with the end of philosophy is that what is
entirely lacking in Sartre is any well-articulated conception of the end of
philosophy, backed up by an account of its history, such as is found in
Heidegger and Derrida.[4]

What is, however, not worked out in Heidegger and Derrida is an
account of that epoch in the history of philosophy which seems of considerable relevance to how the end of philosophy is reached in their own
thinking—the history of phenomenology. Heidegger originally identified
his philosophy as phenomenological, and from Derrida's perspective
Husserl and Heidegger are two philosophers whom "it is up to us to
think about."[5]

Destruktion

A question still remains about the specific relevance of Sartre. It should
not be forgotten that Sartre's philosophy became the occasion for Heidegger in the "Letter on Humanism" to become explicit for the first time
regarding "the Turning" in which his thinking had become involved,
whereby the end of philosophy is being reached. I grant that Sartre's philosophy may have become this occasion only because an issue in the "Letter" is Sartre's (mis)understanding of *Being and Time,* and if any extenuation is allowed Sartre by Heidegger, it is that *Being and Time* may have
lent itself to (mis)understanding in a fashion which it is less likely to do
when "the Turning" is taken into account.

I shall, however, be concerned less with the "Letter" itself than with
the account of (mis)understanding that Heidegger applies there to
Sartre—an account that Heidegger had originally elaborated in *Being
and Time.* The history of philosophy is for Heidegger a tradition, and it
is coming to an end as a tradition. Heidegger interprets Sartre's and Husserl's philosophy alike as at the mercy of tra-dition, which Heidegger ex-

plains in *Being and Time* "takes over what comes down to us and hands it over to *Selbsverständichkeit* (what is taken for granted because of its "obvious understandability"). Tradition thereby becomes an obstruction to understanding's gaining "access" to "the things themselves"[6] and in particular to an understanding of *Being and Time*, over which this principle presides. The *Destruktion* is Heidegger's procedure for coping with this obstruction.

It is Sartre's philosophy, and not Husserl's, that is taken by Heidegger to illustrate another obstruction whereby a philosophy (Heidegger's in particular) can be surrendered to *Öffentlichkeit* ("public obviousness" or "public accessibility"). The question then has to be faced as to the relation between these two different surrenderings, the "traditionalization" of philosophy and its "vulgarization"—if I may adopt a blunter terminology than Heidegger's.[7] They seem to overlap in Heidegger, since he conceived both as processes of transmission, of communication, and since both promote with the "obviousness" that is their outcome an illusion of accessibility and thereby obstruct access to our understanding in a peculiarly perverse fashion.[8]

Presumably they both help explain what Heidegger regards, with respect to his own philosophy, as "the insurmountable difficulty of [securing] understanding."[9] But the relation between these two processes of communication is not readily ascertainable in *Being and Time*. Thus I shall be returning in Volume 3 to the problems I raised in the last two chapters of Volume 1, "Communication" and "Understanding," before I undertook in concluding a transition to the present volume.

In this volume I have provided evidence as to Sartre's (mis)-understanding of Husserl and as to how integral it was to the elaboration of Sartre's own philosophy. Volume 3 will not be a parallel account of Sartre's mis(understanding) of Heidegger. Such an account would not advance much further the elaboration of my own procedures as a historian. Instead, in treating problems of communication and understanding, my focus will largely shift to Heidegger's relation to Husserl—as a much more crucial episode in the history of phenomenology—and specifically to the differences in their conceptions of "communication" and "understanding" as having contributed to the breakdown in communication between them.

Deconstruction

Although Derrida has modeled his deconstruction on Heidegger's *Destruktion*, he has deconstructed Heidegger (to put the matter far too simply) by interpreting him as not having reached with his *Destruktion* the end of philosophy, but as having himself succumbed to the philosophical tradition. Here we encounter a complication. One feature of Heidegger's still succumbing to tradition in Derrida's interpretation is Heidegger's continuing to rely on the categories of "authenticity" and of "inauthenticity." [10] With Derrida's discrediting of these categories, it is not just the French Heidegger who has been discredited—and thereby that phase in the history of phenomenology known as "existential phenomenology," of which Sartre is considered the protagonist. The original German Heidegger also suffers dismemberment and at a juncture decisive for his concepts of "communication" and "understanding" themselves. For with the discrediting of Heidegger's two categories the subcategory *Öffentlichkeit* is also discredited as entering into the constitution of "inauthenticity." [11] What then happens to Heidegger's criticism of Sartre's (mis)understanding of *Being and Time* as evidence of Sartre's succumbing to *Öffentlichkeit?* Or to Derrida's apparently extending this criticism on his own to Sartre's (mis)understanding of Husserl? I raise these questions now in order to argue that my exposition of Sartre in the present volume is not entirely irrelevant to ascertaining later what is at issue in Heidegger's *Destruktion* and Derrida's deconstruction, which are alike involved in reaching the end of philosophy.

Still my main undertaking in the present volume has been to show how the shifts that my own deconstructive procedure exposes are at stake in the relation between one philosophy (Sartre's) and another philosophy (Husserl's). Exposing these shifts poses questions of method, not simply in the narrow sense that I distinguish a shift in *method,* but in the broad sense that includes the other shifts as well. For a further undertaking in the present volume has been to show that Sartre's shift in *method* from Husserl's purely phenomenological method to a phenomenological method that is also a rudimentary dialectic, entails these other shifts. Thus we have seen, for example, that Sartre's transformation of the phenomenological and eidetic reductions with which Husserl purifies his phenomenological analysis entails in *L'imaginaire* a shift in *subject,* in *level,* and in *affiliation.*

Heidegger and Derrida repudiate method as a feature of philosophy that can be discounted, as not surviving the end of philosophy in their own thinking. [12] This repudiation suggests that my continuing to raise questions of method can itself be discounted as traditional and undeconstructive. But how can deconstruction be vindicated as untraditional—and specifically as "not a method"—without taking into account what "method" traditionally has been? It then has to be recognized that differences in method (in my broad sense) have to be acknowledged in accounting for the differences between philosophies, as I have tried to show is the case with the differences between Sartre and Husserl. To attempt to deal with the history of philosophy (or any of its epochs) as if it were a homogenous tradition, unmarked by irreducible differences of method, is as implausible as it would be to deal with the history of art or literature as if its epochs—and individual works within any epoch—were unmarked by irreducible differences of style.[13]

There are also differences between how Heidegger proceeds in his *Destruktion* of the history of philosophy and how Derrida proceeds in its deconstruction—not to mention other deconstructionists. These differences, I suspect, are not reducible simply to differences with respect to the history of philosophy itself. Perhaps even when the centricities of tradition have been eliminated—logo-, phallo-, phono- and so forth—when, more generally, it is no longer feasible to discount another thinker as at the mercy of tradition, eccentric differences may still remain in how different thinkers proceed and may continue to pose problems of communication between them, and thus problems of how such differences are to be understood.

1. The Passage Way

1. Except where otherwise noted, my quotations from Husserl in this chapter are from *Ideen I*, sec. 111.

2. Husserl, "*Nachwort*" to *Ideen I*, in *Ideen 3*, p. 141. I shall employ throughout the present work the term "phenomenological reduction." Husserl and his expositors sometimes refer to this reduction as the "transcendental reduction," (or distinguish from it a reduction that is distinctively "transcendental"), but these complications can be avoided for the purpose of the comparison with Sartre, who was entirely unaware of them.

3. In Volume 1 of *Phenomenology and Deconstruction* (hereafter abbreviated as *P&D* in citations), I have discussed the problem of access with particular reference to Heidegger (see *P&D* 1:138), because his version of the problem is the most exacerbated. In his interpretation of Plato's cave, this exacerbation is hinted by his transferring the adjective which in Plato describes the mouth of the cave as "wide," so that it instead lends additional length to the "passageway" between the inside of the cave and the outside world. He also equips the cave with a "vault," to which there is no explicit reference in Plato but which would seem to add to our sense of confinement (*Platons Lehre von der Warheit*, pp. 6–7, 19).

4. For the distinction here between philosophy and science as drawn by Heidegger, see *P&D* 1:37. For the idiom of "intro-duction" to philosophy as the "leading out" of "confinement" within the natural attitude, which is undertaken by the "re-duction," see Eugen Fink's exposition in "The Phenomenological Philosophy of Edmund Husserl" (p. 105)—an exposition that was warmly endorsed by Husserl (see *P&D* 1:98) and read by Sartre (see n. 4 of Chapter 9 below).

5. Husserl, *The Crisis of European Sciences,* p. 155.

6. Husserl, *Ideas I,* sec. 31.

7. See "Transcendental Freedom" section of Chapter 33.

8. Husserl, *Ideas I,* sec. 111.

9. *L'imagination,* p. 149.

10. Husserl, quoted in Diemer, *Edmund Husserl,* p. 29. See my Vol. 1, pp. 9–10.

11. See my discussion of other difficulties in assessing Heidegger's relation to Husserl (*P&D* 1:14, 63–64, 113, 174).

12. Sartre, *L'imagination,* p. 158.

13. Sartre admits that "the essential procedure" of "the method itself of phenomenology" is "the [phenomenological] 'reduction,' the *epochē*—that is, the bracketing of the natural attitude," but he goes on to explain that in his present undertaking as a "psychologist" he "is not going to carry it out" and that he "is remaining at the level of the natural attitude" (*L'imagination,* p. 140). In Chapter 31 we shall see that he does assume it has been carried out in the conclusion that we shall see he may have added to *L'imaginaire,* but this is not something that need worry us while we are working our way through the body of that work.

14. Plato and Platonists had brought together mental with physical images before but not in such fashion as to constitute a subject. Sartre offers the qualification "termed" probably because he is sensitive here to Husserl's critique of "the image theory," with which (as I shall suggest in Chapter 7) Sartre was acquainted. Husserl warns "one should not speak and think as if what is termed [a mental] 'image' is in the same relation to consciousness as [a physical] image is to a room in which it is placed" (*Logical Investigations* 2:595). Elsewhere, Sartre does not retain the qualification "termed." Husserl's warning is also disregarded when Sartre uses the term *image externe,* though this time he qualifies his usage as *faute de mieux* (*L'imagination,* p. 151). "External image" would seem to imply that a mental image is, in contrast, "internal." Since Sartre ordinarily does not bother with qualifications, I shall refer just as blithely to a "mental image" and a "physical image" (which is my translation for both his *image externe* and *l'image matériel,* which I take to be a translation of Husserl's *das physiche Bild* [*Logical Investigations* 2:566] and of such circumlocutions as *das Bild als physisches Ding* [*Logical Investigations* 2:654]).

15. Italics in original; I shall explain their force later.

16. See my discussion of "direction" (*P&D* 1:38–39).

17. The possibility of this confusion is indicated in Husserl's analysis of the reduction itself (*Ideas I,* sec. 31), where he states that the "bracketing" of the existence of the world "must not be identified with the consciousness termed 'mere imagining'—for example, that nymphs perform a round dance. In the latter consciousness, after all, there is *no excluding* of a living conviction which we accept [emendation in Copy D; italics in original]. So astute a scholar as Paul Ricoeur (in the commentary accompanying his translation of *Ideas I*) apparently overlooks this distinction when he points out regarding section 111 that "the

close relations between imagination and neutralization explain how the imagination could play so large a role in the 'destruction' of the world [one phase of the reduction] which undermines naive belief in existence in itself" (pp. 370–71). I append these comments of my own to suggest: (1) the trouble Sartre spared himself by not becoming concerned with the neutrality modification, and (2) the trouble I am sparing myself and my reader by not now becoming concerned with the neutrality modification that is the phenomenological reduction. But since this reduction is Husserl's ultimate concern, I am also suggesting (3) the very considerable scope of the leeway that is not being taken into account when I use the Dürer passage as a passage way.

18. De Beauvoir, *La force de l'âge*, p. 216.

19. Sartre is, of course, to be dismissed as a careless reader of Husserl if one is concerned simply to expound Husserl, as is Maria Manuela Saraiva in *L'imagination selon Husserl*, who cites this passage as "typical" of Sartre's exegesis (p. 227).

20. The issue of "ambiguity" or "equivocation" which I placed at the start of my Introduction is larger than Sartre's relation to Husserl: it is brought to the fore in Derrida's interpretation; "Husserl has always appealed to univocity as an imperative. Equivocity is [for him] the route of every philosophical aberration" (*L'origine de la géometrie*, p. 101). It will accordingly become an issue in Volume 3, when I deal with Derrida and deconstruction.

21. See *P&D* 1:15–19.

22. See *P&D* 1:39–42.

23. Cairns, *Conversations with Husserl and Fink*, p. 23.

24. Letter from Husserl in 1904 to Franz Brentano, cited by Spiegelberg, *The Phenomenological Movement* 1:89.

25. Husserl, *The Crisis of European Sciences*, p. 153. See also his *Ideas I*, sec. 84.25.

2. The Disciple

1. See *P&D* 1:15–19.

2. See *P&D* 1:194.

3. The phrase is applied by Derrida (*L'écriture et la différence*, p. 130) to Emmanuel Levinas. In Chapter 6 of Volume 1, I argued that this shift in allegiance took place with many of Levinas's French contemporaries, including Sartre (see *P&D* 1:93–96).

4. Sartre, *Les carnets de la drôle de guerre*, pp. 225–26. For Sartre's conversion to Husserl, see *P&D* 1:87, 143–44. I detailed my reasons for basing the comparison of Sartre with Husserl on Sartre's treatment of the imagination in my preceding volume (see *P&D* 1:191). Here we need only remember that with respect to his other prewar writings Sartre (in the citation I have given to the *Carnets*) singles out *l'imaginaire* as "a book" which was "inspired" by Husserl, whereas he men-

tions the "Transcendence of the Ego" as merely "an article." The *Theory of the Emotions* is entitled *A Sketch*.

5. See *P&D* 1:99.

6. De Beauvoir, *La force de l'âge*, p. 216.

7. Husserl, *Ideas I*, sec. 18. The philosophical *epochē* is not to be confused with the "phenomenological *epochē*," which is a feature of the phenomenological reduction.

8. This conclusion provided the title of this investigation, which was by Claude Bonnefoy (*Arts*, 11–17 January 1961), and is cited in *Sartre: écrits de jeunesse*, p. 23.

9. See *Sartre: écrits de jeunesse*, pp. 10, 191.

10. See *P&D*:117.

11. See *Sartre: écrits de jeunesse*, p. 515, footnote 4, referring to the narrator's commitment (p. 145). The early work is *La semence et le scaphandre*.

12. Ibid., p. 192.

13. Of course it was not yet a defeat when Sartre adopted this title. But since we are on the lookout for the later "Sartre," we should bear in mind that in the philosophy he elaborated an *échec* is a decisive moment. Anticipate the apotheosis of defeat in *Being and Nothingness:* "The passion of man is the reverse of Christ's, for man loses himself as man in order that God may be born. But the idea of God is contradictory, and we lose ourselves in vain. Man is a useless passion" (p. 784). See no. 18. in Chapter 23 below.

14. See *Sartre: écrits de jeunesse*, pp. 192–93. One reason it is worth observing that *"Une défaite"* is mainly based on *La jeunesse de Nietzsche, sa vie et sa pensée* [1921–24]) is that the youthful Sartre betrays the same reflexive preoccupation with his own *jeunesse* as (we shall soon see) he does with the prospect of becoming the disciple of a master. He writes to Simone Jollivet (see n. 23 below), "It is not without emotion that I am thinking that in an hour the first page of *une jeunesse* will be written" (cited in *Sartre: écrits de jeunesse*, p. 190, from *Lettres au Castor* 1:13). Contat and Rybalka speculate that Sartre could be referring to *"Une défaite"* or to a section of it. This reflexivity is also illustrated by a passage they cite from Sartre's *Les carnets de la drôle de guerre:* "In short, I wanted to be sure of becoming a great man later, in order to be able to live my *jeunesse* as a *jeunesse* of a great man. . . . I was very conscious of being the young Sartre, as one speaks of the young Berlioz or the young Goethe" (cited in *Sartre: écrits de jeunesse*, p. 25, from *Les carnets*, p. 97). Though Nietzsche has receded from Sartre's recollections (perhaps because he does not want to recall the defeat *"Une défaite"* had been for him) Sartre had been equally self-consciously the young Nietzsche. This proclivity to reflexivity, as we shall see, becomes a philosophical commitment in "Sartre."

15. Frédéric's relation to Cosima is interesting in connection with the vexing topic of Sartre's relation to women, which unfortunately is largely beyond my scope here.

16. See *Sartre: écrits de jeunesse*, p. 194.

17. Ibid., p. 226. I have not omitted any text; the breaks are Sartre's renderings of *Frédéric's* juvenile awkwardness and impatience.

18. Ibid., p. 149. Of course, *maître* can convey different and rather less enslaving implications in French than "master" does in English.

19. Ibid., pp. 213–14. Further evidence of the extent to which this passage is autobiographical are the references that I have omitted to the "Old Friend," who clearly is Sartre's alter ego, Paul Nizan, and to mathematical training Frédéric had received from his father. Sartre's stepfather had unsuccessfully tried to teach him mathematics.

20. Ibid., p. 232–33; italics in original.

21. Ibid., p. 197. The appellation seems to have been a mocking tribute to Sartre's "aggressive voluntarism" (p. 522). Here we can perhaps credit some influence to Nietzsche ("force" is a favorite term in the juvenilia), but in any case voluntarism will become a philosophical commitment of Sartre's. At this time Sartre was tutoring Mme Morel's son, to whom (it is perhaps not irrelevant to my commentary to point out) *L'imaginaire*, is dedicated. For more details see the editors' note, *Sartre: écrits de jeunesse*, p. 522.

22. In *Une défaite* there is also play with the notion of "master." During his conversation with Organte, Frédéric "suffers without interruption the temptation to ask him, 'Would you be my *maître*,' and he immediately recalls "his first *maîtresse*, a whore from the Latin Quarter, fresher and more tender than the others [p. 230]." *Une défaite* begins with Frédéric's feeling himself the "master" in relation to the mistress he has rejected (see below, n. 15 to Chapter 29). Frédéric also compares the way in which "he throws himself into an idea" and the way in which Organte does so, with more force, with *maîtrise*" (ibid. p. 230).

23. Ibid., p. 524, citing *Lettres au Castor et à quelques autres*, p. 14. This letter was written to Simone Jollivet, for whom Sartre may well have written "*Une défaite*," (*Sartre: écrits de jeunesse*, p. 190) and who was, Sartre told the editors, a "model" for Cosima (she was also the model for the Anny of *Nausea*). Sartre's poor judgment should be admitted: he is recommending that she read the biography of Shelley by André Maurois, which is a wretched work. It should also be admitted that the "Sartre" that Sartre eventually became was no Shelley (pp. 213–14).

24. In stressing Sartre's own "identification with the youthful Nietzsche," the editors cite approvingly a psychoanalytic interpretation in which "Sartre's identification with Nietzsche" is explained by their common situation of a "son who lost his father at an early age." This also is taken as explaining "in moments of weakness . . . the call for the Master" (p. 195). But instead of pursuing this analysis, the editors cite Nietzsche [!], "I have to have disciples," before returning to Sartre with the suggestion, "It would be interesting to analyze in the light of "*Une défaite*" the relations between Sartre and Benny Levy." (Levy was a youthful disciple of the aging Sartre.) I find rather extravagant such jumping from the need for a master on the part of the juvenile Sartre (as "the lamentable Frédéric"), who was apolitical, to Sartre's perhaps somewhat senile need for a politically dedicated disciple. There is one respect in which Frédéric's relation to Organte cannot

be compared with Sartre's relation to Husserl: Sartre never sought a personal relation with Husserl. Simone de Beauvoir seems to have dissuaded Sartre from going on from Berlin to Freiburg (see *P&D* 1:85). But, in any case, Sartre kept his philosophical affinities largely separate from the close personal relations he clung to within what he called "the family."

3. The Image

1. I retain the French titles because the title of the English translation of *L'imaginaire*—*The Psychology of the Imagination*—is likely to lead to its being confused with *L'imagination*. The translation of *L'imagination* is adequate; the translation of *L'imaginaire* is completely unreliable. I shall cite the French originals but supply references to the translations, when available, that appear in my anthology, *The Philosophy of Jean-Paul Sartre*.

2. Sartre, *L'imagination*, p. 150.

3. See *Phantasie, Bildbewusstsein, Erinnerung*.

4. See *P&D* 1:18.

5. This is the title of the first chapter of P. N. Furbank's *Reflections on the Word "Image."*

6. Ibid., pp. 1, 9. Later we shall see the extent to which Sartre, in concocting his literary imagery, will rely on physical images.

7. Warnock, *Imagination*, p. 163.

8. I am grateful to Michel Rybalka for allowing me to quote briefly from his typescript of the *diplôme*.

9. De Beauvoir, *La force de l'âge*, p. 17.

10. Sartre, *L'imagination*, p. 147; Husserl, *Ideas I*, sec. 23.

11. See *P&D* 1:28–29.

4. In Passing

1. Sartre, *L'imagination*, p. 143.

2. Thus Sartre not only characterizes Husserl as treating the image "only in passing," but after he has quoted Husserl, Sartre comments, "Such are the brief allusions that Husserl makes to a theory . . . which in *Ideas* remains very fragmentary" [Ibid., p. 150]. It is because Sartre is largely indifferent to Husserl's sustained preoccupation with method, and is preoccupied himself with a theory of the image, that he discovers "allusions" to a theory and considers it "very fragmentary."

3. See *P&D* 1:134–35.

4. Husserl, "*Nachwort*" to *Ideen I*, in *Ideen 3*, pp. 161–62.

5. For how Sartre devoured *Ideas I*, see *P&D* 1:33. So far as is known, Sartre never read any other philosophical work so hungrily. Thus more reliance can be placed on his familiarity with it.

6. See *P&D* 1:190. Having reported his conversion to Husserl, "Voilà enfin la philosophie," Sartre goes on in the next sentence to report his enthusiasm for Jean Wahl's title *Vers le concret* (*Sartre, un film,* p. 39). But Sartre speaks of being "disappointed by the 'toward'" because "we [Sartre is speaking of like-minded contemporaries as well as himself] wanted to start out with the concrete as a whole" (*Questions de méthode,* p. 22). In *L'imagination,* he is starting out with the concrete.

7. See *P&D* 1:148.

8. See *P&D* 1:131–32, 152.

9. *Sartre, un film,* p. 43.

5. Starting Point

1. Elisabeth Ströker has provided a straightforward and lucid exposition in her *Husserls transzendentale Phänomenologie.*

2. Husserl, *Ideas I,* sec. 84.

3. See *P&D* 1:40–41.

4. Husserl, *Ideas I,* sec. 87, 146.

5. Husserl, *Logical Investigations* 2:544.

6. Sartre, *Qu'est-ce que la littérature?,* pp. 269–70.

7. Sartre, *Situations* 9:70.

8. Have I culled this example from a writer? I have always assumed that it was from Alain Robbe-Grillet, but his bibliographer, Michel Rybalka, kindly assures me I am wrong. If I made it up, I can console myself with Husserl's edict, "Fiction is the source from which the cognition of 'eternal truths' is nourished" [*Ideas I,* sec. 70]. Husserl is commenting on the methodological potency that he ascribes to the imagination as applied by the eidetic reduction, which I shall take up in Chapter 13 below.

9. Despite his familiarity with *Ideas I,* Sartre does not employ the term *noēma* in *L'imaginaire* or in the Berlin essay on intentionality. Perhaps he found it too forbiddingly technical for his readers, or he may have recognized that Husserl's clarification of the term in *Ideas I* presumes that the phenomenological reduction has been carried out, as Sartre himself acknowledges in *Being and Nothingness* (p. 9). The status of the *noēma* is controversial, but since Sartre has nothing to contribute to the controversy, I am skirting it, by using the term "intentional object." This term itself Sartre sometimes avoids, for (as we shall see in the next chapter) he assumes that the "transcendent object" is the real object in the external world. Thus my using the term "intentional object" is an attempt to straddle certain epistemological issues that Sartre did not deal with to his own satisfaction until his phenomenology became ontological in *Being and Nothingness,* which is beyond my present scope.

10. Husserl, *Ideas I,* sec. 37.

11. Husserl, *Logical Investigations* 2:563.

12. Husserl, *Cartesian Meditations*, p. 33.

13. Husserl, *Logical Investigations* 2:559.

14. Husserl, *Cartesian Meditations*, pp. 103, 107. Sartre should have been aware of Husserl's paradoxical formulation "transcendence in immanence," since Husserl used it specifically (and in italics) in his brief discussion of the transcendental ego in *Ideas I* (sec. 57); indeed, Sartre attacked this conception in the other essay that he wrote in Berlin. Husserl's use of "transcendent" should not be confused with "transcendental." Sartre's title *The Transcendence of the Ego* suggests that he is playing with Husserl's terminology as if it were ambiguous. On the one hand, the ego (the self of which I am conscious when I am self-conscious) is in Sartre a "transcendent object" in that it transcends my consciousness of it, just as does any other object of intentional reference (for example, the chair or the centaur). But it is not a transcendental ego, in the sense that it survives the phenomenological reduction with which we enter the transcendental realm. Such a play with ambiguity Husserl would have found intolerable (see the "Ambiguity" section of my Chapter 1).

15. The argument is Heidegger's in "The Origin of the Work of Art" (1936), in *Basic Writings*. I cite it because the argument is still phenomenological, although by this date Heidegger has abandoned the label and usually is presumed to have turned his back on phenomenology.

16. Husserl, *Logical Investigations* 2:650.

17. See *P&D* 1:44–45.

18. Husserl, *Ideas I*, sec. 41.

6. A Fundamental Idea

1. Sartre, *L'imagination*, p. 148. Sartre's negative formulation ("nothing precludes") may be an admission that Husserl fails to treat the image except in passing. But see Sartre's use of "invitation" in my next quotation.

2. Ibid., p. 14.

3. Husserl, *Nachwort* to *Ideen I* in *Ideen 3*, p. 140. Heidegger is not mentioned by name, but Husserl clearly had him in mind. See Cairns, *Conversations with Husserl and Fink*, p. 43.

4. Unless otherwise indicated, references to "the Berlin essay" will be to this essay. Though it was written in Berlin, it was not published until 1939 (in volume 1 of Sartre's *Situations*). Since it is less than five pages long, I shall not furnish page references.

5. Husserl, *Logical Investigations* 1:563.

6. Sartre's claim is reported by his editors (*Oeuvres romanesques*, p. 1664. In *Being and Nothingness* Sartre will transform Husserl's intentional reference into an ontological proof (pp. 22–24). The "things themselves" then are not just intentional objects but are things that really exist. The "obstinate existence" that Frédéric credits to them (in the passage I am about to quote) will thus be vindicated. But Sartre is also bridging the gap between Husserl's phenomenology and

Heidegger's ontology and for this purpose is employing the term "transcendence" both in the sense that transcendence is a trait of the intentional object of consciousness and in the sense that it is a trait of being-there in Heidegger who himself employs the term to describe a more fundamental reference to the world than intentionality. This conflation of senses is promoted by Sartre's principle "to the concrete" as warranting the assumption that the differences he is overriding are abstract and do not make any difference concretely. Accordingly, the direction of his philosophy "toward the concrete" can itself be conflated with the direction of Husserl's "to the things themselves." (See *P&D* 1:190–93, and for the conflation of "transcendence" itself with other terms, see accompanying note 23.) What is a legitimate conflation in Sartre would be sheer confusion in Husserl, as we shall see in Chapters 8 and 11 below.

7. *Sartre: écrits de jeunesse,* p. 220.

8. *Situations* 4:249.

9. See *P&D* 1:122.

10. See *P&D* 1:53, 192–93. Sartre has in mind a novel that deals with social history (see *P&D* 1:163) I think he would extend his claim to other problems.

11. See the "Priority" section of Chapter 18.

12. See *P&D* 1:11.

13. See *P&D* 1:88, 101.

14. Cited in introduction to *Husserliana* 23:xxxv-vi.

7. The Illusion of Immanence

1. I quote the 1986 edition of *L'imaginaire.* The pagination differs from earlier editions, so I shall often supply a reference to a chapter or a section. Since my sampling follows Sartre's sequence of topics (see Chapter 15 below), the reader will be better able to follow and assess my interpretation if she reads *L'imaginaire* first, up to p. 112.

2. Although Sartre usually dismisses the distinction between *L'imagination* and *L'imaginaire,* as due simply to the hazard of a publisher initially accepting one portion of his manuscript and rejecting the rest, some justification for my interpretation of the title can be found in the first sentence of his *prière d'insérer* for *L'imaginaire:* "La Psychologie des Facultés en s'effondrant sous les critiques de la psychologie positive entraîna dans sa ruine L'Imagination ou faculté de former des images" (see Contat and Rybalka, *Les écrits de Sartre,* p. 77). This *prière* would have been written by Sartre two or three years after the original manuscript.

3. See Husserl, *Logical Investigations* 2:593–96. John Sallis makes the claim that "Husserl's stand against the image theory is dictated by its conflict with the concept of intentionality," and he reaches the conclusion, "The consequence is momentous: the issue of images is decisively removed from the center of phenomenological concern" ("Image and Phenomenon," pp. 64–65.) The same claim is implicit in Sartre, but he reaches the opposite conclusion. Or to put the issue in

my terminology: in both cases a shift in *subject* takes place, but in completely different directions. One ambiguity here is, of course, that Husserl is taking his stand primarily against the image theory of perception, whereas what is moved to the center of phenomenological concern in Sartre is the image itself. There is another ambiguity inasmuch as Husserl at the time he wrote the *Logical Investigations* does assume a mental image in the case of imagination (but not in the case of perception) as well as an imagined object, even though it is the latter that is, strictly speaking, intended. The distinction here is drawn most clearly in a *Beilage* dating from 1898: "In imaginative representation two objects are apprehended. There is the mental image [*Phantasiebild*] and, represented by it, the imagined object [*Bildsujet*], which is the represented in the strict sense. Perceptual representation represents its object directly; imaginative representation indirectly" (Husserl, *Phantasie*, p. 112). By the time of *Ideas I*, Husserl has dropped this "two object" analysis, and representation becomes direct in the case of the imagination as in the case of perception. For a summary of this development, see Eduard Marbach's introduction to Husserl's *Husserliana* 23:liv–lix. If I am not considering the development of Husserl's analysis of the image, it is because Sartre was not only unaware of it but was also largely insensitive to the problems Husserl was facing—thus we do not find in Sartre comparable distinctions. Accordingly, in the next chapter, I will focus on a more general comparison between how Husserl draws distinctions and how Sartre disregards them.

4. Husserl, *Ideas I*, sec. 24.

5. Husserl, *Logical Investigations* 1:265. With this philosophical *epochē*, Husserl makes the transition from the *Prolegomena* of Volume 1, in which he does take previous theories into account, to the strictly phenomenological investigations of Volume 2. The apparently corresponding distinction between *L'imagination* and *L'imaginaire* seems rather to have been forced on Sartre (as I have already indicated) by the publisher's acceptance of the historical stretch of Sartre's longer work and rejection of the rest.

6. Sartre, *L'imaginaire*, p. 20.

7. Husserl, *Ideas I*, sec. 66.

8. Sartre, *L'imagination*, p. 158.

9. See *P&D* 1:107–11. Sartre's obviously significant immersion was as a prisoner of war. See *P&D* 1:121 and *Starting Point*, p. 113.

10. See *P&D* 1:108. I use "academicization" in the higher-order sense that even Sartre's assimilation of the "barbaric" (and thus nonacademic Heidegger) can be regarded as an "academicization" of Sartre's war experience. During the war Sartre was too busy with *Being and Nothingness* (in emulation of Heidegger's *Being and Time*) and other writings to find time to participate in the only Resistance cell that was half prepared to trust him. (Some of the evidence is summarized by Bair, in her *Simone de Beauvoir*, pp. 158–260.) I make this point, not because too many Americans are still under the impression that Sartre played some role in the French Resistance, but because Sartre's bookishness is most striking under the circumstances of wartime. My present point is that Sartre's important prewar experience were also mainly experiences of reading and writing.

11. *Sartre, un film,* p. 130. One reason I would characterize Sartre's predicament as "academic" is that *professeur* of course designates any "teacher," not merely a college professor, which Sartre never was.

12. Sartre, *Les mots,* p. 29. It is necessary to take one step beyond Sartre's bookishness and take into account the kind of books he tended to read. He apparently required the guidance of Aron's account of German philosophy of history to prepare him for Heidegger, whom he read initially in the anthology translated by Corbin (1938). Soon when he was working on *Being and Nothingness* he was also reading Hegel, but only "a few pages" and again in a translated French anthology, which was published in 1939, a year after the Corbin (see Jean Launay, "Sartre lecteur de Heidegger," p. 414), though Sartre was also aided by de Beauvoir, who apparently read some works of Hegel on Sartre's behalf. Sartre did secure a copy of *Being and Time* while a prisoner of war, but there is no clear evidence that he did not continue to rely in *Being and Nothingness* largely on Corbin and secondary works—in particular Jean Wahl's *Etudes kierkegaardiennes* (published the same year as Corbin and the year Sartre began *Being and Nothingness*) for the crucial issue of anxiety in Heidegger (see *Being and Nothingness,* p. 65). Of course it's quite possible that if Sartre had been able to come to closer grips with Heidegger or Hegel, he would not have been able to digest them into a philosophy of his own. Since he did in fact spend most of a year in Berlin devouring *Ideas I* in German, his relation to Husserl demands the attention I am giving it as the most intimate relation between his philosophy and another philosophy.

13. Aside from the bookishness, I would not want to press too hard an analogy between Sartre's relations to women and his relations to other philosophers. In both cases he displays remarkable lack of scruple, but this need not entail complete randomness. A pattern can still be discerned in his unscrupulous exploitation of the texts of other philosophers (in this volume, those of Husserl), just as there may well be some pattern discernible in his exploitation of women.

14. *Sartre: écrits de jeunesse,* p. 261. Frédéric proceeds to "pout." Cosima goes on to warn him he is running the risk that he will "become a *professeur,* without a future, without happiness" (263). This was the youthful Sartre's own fear, and he provided a devastating portrait in *Jésus la chouette* of a *professeur* he had known who had lived without a future and without happiness. Throughout the conversation between Frédéric and Cosima Sartre may be self-ironizing on behalf of Simone Jollivet (see n. 23 in Chapter 2), who must have complained at times over Sartre's lecturing her and his getting her to read books. Sartre may also be mocking de Beauvoir who was devoted to Meredith. But penetrating these layers of irony is still the general point that Sartre's participation in amorous experiences was perhaps not much more "existential" than his participation in the French Resistance.

15. See *P&D*: 110.

16. See "The Master" section of Chapter 2 above.

17. In a speech at a celebratory dinner, reported by Boyce-Gibson in the "Excerpts from a 1928 Freiburg Diary," Husserl extolled the ethos of *absolute*

Redlichkeit and *absolute Ehrlichkeit* "in all relations of life and thought" (p. 70) and these demands on his thought is evident to any reader of his writings. It is of course difficult to visualize Sartre as condoning *Redlichkeit* and *Ehrlichkeit,* and the reference to a master who was "upright" may mock one of his professors.

18. The term "vulgarization" is Sartre's, but he reserves it as a requisite for political action (see *P&D* 1:71). My general application of the term receives some encouragement from Heidegger's and Derrida's criticisms of Sartre (see *P&D* 1:70, 189–90). In now applying the term to Sartre's relation to Husserl, I am adding evidence that "vulgarization" is not inconsistent with bookishness.

19. Sartre quoted in de Beauvoir's *Entretiens avec Sartre,* p. 167.

20. *Sartre: écrits de jeunesse,* p. 224.

21. Ibid., pp. 87.

22. Husserl, *Logical Investigations,* 1:43.

23. Sartre, *Les carnets de la drôle de guerre,* p. 175.

24. See *P&D* 1:117–26.

25. *Sartre, un film,* p. 130.

26. Sartre, *La mort dans l'âme,* p. 193. The character whose exploit is being described, Mathieu, is clearly a stand-in for Sartre and a vehicle for Sartre's reflections even though Sartre never could emulate his belligerent behavior.

27. *Sartre, un film,* p. 63. This was de Beauvoir's response to a question addressed to Sartre as to why he had not fought in the Spanish Civil War. The best survey of Sartre's political activism is Michel-Antoine Burnier's "On ne peut pas être sartrien, on ne peut pas être anti-sartrien." It provides several previously unpublished illustrations of his verbal commitment to violence.

28. Husserl, *Cartesian Meditations,* p. 157.

29. Though in this instance there is a sustained opposition in direction, it should not be supposed that a philosopher simply proceeds along one track in a single direction, not even when "everything is outside" or if the way followed leads into the "inner man." Thus we are led back in Husserl in two distinct directions to two distinct levels—to the level of essences by the eidetic reduction and to the transcendental level by the phenomenological reduction. Of course, philosophers have sometimes proposed following "the straight path," as Descartes does (such a proposal is often inspired by a deductive mathematical model), but the sense in which a philosopher follows a single direction has to be distinguished from the sense in which he may change direction, as Descartes does several times in the course of his *Metaphysical Meditations.* For the idiom of "direction" see my *Starting Point,* esp. pp. 148–151. Needless to say, I shall take up the idiom again when I deal with Heidegger's *methodos* as the "following of a way."

8. The Shift in Method

1. See n. 5 below.

2. Sartre, *L'imaginaire,* p. 21; italics in original.

3. See Husserl, *Logical Investigations,* pp. 557–58.

4. Sartre *L'imaginaire*, p. 23; see also *The Philosophy of Jean-Paul Sartre*, p. 77. In the 1987 reissue of *L'imaginaire*, (edited by Sartre's adopted daughter), although there is no indication of alterations in the text, *Abschattungen* has been removed, despite Sartre's having called the German designation a *terme heureux*. Sartre is obviously thinking of the failure of the French translation to convey the etymology of the German.

5. Husserl, *Cartesian Meditations*, p. 41. Christina Howells complains, "One of the problems with *L'imaginaire* is that it opposes imagination and perception without giving even an outline account of the latter" (*Sartre: The Necessity of Freedom*, p. 11). What is obvious from the present section, where Sartre is opposing imagination and perception (and obvious, as well, from his insistence on his debts to Husserl in *L'imagination*, etc.), is that he is presupposing Husserl's analysis of perception, at least in outline, and in particular Husserl's analysis of the "synthesis of identification"—which later we shall see Sartre latches onto, inasmuch as it lends itself to his transformation of Husserl's intentional analysis into a relational analysis. Howells should have asked the question, How could Sartre have supposed he could conduct an analysis in which he is opposing imagination and perception without giving even an outline account of the latter? When Howells does refer to Sartre's relation to Husserl she apparently has in mind the Berlin essay and *L'imagination*, though she misdescribes "Husserl's notion of intentionality" as "a direction of attention" (p. 10), thus attributing to him Sartre's notion. But then she states, "In *L'imaginaire*, Sartre will start where Husserl leaves off and elaborate a full-scale phenomenological psychology of the imagination." This statement suggests an inert relation between Sartre and Husserl. But it can be learned from the history of philosophy that a philosopher usually does not start from where some predecessor leaves off—perhaps especially not when he is "inspired" by that predecessor, as Sartre says he is by Husserl in *L'imaginaire*. My argument in this volume is that Sartre does not leave Husserl's philosophy intact when he borrows from Husserl and that what Sartre himself is specifically up to as a philosopher can often more readily be understood when what he does to Husserl's philosophy is taken into account. The same argument can be pursued regarding Sartre's relation to Heidegger (see "The Gas Leak" section of Chapter 33 below).

6. For an example of a conflation that such sliding can promise, see *P&D* 1:235 n. 23.

7. Husserl, *Logical Investigations* 2:558.

8. Husserl, *Ideas I*, sec. 35; Sartre, *L'imagination*, p. 1.

9. Husserl, *Logical Investigations* 2:563.

10. Sartre, *L'imaginaire*, pp. 172–75.

11. Ibid., p. 30. I am deferring consideration of this characteristic of the imagination until Chapter 32.

12. Ibid., pp. 177–82.

13. Ibid., p. 240.

14. Sartre, *Being and Nothingness,* p. 116; see also *The Philosophy of Jean-Paul Sartre,* p. 166.

15. See "Commotion" section of Chapter 6 above.

16. See *Sartre: écrits de jeunesse,* p. 285. Frédéric has other illusions: "He is treated as affected, and he only lives his error, takes pleasure in the thick and damp growth of illusion" (p. 222). Here the illusory affectation is that he could be elegant: "He raised his head, exaggerated the suppleness of his gait, in order to obtain the pleasure of feeling himself supple, and little by little his old image, which he was keeping closed up, the image that summed up his desire of elegance, reopened." A preliminary note indicates the part supposedly played by an image in constituting this illusion: "He believes himself to be elegant. He feels himself live his image" (p. 526). This is not just Frédéric playing with his body image but Sartre ironizing over the illusion he could be as elegant as his famously elegant alter ego, Paul Nizan. In emulating Nizan, he is also mocking him and, presumably, also their relation. For further implications of this example, see the "Doubling" of Chapter 26.

17. *Sartre: écrits de jeunesse,* pp. 501–2; for the *salaud,* see "Nausea" section of Chapter 23 below.

18. Sartre, *Les mots,* pp. 4–5.

19. Though Sartre seems to have been guilty of this confusion in the Berlin essay on intentionality, he would seem to be trying to remove it in *L'imaginaire:* "Transcendence does not mean exteriority: it is the thing represented that is external, not its mental 'analogue.' The 'illusion of immanence' consists in transferring to the transcendent mental content exteriority, spatiality, and all the sensible qualities of the thing" (p. 110). But then the mental image would seem to be neither inside nor outside, so that Sartre's conclusion in the Berlin essay that "everything is outside . . . : in the world" seems to be undermined. Yet Sartre published this essay *after* he had written *L'imaginaire.* A possible explanation is that he was by then committed to Heidegger's "being-in-the-world," which was not much more than a catchy phrase to him when he originally wrote the essay in Berlin. But in Heidegger, "being-there takes up space, and this is to be taken literally" (see my *Starting Point,* p. 103). This is one of many issues that Sartre apparently never tried to resolve in his ostensible reconciliation of Husserl and Heidegger in *Being and Nothingness.*

20. Sartre, *L'imaginaire,* p. 19.

21. Ibid., p. 36.

22. Ibid. At this juncture, the contrast between Sartre and Husserl would have been less reliable if *Ideas I* had not been the work of Husserl's that Sartre had devoured. In *Ideas I,* Husserl admits that with regard to "time," which is "a rubric for a *set of problems that are completely delimited,* our previous analyses have, to a certain extent, remained silent and must, of necessity, remain silent in order to protect against confusing what, first of all, is alone visible in the phenomenological attitude and what, disregarding the new dimension ['time'], makes up a closed domain of investigation" (sec. 81; italics in original). As Derrida points

out, "Despite the very great importance acquired by the analyses of the consciousness of time [which Husserl is anticipating in his admission, and with which Sartre had some acquaintance, Husserl's problems remain up to 1919–20 problems of 'static' constitution" (*Le problème de la genèse dans la philosophie de Husserl*, p. 107). Derrida also points out that "with Husserl's rejection of psychologism, genesis became confused with psychophysiological causality" and accordingly was eliminated from consideration by the reduction (ibid., p. 37). I have expounded Husserl's "static" analysis not only because this analysis enjoys with Husserl a priority that is more fundamental than the chronology of his development (as is indicated by my first quotation in this note) but also because the problems of the relation between the "static" analysis of *Ideas I* and the genetic analyses he later undertook are too difficult to take on here. Again I cite Derrida: "It is impossible to decide if the emergence of genesis as a theme after *Ideas I* amounts to a fulfillment of or a revolution in Husserl's earlier philosophy" (ibid., 177). In any case, it would be at best injudicious to try to deal with this question in the context of Sartre's relation to Husserl. Indeed, this is a good illustration of the kind of question in one philosopher that should be skirted by an expositor who is committed to dealing with this philosopher in terms of his relations to other philosophers.

23. *Sartre: écrits de jeunesse*, pp. 224, 231. The same commitment to fluidity emerges in Sartre's *Apologie pour le cinéma* (1924 or 1925). Perhaps a sufficient illustration will be a sample of the opposition between the static and the mobile that he starts out by setting up: "To Alain ... nothing is beautiful except the [immobile. He gets] his pleasure out of looking at the frozen bodies of Greek statues. ... Is there no charm in the fluidity of the kaleidoscope? ... The cinema provides the formula for a Bergsonian art. Bergson inaugurates mobility in aesthetics" pp. 388–89). In Chapter 17 below, we shall watch Sartre gain fluidity for his analysis by borrowing from Bergson.

24. Sartre's methodology here betrays his own sensibility. By virtue of the fluidity of water, water-skiing is regarded by Sartre as more exhilarating than other kinds of *glissement*, such as skiing and skating (*Being and Nothingness*, p. 746; cf. 774). Or perhaps his methodology dictates his sensibility, since I don't remember any reported occasion on which he went water-skiing.

25. I have been using the term "transformation" (see *P&D* 1:9) as well as "transition," although I have retained, in the titles of this chapter and the next chapter, the brusque term "shift," which I justified in Volume 1 by reference to the "lurch" that takes place in Heidegger's relation to Husserl at the start of *Being and Time*. My present usage is not merely a matter of my proceeding now in low gear, as compared with my pace in Volume 1, with the result that the differences between the "structures" of their two philosophies are slower to emerge. Unlike Heidegger, Sartre borrows generously from Husserl, and the development of Sartre's analysis in *L'imaginaire*, seems as if it were a gradual transformation of Husserl rather than a sudden lurch. However, in Chapter 15 below, we shall reach a juncture in *L'imaginaire*, where we shall find Sartre aware himself of his making a sharp break with Husserl.

9. The Shift in Subject

1. Sartre, *L'imaginaire*, pp. 40–41; see also *The Philosophy of Jean-Paul Sartre*, pp. 79–80.

2. Sartre, *L'imaginaire*, pp. 46–47; see also *The Philosophy of Jean-Paul Sartre*, p. 81.

3. See Husserl, *Ideas I*, sec. 94.

4. Fink is particularly explicit about our predicament; see his essay "The Phenomenological Philosophy of Edmund Husserl." Not only did Husserl warmly endorse Fink's essay, but it also seems to have been the only item of secondary literature in German that commanded Sartre's attention—presumably because it came out while he was in Berlin. Thus a pertinent statement is worth quoting here: "This concept [of the natural attitude] is not at all a worldly one that is in some way already given. Rather, it is a 'transcendental' concept. We are, in the natural attitude, confined and absorbed within it, so that we are not at all able to disengage ourselves from it without breaking out of it completely. The phenomenological reduction is this very breakthrough." The scope of the natural attitude is further stressed by Fink's claim, "All human attitudes remain in principle *within* the natural attitude" (p. 107; italics in original). In Sartre, this distinction in *level* largely disappears, but the concept of attitude retains more than its ordinary scope. When I refer to Sartre as "renaturalizing" a concept of Husserl's, I am extending to Sartre one of Husserl's complaints against Heidegger (see *P&D* 1:9–10, 44–45). The renaturalization also illustrates one respect in which the movement of Sartre's philosophy is "toward the concrete."

5. Sartre, *L'imaginaire*, p. 62; and see *The Philosophy of Jean-Paul Sartre*, p. 85.

6. Husserl, *Logical Investigations* 1:43.

7. Husserl, *Logical Investigations* 2:650–51.

8. Ibid., p. 563.

9. Sartre, *L'imaginaire*, p. 51.

10. I analyzed *interplay* in my *Starting Point*, which is an exposition of dialectical method and a companion volume for the present exposition of phenomenological method (see *P&D* 1:151–52). In *Starting Point*, I demonstrate that Kierkegaard uses a more purely dialectical method than is employed by Sartre, whose method in *Being and Nothingness* retains a phenomenological component. Since an image is involved, consider the following example from *Either/Or* of *interplay* between levels: "How beautiful it is to be in love [level of immediacy], how interesting to be conscious of being in love [level of reflection]. Lo, that is the difference. I could be bitter at the thought that . . . I have lost sight of her and yet in a certain sense it pleases me. The image I now have of her hovers indeterminately between her actual and her ideal form" (*Starting Point*, p. 108). There is probably some allusion here to Hegel's treatment of "imaginative representation" (*Vorstellung*) as between "sense perception" (*Anschauung*) and thinking (for Hegel's treatment and a portion of Kierkegaard's critique, see *Starting Point*, pp. 106–8). In any case, Kierkegaard is playing with the aesthetic category of the interesting.

Kierkegaard's dialectic is a relational analysis in which "consciousness is relation and brings with it interest, a duality that is fully expressed with the pregnant double meaning of the word *interesse*" (*Starting Point,* pp. 161). In other words, what is interesting is interesting by virtue of its "in-betweenness," which permits indulging an interesting *interplay.*

11. Sartre, *L'imaginaire,* pp. 52–53.

12. Ibid., pp. 270–73.

13. Eventually, Sartre's favoring examples of consciousness of some*one* over examples of consciousness of some*thing* will find its general justification with his assertion: "Relations with things are always originally human relations" (*L'idiot de la famille* 1:340).

14. See *P&D* 1:120–21.

15. See my *Starting Point,* pp. 315–16.

16. What I referred to as "levels" in n. 10 above are also the "stages" of "immediacy" and "reflection"; see also my *Starting Point,* chap. 6.

17. We see a broad contrast here between Sartre's mixture of a phenomenological method and a dialectical method and Kierkegaard's more purely dialectical method. The lyrical "aphorisms" with which *Either/Or* starts out implement the a-phoristical procedure (form) of (etymologically) "separating off" from the rest of experience whatever experience (content) can be taken as "essential" to the "mood" of the "moment." Their separateness provides the dialectical opposite of a relational analysis, yet they are also "provisional glimpses of what the longer essays develop more connectedly [*sammenhaengende*]." The first of the longer essays presents "The Immediate Stage of the Erotic;" the later essays, the reflective stages (see *Starting Point,* pp. 249–261). In *L'imaginaire,* however, it is only after the first chapter of phenomenological description that the analysis becomes a rudimentary dialectic.

10. Expression and Meaning

1. Husserl, *Logical Investigations* 1:43–44.

2. See *P&D* 1:28, 34–35, 42.

3. Husserl, *Logical Investigations* 1:282–83.

4. Sartre, *L'imaginaire,,* pp. 47–48.

5. Husserl, *Ideas I,* sec. 124.

6. Husserl, *Logical Investigations* 1:275.

7. Sartre, *L'imaginaire,* p. 55.

8. Sartre, *La nausée,* p. 32, 136.

9. The two essays have been reprinted in *Les écrits de Sartre,* ed. Contat and Rybalka, pp. 557–64; my quotation is from p. 558.

11. The Priority of Method

1. Husserl, *Logical Investigations* 1:269.

2. See Derrida, *La voix et le phénomène,* pp. 17–21.

3. Sartre, *L'imaginaire*, pp. 143, 150.

4. *Husserliana* 10:343.

5. *Husserliana* 23:xxviii.

6. De Beauvoir, *La force de l'âge*, p. 216.

7. Husserl, *Logical Investigations* 1:43–44.

8. Ibid., p. 254.

9. *Husserliana* 23:602.

10. Ibid., p. 18. The quotation will be given in full at the beginning of Chapter 12 below.

11. Ibid., p. xxxi.

12. Husserl, cited in Spiegelberg, *The Phenomenological Movement* 1:89.

13. Husserl, *Logical Investigations* 2:435.

14. See *P&D* 1:48–49.

15. Levinas, cited in Schumann, *Husserl-Chronik* 1:2.

16. Husserl, *Logical Investigations* 2:566.

17. Ibid., pp. 567–68 hr. n.

18. Ibid., p. 559.

19. Ibid., pp. 566–67.

20. Ibid., p. 567.

12. Relations

1. Sartre, *L'imagination*, p. 148. Seeking a rapprochement is, of course, not in itself a reliable clue that a relational analysis is under way. Any philosopher will bring items together for one purpose or another. Husserl himself does so, if often only to separate them more clearly. The clue becomes rather more reliable when a philosopher brings together, as Sartre does here, "what previous philosophers . . . have separated."

2. *Husserliana* 23:18; my italics.

3. Heidegger, *Being and Time*, p. 40.

4. Husserl, *Logical Investigations* 1:48.

5. Ibid., p. 49.

6. Husserl, *Logical Investigations* 2:463.

7. Ibid., pp. 437–39.

8. Heidegger, *Being and Time*, p. 40.

9. Husserl, *Logical Investigations* 2:449.

10. See *Les écrits de Sartre*, ed. Contat and Rybalka, p. 228.

11. Sartre, *Being and Nothingness*, pp. 33–34. The ordinary sense of "naïveté" is probably stiffened here by a reminiscence of the "naïveté" that is an explicit attribute in Husserl of "the natural attitude" but that is recognized only when the phenomenological reduction is carried out (see n. 4 of Chapter 9

above), which Sartre is arguing here is not to be carried out. Here, as often elsewhere in Sartre, it is hard to be sure if what we come up against is the ordinary sense of a word or a vulgarization of a technical philosophical term, involving a shift in *level*.

12. Sartre, *Being and Nothingness,* pp. 44–45.

13. Merleau-Ponty, *Sense and Non-Sense,* p. 72.

14. Merleau-Ponty, *Phenomenology of Perception,* p. viii.

15. Merleau-Ponty, *Le visible et l'invisible,* pp. 321–22.

16. Merleau-Ponty, *Phenomenology of Perception,* pp. viii, ix, x, xii, 166.

17. Merleau-Ponty, *The Structure of Behavior,* p. 168.

18. "The wonder of interrelated experiences" is Merleau-Ponty's version of the "'wonder' in the face of the world" which he cites as "the best formulation of the [phenomenological] reduction" (*Phenomenology of Perception,* p. xiii). Eugen Fink, whom Merleau-Ponty is citing, Husserl, and Heidegger all echo the Platonic and Aristotelian conception of "wonder" (or "astonishment") as the "starting point" of philosophy.

19. Merleau-Ponty, "Le philosophe et son ombre," *Signes,* p. 202; my italics.

20. I skip over Merleau-Ponty's distrust ("not nothing") of Sartre's rendering as negation ("Omnis determinatio est negatio") the process of discrimination that produces the discrete.

21. In Volume 1, my attention was restricted to how the relations between Sartre's and Merleau-Ponty's philosophies are differently envisaged in their respective philosophies in conformity with the different conception each upholds there of the relation between the individual and the other (see *P&D* 1:170–72); now these relations can be seen to conform to the different conception each upholds of the relations between *relata* in general.

22. See *P&D* 1:124–26.

23. When Husserl does employ an analogy, it is often to an artificial operation. Recall his analogy to a "lever," which I examined in Chapter 11. More recently we have encountered analogies to construction. Husserl characterized the difficulties he ran into in his analysis as due to phenomena being "built intricately upon one another in multiple ways" (*Logical Investigations* 1:254). The analogy is awkward—even implausible—as an analogy, and thereby conveys the difficulties analysis encounters in disentangling relations. Yet, since it is an analogy to construction, it implies that analytic separation is still feasible: what has been "built" can be taken apart. Another example was Husserl's treating sense-data as "building stones." Again the analogy encouraged him to separate sense-data from the intentional reference organizing them. The plausibility of his "hylomorphic" analysis was thereby enhanced. It may be worth remembering that this distinction between "form" and "matter" itself was obtained by Aristotle from the analogy to artificial operations and generalized to psychological and other phenomena.

24. A detailed comparison between Husserl's and Heidegger's handling of expression and meaning, I am postponing to Volume 3. In the present chapter I am settling for the easier comparison of Husserl with Sartre and Merleau-Ponty.

25. Merleau-Ponty, *Phenomenology of Perception,* p. 452.

26. Sartre, *L'existentialisme est un humanisme,* pp. 84–85.

27. Sartre, *La nausée,* p. 129. If engineering seems to acquire more salience here than is usually associated with the bourgeoisie, it should be remembered that the detested father-in-law, who had deprived Sartre of his monopoly of his sisterly mother, was an engineer.

28. I am quoting Arion Kelkel, *Maurice Merleau-Ponty, le psychique et le corporel,* p. 17. Kelkel is contrasting Merleau-Ponty with Husserl, but at this juncture a similar contrast holds with Sartre.

29. I translate *empiètement* (*Le visible et l'invisible,* p. 256; italicized in original) as "overlapping," but I am also thinking of Merleau-Ponty's use of the terms *enveloppe-enveloppant* and the German *Ineinander* (p. 321).

30. Merleau-Ponty, *Phenomenology of Perception,* p. 121.

31. The quotation is from the concluding chapter of *Phenomenology of Perception,* "Freedom." This chapter was written at a time when *Being and Nothingness,* published three years before, was coming into vogue. The chapter contains considerable criticism of Sartre. The English translation unfortunately renders *condamné* as "doomed." But Merleau-Ponty is reasserting, as he nears the end of the chapter, the formula he flourished in his preface against Sartre's "we are condemned to be free"—"we are *condemned to meaning*" (p. xix; italics in original). As usual Merleau-Ponty does not actually name Sartre.

13. The Eidetic Reduction

1. Husserl, *Logical Investigations,* 2:559.

2. Ibid., 1:45.

3. I use the word "structure" because Husserl himself uses it. See, e.g., his mention of "the main structures [*die Hauptstrukturen*] of pure consciousness" (*Logical Investigations,* 1:45]). The structure of intentional reference is not a *relational* structure such as is found in our three other phenomenologists.

4. Husserl, *Ideas I,* sec. 3.

5. Husserl, *Logical Investigations* 2:557–58. Husserl acknowledges that "no term in descriptive psychology is . . . more controversial than the term 'act,' and doubt, if not prompt rejection, may have been aroused by all passages . . . where we have made use of the notion of 'act'" (*Logical Investigations,* 2:534). The reader of my exposition may likewise have been aroused.

6. Ibid., p. 554.

7. Husserl, *Experience and Judgment,* p. 341.

8. Ibid., p. 342.

9. *Ideas I,* sec. 70.

10. See the final clause of the following characterization of the eidetic reduction: "What necessarily persists throughout this free and always repeatable variation comes to the fore: the *invariant,* the indissolubly identical in the different

and ever again different, the *essence* common to all, . . . by which all 'imaginable' variants of the example are restricted. This invariant is . . . the *eidos,* corresponding to the example, in place of which any variant of the example could have served equally well" (*Formal and Transcendental Logic,* p. 248). The emphasis of this last clause is reaffirmed in the next paragraph: The eidetic reduction "is a method that can be followed, no matter what conceivable object is taken as an initial example."

11. See *P&D* 1:102.

12. Husserl, *Logical Investigations,* 1:47.

14. Dialectical Correlation

1. Husserl, *Ideas I,* sec. 36.

2. Husserl, *Experience and Judgment,* p. 341.

3. Sartre, *Being and Nothingness,* p. 362.

4. Ayer, *Metaphysics and Common Sense,* p. 3.

5. Sartre, *L'imaginaire,* p. 558.

6. Husserl, *Logical Investigations,* 2:563.

7. Sartre, *L'imagination,* p. 151; Husserl, *Logical Investigations* 2:680.

8. Husserl, *Ideas I,* sec. 131. This section is entitled "The 'Object,' the Determinable X in the Noematic Sense." From this section Sartre makes his longest citation from Husserl (see Sartre's *La transcendance de l'ego,* p. 55).

15. Sequential Analysis

1. Sartre, *L'imaginaire,* p. 60.

2. Husserl, *Logical Investigations,* 1:261.

3. Husserl, *Ideas I,* sec. 65.

4. Ibid., sec. 84, 87.

5. *Husserliana* 23:383.

6. Though either example would serve, Husserl probably employs both because their considerable differences permit what is implicitly an eidetic reduction, which renders these differences (including the movement of the actors) irrelevant.

7. Sartre, *L'imaginaire,* pp. 106, 58.

8. Husserl, *Ideas I,* sec. 111.

9. Sartre, *L'imagination,* p. 148. Sartre is apparently sliding over Husserl's distinction between the sense in which the *hylē* is the "matter" (sense-datum) of the image and the sense in which any intentional act has a "matter" (content). I have not dealt with "matter" in this second sense, which emerges in Husserl with an eidetic reduction whereby it is recognized that two acts may differ in "quality" (one may be a judgment, another a question or a wish, etc.) but still have "the same content" (*Logical Investigations* 2:586).

10. Sartre, *L'imagination,* pp. 158, 152. The serious ambiguity of which Sartre

is apparently unaware is the possibility that the genetic analysis Husserl later undertakes may undercut the duality of intention and sense-data in the "hylomorphic" analysis that Sartre is taking for granted here. See Chapter 8 note 22 above.

11. Ibid., p. 151.

12. Sartre, *L'imaginaire*, p. 106.

13. Ibid. p. 104; *L'imagination*, p. 105. The question-begging phrase here is "in the last analysis [*finalement*]." If Sartre is referring to the *hylē* of the image as deriving initially from perception, then the answer is that it is "the same *hylē*," but it is modified when it becomes the *hylē* of the image and Husserl adopts for it a different term, *phantasma*, which he takes over from Aristotle, as he does *hylē*—though without much regard for Aristotle's usage. In *L'imagination selon Husserl*, Saraiva observes that "Husserl never hesitates to draw the necessary distinctions," but finds that there is "here an ambiguity that Husserl has not suppressed because it is real, because due to the nature of things" (pp. 138–39). In my own interpretation, the issue is rather the scope of a phenomenological analysis; the process whereby the *hylē* of perception is modified to become a *phantasma* has to be left to empirical psychology to trace, even though we are conscious of differences to which Husserl's different terms allude.

14. Sartre, *L'imaginaire*, pp. 104, 56. Husserl never had to confront *L'imaginaire*, since it was published after his death. In his absence, permit me to slip in the appropriate comment regarding Sartre's "leaving behind the secure terrain of phenomenological description." I am quoting Jean Héring, a pupil of Husserl's of the first generation, who helped with the proofs of the second edition of the *Logical Investigations*, introduced phenomenology into France (when Strasbourg went back to France after World War I), and sponsored Levinas (*via* whom Sartre came to phenomenology). In a review of *L'imaginaire*, Héring reports not only Sartre's titles for Part 1, "The Certain," and for Part 2, "The Probable," but he also attributes to Sartre a title for Part 3, "The Doubtful," for which there is no textual warrant. One comment is sufficient to illustrate how confusing he finds the second and third parts: their "largely psychological investigations . . . partly comprise, partly presuppose, and—perhaps unfortunately—partly also modify phenomenological analyses by interpretation, so that it is often left to the reader to distinguish in the particular case between phenomenological à priori, psychological à posteriori, and theoretical-constructive expositions" ("Concerning Image, Idea, and Dream," p. 188). These are distinctions Husserl himself might well have tried to draw, though he would soon have discarded *L'imaginaire* in dismay.

15. Sartre, *L'imaginaire*, p. 47.

16. Ibid., p. 112.

17. If I seem to give unwarranted attention in this chapter and in the following chapters to the sequential character of Sartre's analysis, it should be anticipated that I am preparing to deal in Volume 3 with difficult questions raised by Heidegger's conception of method as the following of a sequence—a *Schrittfolge* (see *P&D* 1:132–33).

16. The Plug

1. See Sartre, *L'imaginaire*, p. 55.

2. Sartre, *L'imagination*, p. 139.

3. Sartre, *Situations* 9:70.

4. Ibid.

5. Sartre, *Being and Nothingness*, p. 53 (and see "Toward the Concrete" section of Chapter 32 and n. 13 in the same chapter below). For the human "project" of plugging holes in being, see Joseph P. Fell, *Heidegger and Sartre*, pp. 168, 211, 420.

6. The active role of plugging holes is correspondingly particularizable and vulgarizable as male! "The ideal of the hole is . . . an excavation which can be carefully moulded about my flesh in such a manner that by squeezing myself into it and fitting myself snugly inside it, I shall contribute to making a fullness of being exist in the world. Thus to plug up a hole means originally to make a sacrifice of my body in order that the plenitude of being may exist. . . . Here . . . we grasp one of the most fundamental tendencies of human reality—the tendency to fill. . . . Conversely, the obscenity of the feminine sex organ is that of everything which 'gapes open.' It is *an appeal* to being as all holes are. . . . Woman senses her condition as an appeal precisely because it is 'in the form of a hole'" (*Being and Nothingness*, pp. 781–82; [Sartre's italics]; *Philosophy of Jean-Paul Sartre*, pp. 349–50).

7. See *P&D* 1:44.

8. In a prefatory note, "The Intentional Structure of the Image," at the beginning of *L'imaginaire*, Sartre explains, "I have allowed myself to employ the term 'consciousness' in a sense a little different from that ordinarily accepted." He wants to avoid the implication that "with respect to psychic structures there is a kind of inertia, of passivity, that appears to me incompatible with the givens of reflection." He again has trouble with ordinary usage when what is specifically in question is the imaginative consciousness: "For convenience I shall employ turns of expression that seem to accord the object imagined causal power *over* consciousness. It remains of course only a matter of metaphor. The real process is easily reestablished. For example, an image has no persuasive power, but we persuade ourselves by the very act with which we constitute the image" (p. 187). It apparently does not remain only a matter of ordinary usage and metaphor; instead, it would seem in *Being and Nothingness* to become a matter of surrendering our responsibility for our acts of consciousness to "bad faith." In *L'imaginaire*, which is my present concern, the opposition between imagination and perception toward which Sartre pushes yields a treatment of the imagination as active while perception is treated as passive. I am not going on to the problem of reconciling this opposition with his general conception of consciousness as active, since the problem, as I have suggested, can hardly be treated without taking up *Being and Nothingness*. Here I have merely mentioned a possible debt to Husserl's conception of a logical "act"—I can only add that there seems a more ob-

vious debt to Husserl's distinction between consciousness as the subject of phenomenology and psychology as a causal inquiry.

9. For Sartre's "aggressive voluntarism," see n. 21 in Chapter 2 above. Derrida suggests that "without forcing Husserl's intention, *bedeuten* [which Derrida would translate by "to mean" in English] could be defined, if not translated by *vouloir-dire*" (*La voix et le phénomène*, p. 18). I leave the *dire* out of present account, but the *vouloir* would blur the issue I am raising between what "meaning" means in Husserl and its more obviously active, voluntaristic meaning in Sartre. A similar issue over the meaning of "meaning" will come up in "The Shift in Subject" section of Chapter 17.

10. Sartre's philosophy may have further encouraged him to identify Husserl's treatment of "passive genesis" as extraneous because the work of Husserl's that Sartre devoured was a "static" analysis, to which his own developmental analysis is opposed. I shall reexamine this opposition in Chapter 25 below. For the way in which Husserl's segregation of a genetic analysis lends itself to criticism as extraneous, see n. 22 in Chapter 8 above.

11. See *P&D* 1:153. For the criterion of consistency, see *P&D* 1:156, 161, 226, n. 5.

12. See *P&D* 1:166.

13. Sartre, *L'imaginaire*, p. 60.

14. See *P&D* 1:93–95.

17. Toward the Concrete

1. Sartre, *L'imaginaire*, p. 62.

2. See *P&D* 1:36–38.

3. Husserl, *Experience and Judgment*, p. 358.

4. Sartre, *L'imagination*, p. 140.

5. Ibid., pp. 1–2.

6. See *P&D* 1:102.

7. Hegel, *Phenomenology of Spirit*, pp. 34–35.

8. Husserl, *Ideas I*, sec. 70.

9. See *P&D* 1:158–64.

10. See Sartre, *Situations* 10:175; also *P&D* 1:106–26.

11. See *P&D* 1:138.

12. Heidegger, *On Time and Being*, p. 64; *Ontologie*, p. 42. See *P&D* 1: 147–57.

13. See my *Starting Point*, chap. 5.

18. Literature

1. *Sartre, un film*, p. 42.

2. See *P&D* 1:10.

3. Sartre, *Qu'est-ce que la littérature?* pp. 269–70.

4. A deconstructive question can be posed here. Derrida has argued that "phenomenology" as "a metaphysics of presence in the form of ideality [e.g., the ideality of essences] is also a philosophy of life." He is drawing our attention to how the application of such "fundamental concepts" as *Leben, Erlebnis,* and *Lebendigkeit* "survives the phenomenological reduction," which discloses "the transcendentality" of "the living present"—which I have been referring to as what is "immediately given." Then Derrida complains that Husserl "nonetheless fails to pose the question of the unity of the concept of life" (*La voix et le phénomène,* p. 9). This unity seems at risk in a way that can be brought out by the comparison with Sartre. When Husserl upholds *Lebendigkeit* ("liveliness") as a criterion, it can apply, for example, to a "painting executed in living details" (*Logical Investigations* 2:721). Husserl is referring to the filling in of perceptual "details" that are absent from a mere "sketch." But Sartre has introduced the criterion with the challenge of the impersonation: "I must lend life to these arid schemata." Here, perceivable details are lacking, as they are in the Husserl sketch, but the liveliness is to be contributed by our affective reaction, which is to compensate for this lack. The comparison is feasible because Sartre at this juncture is inheriting from Husserl the problem of fulfillment. The difference between them is roughly the same as the difference (taken up in Chapter 17 above) between Husserl's conception of meaning as cognitive and Sartre's conception of meaning as, in considerable measure, affective. I shall return to this difference in my Conclusion.

5. I have taken over from Sartre this idiom of "privilege"; he makes a transition in *L'imagination* to his concluding chapter by raising the question, "Does there exist a type of privileged experience that puts us immediately in contact with the law [in psychology]? A great contemporary philosopher has believed this, and we are going to ask him now to guide our first steps in this difficult science" (*L'imagination,* p. 138). The great philosopher is, of course, Husserl, who has hardly managed to guide Sartre's first step, as is evident from Sartre's replacing the "essence," which is immediately given, with a "law." Sartre is drawing a contrast with a scientific law, which is only established in the long run by an "induction." He conceives of the privileged experience with which the phenomenologist is immediately in contact as "an experience that precedes all experimentation" (p. 143). Sartre may well have in mind the contrast Husserl drew between "the principle of principles," whereby the immediately given is a "validating source of [the] cognition [of essences, "to which the word 'principle' is commonly limited"]" (*Ideas I,* sec. 24). but the "principles" we have watched Sartre adduce are lawlike: "Every perception is accompanied by an affective reaction; every feeling . . . projects on its object a certain quality."

6. Sartre, *L'imaginaire,* pp. 140–41; Husserl, *Ideas I,* sec. 70.

7. Sartre, *Situations* 9:70.

8. One reason Sartre may not earlier make much of Husserl's conception of phenomenology as scientific is that he was himself so hostile toward science. Organte asks Frédéric about his attitude toward science, and Frédéric retorts " 'La science, je m'en fous.' with a timid smile—in order to get away with the 'je m'en

fous,' not the idea" (*Sartre: écrits de jeunesse,* p. 230). One of the comments by the editors of Sartre's juvenilia is that "Sartre had found strictly philosophical justifications for it ["the hostility of the young Sartre toward science"] that have to do no doubt with the lag in the philosophy of the sciences in the 1920s and the 1930s in relation to phenomenological thought, for instance" (p. 528). Sartre would have scoffed at this explanation, as would philosophers of science—from their different perspective.

9. Sartre, *Situations* 9:100.

19. The Work of Art

1. De Beauvoir, *La force de l'âge,* pp. 209, 219.

2. *Sartre, un film,* p. 59.

3. Ibid., p. 42.

4. Sartre, *Being and Nothingness,* p. 404.

5. Sartre, *Oeuvres romanesques,* p. 1668.

6. *Sartre, un film,* p. 56–57. See also Sartre, *Carnets de la drôle de guerre,* p. 82.

7. Sartre's editors, Michel Contat and Michel Rybalka, report "Sartre himself asserted several times that his first ideas on contingency were suggested by the impression of necessity produced by film images and the feeling of absurd arbitrariness involved in the flow of real life" (*Oeuvres romanesques,* p. 1661). But "contingency" is not one of the long list of topics included in *Le carnet Midy,* and if the "idea" of contingency was still "something quite vague" when he wrote *Nausea,* it must have been even vaguer—I am arguing—before he read Heidegger's *What is Metaphysics?* (translated in 1931, the year he began the "*factum* on contingency," which would become the novel).

8. *Sartre: Les écrits de jeunesse,* p. 28.

9. *Sartre, un film,* p. 58.

10. See the "Commotion" section of Chapter 6 and the "Bookishness" section of Chapter 7 above.

11. See *P&D* 1:100–101 for Sartre's sense of relief that the originality of his treatment of contingency vis-à-vis Husserl is intact. But for his debt to Heidegger, see *P&D* 1:103–4. Thomas Busch finds in the nauseous vision of contingency in the public park a debt to Husserl's reductions (see "*La nausée:* A Lover's Quarrel"). This seems to me entirely possible, but Busch defends Sartre's originality by arguing that the vision is an implicit criticism, on Sartre's part, that "Husserl's eidetic and transcendental reductions evade the issue of facticity or contingency" (p. 5). It is with respect to his philosophical sensitivity to this issue, I argued in Volume 1, that Sartre is indebted to Heidegger. If Busch is right about the debt to Husserl too, the vision can be regarded as a conflation of Husserl and Heidegger, such as I shall myself find in *Nausea* (see Chapter 23 below). Aron has reported that Sartre dealt with contingency as a student in a Sorbonne seminar presentation of Nietzsche (*Sartre: écrits de jeunesse,* p. 190). But I agree with the editors

of that collection that "Sartre does not feel any profound philosophical affinity with Nietzsche" (p. 194). However, he may have been indebted to Nietzsche for the word "nausea" itself. The earliest use of it of which I am aware is the following: "An insurmountable nausea clutched my throat and my body suffered more than my soul, for I was no longer thinking of anything. I was suddenly invaded by a great pity for myself. I saw all my hopes disappointed, I saw myself as I was, a poor traveler who was overwhelmed" (p. 377). It may be tempting to detect here a premonition of the protagonist of *Nausea,* who had been a traveler, but the slack, almost sniveling style of *"Andrée"* (around 1924) is not his. The protagonist of *"Andrée"* may be (as the editors propose) Sartre's alter ego, and he is rebuked by his mother, "You stuff you head with Nietzschean literature" (p. 376). But although the writer of what I have quoted may well have been Sartre, *"Andrée"* was written in collaboration with Nizan, who was in real life Sartre's alter ego, and *his* head was much more stuffed with Nietzsche than was Sartre's. In any case, the most obvious evidence of Nietzsche's influence is "the aggressive voluntarism" of "the lamentable Frédéric." But the inspiration here is not just Nietzsche's *volonté de puissance* but also *un homme de volonté,* as incarnated by the actor Erich von Stroheim (p. 371). With respect to Nietzsche as a source at least for the word "nausea," it should be remembered that word disappears in the earliest documentary evidence for *Nausea.* This is a notebook dated by the editors as "probably 1932"; there the place of "nausea" is taken by *ennui,* which just possibly could also betray Heidegger's influence, since "What is Metaphysics" (Translated, as I've indicated in 1931) *Langeweile* is translated *ennui.* See *P&D* 1:115 and 219 n. 20.

12. *Sartre, un film,* p. 59.

13. Sartre, *Carnets,* p. 102. "O" was Olga Kosakiewicz. For Sartre's "passion" and her story, see Cohen-Solal, *Sartre,* pp. 156–60.

14. *L'image,* I remind the reader, was the title of Sartre's *diplôme* (but to avoid confusion, I always refer to it as the *diplôme*), which he retained for the manuscript he wrote after his stay in Berlin. The first part of it was published as *L'imagination,* and the second part was published later as *L'imaginaire,* but with added chapters. There the influence of Heidegger is decisive, as we shall see later.

15. *Sartre: écrits de jeunesse,* p. 330. The editors state that "Er l'Arménien" was "written after 'Une défaite' and perhaps in 1928" (p. 288).

16. *Sartre, un film,* p. 59. The last two sentences occur in a passage scrubbed from the film (too many essences?), but they are printed in *Oeuvres romanesques,* p. 1699.

17. Sartre, *La nausée,* pp. 245–46.

18. This is the title of chapter 1 of *Ideas I.*

19. See Sartre, *Oeuvres romanesques,* pp. 1667–68.

20. De Beauvoir, *La force de l'âge,* pp. 292, 308.

21. See Panofsky, *The Life and Art of Albrecht Dürer,* pp. 167–70. Panofsky's interpretation was available to Sartre in Panofsky and Saxl's *Dürers Kupferstich*

"Melencolia I," which had been published in 1923, but I know of no definite evidence that Sartre had read this work.

22. The end of the novel (its prospective "starting point," as we shall see) is related to the start of the journal kept by Roquentin: there the train arrives from Paris; at the end of the journal he is about to leave for Paris, with the prospect of "arriving" (we shall also see) at self-acceptance by writing the novel. Roquentin's uncertainty regarding this prospect (which I am interpreting by reference to *Melancholia I*) echoes the first reference to a novel, when Roquentin is disheartened over the prospect of continuing to write a biography of the Marquis de Rollebon: "I have the impression I was involved in a work that was purely imaginary. Am I sure that the characters in a novel would seem truer, would, at any rate, be more appealing" *La nausée,* p. 26). This is the ending of an entry in Roquentin's journal that began when he "first reread with melancholy" a historian's footnote, which had once inspired him to start the biography. Presumably his melancholy is due to his uncertainty now that he can get on with it. This possible allusion to *Melancholia I* thus prepares us for the ambiguity of the end of the novel itself.

23. Sartre, *Nausea,* p. 249.

24. See Sartre, *Oeuvres romanesques,* p. 1718; Sartre did not remember having requested these deletions.

25. Ibid., pp. 1659–60.

26. Sartre, *Nausea,* p. 245.

27. Ibid., p. 249.

20. In Person

1. See *P&D* 1:51–57.

2. Husserl, "Persönliche Aufzeichnungen," p. 300.

3. Husserl, quoted in Spiegelberg, *The Phenomenological Movement* 1: 89–90.

4. Panofsky, *Life and Art of Dürer,* p. 152.

5. Panofsky, *Life and Art of Dürer,* pp. 151, 156, 150, 154.

6. Sartre, *Les mots,* p. 29; *Situations* 10:164.

7. See "The Example" section of Chapter 1 above.

8. *Husserl-Chronik,* ed. Schumann, p. 261.

9. Husserl, *Logical Investigations,* 1:48.

10. This explanation would supplement the explanation offered in "The Engraving Section" of Chapter 13.

11. Sartre, *Les mots,* pp. 208–9.

12. *Sartre, un film,* p. 27.

13. Sartre, *Carnets de la drôle de guerre,* pp. 96, 107.

14. De Beauvoir, *La force de l'âge,* pp. 72, 78; Sartre, *Oeuvres romanesques* 1:1667.

15. Sartre, *La nausée*, p. 206.

16. Sartre, *Les mots*, p. 38; Sartre's italics.

17. Sartre, *La nausée*, p. 306.

18. *Sartre, un film*, p. 42.

19. *Husserliana* 23:16; my italics. See also *Ideas I*, sec. 43.

20. Sartre, *L'imaginaire*, p. 53.

21. Husserl, *Ideas I*, sec. 85.

21. A Moral Theory

1. See "The Prophet" section of Chapter 7 above.

2. This is the final push in what I would guess had been *L'image* (that is, the original manuscript of *L'imaginaire*). There is an even further push in the chapters that were added later and that I shall not reach here until Chapter 31 below.

3. Sartre, *L'imaginaire*, p. 282; *Philosophy of Jean-Paul Sartre*, p. 90.

4. Sartre, *L'imaginaire*, p. 283; *Philosophy of Jean-Paul Sartre*, p. 90. "Apprenticeship" is the idiom that Sartre uses of the inductive process of learning about further "aspects" of the cube from bona fide observation as opposed to quasi observation, which is an essential trait of the imagination.

5. Sartre, *L'imaginaire*, p. 64. Sartre seems to wobble in his handling of this issue. On page 64 he states: "The image according to Husserl is a 'fulfillment' of meaning. The investigation of the impersonation leads us rather to believe that the image is a degraded meaning that has descended to the level of intuition." On page 118, where he is shocked, he first refers to the "empty" meaning conveyed by the sign, becoming, "if the [corresponding] image appears," a "full consciousness." Then he goes on to ask, "Is it quite certain that knowledge when it passes from a free condition [Husserl's idiom] to that of the intentional structure of an imaginative consciousness does not undergo any other alteration besides a fulfillment?" I cannot resolve the discrepancy, but his carelessness can perhaps be explained by his emphasis: "What preoccupies me above all is what could be called the question of the degradation of knowledge." I shall take up this question in Chapter 30.

6. Husserl, *Ideas I*, sec. 67.

7. Husserl, *Logical Investigations*, 2:728.

8. Sartre, *La nausée*, pp. 48–49; *Les mots*, p. 38.

9. Sartre, *L'imaginaire*, p. 268. In Sartre's paraphrase of the passage in *Logical Investigations* (2:680–83) in which Husserl distinguishes, with the example of the blackbird, between reference with a sign and perception, Sartre initially introduced the idiom "je peux penser à vide," to characterize "une intention signifiante fixée sur le mot 'alouette.'" He then goes on, "But to fill this empty consciousness and transform it into an intuitive consciousness, it makes no difference whether I form an image of the lark or look at one in person (*L'imagination*, p. 151). The issue at this juncture seems only to be whether the "matter" of the image and

perception is "the same" (p. 153). The further assertion that, in the case of the image, "there is no fulfillment" is made for the first time (*L'imaginaire*, p. 65) after the example of the impersonation and may well have been prompted by that example.

10. Husserl, *Ideas I*, sec. 124.

11. Husserl does not deny the colloquial origin of his idiom: "An intention aims at its object—as it were, yearns for it (*Ideas I*, sec. 726). But an eidetic reduction intervenes: "The syntheses of fulfillment in the cases of wanting and willing intentions . . . differ profoundly from those taking place . . . in the case of meaning-intentions" (sec. 708). Here, as often elsewhere, what Husserl regards as a profound difference, Sartre slides over, allowing scope for the wanting and willing intentions that Sartre, with his "aggressive voluntarism," would incorporate in "meaning-intentions."

12. I shall return to this issue in Volume 3.

13. Sartre, *L'imaginaire*, p. 241; *Philosophy of Jean-Paul Sartre*, p. 88. Having used Husserl's idiom of "fulfillment," Sartre provides an example with which he translates the analysis into terms of what we shall see below in Part 6 is his own distinctive idiom of playacting: "If I desire to see a friend, I make him appear unreally. This is a way of playing at satisfying my desire. But the satisfaction is only playacting, for in fact my friend is not really there" (ibid.).

14. Sartre, *Les mots*, pp. 38–39.

15. Ibid., pp. 46–47. The mise-en-scène of a "symbolic sixth floor" apparently goes back to the time Sartre lived there. In a story his editors date to 1921 or 1922, there was a pharaoh who lived on a sixth floor in Paris and delivered philosophical discourses to a young woman. The editors are citing *La cérémonie des adieux* (pp. 168–69) and comment that it sometimes happened that "Sartre invented his memories a little" (*Sartre: écrits de jeunesse*, p. 22).

16. *Sartre, un film*, p. 42.

17. Sartre, *Les mots*, p. 213.

18. Sartre, *Carnets de la drôle de guerre*, p. 101; *Sartre, un film*, p. 112.

19. See the "Salvation" section of Chapter 19 above.

22. Presenting an Object

1. Sartre, *L'imaginaire*, pp. 132, 129–30. Sartre admits "the poverty of the images that accompany reading" (p. 126). He explains that "the imaginative knowledge" involved is presented . . . as a will to arrive at the intuitive, as an *attente d'images*" (p. 132). In other words, while reading (that is, grasping the meanings of signs), we are usually on the verge of constituting mental images, rather than actually constituting them. An obvious comparison is feasible here with our *attente* of the image the impersonator would constitute in our consciousness (e.g., at the moment she puts on the straw hat and we grasp its meaning only as a sign), but there the impersonator in movement is about to provide us with physical imagery, and her undertaking need not be as elaborate as *le travail du style* that we shall be watching the writer undertake.

2. Sartre, *L'imaginaire*, pp. 47–48, 51–53.

3. Sartre, *Situations* 10:138.

4. Husserl, *Ideas I*, sec. 124.

5. Sartre, "Penser l'art," p. 15.

6. *Sartre: écrits de jeunesse*, p. 38.

7. Sartre, *L'imaginaire*, p. 361.

8. In an interview, Sartre was asked, "Do you have an aesthetics?" He replied, "If I have one—and I have somewhat of one—it is entirely in what I have written and can be found there. I judged that it was not worthwhile to do an aesthetics the way Hegel did." He then asserts that an aesthetics was "never" his ambition. He goes on to agree with his interviewer that his aesthetics "is [implicit] everywhere," and to reemphasize, "I never wrote a book on aesthetics, and I never wanted to write one" (*The Philosophy of Jean-Paul Sartre*, ed. Schilpp, p. 15). Sartre has either forgotten his youthful aspiration to "a complete aesthetics" or he regards the aspirations of his youth as "those of a stranger he had known long ago" (see "The Inventor" section of Chapter 2 above). In any case, I take these pronouncements as evidence that he is only secondarily a philosopher when his literary undertakings are in question; as a result, our primary evidence for the aesthetics that is implicit "everywhere" is his literary style and his incidental comments on his style, which usually have to be elicited by an interviewer.

9. Sartre, *L'imagination*, p. 149.

10. Sartre, *Situations* 9:71.

11. Sartre, *L'imagination*, p. 158.

23. Le Travail du style

1. Sartre, *Situations* 9:45.

2. Sartre, *L'imaginaire*, p. 132.

3. See Sartre, *Oeuvres romanesques*, p. 1664. The editors (Michel Rybalka and Michel Contat) state what they mean by the appellation: "*Nausea* is a phenomenological novel by virtue of the status it establishes for consciousness *via* the person of Roquentin, by the dissolution of the subject that it undertakes, by its repudiation of psychology—Roquentin has no 'character,' no substantial ego; he is pure consciousness *of* the world; his experience is not a voyage to the depths of interiority; it is, to the contrary, an explosion toward things; everything is outside; nausea is not *in* Roquentin; he is dissolved in it" (p. 1664). Their first statement could as plausibly be made about the narrators of some of Henry James's novels, as well as about other novels that are also very different from *Nausea*. The remaining statements are a somewhat too literal transcription of theses the editors would derive from the two philosophical essays Sartre wrote in Berlin while writing the second version of *Nausea*. I have my doubts regarding the purity of Roquentin's consciousness of the world, and it is obvious that he has a "character." Anny characterizes him, and she has a definite character too, so that Sartre is able to compare her "character" with that of her real-life model (*Oeuvres ro-*

manesques, pp. 1790–91). The Autodidact also has a "character," granted that he is caricatured. What Sartre's editors fail to recognize is that the "The Transcendence of the Ego" (one of the two essays written while Sartre was at work on *Nausea*) is not simply a refutation of Husserl's transcendental ego (the "substantial ego"); it is an exposure of the illusion of selfhood, in which Roquentin and the others in various ways indulge and which is an instance of the illusion of immanence, which in turn is exposed in *L'imaginaire*. To be specific, Roquentin's keeping a journal, his initial identification with the M. de Rollebon, entails a measure of self-consciousness, and the self implicit in this consciousness displays traits of character.

4. Cited in *Sartre: écrits de jeunesse*, p. 29. Remember that Sartre's method is also "hétéroclite," mixing phenomenology and dialectic, Husserl and Heidegger, in a *salade*. See *P&D* 1:153.

5. The homophony has been recognized by Michel Rybalka.

6. This phrase is from the title of section 67 of *Ideas I*.

7. De Beauvoir, *La force de l'âge*, p. 141.

8. Husserl, *Ideas I*, sec. 41.

9. Heidegger, *Basic Writings*, pp. 102–3. It is strange that Rybalka and Contat ferret out several more or less plausible literary precedents for what goes on in *Nausea* but do not cite Heidegger. See *P&D* 1:103–4.

10. Heidegger, *Being and Time*, pp. 186, 189.

11. Ibid., pp. 69, 74.

12. Before considering more extravagant instances of tactile experience in *Melancholia,* I would compare a philosophically sober example in *L'imaginaire* with an example of merely visual experience in *"Une défaite."* This earlier example is, in the first instance, an illustration of how before Sartre's conversion to phenomenology, it "had been his fervent wish—to speak of things." His fervor can be surmised from the sense of defeat "the lamentable Frédéric" suffered. While waiting for Organte, he is looking at the color of the fabric on an armchair: "Once again he had to concede his defeat, and tell himself, poor observer: 'That green there is . . . it is like the green of alpine meadows . . . no, more like the green of a meadow lit by a large sun, then suddenly dimmed by the shadow of a cloud'" (*Sartre: écrits de jeunesse*, p. 224). We recognize the Sartre of the *diplôme* who is still taken up with landscapes, as well as the fact that his description is preposterous. Now to discover if there has been any adjustment, once he is assisted in his observation by intentional reference, we can turn to a comparable example in *L'imaginaire*, which likewise involves color and a fabric. Sartre is discussing a painting by Matisse: "The artist . . . has selected in particular a carpet in order to enhance [*redoubler*] the sensual value of this red: tactile elements, for instance, must be intended *via* this red; it is a red which is *wooly*" (*L'imaginaire*, pp. 364–65; Sartre's italics). This example is used in the added chapter, "The Work of Art," where we shall later see the influence of Heidegger is decisive.

13. "Muck" is an idiom that could easily have occurred to Sartre, especially since the actual locale was dank Le Havre. He could also have found encourage-

ment in generalizing its implications from the Latin poem that Heidegger cites in *Being and Time* on the creation of the human being, which begins, "Once when Care was crossing a river, she saw some muck [*lutum/Erdreich*], rich in clay, and she thoughtfully took up a piece and began to shape it" (p. 198).

14. See Sartre, *Nausea*, pp. 119–36. Partly because Sartre's most vehement criticism of Husserl in *L'imaginaire* is of his conception of imaginative fulfillment, I have made more than Husserl does of the distinction between the in-tentional "aiming at" a target emptily and the in-tentional "hitting" of the target in fulfillment. The "muck" in the "Feuillet" is the starting point of a development that culminates in *Being and Nothingness* when the clean and neat in-tentionalist idiom of "aiming at" and "hitting" is superseded by the "project" to "slide over" in order to escape getting "stuck"—which is the menace of the "slimy" (*Being and Nothingness*, pp. 743–47, 770–80; *Philosophy of Jean-Paul Sartre*, pp. 314–16, 338–48). There are variations in the idiom into which I cannot go here.

15. *Sartre: écrits de jeunesse*, p. 526.

16. Ibid., p. 220.

17. Heidegger, *Basic Writings*, p. 103.

18. I am not implying that the thwarting of intentional reference is simply the outcome of Sartre's half-shifting his allegiance from Husserl to Heidegger. The moment of *échec* when one is thwarted assumes its own significance in Sartre's philosophy, but I cannot go into this more fully here, since the *échec* receives extensive analysis (as "loser wins") only in Sartre's late work *L'idiot de la famille*, and since the *échec* is a juncture that can receive this analysis only when Sartre's method becomes more dialectical. (Unfortunately, I have found it difficult throughout to avoid the comparative when speaking of the increasingly dialectical character of Sartre's method.) At least it can be recognized here that Sartre's commitment to an *échec* antedates his discovery of phenomenology. "*Une défaite*" is an *échec* with respect to Frédéric's relation with his master and with Cosima, and with respect to Organte's relation to his disciple. *Nausea* can be said to end in an *échec*, for even if the novel may be written and Roquentin saved by art, he will "only" be saved with respect to what he has been "in the past." In *The Wall* (a prewar collection of short stories) the theme of *échec* is stated in Sartre's *prière d'insérer*: "No one can confront Existence. [This is the *échec* we have seen involved in the experience of anxiety.] Here are five *déroutés* ["misdirected" and "dislocated" types] with respect to Existence. Pablo, who is going to be shot, would cast his thought to the other side of Existence and conceive his own death. In vain. Eve tries to get together with Peter in the unreal and closed world of madness. In vain. . . . Lola lies to herself: between herself and the look that she cannot cast on herself, she tries to slip a light fog. In vain; the fog immediately becomes transparence. . . . All these flights are halted by a Wall: to flee Existence is to exist still" (*Oeuvres romanesques*, p. 1807). In the first story, itself entitled "The Wall," the wall is death; in the other stories, it becomes the *échec* that thwarts a flight. (For "flight" as a concept of Heidegger's that Sartre took over, see the "Flight" section of Chapter 33 below. In the stories of Eve and Lola (Lulu), the *échec* can be regarded as thwarting a phenomenological analysis. But

the theme of *échec* itself is so baldly stated that it belongs rather to a philosophy of the absurd. The rendering of the *échec* becomes more dialectical in *Being and Nothingness*. I have already quoted its climax: "The passion of man is the reverse of that of Christ, for man loses himself as man in order that God may be born. But the idea of God is contradictory and we lose ourselves in vain. Man is a useless passion" (p. 784). I have retained the French *échec* as having a broader range of implications than any possible English translation: "check," "reverse," "defeat," "failure."

19. Since Sartre's commitment to *échec* antedates his reading of Heidegger, the thwarting of an intentional reference is not necessarily a debt to Heidegger. Consider the following example: "His eyes are glassy. In his mouth I watch a somber, rosy, mass stir" (*Oeuvres romanesques*, p. 623). Here the reader is supplied with the qualities of the sense-data (the *hylē*)—somberness, rosiness, massiveness; but the meaning-endowing act (it's a tongue) is withheld—the synthesis of identification, whereby in Husserl's terminology the predicates as "predicates of 'something'" are tied in with "their central point of unity" (*Ideas I*, sec. 131, which I have already noted Sartre quotes in *La transcendance de l'ego*, p. 55). As this example illustrates, the reader of Sartre's literary works is somewhat handicapped if he is not familiar both with Husserl's phenomenological analysis and with Sartre's revision of it. (See also the example I provide in note 5 of Chapter 24.) We have learned that in Husserl it is the meaning which is immediately given; the sense-data are not data—that is, are not given as ("immanent contents") without the intentional reference having been already locked in to its object. This *échec*, the reader is prepared for (to be somewhat labored about the analysis) by another *échec*, that has already promoted an "affective reaction" (in Sartre's terminology) on the part of the reader. The predicate attached to the eyes, "glassy," implies that they fail to see, and this failure helps divert the reader's attention to what can be seen—the somber, rosy mass stirring. Presumably there is some *interplay* between the two *échecs*, to reinforce the reader's sense that normal, functional experiencing is being subverted. I will return in my conclusion to the way in which cognitive meanings (he's looking at me, it's a tongue) are no longer readily available in Sartre, so that meanings become predominantly affective and imaginative.

24. En Surcharge

1. Sartre, *La nausée*, p. 177.

2. Husserl, *Ideas I*, sec. 35; *Logical Investigations*, 2:565.

3. Husserl, *Cartesian Meditations*, p. 41; Sartre, *L'imaginaire*, p. 23.

4. Sartre, *L'imaginaire*, p. 23.

5. I have already indicated (n. 19 in Chapter 23) that it may be left to the reader to carry out a thwarted intentional reference and identify the "something" consciousness is of. It may also be left to the reader to carry out the transition from being conscious of something to being self-conscious. At the beginning of the story about Eve (see Chap. 23, n. 18) we are introduced to her mother, whose self-consciousness is apparently even more befogged than Lola's by what Sartre

will later term "bad faith." Phenomenologically speaking, the mother is carrying out a "synthesis of identification"—becoming conscious of something by carrying out a synthesis in which qualities are successively identified as its predicates: "Madame Derbedat held a Turkish delight between her fingers. She lifted it with great care toward her lips and held her breath for fear that the powdered sugar with which it had been sprinkled would be scattered by her breathing. 'It's rose-flavored,' she thought. Brusquely she bit into the glazed tissue and a stagnant flavor filled her mouth. 'It's curious how illness sharpens one's sensations.' She began to think about mosques, about obsequious orientals (she had been in Algiers during her honeymoon), and a faint smile stirred on her pale lips: the Turkish delight was obsequious too" (*Oeuvres romanesques*, p. 234). Again I risk ham-fistedness by suggesting that the "faint smile" was phenomenological satisfaction over completing the synthesis of predicates with a final identification of the crucial predicate of something. But this "predicate" is transferred to the something from persons ("orientals"), thus encouraging the reader to continue the process of identification back to the person doing the identifying. In other words, her elaborate consciousness of something (especially since it includes what it reminds her of) serves predominantly a reflexive reorientation, whereby predicates of her character are disclosed to the reader as implicit in this consciousness—her self-indulgence, snobbishness, racism. I offer this as a succinct example not only of the extent to which Sartre's style here can be construed in terms of his phenomenological method but also of why it is impossible to agree with Sartre's editors that "the dissolution of the subject that it [nausea] undertakes" (that "stagnant flavor" filling her mouth is a transition to personal reminiscences, but at the same time the reader finds himself at least on the edge of nausea) is occurring in such a way that a person can have "no 'character'" but remain "pure consciousness of the world" (see n. 3 in Chapter 23 above). Roquentin has even more of a "character" than Mme Derbedat, and as much of his characterization, likewise, is implicit in what he is conscious of. Consider another instance in which the reader's intervention is solicited: "Daniel looked at her shoulders and neck hungrily. That stupid obstinacy annoyed him; he wanted to break it. He was possessed by a desire that was huge and awkward: to rape this consciousness, to sink with it into the depths of humility. But it wasn't sadism; it was more groping, and more humid, more fleshly. It was kindness" (*Oeuvres romanesques*, p. 570). Daniel is identifying an "aspect" of Marcelle's character—"stupid obstinacy"—but since this attitude is an *échec* for him and remains fixed, the reader is prepared to participate in Daniel's reflexive reorientation and to refocus on predicates of his attitude toward her. For a moment the reader may accept the impression that Daniel's looking "hungrily" is a conventional male reaction to female shoulders and neck, but the reader already knows that sexual hunger is out of place, since Daniel is gay. The reader's impression is definitely disconfirmed when the "desire that was huge and awkward" is displaced by hostility. Further evidence accumulates that Daniel is doubling himself with these metaphors in a fashion similar to the example in *L'imaginaire* of resorting to "unreal hands." However hostile one's reaction to someone, how does one in the real physical world "break an obstinacy"? Raping a consciousness is also a difficult feat: rape is an arrantly physical act, so its metaphorical extension to a consciousness brings out Daniel's potential for moral violence, especially since he is violating conventional linguistic usage. But if in his *monde imaginaire,* he could bring off the feat of raping a consciousness, his aspiration would be assumed conventionally to be exultant domination, not the prospect of sinking with that consciousness into the depths of humility. Conventionally, it would also be thought incompatible with this humility for Daniel to envisage "sadism" in identifying how he feels, just as "sadism" in turn will seem incompatible with "kindness." The reader's sense of this incompatibility is reinforced by the predicates "more groping, and more humid, more fleshly," which lead us on toward the climax, "It was kindness." By now more than Daniel's attitude and character are being delineated here, for once the climax of his effort is reached with his identifying his feeling as "kindness," there is a culminating *échec* and a reversal in the synthesizing of contradictory implications that the reader has had to follow out. For "kindness" (*bonté*) in the conventional sense can hardly subsume the predicates "more groping, and more humid, more fleshly," which have been offered as differentiating it from "sadism," and we do not conventionally think of "kindness" as differing only in degree from "sadism." What began for the reader as the prospect of sexual intercourse has become subversive of human intercourse and of the norm of "kindness" as presiding over it. Havoc is at the same time wreaked on the intentional reference itself, which in the case of perceptual consciousness of something is the carrying out of a synthesis of identification—but this synthesis multiplies contradictions. For a fuller exposition of the session between Daniel and Marcelle, see my *Starting Point,* pp. 347–55 and 370–79. For Sartre's commitment to subversion, see Chapter 29 below.

6. Husserl, *Logical Investigations* 2:700; Husserl's italics.

7. Sartre, *Oeuvres romanesques,* p. 1719; italics in original.

8. Ibid.

9. Sartre, *Situations* 10:137–39.

10. In 1965, nearly thirty years after writing *Nausea,* Sartre will retain the same word his fictitious editors were not sure of: "The philosophical writer's goal is . . . to *forge* notions that become progressively heavier and heavier" (*Situations* 9:67; my italics). Thus, adding weight is an aesthetic feature of the movement "toward the concrete," just as putting on "lead shoes" is a moral feature of this movement.

11. Sartre, *Situations* 9:55.

12. Hegel, *Aesthetics* 1:31.

13. Sartre, *Oeuvres romanesques,* p. 1666.

14. See the "Contingency" section of Chapter 19 above.

15. Spiegelberg, *The Phenomenological Movement,* 1:82. If the formula oversimplifies what Husserl was up to in the *Logical Investigations,* it is more plausibly applicable to Sartre.

16. Sartre, "Penser l'art," p. 15.

17. Sartre, *Being and Nothingness,* pp. 141–42; *Philosophy of Jean-Paul*

Sartre, p. 173. The "turn to the object" in Sartre is a turn to a solid object (an "in-itself") and sometimes more specifically to a solid art object. Our first premonition of this turn was Sartre's turning to a physical image in order to treat in conjunction with it the mental image. Although Sartre found a precedent for this turn in Husserl's example of the Dürer engraving, we now have more evidence of why this example could not have had the significance for Husserl that it had for Sartre. Because Husserl's analysis is "directed by general logical interests" (and not by the kind of aesthetic interest we have been watching emerge in Sartre), Husserl stretches the colloquial conception of an "object" (much as he does the colloquial conceptions of "fulfillment" and "frustration") and, in effect, weakens it. Thus if the eidetic reduction is to be feasible in Husserl, it is necessary for an essence to be an "object." He notes "that object is always understood by me in the broadest sense, which comprehends all syntactical objectivities" (*Formal and Transcendental Logic,* p. 248). Often he instead prefers to "make use of the vaguer expression 'objectivity,' since we are never limited to objects in the narrower sense" (*Logical Investigations* 1:281). Sartre is in effect regaining the narrower, colloquial sense (as we have watched him do with other terms taken over from Husserl), and (here as elsewhere) he is able to do so because he is weakening the distinction in *level* that in Husserl upholds the essence. What is not colloquial but Sartre's own philosophical elaboration is that an art object becomes the privileged instance of what one aspires to shape oneself into, even when one is a writer. Thus Baudelaire "spent his life attempting to make himself a thing in the eyes of others and in his own eyes. He wanted to set himself up aloof from the great social festival, like a statue—definitive, opaque, unassimilable. In a word, it can be said he wanted *to be,* by which I mean the obstinate, rigorously defined, being of an object" (*Baudelaire,* p. 90; Sartre's italics).

18. Sartre, *Situations* 9:53–54, 82.

19. Sartre, *Qu-est-ce-que la littérature?,* p. 21; *Philosophy of Jean-Paul Sartre,* p. 371.

25. Playacting

1. See *P&D* 1:15–17.

2. See *P&D* 1:167.

3. Now that I have finished dealing with the relation between the novel and *Melancholia I* as a physical image, I am allowing the novel to resume its published title.

4. Sartre, *L'imaginaire,* p. 367; *Philosophy of Jean-Paul Sartre,* p. 93.

5. Ibid., p. 62.

6. Husserl, *Logical Investigations* 1:284.

7. Sartre, *Being and Nothingness,* p. 90; *Philosophy of Jean-Paul Sartre,* p. 140.

8. Sartre, *L'imaginaire,* pp. 63–64; *Philosophy of Jean-Paul Sartre,* p. 86.

9. Husserl, *Ideas I,* sec. 46.

10. Sartre, *La transcendance de l'ego,* p. 66; *Being and Nothingness,* pp. 523–24. See my *Starting Point,* p. 204.

11. Sartre, *L'imaginaire,* p. 240.

12. Sartre, *Being and Nothingness,* 88–89; *Philosophy of Jean-Paul Sartre,* pp. 139–40. I retain the French *personnage* because it carries a wider range of references than the English equivalent. Here it refers to "the character" (one of the dramatis personae); it can also refer (as we shall see) to "the character" as the "role" the actor plays. If my jumping from *L'imaginaire* to this episode of play-acting in *Being and Nothingness* seems to overlook too many alterations in the setup of Sartre's analysis, *L'imaginaire* itself provides an example of how the advance in its analysis beyond the impersonation is an advance in reflexivity, even before the actor is reached in the added chapter. With the example of the schematic design (introduced by Sartre as a further stage beyond the impersonation in the successive impoverishment of the perceptual evidence on which the image is based), I become myself the performer, and it is my body which "adopts certain attitudes, acts out a certain pantomime in order to animate [a] set of lines" (*L'imaginaire,* p. 67).

13. Sartre, *L'imaginaire,* 367–68; *The Philosophy of Jean-Paul Sartre,* p. 194.

14. De Beauvoir, *Entretiens,* p. 231.

15. See *P&D* 1:149.

16. *Philosophy of Jean-Paul Sartre,* pp. 75–76.

17. Sartre, *Being and Nothingness,* 101–2; *Philosophy of Jean-Paul Sartre,* p. 152.

18. Sartre, *Being and Nothingness,* p. 103; *Philosophy of Jean-Paul Sartre,* p. 153.

19. Ibid.

20. Ibid., pp. 96–97; *Philosophy of Jean-Paul Sartre,* p. 147. For another illustration of how Sartre's dialectic, anchored as it is to a first-person *cogito* (see *P&D* 1:170), prompts him to design examples in which the attitude of the other party is held fixed so that the attitude of the first party can undergo development, consider how Marcelle's attitude remains fixed by virtue of "the stupid obstinacy" that Daniel attributes to her (see n. 5 in Chapter 24 above).

21. The only occasion of which I am aware of this issue of the hybrid character of Sartre's method having almost been raised was by the Hegelian scholar Jean Hyppolite, who challenged Sartre, "What I have difficulty in understanding is . . . [the] stage that is neither immediate nor mediation." In reply, Sartre explained, "Isn't this due to your tendency to adopt the point of view of categories (which, moreover, are true) like those of Hegel and not the point of view of a pure and simple discovery?" Sartre then identified Husserl as the "first philosopher to have discussed [this] dimension that is distinctive of consciousness . . . and is not a kind of indefinite progress of the mind . . . but a consciousness of itself" that is "given without movement" (*Conscience de soi et connaissance de soi,*" pp. 88–89). In my terms, Sartre is defending a phenomenological conception of immediacy ("a pure and simple discovery" of what "is given without movement") that is caught

up in an ensuing dialectic development. This ambiguity, though its methodological implications are not probed, is crucial to Howells's interesting defense of Sartre against Derrida's saddling him with the traditional metaphysical commitment to presence: "Sartre cites Husserl as evidence that even the most determined philosopher of presence cannot entirely overcome the reflexivity implicit in all consciousness. Presence is precisely what prevents identity: 'S'il est présent à soi, c'est qu'il n'est pas tout à fait soi' " (*Sartre: The Necessity of Freedom*, p. 196).

26. The True Novel

1. Heidegger, "Interview" in *L'Express*, p. 85.

2. Reported by Frederic de Towarnicki (who was the go-between), "Sartre-Heidegger: Le rendez-vous manqué," *Le Figaro* 28 May 1990; cited in Jean Launay, "Sartre lecteur de Heidegger."

3. See *P&D* 1:70.

4. Jean Cau is reporting Sartre's account of his visit to Heidegger in "Croquis de mémoire."

5. See *P&D* 1:185.

6. Heidegger, *Poetry, Language, Thought*, p. 4.

7. Ibid., p. 40.

8. Contat and Rybalka, *Les écrits de Sartre*, p. 243.

9. Sartre, *Situations* 10:94. Sartre also refers to *The Family Idiot* as a "un *vrai* roman" (9:123). He means that it is truly a novel in that he resorts to "fiction" and "invents to an extent" Flaubert as a "character" (*personnage*). In both usages, *vrai* is italicized. The opposing emphases ("a novel that is *true*)," and "a *true* novel") suggest that the structure of the work is "metastable."

10. Sartre, *Situations* 9:100.

11. Sartre, *L'imaginaire*, pp. 372–73; Sartre's italics; *Philosophy of Jean-Paul Sartre*, pp. 96–97.

12. Sartre, *L'idiot de la famille* 3:540. Here the ambiguities and contradictions of Flaubert's affective/imaginative reaction to the princess are pointed up with the citations Sartre intrudes from the Goncourts, in order to oppose a realistic reaction. The effect on us is a "metastable" structure comparable to that produced by Franconay's performance when we "slide from the level of the image to that of perception." It should also be observed how there still survives in the passage the terminology from Husserl that Sartre had favored forty years before in *L'imaginaire*—"analogue," "aiming," "essence." The giveaway is *analogon*, which Sartre claims is his own term. Presumably he does not remember having taking it over in *L'imaginaire* from Husserl.

13. *Sartre: écrits de jeunesse*, p. 274. See the similar use of "behind" in passages I cited from *Nausea* in Chapter 19.

14. Ibid., p. 378.

15. The *carnet* bore the rubric, "*Suppositoires Midy*," and Sartre's editors as-

sume it was supplied to doctors (*Sartre: écrits de jeunesse*, p. 437). Sartre happened to pick up a clean copy in the *métro* and entered in it his thoughts, his projects, and citations.

16. *Sartre: écrits de jeunesse*, pp. 221–22. One feature of Sartre's analysis that I have skipped over is his preoccupation with play itself (in addition to playacting), which also antedates his conversion to Husserl. Sartre wrote a poem "in 1926 or 1927" on playing (*le jeu*), inspired by James Barry's *Peter Pan; or, The Boy Who Wouldn't Grow Up* (see *Sartre: écrits de jeunesse*, pp. 407–10). In the poem, Sartre claims, "Nothing is serious in the world" and announces, "I can play with the institutions of man." This is a foretaste of his later critique of *l'esprit de serieux* in *Being and Nothingness*, pp. 74–78; *Philosophy of Jean-Paul Sartre*, pp. 124–29.

17. *Sartre: écrits de jeunesse*, p. 281. It is not always easy to draw a distinction between playacting and playing. This quotation is from a section entitled "*Règles du jeu commentées.*"

18. *Sartre: écrits de jeunesse*, pp. 204–5. Note the possibly dual implication of *composer*: the reference to the pose Frédéric is adopting might also carry an allusion to its place in the novel that he is composing. Be this as it may, the initial theme is picked up again in one of the last fragments, in which Frédéric is this time parting from Cosima. When "she smiled at him," he "suddenly had the painful impression it was for her only a game [*un jeu*] that she was playing at the sadness of goodbyes, that she was surrendering to the *comédie* of separation in order to provide her soul with a reason to be melancholy. . . . How could she be sad except by feigning it, by *jeu d'artiste*. . . . As he left, she called him back: 'It was not only *le jeu de la tristesse;* it was also *le jeu de l'amour.* It is a game I play only on days of parting" (p. 280). When Frédéric then lingered, "she said to him impatiently, 'You're going to spoil everything.'" Presumably he had failed to play the game. (It is the next fragment that is entitled "*Règles du jeu commentées.*") This will be Anny's complaint about Roquentin in *Nausea*, but he finally comes round, at least in her appraisal (see n. 10 in Chapter 27 below).

19. Cau, "Croquis de mémoire," p. 1114.

20. De Beauvoir, quoted in *Sartre: écrits de jeunesse*, p. 18.

21. See the "Embodiment" section of Chapter 17 above.

22. *L'idiot de la famille* 1:791.

23. The process of synthesis, abstracted by itself, can be dialectical in the sense that the opposition is more or less overcome—e.g., between what is perceived and what is imagined in the case of the impersonation. Or it can, as the result of the strain of the oppositions, more or less come apart—e.g., in the case of Daniel's identification of "kindness" (see n. 5 in Chapter 24 above).

24. See the "Intuitive Content" section of Chapter 22 above.

25. Sartre, *L'imaginaire*, p. 372; *Philosophy of Jean-Paul Sartre*, p. 96.

26. *Sartre: écrits de jeunesse*, p. 190. Simone Jollivet was the original except in name. Presumably Sartre did not want to have his heroine confused with Simone de Beauvoir. At any rate, he called her "Anny" in memory of one of his first loves,

a cousin who had died. The cousin's real name, Annie, survives in examples from Sartre's philosophical works (e.g., in the passage I have cited from *L'imaginaire*— "I wanted Annie to come" [see "The Shift in Subject" section of Chapter 21 above]) but the name is anglicized in *Nausea,* presumably for the snob-appeal that went with the character's being an actress.

27. The Writer

1. I am only sampling this one process and expounding certain of the respects in which *L'idiot de famille* can be regarded as a "sequel" to *L'imaginaire*. In particular, I single out "metastable" structures. These proliferate in *L'idiot,* and a more detailed examination of Sartre's dialectic would have to sort out the variants.

2. This famous proclamation "Mme Bovary, c'est moi," is cited by Sartre in *Questions de méthode,* and Sartre's preoccupation with it illustrates an advance in dialectical complexity beyond his general discovery in *La transcendance de l'ego* that the self is "a contradictory composite" (p. 66). Not just the image of the Princess (as constituted by Faubert's reaction to her) but this *moi* (of "Mme Bovary, c'est moi") is a "metastable" structure.

3. Sartre, *L'idiot* 1:661–62.

4. Earlier in *Being and Nothingness* (p. 714), Sartre is already preoccupied with the implications of Flaubert's statement, "I could have been a great actor." Speaking of himself in *Les mots* as a child, Sartre emphasizes, "I have the princely freedom of the actor who keeps his audience panting and refines his role" (p. 19). Again, "Playacting deprived me of the world and of men; I saw only roles and props" (pp. 67–68). Sartre quotes Flaubert, "I am nothing other than the roles [*rôles*] that I play," and "I am a being whose real function is to play roles" (*L'idiot* 1:785). Sartre's interest in Jean Genet as a candidate for psychoanalysis must have been prompted to some extent by Genet's own preoccupation with playacting. In an appendix to *Saint Genet,* Sartre reviews Genet's play *The Maids,* in which a man plays a woman who is playing a maid who is playing her female employer playing a proper wife. But Sartre himself is restrained from indulging in such pile-ups by his commitment to oppositions.

5. Sartre, *Situations* 10:151.

6. Sartre, *L'idiot* 1:658.

7. Sartre, *Situations* 10:138.

8. Sartre, *L'idiot* 1:662.

9. Ibid.

10. Sartre's preoccupation with playacting or role playing is a general philosophical preoccupation, and it is not restricted to plays or to the psychoanalysis that is "the true novel." When we examined intentional reference in the initial "Feuillet," we were still close to Husserl, as we were when we examined it at the start of *L'imaginaire.* Just as Sartre's distinctive preoccupation there as a phenomenologist emerges only with the impersonation, so it emerges only later in *Nau-*

sea. Anny is an actress both on the stage and in relation to Roquentin, and when she finally parts company with him she accords him only one real regret: "The poor jerk! He has no luck. The first time he plays his role, he gets no gratitude" (p. 216). Roquentin also attempts to identify with the Marquis de Rollebon. (They share the same initials.) Although the editors offer interesting speculations on Roquentin's name, they neglect the Marquis. Does not his name perhaps suggest that he was a good role player? After all, "he engages in intrigues, plays a very ambiguous [*louche*] role in the Collier affair" (p. 24). Though Roquentin is reluctant to assign him "a melodramatic role" in the assassination of Paul I, one of the authorities reports he "acted out [*mimait*] the scene with incomparable power" (p. 29). The implication that he is a role player would help explain his completely eluding Roquentin ("not a glimmer of light comes from Rollebon himself)," so that Roquentin has problems determining his identity (the "testimonies do not seem to have to do with the same person" [p. 25]), is left with "the impression of being engaged in a purely imaginary undertaking," and suspects that "characters in a novel would seem truer" (p. 26). This is our first premonition that Roquentin may undertake a novel.

11. *Les écrits de Sartre,* pp. 268, 270.

12. Sartre, *L'idiot* 1:783, 776. *Selbständigkeit* is a term Sartre probably took over from Heidegger.

13. Ibid., p. 693. The example is a more precise rendering, transferred to an actress, of what is pretty much the same point Sartre made in the *Carnet Midy* and again in "*Une défaite*" regarding mature women (see the "Originality" section of Chapter 26 above).

14. Ibid., p. 684.

15. Ibid., p. 694.

16. *Sartre, un film,* p. 58. From *La nausée* as a starting point the problem has evolved in its generality. Sartre explains that "the reasons I wrote *La nausée* rather than another book are of little importance. What is interesting is the emergence of the decision to write" (*Situations* 9:134). I am accordingly somewhat skeptical of his editors' hypothesis, "If Sartre had continued his autobiography [i.e., *Les mots*], he would have replied to the question that follows: How did I become this writer who had produced precisely these texts?" (*Sartre: écrits de jeunesse,* p. 7).

17. Sartre, *Situations* 9:116.

18. Sartre, *L'idiot* 1:693.

19. Ibid., p. 694.

20. Ibid., pp. 714, 704–5.

21. Sartre, *Critique de la raison dialectique,* p. 89.

22. Sartre, *L'idiot,* 1:912. I have argued that an advance in reflexivity takes place during the development of the analysis in *L'imaginaire,* in *Being and Nothingness,* as compared with *L'imaginaire,* and during the development of *Being and Nothingness* itself. But undoubtedly the convolutions are carried out much further in *The Family Idiot.* Not only is this particular self-identification, "Ma-

dame Bovary, c'est moi" a "metastable structure" (as "the self" as such has been for Sartre, at a more fundamental level, ever since *La transendance de l'ego* [see n. 2 this chapter]), but Flaubert cannot be identified exclusively with Madame Bovary: "Who . . . can Flaubert be, who must he be, to objectify himself in his work a few years apart in the guise of a mystical monk [i.e., in *The Temptation of Saint Antony*]" and in the guise of Madame Bovary? (*Critique de la raison dialectique*, p. 90).

28. The Conversion to Dialectic

1. Sartre, *Situations* 9:118; *L'idiot de la famille* 1:7.

2. Sartre, *Critique de la raison dialectique*, pp. 38–39. Observe how the example of the actor is interpolated in much the same fashion as the elderly actress was interpolated in the long passage I quoted from *L'idiot de la famille* in Chapter 27.

3. Sartre, *Situations* 9:12.

4. Ibid. 10:100. Needless to say, I am not pretending to deal directly in any way with the horrendous problems of method Sartre faces in employing these two methods conjointly in the *Critique* and *L'idiot*. I am merely demonstrating the continued relevance of *L'imaginaire* to a phase of the social analysis in the *Questions de méthode*, as I have already demonstrated in the last chapter its relevance to a phase of his psychoanalysis in *L'idiot*.

5. Sartre, *Questions de méthode*, p. 30.

6. Ibid. Sartre also derives from Heidegger's *Entwurf* the term *pro-jet* which he links to being "thrown back" as its dialectical opposite. For another dialectical linkage, see the "Flight" section of Chapter 33 below.

7. Sartre, *Critique*, p. 364; Sartre's italic; *Philosophy of Jean-Paul Sartre*, pp. 462–63.

8. Sartre, *L'imaginaire*, p. 64; Sartre's italics.

9. Sartre, *L'idiot*, p. 7.

10. Sartre, *Questions de méthode*, p. 96; *Philosophy of Jean-Paul Sartre*, pp. 413–14.

11. Ibid.

29. Le Travail de la Rupture

1. "An Interview with Sartre," in *The Philosophy of Jean-Paul Sartre*, ed. Schilpp, p. 24.

2. Sartre, *Situations* 9:99.

3. Sartre, *Questions de méthode*, pp. 22–23. See also his pronouncements that "it is impossible to struggle against the working class without becoming the enemy of mankind and of oneself" (*Situations* 6:86–87; my italics), and that "the truth of a dialectical movement can be established only . . . if one is oneself drawn into the movement" (7:21).

4. Sartre, *Situations* 4:249.

5. Ibid., pp. 248–49.

6. The term "traitor," with this connotation, Sartre apparently expanded from its use by his dead alter ego Paul Nizan (*Situations* 4:248), but the term becomes recurrent in Sartre. "I became a traitor," he announces, "and I have remained one" (*Les mots*, p. 198). The moment of *rupture* is at once the reflexive moment of "self-contestation" and the moment more broadly of a "dialectical reversal," which is "a form of proceeding that is absolutely necessary to dialectic" (*Situations* 9:77).

7. Sartre, *Les carnet de la drôle de guerre*, pp. 329, 19.

8. Sartre, *Situations* 10:175.

9. Sartre, *L'âge de la raison*, p. 307; italics in original. One justification (though it is rather difficult to pin down) for comparing the swearing hatred passage with the Mathieu's reflection on Daniel's decision is that the title Sartre had initially planned for the novel was *Le serment*. This idiom for a commitment he will revive in the *Critique*.

10. *P&D* 1:123–24.

11. Sartre, *Les mots*, p. 210.

12. Sartre, *Les carnets de la drôle de guerre*, pp. 225–26. See *P&D* 1:87, 178.

13. Sartre, *Situations*, 4:242.

14. Ibid., p. 260.

15. Ibid., p. 189.

16. Sartre, "Merleau-Ponty," p. 20. This was the earlier draft of the essay on Merleau-Ponty that I have been quoting from volume 4 of Sartre's *Situations*. In this earlier draft, Sartre sets up the opposition between them by recalling how "I used to blame him for his half-shadows, his continuities; he used to blame me for my breaks [*cassures*], my voluntarism, my brutality" (p. 16).

17. Sartre, *Situations* 4:258.

18. Sartre, *Questions de méthode*, p. 20. *Le travail du style* similarly refers to working over language, whose inertia offers its own reemerging resistances. This *travail* also has its reflexive dimension. The passage I quoted at the end of Chapter 24 above from *Qu'est-ce que la littérature?* goes on to acknowledge this dimension: "To that must be added the insidious attempt at biography. For me, Florence is also a certain woman, an American actress who played in the silent films of my childhood, and about whom I have forgotten everything except that she was as long as an evening glove and always rather tired, and always chaste and always married and misunderstood" (*Qu'est-ce que la littérature*, p. 21; *Philosophy of Jean-Paul Sartre*, p. 371). At least one of these attributes Sartre must have ruminated, for Cosima was "tired" (*lasse*) too during their crucial encounter (*Sartre: écrits de jeunesse*, pp. 234–35).

19. *Sartre: écrits de jeunesse*, p. 204.

20. Sartre, *Les mots*, p. 193.

21. Sartre, "Merleau-Ponty," p. 20.

22. Sartre, *Situations* 4:268. I have already explored the different implications

of their respective conceptions of dialectic for their relation and, indeed, for their general analyses of the individual's relation to the other (see *P&D* 1:169–75).

23. Sartre, *Situations* 1:39.

24. Sartre, *Les carnets*, p. 111.

25. Sartre, *Les mots*, pp. 197.

26. Sartre, *Being and Nothingness*, p. 612; *Philosophy of Jean-Paul Sartre*, pp. 262–63.

27. Sartre, *Situations* 1:42. See "The Inner Life" section of Chapter 7 above.

28. For another "image . . . of freedom" that is also contradictory and metastable, see my *Starting Point*, p. 201.

29. See *P&D* 1:38.

30. Sartre, *Les mots*, p. 198.

31. *Sartre, un film*, p. 41.

32. Sartre, *Situations* 4:100. Sartre is describing his writing of *"Les communistes et la paix"*—one of his more extreme efforts to fellow-travel.

33. Sartre, *Situations* 9:133–34.

34. See section "Astonishment" in Chapter 26.

35. *Sartre, un film*, p. 89.

36. In his discussion of conversions in *Being and Nothingness* from which I have quoted, Sartre refers to how they "make me metamorphose my original project." He uses the term "metamorphosis" to stress the completeness of the transformation involved. The term itself is probably taken from Kafka's title.

37. Sartre, *L'idiot de la famille*, 2:2001; Sartre's italics.

38. Ibid., pp. 1996, 1920.

39. *Sartre: écrits de jeunesse*, p. 286.

40. Sartre, *Les mots*, p. 213.

41. Sartre, *Les carnets*, pp. 43–44.

42. See "The Ending" section of Chapter 19.

43. Sartre as quoted in an unpublished interview (*Oeuvres romanesques*, p. 1876).

30. Radical Renovation

1. Sartre, *L'imagination*, pp. 158, 152.

2. Sartre, *Situations* 9:10.

3. See Coleridge, *Biographia Literaria*, chap. 13. Sartre seems entirely unaware of Coleridge, but it may be worth remarking on how strenuously both believed in the imagination as creative, despite the extent to which they were both, as theorist, vulgarizers who derived their theories generally from previous thinkers. For an exposition of Coleridge's theory, see Mary Warnock, *Imagination*, chap. 3. For the place in British Romanticism of Coleridge's conception of the creative imagination, see M. H. Abrams, *The Mirror and the Lamp*. For one

illustration of the influence of this conception, see my *Human Nature and History* 2:275–85.

4. Sartre, *L'imagination*, p. 21. Sartre's commitment to the new is well illustrated by the application of this criterion to the then-reigning philosopher, who was often credited in France with the renovation of psychology: "The solution that Bergson gives to the problem of the image provides absolutely nothing that is new . . . ; "he does not enrich the psychology of the image with any new insight" (p. 63).

5. Ibid., pp. 21–22.

6. Ibid., p. 22.

7. This is the Belgian H. Ahrens, who had been influenced by the post-Kantians and taught at the Sorbonne from 1834 to 1836 (*L'imagination*, p. 22).

8. Sartre, *L'imaginaire*, pp. 64, 118.

9. Ibid., p. 118.

10. Ibid., p. 62.

11. Husserl, *Logical Investigations* 2:719–21. Sartre has employed the term casually in the historical survey in *L'imagination*. He uses it in his brief exposition of Spinoza: "The image is . . . a confused idea that presents itself as a degraded aspect of thought" (p. 9). Though he could have derived the implication of a change in level from Spinoza, it seems more likely to have come from Husserl, since it is Husserl he is now criticizing.

12. Sartre, *L'imaginaire*, pp. 282–83, 241.

31. Radical Conversion

1. Sartre, *L'imaginaire*, p. 343. Sartre himself reports the same year that *L'imaginaire* was published (when his memory should have been fairly accurate), "I wrote an entire book (less the last chapters) inspired by Husserl" (*Carnets de la drôle de guerre*, p. 226). The parentheses would seem to refer, in the first instance, to the last two chapters of the third and last part ("The Imaginary Life"), "The Pathology of the Imagination" and "The Dream," which are topics Husserl did not treat, so I am not taking these chapters into account. (Anyway, they are of little interest.) The parentheses would also seem to refer, in the second instance, to the second chapter in the "Conclusion"—the chapter added later, "The Work of Art." But the first chapter here, which we are now considering, we shall see is inspired by Husserl, even though he is not named. Sartre may have thought of it as inspired by Heidegger, who is regularly named.

2. Sartre, *L'imaginaire*, p. 343. No one seems to have been surprised by this placating of neo-Kantianism, even though in the Berlin essay (written in 1933–34 but published in 1939, only the year before *L'imaginaire*) Sartre had denounced the neo-Kantianism then dominant in France.

3. Ibid., p. 345.

4. Ibid., p. 351.

5. *Dévoiler* and *révéler* are used by Henry Corbin to translate Heidegger's *erschliesen* (see *Qu'est-ce que la métaphysique?*).

6. Corbin's translation of *Was ist Metaphysik?* had been published separately in 1931, but Sartre confesses to not having understood it then (see *P&D* 1:115). Sartre rereading may explain why he regards himself as having reached in his conclusion a "metaphysical question." Simone de Beauvoir traces Sartre's "idea of nothingness" back to *L'imaginaire*, but she acknowledges no debt on Sartre's part to Heidegger. Sartre responds, "I expressed in *L'imaginaire* my essential idea" (*Entretiens*, p. 205; my italics)—this is apparently the "idea of nothingness," but he also does not acknowledge the debt to Heidegger.

7. Sartre, *L'imagination*, p. 140.

8. Sartre, *L'imaginaire*, p. 362.

9. *Les écrits de Sartre*, p. 77.

10. See Chapter 19 above.

11. Sartre, *Les mots*, p. 200.

12. In the original analysis of imagining Charles VIII on the basis of his portrait (see Chapter 9 above), the dialectical doubling involved an "object" that "is posed as absent," but the perceptual "impression is present"—Charles VIII, who has "disappeared[,] is there present in front of us." There is no resort in the analysis to negation. In the first chapter of *L'imaginaire*, "the imaginative consciousness poses its object as a nothingness" (p. 30), but in the instances when it poses it, there is no implication that this "nothingness" is to be taken "in relation to the totality of the real." It is not until the "Conclusion" and in the *prière d'insérer*, that "the imaginary could occur only against the background of the nihilation of the world."

13. Sartre, *L'imaginaire*, p. 352.

32. Nothingness

1. Husserl, *Ideas I*, sec. 49.

2. Heidegger, "What is Metaphysics?" in *Basic Writings*, p. 105; *Qu'est-ce que la métaphysique?*, trans. Corbin, p. 33.

3. *Sartre, un film*, p. 130.

4. Sartre, *Being and Nothingness*, p. 62.

5. Ibid., p. 53.

6. See "Access" section of Chapter 1 above.

7. Sartre blurs the issue here between himself and Husserl. I have tried to state it in terms of how he handles the two reductions. What remains elusive is what happens in Sartre to Husserl's commitment to ideality of meaning—a controversial issue itself in Husserl. I have only been able to argue that Sartre does not maintain Husserl's sharp distinction between "factual reality" and the essence as ideal. The distinction as maintained by the eidetic reduction is a distinction between the imaginative operation of constructing and varying examples and the

cognitive operation by which the essence is itself grasped as invariant. Here we come up against the extent to which methodologically this reduction becomes in Sartre a rudimentary dialectic in which meaning does not emerge as invariant from the relations in which it is caught, and we come up against the extent to which substantively the essences that interest Sartre are imaginary. (In an effort at clarity I am separating the methodological and the substantive—the separation I otherwise disavow as inapplicable to Sartre.) He is also not sufficiently interested in the theory of knowledge to clarify this issue. I suspect the status of knowledge cannot be clarified in terms of his relation to Husserl (though I return to it in my conclusion) but only in *Being and Nothingness* and in his increasingly dialectical later writings. The best attempt to deal with the issue is Christina Howells', and she runs into difficulties. One of the difficulties she faces is "the *compréhension/ connaissance* distinction." She regards Sartre's introduction of this distinction as "evidently due to the increasing flexibility of Sartre's attitude towards the unconscious, and his increasing awareness of the need to make distinctions within his own all-pervading notion of 'consciousness'" (*Sartre,* p. 151). But more than flexibility is at stake here, and *compréhension* is stiff with meaning as a translation of Heidegger's *Verstehen.* For Sartre is aware of Heidegger's effort with this concept to undercut Husserl's restriction of phenomenology to the analysis of the deliverances of consciousness. Howells claims that "the Lacanian interpretation of Freud . . . lies at the root of Sartre's new terminology [the *compréhension/connaissance* distinction]." I would not deny that the Lacanian interpretation is involved, but I am not sure that it "lies at the root." I suspect a tangle of roots. The distinction Sartre would redraw, he had originally drawn in an effort to reconcile Husserl and Heidegger in *Being and Nothingness.* There Sartre protests against Heidegger's effort to undercut consciousness with a concept of human "self-understanding" as "the pro-ject of its own possibilities" (p. 120). Yet he also retains and elaborates on Heidegger's concept of "pro-ject," which he continues to utilize in his later writings. Because Howells overlooks Sartre's terminological debt to Heidegger here, she misses its relevance to Sartre's concept of *compréhension.* In the next chapter I shall glance at "project" in Sartre's later works. But the issues are more than terminological and beyond my present scope.

8. See the "Embodiment" section of Chapter 17 above.

9. Sartre, *La transcendance de l'ego,* p. 84.

10. Ibid., pp. 80–81. The case is borrowed from Pierre Janet.

11. Ibid., p. 83. Observe that the *epochē* is compared with a conversion in Plato.

12. Sartre's facile reconciliation of Husserl and Heidegger here comes at the very juncture where there is a major breakdown of communication, with Husserl remonstrating that Heidegger never understood the phenomenological reduction and Heidegger criticizing the tradition for "having lept over the phenomenon of the world" (*Being and Time,* p. 100). I shall return to this juncture in Volume 3.

13. In addition to the shift in *level,* these mundane "pools" introduce plurality into what Sartre construes as Heidegger's transcendental nothingness. Other illustrations of this introduction of plurality are a misquotation from Heidegger

whose *ein Wesen der Ferne* (which Corbin translates as *un être du lointain*) becomes in Sartre an attribute of man as *un être des lointains*.

33. Freedom

1. Howells, *Sartre,* p. 1; Busch, *The Power of Consciousness,* p. 1.

2. See the "Discontinuity" section of Chapter 29 above.

3. See Sartre, *Situations* 9:99. The last word in this paragraph is intriguing. Sartre is describing "la situation de l'homme parmi les choses, que j'ai appelée l'être-au-monde.'" Ordinarily Sartre employs "l'être-dans-le monde" as a translation for Heidegger's "in-der-Welt-Sein." It is not intriguing that Sartre should say "j'ai appelée." He never admitted that he had borrowed from Heidegger the term "situation," which provided Sartre with not only an important category in *Being and Nothingness* but also the title for ten volumes of his occasional essays (see especially *Being and Time,* p. 299). What is intriguing about the "j'ai appelée" (and about Sartre's departure from his ordinary terminology) is not just that "l'être-au-monde" is a term of Merleau-Ponty's, who uses it to translate Heidegger—e.g., in the *Phenomenology of Perception,* page 430. There it is translated into English "being-in-the-world," though I would suppose that Merleau-Ponty is translating into French, Heidegger's "'Sein-bei' der Welt" (*Being and Time,* p. 54). (In Volume 3 I shall deal with the implications for Heidegger of the two different prepositions.) What is even more intriguing is that "l'être au monde" is a term to which Merleau-Ponty resorts in criticizing Sartre (though characteristically not mentioned him by name—see *P&D* 1:229 n. 18) and in particular his concept of absolute freedom. Presumably prompted by Sartre's own linking of situation and freedom ("there is freedom only in a situation, and there is a situation only through freedom" (*Being and Nothingness,* p. 629; *The Philosophy of Jean-Paul Sartre,* p. 270), Merleau-Ponty argues, "The idea of situation excludes absolute freedom at the source of our commitments" (p. 454). In then winding up his argument, he distinguishes between our being "au monde" from being "dans le monde, as things are" (p. 456). Sartre's using the term "l'être-au-monde" in the paragraph I have quoted may well suggest that his "progression" from "absolute freedom" to his "mature position" was encouraged by Merleau-Ponty's sustained criticism of Sartre's conception of freedom. Howells mentions Merleau-Ponty only once and only in connection with his later "devastating polito-philosophical dismantling of Sartre's arguments" in defense of his fellow-traveling (p. 99), but by this time Sartre's "progression" had been completed. If in the quoted paragraph Sartre does have Merleau-Ponty's criticism in mind, it is more than merely intriguing in two connections. First, I suspect that in spite of their fairly close collaboration, Merleau-Ponty had less philosophical influence while still alive on Sartre that he obtained after his death. Second, (and here my own slant comes into play), it is striking that Sartre, who seems more indebted to other philosophers than perhaps any other philosopher as influential as he has been, should be so explicitly unimpressed by other philosophers when they criticise him. (I am drawing attention to his contention that he never "learned anything" from anyone's writing on him (*Situations* 10:188). It is a general paradox,

which no expositor has examined, that a philosophy so pervious to other philosophers' philosophies, should be so impervious to other philosophers' philosophical criticisms. Why does he not concede in the quoted paragraph Merleau-Ponty's contribution to his "progression"? Why will he assign de Beauvoir the chore (as he assigned so many other chores to her) of replying to Merleau-Ponty, when he eventually will criticise Sartre by name.

4. *Being and Nothingness,* p. 34; *The Philosophy of Jean-Paul Sartre,* p. 110; see *P&D* 1:192.

5. See *P&D* 1:98.

6. See section "Idealism" of Chapter 21 above.

7. Sartre, *Situations* 9:100; cited by Howells, *Sartre,* p. 94, and by Bush, *The Power of Consciousness,* p. 41.

8. See section "Conversion" of Chapter 29 above.

9. Ibid.

10. The term *projet* is regularly used in *Being and Nothingness,* not in *L'imaginaire;* see *P&D* 1:183. The thrust of the *jet* (the *wurf* of Heidegger's *Entwurf* is assimilated by Sartre to "transcendence" in Heidegger; see note 28 below for Sartre's interpretation of the prefix. Since Heidegger had argued in *Vom Wesen des Grundes,* which Corbin had translated in part, that "transcendence" is the ontological structure (whereby being-there is being-in-the-world), underlying the phenomenon of intentionality, Sartre can continue to cling to intentionality, even after he "turns toward Heidegger" in *Being and Nothingness.*

11. Howells, *Sartre,* p. 14; italics mine. Howells is quoting *L'imaginaire,* p. 358.

12. *Being and Nothingness,* pp. 15, 42; *The Philosophy of Jean-Paul Sartre,* pp. 105, 108–9.

13. Heidegger, *Being and Time,* p. 41; see also section "Parts" Chapter 12 above. I have cited Sartre's quotations from Heidegger from the introduction to *Being and Nothingness.* It is true that philosophers often do get started in terms of their relations to other philosophers whom they quote, but from then on their advances are often more on their own. Sartre, however, moves on from his introduction (entitled "The Pursuit of Being") to his first chapter (entitled "The Origin of Negation," where he analyzes Hegel's "Dialectical Concept of Nothingness" and Heidegger's "Phenomenological Concept of Nothingness." In Part 2 he starts out by pitting Heidegger and Husserl against each other, and goes on to quote again the definition of consciousness he obtained from Heidegger in the Introduction (pp. 119–20. In Part 3, he lines up "Husserl, Hegel, Heidegger" on the Other.

14. See Volume 1, pp. 15–19.

15. Sartre, *Situations* 9:99. One philosopher Howells is concerned to see Sartre in relation to is Kant. In her exposition of *L'imaginaire* Howells observes, "Sartre has been criticized for omitting a discussion of Kant from *L'imagination.*" She explains that in *L'imaginaire* "Sartre is implicitly refuting Kant's view of perception as necessarily implying an element of imagination" (p. 11). (What

is peculiarly Kantian about this view? Is it not the mainstream traditional view?) She asserts that "Sartre does refer to him [Kant] on several significant occasions." But her general conclusion is that "the overall omission [apparently of more frequent or of explicit references to Kant] is nonetheless revealing [How? Why?], and it will become progressively clearer that Kant is an opponent with whom Sartre has a permanent (albeit oblique) battle in the domain not only of aesthetics but also of ethics and arguably epistemology" (p. 11)." A significant occasion would seem Sartre's starting out his "Conclusion" to *L'imaginaire*. There Sartre admits (and I quoted his admission at the beginning of Chapter 31) that "our minds" are "habituated to pose philosophical questions from Kantian perspectives." All that Sartre is admitting is that Kantianism is the dominant philosophy in France, and his Berlin essay on intentionality is ample evidence that as soon as he was converted to Husserl and phenomenology his own contempt for neo-Kantianism was complete. (There is no clear evidence of which I am aware that Sartre was particularly concerned to distinguish Kant himself from the Kant expounded by French neo-Kantians.) Sartre's concession to this habituation of "our minds" is a reformulation of the problem of the imagination in terms of a Kantian regressive analysis. But he promptly insists, "But truly, the most profound meaning of the problem can be grasped only from a phenomenological point of view." Howells apparently makes nothing of Sartre's insistence as an effort to distinguish the phenomenological from the Kantian point of view. Instead she presents the Kantian point of view as if she were expounding phenomenology: "Phenomenological intuition seeks to determine the essence of the structures of (transcendental) consciousness—the essence not in any Platonic sense but simply in the sense of the necessary conditions of, say, an image or an emotion" (p. 8). This presentation approximates the stereotypical Kantian formulation that Sartre himself had employed as a concession: "We shall see if the necessary conditions for actualizing an imaginative consciousness are *the same as* or *different from* the conditions of the possibility of a consciousness in general" (*L'imaginaire*, p. 345; Sartre's italics). But Sartre goes on to grasp "the most profound meaning of the problem" by borrowing from Husserl and Heidegger. To them Sartre declares allegiance; it is with them as opponents that he does battle, explicitly and not obliquely. I can think of only one plausible explanation for Howells making more extensive references to Kant than to either Husserl or Heidegger: Kant is the last Continental philosopher (except for Frege and sometimes Marx, who are hardly relevant in the present context) to enjoy general favor as an acceptable point of reference in England. The irony is in that this is almost as much a matter of the habituation of many English minds, as Sartre admits it was, back before World War II, for "our [French] minds." But Howells does not offer this explanation. If she had only acknowledged Sartre's insistence on distinguishing from "Kantian perspectives" the "phenomenological point of view," as yielding "the most profound meaning of the problem," there would be no objection to her respecting a landmark to which her English audience was habituated. My resort to habituation by way of an explanation seems confirmed by her next sentence after her reference to Kant: "An implicit and traditional (Aristotelian) hierarchy seems to underlie much of Sartre's discussion of imagination: that of knowledge, imagination, affectivity. He refers repeatedly to imagination as a form of 'degraded knowledge.'" But what, I ask, is distinctively "Aristotelian" about this hierarchy? The parentheses have been opened up, I suspect, not because she had in mind some significant contrast with any other prominent tradition, but because Aristotle, like Kant, is a habitual landmark in English philosophy. Otherwise he could not blot out of her view Sartre's own reference to Husserl, whom Sartre *explicitly* criticizes in introducing his own conception of "the image" as "a degraded meaning that has descended to the level of intuition." I have already shown (see "The Lurch" section of Chapter 21 above) that Sartre is elaborating here a criticism of a specific doctrine of Husserl's, which he finds "shocking." (This should arrest attention, since he is being "inspired by Husserl" in *L'imaginaire*.) The criticism has consequences I have tried to bring out, both for Sartre's aesthetic theory (more specifically, for his *travail du style*) and for his moral theory as a critique of the doctrine of salvation by art. Of course the "hierarchy" is "traditional," but Sartre's dismantling of it (to which I shall return in my Conclusion) is best understood in terms of the philosopher whom he had devoured.

16. There are, of course, philosophies that do not lend themselves to exposition in terms of their relations to other earlier philosophers to the extent that Sartre's does—Husserl's and Wittgenstein's, for example.

17. Sartre, *L'imaginaire*, pp. 353–54.

18. Husserl, *Ideas I*, sec. 31.

19. Ibid.

20. Sartre, *L'imaginaire*, p. 358.

21. Like most expositors of Sartre, Busch is well aware of how concerned Sartre is with the phenomenological reduction. He cites the crucial passage in *Being and Nothingness* where Sartre mentions the prospect of "a radical conversion" to be carried out by "purifying reflection," and he recognizes "that pure reflection would function as Husserl's *epochē*" (p. 33). But perhaps because he is focusing on what happens with "the power of consciousness" later in Sartre, he does not deal with *L'imaginaire* or cite the parallel passage there on "a radical conversion." Thus he does not explicitly recognize that the extent to which "the power of consciousness" is in Sartre an exercise of *le pouvoir d'arrachement*, which (if perhaps vulgarized) is still the freedom that is associated with the phenomenological reduction in Husserl but that in *L'imaginaire* is also implemented by an act of the imagination.

22. *Sartre: écrits de jeunesse*, p. 328. The appropriate commentary on these equations is given in Sartre's preceding paragraph: "I was going without interruption from one term to the other . . . and my thought went around like a sheep who has the staggers [*le tournis*]." Although this is presumably self-mockery, it is also a foretaste of the *tourniquets* that will become so extravagant in *Saint Genet* and *L'idiot de la famille*. It also suggests Sartre's predisposition to dialectic, which seems to have been somewhat tamed by the encounter with Husserl but which will become more pronounced in *Being and Nothingness*.

23. Sartre goes on after the passage I have cited to reach what he outlines as

"The End of Er the Arménian." It begins with the announcement, "A moral philosophy, what a stupidity! But keep the desire to create a work of art." The conclusion is reached, "Your true goal is the book, the statue that will be born under your fingers." The conjunction of "the book, the statue" is a premonition perhaps of Sartre's later desire to have an aesthetics where "the literary art would have its place, but in relation to the others arts," which "create a certain way of presenting an object" (see the "Intuitive Content" section of Chapter 22 above)—and, in particular, the three-dimensional way the plastic arts present an object (see "The Turn of the Object" section of Chapter 24 above).

24. See "The Shift in Subject" section of Chapter 21 above.

25. Sartre, *Situations* 9:118.

26. Sartre, *Being and Nothingness*, p. 78; *The Philosophy of Jean-Paul Sartre*, p. 129; Heidegger, *Being and Time*, pp. 184–86. Sartre himself does not mention Heidegger at this juncture.

27. Howell, *Sartre*, p. 149.

28. The transition from Husserl to this dialectical flip-flop deriving from Heidegger is well illustrated by a prouncement in *Les mots:* "Our profound intentions are projects and flights inseparably linked" (p. 160). Intentions are never profound in Husserl, but their becoming profound may have helped Sartre make the transition. The translation *projet* is Corbin's, and Sartre sometimes follows Corbin in hyphenating—*pro-jet*. Sartre also reads into the French prefix purposive implications that are not found in the German prefix (see *P&D* 1:183) but that perhaps recall the "aggressive voluntarism" first detected in Sartre's youth, when it prompted the appellation "the lamentable Frédéric." That Heidegger singles out for criticism Sartre's interpretation of *Entwurf* as *projet* (*Basic Writings*, p. 207) gives additional interest to Sartre's reliance on the term.

Conclusion: Questions of Method

1. Husserl, *Ideas I*, sec. 35.

2. Ibid., sec. 70. The issue of priority comes up in this section, as is indicated by the full section title, "The Role of Perception in the Method of Eidetic Clarification: The Priority of Free Imagining." Thus having explained his preference (as we shall see) for examples taken from perception, Husserl concedes a certain priority to free imagining in the eidetic reduction (see the "Free Variation" section of Chapter 13 above).

3. *Husserliana* 23:18.

4. Sartre, *L'imagination*, pp. 148–49.

5. Husserl, *Ideas I*, sec. 67.

6. Ibid., sec. 70.

7. Sartre, *Situations* 1:42.

8. De Beauvoir, *Entretiens*, p. 231.

9. Sartre, *L'imaginaire*, p. 64.

10. Ibid.

11. See the "Shift in Subject" section of Chapter 25 above.

12. See the "Feeling" section of Chapter 16 above.

13. Sartre, *L'imagination*, p. 22. With this denial of external relations, the most important impediment to the fluidity of Sartre's analysis is removed.

14. Ibid., p. 161.

15. Ibid., p. 162.

16. Ibid., p. 82. The only treatment of synthesis in *L'imaginaire*, besides those I am about to take up, is in the instance of the impersonation. But the concept Sartre defends there, against the mechanistic concept of external relations, is presented as appropriate not just to the image but to consciousness in general. In dealing with the relation between the consciousness of the sign and the consciousness of the image, Sartre argues "that the image, like the sign, is a consciousness, and that there can be no external link between them. A consciousness does not have an opaque and unconscious surface by which it can be grasped and so attached to another consciousness. . . . A consciousness is entirely synthesis, carried out entirely within itself; only from within this synthesis can a consciousness join itself, by an act of retention or protention, to a preceding or succeeding consciousness. . . . There are no passivities, only internal integrations and disintegrations [as I have put it, fluid, metastable structures] at the heart of intentional synthesis" (*L'imaginaire*, p. 57; *The Philosophy of Jean-Paul Sartre*, p. 82). In *La transcendance de l'ego* the distinctive character of Sartre's methodological commitment emerges somewhat more definitely from Sartre's criticism of Husserl. There Sartre quotes *Ideas I*, section 131: "Predicates are the predicates of *something*. . . . It is the point of attachment for the predicates, their support. . . . [But] it must necessarily be distinguished from them" (p. 56; italics Husserl's). In other words, Sartre paraphrases, "Undoubtedly, this tree, this table are synthetic complexes and each quality is linked [as a predicate] to each other quality. But it is linked to it *in so far as it belongs to the same object X*. What is logically prior are the unilateral relations according to which this quality belongs . . . to this X, as a predicate to a subject. The result is that analysis [analytic separation] is always feasible" (italics Sartre's). Sartre then protests on behalf of his thoroughgoing relational analysis: "This concept [of synthesis] is most questionable. But this is not the place to examine it. What matters to us is that a synthetic totality which cannot be dissolved and which would support itself would not need any support from an X." He cites as an example "a melody" that does not require an X to serve as the support for its different notes. But the methodological issue does not emerge fully, because there is a shift in *subject*. The X that concerns Sartre is not the object of consciousness (e.g., of an object to which a perceptual consciousness in Husserl assigns its qualities) but the subject, and the self as subject is not comparable in structure to an object. Indeed, since the self soon turns out to be a "contradictory composite" (p. 66), Sartre's analysis of it becomes a rudimentary dialectic. This is not the place for me to examine Sartre's concept of the self or of consciousness in general, for any serious examination would have to take *Being and Nothingness* into account.

17. See *P&D* 1:134–35. Though simplistic, Sartre's relation to Husserl here

provides some measure of preparation for the very much more complicated issues raised by Heidegger's rejection of Husserl's commitment to method.

18. Sartre, *Questions de méthode*, p. 23. See *P&D* 1:190–93.

19. See Chapter 8 above.

20. See the "Commotion" section of Chapter 6 and the "Bookishness" section of Chapter 7 above.

21. See the "Leeway" section of Chapter 1 above.

22. Husserl, *Logical Investigations*, 1:43. See the section "Difficulties" of Chapter 11 above.

23. Husserl, *Logical Investigations*, 2:528.

24. Ibid., 648.

25. Sartre, *L'imaginaire*, pp. 140–41.

26. Ibid., p. 271. Sartre's denial of the primacy of representation blends with his denial of the primacy of knowledge—the denial we have already encountered in the Berlin essay on intentionality (see "The Prophet" section of Chapter 7 above). The denial is repeated in *Being and Nothingness,* when Sartre makes a reflexive move from phenomenology to ontology: "By abandoning the primacy of knowledge, we have discovered the *being* of the *knower*" (p. 17). When Sartre turns from Husserl and Heidegger to Hegel in order to deal with the problem of The Other, he again denies the primacy of knowledge (pp. 322–23).

27. Sartre, *L'imaginaire*, pp. 141–42.

28. Ibid., p. 143. This "synthesis of affectivity and knowledge" is fluid and illustrates how Sartre endorses the fluidity of the structure that Husserl would take as "built" up and susceptible of being taken apart by an analysis.

29. Ibid., pp. 135, 138.

30. This *sur* is the juncture at which the idiom of "sliding," as over against bogging down and getting "stuck," can come to the fore and to a degree displace Husserl's idiom of "aiming at" a target and "hitting" it. See "The Lurch" section of Chapter 21 above.

31. Sartre, *L'imaginaire*, p. 139. Sartre is citing Lawrence's "The Woman who Rode Away" (see *The Later D. H. Lawrence*, p. 309).

32. Sartre, *L'imaginaire*, p. 139.

33. See "The Shift in Subject" section of Chapter 17 above.

34. Sartre, *L'imaginaire*, p. 145. This citation from *La vie de Henri Brulard* is found not only in the *diplôme* but also in some loose pages that seem to have been an initial revision of the *diplôme* or of the original manuscript that later became *L'imaginaire.*

35. My citations from Sartre's juvenilia demonstrate that memories and affective reactions already have an assured place there. The attendant distrust of cognitive reliability is illustrated by Sartre's title *La légende de la vérité*. If I have not taken this prephenomenological work into account, it is because its main interest is as evidence of the youthful Sartre's concern with the social dimension, which has remained marginal in my exposition, as it is in the phenomenological writings

of Sartre himself. Recall his claim that what is ostensibly a social role is not fundamentally social. See "The Waiter" section of Chapter 25 above.

36. See "Vulgarization" section of Chapter 21 above.

37. Sartre, *L'imaginaire*, pp. 62–63.

Epilogue: The End of Philosophy

1. *The Crisis of European Sciences*, p. 389. See *P&D* 1:7.

2. Sartre, *L'imagination*, p. 152; Heidegger, *Being and Time*, p. 38. See vol. 1, p. 28.

3. "Jean-Paul Sartre," *L'arc* 30, p. 94. The interviewer is Bernard Pingaud.

4. Throughout this epilogue, it should be remembered that I leave undefined what is to be meant by "end," though it is certainly not to be taken in any superficial chronological sense. As I explained at the beginning of Volume 1, "How we conceive the end of philosophy depends on how we conceive philosophy—and upon the account, in justifying this conception, we give of its history. There is no simple elucidation of the end of philosophy, since there is no simple elucidation of the multifarious evidence of what has gone on during the history of philosophy (*P&D* 1:3)."

5. Derrida, *Du droit à la philosophie*, p. 516.

6. Heidegger, *Being and Time*, pp. 4, 21, 28.

7. Heidegger, *Basic Writings*, p. 197; and see *P&D* 1:70–71.

8. See *P&D* 1:187–89.

9. Ibid., p. 177.

10. See *P&D* 1:233, n. 9.

11. Ibid., pp. 188–89.

12. In Volume 1 I commented on Derrida's statement, "Deconstruction is not a method and cannot be transformed into a method" (p. 140). For Heidegger's repudiation of method, see *P&D* 1:142.

13. See Vol. 1, pp. 160–64.

WORKS CITED

Abrams, M. H. *The Mirror and the Lamp: Romantic Theory and the Cultural Tradition.* New York: Norton, 1958.

Ayer, A. J. *Metaphysics and Common Sense.* San Francisco: Freeman, Cooper, 1970.

Bair, Deirdre. *Simone de Beauvoir.* New York: Simon and Schuster, 1990.

Beauvoir, Simone de. *La cérémonie des adieux, suivi de entretiens avec Jean-Paul Sartre.* Paris: Gallimard, 1981.

———. *La force de l'âge.* Paris: Gallimard, 1960.

———. *Lettres à Sartre.* 2 vols. Paris: Gallimard, 1990.

———. "Merleau-Ponty et le pseudo-sartisme." In *Privileges.* Paris: Gallimard, 1955.

Boyce-Gibson, W. R. "From Husserl to Heidegger: Excerpts from a 1928 Freiburg Diary." Edited by Herbert Speigelberg. *Journal of the British Society for Phenomenology* 2 (Jan. 1971).

Burnier, Michel-Antoine. "One ne peut pas être sartien, on ne peut pas être anti-partrien." *Les temps modernes* 2 (1990): 531–33.

Busch, Thomas W. "*La Nausée:* A Lover's Quarrel with Husserl." *Research in Phenomenology* 11 (1981): 1–24.

———. *The Power of Consciousness and the Force of Circumstances.* Bloomington: Indiana University Press, 1990.

Cairns, Dorion. *Conversations with Husserl and Fink.* The Hague: Martinus Nijhoff, 1976.

Cau, Jean. "Croquis de mémoire." *Les temps modernes* 2 (1990).

Cohen-Solal, Annie. *Sartre 1905–1980.* Paris: Gallimard, 1985.

Coleridge, S. T. *Biographia Literaria.* Edited by J. Shawcross. Oxford: Clarendon Press, 1907.

Contat Nichel and Michel Rybalka, (Editors). *Les écrits de Sartre*. Paris: Gallimard, 1970.

Cumming, Robert Denoon. *Human Nature and History: A Study of the Development of Liberal Political Thought*. 2 vols. Chicago: University of Chicago Press, 1969.

———. *Starting Point: An Introduction to the Dialectic of Existence*. Chicago: University of Chicago Press, 1979.

Derrida, Jacques. *Du droit a la philosophie*. Paris: Galilee, 1990.

———. *Le problème de la genèse dans la philosophie de Husserl*. Paris: Presses Universitaires de France, 1990.

———. *La voix et le phénomène*. Paris: Presses Universitaire de France, 1967.

———. *L'écriture et la différence*. Paris: Editions du Seuil, 1967.

Diemer, Alwin. *Edmund Husserl*. Meisenheim am Glan: Hain, 1956.

Fell, Joseph P. *Heidegger and Sartre: An Essay on Being and Place*. New York: Columbia University Press, 1979.

Fink, Eugen, "The Phenomenological Philosophy of Edmund Husserl and Contemporary Criticism." In *The Phenomenology of Husserl*. Edited by R. O. Elveton. Chicago: Quadrangle Books, 1970.

Furbank, P. N. *Reflections on the Word "Image."* London: Secker and Warburg, 1970.

Hegel, G. W. F. *Aesthetics*. Translated by T. M. Knox. Oxford: Clarendon Press, 1975.

———. *Phenomenology of Spirit*. Translated by A. V. Miller. Oxford: Clarendon Press, 1977.

Heidegger, Martin. *Basic Writings*. Edited by David Farrell Krell. New York: Harper and Row, 1977.

———. *Being and Time*. Translated by John Macquarrie and Edward Robinson. New York: Harper and Row, 1962.

———. "Interview." *Express*, (October 1969): 20–26.

———. *Of Time and Being*. Translated by Joan Stambaugh. New York: Harper and Row, 1972.

———. *Ontologie*. Gesamtausgabe 63. Frankfort: Vittorio Klostermann, 1988.

———. *Poetry, Language, Thought*. Translated by Albert Hofstadter. New York: Harper and Row, 1971.

———. *Qu'-est-ce que la métaphysique?* Translated by Henry Corbin. Paris: Gallimard, 1938.

———. *Platons Lehre von der Wahrheit*. Bern: A. Francke, 1947.

Héring, Jean. "Concerning Image, Idea, and Dream." *Philosophy and Phenomenological Research* 8 (1947).

Howells, Christina. *Sartre: The Necessity of Freedom*. Cambridge: Cambridge University Press, 1988.

Husserl, Edmund. *Briefe an Roman Ingarden*. Edited by Roman Ingarden. The Hague: Martinus Nijhoff, 1968.

———. *Cartesian Meditations: An Introduction to Phenomenology*, translated by Dorian Cairns. The Hague: Martinus Nijhoff, 1977.

———. *The Crisis of European Sciences and Transcendental Phenomenology*, translated by David Carr. Evanston, Ill.: Northwestern University Press, 1970.

———. *Experience and Judgment*. Translated by James S. Churchill and Karl Ameriks. Evanston: Northwestern University Press, 1973.

———. *Formal and Transcendental Logic*. Translated by Dorian Cairns. The Hague: Nijhoff, 1969.

———. *Ideas Pertaining to a Pure Phenomenology and to a Phenomenological Philosophy*. Vol. 1. Translated by F. Kersten. The Hague: Martinus Nijhoff, 1983.

———. *Idées directrices pour une phénoménologie*. Vol. 1. Translated by Paul Ricoeur. Paris: Gallimard, 1950.

———. *Ideen 3*. Husserliana 5. Edited by Marly Biemal. The Hague: Martinus Nijhoff, 1952.

———. *Logical Investigations*. Translated by J. N. Findlay. 2 vol. New York: Humanities Press, 1970.

———. *L'origine de la géométrie*. Translated and introduced by Jacques Derrida. Paris: Presses universitaires de France, 1974.

———. *Phantasie, Bildbewusstsein, Erinnerung 1898–1925*. Husserliana 23. Edited by Eduard Marbach. The Hague: Martinus Nijhoff, 1980.

———. "Persönliche Aufzeichnungen." *Philosophy and Phenomenological Research*. 16 (March 1956).

Hyppolite, Jean. "Comment on Sartre's 'Conscience de soi et connaissance de soi.'" *Bulletin de la société française de philosophie* 3 (April-June 1948).

Kierkegaard, Søren. *Either/Or*. Vol. 1. Translated by David F. Swenson and Lillian Marvin Swenson. Princeton: Princeton University Press, 1971.

Kelkel, A. *Maurice Merleau-Ponty, le psychique et le corporel*. Paris: Aubier, 1988.

Launay, Jean. "Sartre lecteur de Heidegger," *Les temps modernes* 1 (October-December 1990): 531–33.

Lawrence, D. H. "The Woman who Rode Away." *The Later Novels of D. H. Lawrence*. New York: Knopf, 1952.

Merleau-Ponty. *Humanisme and Terror*. Translated by John O'Neill. Boston: Beacon Press, 1969.

———. *The Phenomenology of Perception*. Translated by Colin Smith. New York: Humanities Press, 1962.

———. *Le primat de la perception*. Grenoble: Cynara, 1989.

———. *Sense and Non-Sense*. Translated by Hubert L. Dreyfus and Patricia Allen Dreyfus. Evanson, Ill.: Northwestern University Press, 1973.

————. *Signes*. Paris, Gallimard, 1960.

————. *The Structure of Behavior*. Translated by Alden L. Fischer. Boston: Beacon Press, 1968.

————. *Themes from the Lectures at the College de France, 1952–1960*. Translated by John O'Neill. Evanston, Ill.: Northwestern University Press, 1970.

————. *Le visible et l'invisible*. Paris: Gallimard, 1964.

Panofsky, Erwin. *The Life and Art of Alberecht Dürer*. Princeton: Princeton University Press, 1971.

Panofsky, Erwin, and F. Saxl. *Dürers kupferstich "Melencolia I"; Einen quellen-und-typengeschichtliche Untersuchung*. Leipzig: Teubner, 1923.

Sallis, John. "Image and Phenomenon." *Research in Phenomenology* 5 (1975).

Sartre, Jean-Paul. *Baudelaire*. Paris: Gallimard, 1947.

————. *Being and Nothingness*. Translated by Hazel Barnes, New York: Philosophical Library, 1956.

————. *Cahiers pour une morale*. Paris. Gallimard, 1983.

————. *Les carnets de la drôle de guerre*. Paris: Gallimard, 1983.

————. "Conscience de soi et connaissance de soi." *Bulletin de la société française de philosophie* 3 (April-June 1948).

————. *Critique de la raison dialectique, précèdé de Questions de méthode*. Paris: Gallimard, 1960.

————. *L'existenialisme est un humanisme*. Paris: Nagel, 1970.

————. *Esquisse d'une théorie des émotions*. Paris: Hermann, 1939.

————. *L'idiot de la famille* 3 vols. Paris: Gallimard, 1971–72.

————. *L'imaginaire*. Edited by Arlette Elkaim-Sartre. Gallimard, 1986.

————. *L'imagination*. Paris: Alcan, 1936.

————. "An Interview with Sartre." In *The Philosophy of Jean-Paul Sartre*. Edited by Paul Arthur Schilpp. La Salle, Ill: Open Court Press, 1981.

————. "Itinerary of a Thought," in *New Left Review* 58 (Nov.-Dec. 1969).

————. "Jean-Paul Sartre repond." In *L'arc* 30 (1966).

————. *Les mots*. Paris: Gallimard, 1963.

————. *Lettres au Castor et à quelques autres*. 2 vols. Paris: Gallimard, 1983.

————. "Merleau Ponty," *Revue internationale de philosophie* 152–153 (1985).

————. *La mort dans l'âme* Paris: Gallimard, 1949.

————. *La nausée*. Paris: Gallimard, 1938.

————. *Nausea*. Translated by Lloyd Alexander. New York: New Directions, 1964.

————. *Oeuvres romanesques*. Paris: Pleiade, 1981.

————. "Penser l'art." In *Sartre et les arts*. *Obliques* 24–25 (1981).

————. *The Philosophy of Jean-Paul Sartre*. Edited by Robert Denoon Cumming. New York: Vintage, 1972.

————. *Qu'est-ce que la littérature?* Paris: Gallimard, 1948.

———. *Saint Genet, comédien et martyr.* Paris: Gallimard, 1952.

———. *Sartre: écrits de jeunesse.* Edited by Michel Contat and Michel Rybalka. Paris: Gallimard, 1990.

———. *Sartre: un film réalisé par Alexandre Astruc et Michel Contat* Paris: Gallimard, 1977.

———. *Situations.* 10 vols. Paris: Gallimard, 1947–76.

———. *La transcendance de l'ego* Paris: Vrin, 1965.

———. "Une idée fondamentale de la phénoménologie de Husserl: Intentionalité." In *Situations,* vol. 1. Paris: Gallimard, 1947.

Saraiva, Maria Manulla. *L'imagination selon Husserl.* The Hague: Nijhoff, 1970.

Schuhmann, Karl, ed. *Husserl-Chronik,* volume 1. The Hague: Nijhoff, 1977.

Spiegelberg, Herbert. *The Phenomenological Movement.* 2 vols. The Hague: Nijhoff, 1981.

Ströker, Elisabeth. *Husserls tranzendentale Phänomenologie.* Frankfort: Klostermann, 1987.

Taylor, Charles. Review of *La philosophie analytique. Philosophical Review* 73 (1964).

Wahl, Jean. *Etudes kierkegaardiennes.* Paris: Aubier, 1938.

———. *Vers le concret* Paris: Vrin, 1932.

Warnock, Mary. *Imagination.* Berkeley and Los Angeles: University of California Press, 1978.